Trade and Development

Trade and Development

Directions for the 21st Century

Edited by

John Toye

Visiting Professor, Department of Economics,
University of Oxford, UK

The work is published for and on behalf of the United Nations

Edward Elgar

Cheltenham, UK • Northampton, MA, USA

Published by
Edward Elgar Publishing Limited
Glensanda House
Montpellier Parade
Cheltenham
Glos GL50 1UA
UK

MIK

Edward Elgar Publishing, Inc.
136 West Street
Suite 202
Northampton
Massachusetts 01060
USA

A catalogue record for this book
is available from the British Library

Library of Congress Cataloging in Publication Data
Trade and development : directions for the 21st century / edited by John Toye.
    p. cm.
    Papers presented at the Round Table of Eminent Economists at the opening session of the U.N. Conference on Trade and Development (UNCTAD X) in Bangkok, Thailand in February 2000—Introd.
    "The work is published for and on behalf of the United Nations".
    Includes index.
    1. International trade—Congresses. 2. Economic development—Congresses. 3. Economic history—1990– —Congresses. I. Toye, J.F.J. II. United Nations Conference on Trade and Development.

    HF1379 .T6875 2003
    338.9—dc21
                                                                2002034702

ISBN 1 84376 044 4
Printed and bound in Great Britain by MPG Books Ltd, Bodmin, Cornwall

Contents

Contributors

Alice H. Amsden, Massachusetts Institute of Technology, Cambridge, USA.
Hans Binswanger, Director of Rural Development and Environment for Africa, The World Bank.
Kwesi Botchwey, Harvard University, Cambridge, USA.
Bernard Chavance, University of Paris VII, France.
Peter Evans, University of California, Berkeley, USA.
Ernst Lutz, Senior Sector Economist, Rural Development and Environment for Africa, The World Bank.
Alfred Maizels, Oxford University, UK.
Deepak Nayyar, Vice Chancellor, University of Delhi, India.
Carlota Perez, Honorary Research Fellow, SPRU – Science and Technology Policy Research, University of Sussex, UK, Adjunct Senior Research Fellow, INTECH/UNU, Maastricht, The Netherlands and Visiting Scholar 2002, Cambridge University, UK.
Jean-Philippe Platteau, Department of Economics, Centre de Recherche en Economie du Développement, University of Namur, Belgium.
Frances Stewart, Oxford University, UK.
John Toye, Visiting Professor, Department of Economics, University of Oxford, UK.
L. Alan Winters, University of Sussex, UK.
Ippei Yamazawa, Hitotsubashi University and Institute of Developing Economies/JETRO, Tokyo.

Bk Title!

1. Introduction

Fi 4
o\9

John Toye

When the tenth session of the UN Conference on Trade and Development (UNCTAD X) took place in Bangkok, Thailand, in February 2000, it was the first major international conference of the twenty-first century. Given its position of honour in the diplomatic chronology of the millennium, it seemed an appropriate occasion to generate some broad reflections on the theme that has animated UNCTAD since its establishment as an organ of the UN in 1964. Its mission was to correct the situation in which problems of international trade policy were dealt with separately from issues of development and of international finance. Stated in the boldest of terms, then, two questions needed to be addressed. First, what can now be said with confidence about the interdependence of trade and development? Second, what national and international policies should flow from that understanding?

It was my great privilege to be invited by Rubens Ricupero, the Secretary General of the Conference, to organize a Round Table of Eminent Economists at the opening session of UNCTAD X. The aim of the round table was to place before the conference a set of papers representing the research and experience of some of the leading economists around the world on the subject of the policy implications of the links between international trade and development. Mr Ricupero wanted the delegates to be given a sense of the way in which academic opinion on the trade and development nexus had developed over the previous half-century, of where it stood at the start of the new millennium and of the implications for the future of international economic policy.

In order to try to fulfil this mandate, I immediately had to confront a painful problem of selection. No dozen authors, however distinguished, could possibly cover what is a vast field, encompassing a multitude of topics, on all of which exist many fine shadings of opinion. Any such team of scholars would necessarily fail to represent the full range of available opinion, exclude important issues and simplify significant nuances. Nevertheless, I did not advise that the enterprise was hopeless and that nothing could be done. It seemed to me better to take the opportunity that I was offered, and to try to use it to maximum advantage, than to throw in my hand because the task could not be carried out to perfection.

Inevitably, personal judgement entered into making the choice of participants. I decided steadfastly to ignore the UN's political and administrative concerns with geographical and gender representation. I allowed myself to be guided by my own understanding of merit in this very competitive field. I was greatly gratified that so many of those who were originally invited were able to agree to make presentations in Bangkok. This volume contains the twelve papers on which the Bangkok presentations were based.

Part of the guidance that I gave to the authors was negative. I suggested that they did not attempt either to produce full reviews of the academic literature on their assigned topic or to write new academic papers that would add substantively to that literature. Instead, I wanted them to state, within what must have seemed to them an extraordinarily tight word limit, the main messages of value that they thought should be the starting point for thinking about trade and development in the twenty-first century. I thought about the task as one of winnowing the academic literature of the last fifty years. The criterion of the authors' success would be the wholesomeness of the intellectual grain, and its capacity to provide nourishment and inspiration to the future policy makers of the international economy.

Since the round table was the initial event of UNCTAD X, it provided a framework for the subsequent official intergovernmental deliberations in Bangkok, or at least a context of ideas that many of the later contributions tried to address. The official deliberations of the conference were inevitably diverse and wide-ranging. Those present heard ideas and opinions coming to them from all points of the compass of international governance – from heads of state and heads of government, from the delegations of the member states of UNCTAD, from the leaders of the international financial institutions, from ministers, from representatives of parliaments and of non-governmental organizations, from entrepreneurs in both small and multinational enterprises, from the directors of the agencies and regional commissions of the United Nations system, as well as from academic experts. It turned out to be a very rich and varied diet of speech making. Because of this richness and variety, it would be misleading to try and summarize the message of either the round table or the later contributions to UNCTAD X under any simple label.

In the policy discourse on economic development, the dominating voices of the last two decades of the twentieth century were those articulating and praising the so-called 'Washington Consensus'. This was nothing less ambitious than a statement of twelve rules of economic policy for development with which all sensible economists were supposed to agree, and which therefore could be safely implemented when they, or their supporters, happened to find their way to political power. However, this digest of policy rules was gradually seen to be too limiting. Even within the World Bank, that pillar of the Washington Consensus, rumblings of dissent were eventually heard. Joseph Stiglitz, then the bank's chief economist, began to adventure 'toward the Post-Washington Consensus'.[1] Stiglitz went on to push outward the boundary of sensible economic thinking, and in the course of doing so quit the bank in 1999.

Politicians, too, have been abandoning the Washington Consensus. The British Chancellor of the Exchequer, Gordon Brown, did so in early 2000. He said:

> we need to move beyond the Washington Consensus of the 1980s, a creature of its time that narrowed our growth and employment objectives. Which assumed by liberalising, deregulating, privatising and getting prices right, private markets would allocate resources efficiently for growth. This has proven inadequate for the insecurities and challenges of globalisation ... We need to find a new 2000 paradigm.[2]

Here then was an open invitation to a lively academic entrepreneur to come up with a 'new consensus'. From the political point of view, it would be very tempting for me to claim that the deliberations at UNCTAD X constituted the arrival of a 'Bangkok Consensus'. This could be neatly packaged into another set of twelve points – rather different points, of course – and touted around as a recipe for development policy on which all sensible economists could henceforth agree.

The fate of previous consensuses on economic policy, however, suggested to me that to accept this implicit invitation would be unwise. Consensuses have a vexing and perplexing habit of self-destructing. This may not matter much to politicians, to whom all consensuses are grist to their mill, and the erosion of one consensus is but the opportunity for fashioning another. For intellectuals, though, it is criticism that is the lifeblood of the evolution of ideas, and to them the declaration of a new consensus seems rather like a polite request to abandon the habit of thinking.

However, even those who, as I do, react badly to consensus mongering, accept that in recent years some convergence of views among economists has taken place on the subject of economic policies for development. This is largely because there has been some attrition at both of the extreme ends of the ideological spectrum. In this introduction, I shall point out some of the important ways in which the spectrum of economic opinion about trade and development has in fact narrowed in recent years. This is most notable among academic experts, but it follows a broader movement of politics in the 1990s, that combined Democratic occupancy of the US White House with a growing social democratic hegemony in Europe. This political phase also saw the softening of postures of those leaders of international organizations who (like Michel Camdessus) were appointed in the 1980s and remained in office through the 1990s.[3] This phase may well have ended with the Presidency of George W. Bush and the events of 11 September 2001.

The papers for the round table each made their own contribution by illuminating how and why the intellectual spectrum on development policy has tended to narrow. I shall indicate very briefly the nature of each author's contribution as I explore the theme of the narrowing intellectual spectrum. Its historical context was the key event of our time, the ending of the Cold War. Those of us who have lived most of our professional lives under that great geopolitical stalemate had our mental horizons imprinted by it, and find it a slow process to think outside the blinkers that it fashioned. The starting point for the exercise of intellectual reorientation is to fathom what those blinkers prevented us from understanding. Was the Cold War simply a power struggle between two large states, both in command of the weaponry of mass destruction, a power struggle which one state lost? Or was it a competition between two fundamentally different social and political systems, which one system (capitalism) won because the other (socialism) proved itself to be, in some sense, not historically viable?

The latter interpretation was certainly eagerly seized on at the end of the last century, when an unusually long boom in the American economy buoyed up a public mood of capitalist triumph. Nevertheless, it is too simple a story, and is in need of refinement. The gulf between capitalism and socialism is easily exaggerated, given that they shared an underlying view of what constitutes the good society. The nature of their opposition can easily be misunderstood, given that – far from being fixed and unchanging – they evolved together, and that each was modified continuously by their mutual engagement. In Chapter 2 of this volume, Bernard Chavance brings out the implications of this process of mutual adaptation with considerable skill. He presents an explanation of the relative failure of socialism, the variety of paths out of socialism and the strengths and weaknesses of the form of capitalism that, simply by surviving, constitutes the modern sociopolitical and ideological context of development.

Early on in the Cold War, a group of important developing countries decided to declare their neutrality. They became known as the 'third world', and, as decolonization proceeded, they formed a collective entity, originally the Group of 77, that raised the issue of the interdependence of trade and development. The issue, simply put, is that the rules that govern the world trading system do not sufficiently take account of the interests of countries that are poor and in the process of development. UNCTAD was established as the international organization that is the forum for the discussion of this issue and its various agendas. The end of the bipolar world of the USA and the Soviet Union as superpowers has undermined the political identity and resources of the old 'third world' that at times succeeded in standing apart from both power blocs and championing a trade policy that supported development.

Remarkably swiftly after the liberal revolution of 1989 in Eastern Europe and the end of the former Soviet Union, the World Trade Organisation was conceived and born. In part, the WTO represented a reversion to the plan for a more substantial regulatory framework for world trade, which had been abandoned when the USA finally failed to ratify the 1948 Havana Charter that would have set up an International Trade Organisation. Although he advocated a universal membership organization for trade, Raul Prebisch regarded the Havana Charter as a backward-looking attempt to set down rules of the game in order to recreate an earlier economic order. He thought that the trade regime should be directed by policies rather than by rules. So the formation of the WTO was a defeat for his idea of a new international economic order. It was also a posthumous and pyrrhic victory for the Soviet Union, which since 1955 had campaigned for the establishment of the International Trade Organisation.

In part, however, the WTO was a move to incorporate into a stronger regulatory framework new issues that had grown in importance to industrial countries during the long interregnum when the General Agreement on Tariffs and Trade (GATT) had held sway, issues such as intellectual property rights and trade in services. The arrival of the WTO presented the former third world countries with a new set of problems. Ever since, they have had to redefine themselves in relation to the challenge of globalization. That is to say, they now face a strategic choice of whether they accept or reject a growing integration into a single system of trading and financial relations, in which the most powerful participant country is the USA and in which their voice, both individually and even collectively, is very weak.

Thus one important effect has been to put the phenomenon of globalization in a new light. By 'globalization' I do not mean the well-known and long-standing facts of the acceleration of the speed of transport and communications. I do not use the term to mean some unstoppable form of technical change spreading inevitably across the face of the world. Neither do I mean by 'globalization' a process of cultural blending that is currently most strongly coloured by American companies, images and artefacts. For me, globalization is the outcome of global institution building, which occurs when national states agree to limit their own power to make law in certain economic fields. The WTO is the major post-Cold War example of this voluntary self-limitation. Much of what is popularly referred to as 'globalization' is rightly called 'regionalization', the making of new agreements to limit national powers in certain economic fields within a region, like the European Union or the North American Free Trade Area.

Globalization has to be seen as the outcome of the choices that governments have to make about their global economic integration. On the one hand, this points to the need to examine the circumstances under which small and poor countries have to make those choices, and on the other it points to the possibility of contradiction between choices made at the regional and at the truly global level.

Chapter 3 by Deepak Nayyar treats globalization as an historical phenomenon of the last twenty years, and points to its mixed harvest. Market opportunities for some and market exclusion for others is a recipe for growing inequalities, and these can easily foment an increase in social and political instability. This would be especially so if crime and identity politics become the refuges of the excluded. (That particular observation has been given an added resonance by the events of 11 September.) The downside risks associated with globalization that many policy makers in developing countries perceive are explained articulately in this chapter. Reluctance to take further steps towards economic integration is justified here with reference to the marginal position of developing countries in setting the rules of the international game, and to the asymmetrical rules that result from the dominance of the industrial countries in the rule-making process. The essentials of specific problems, such as restrictions on the mobility of labour, the outlawing of industrial policy instruments and the encouragement of a race to the bottom for foreign investment are laid out. The responses to these risks and problems by the international community continue to be slow and inadequate, indicating – paradoxically – the need for greater political commitment to new institution building in the international sphere.

Despite the unattractive features of the choice that developing countries now face, it is likely that they will have to continue to integrate somehow or other. The popular belief that the cutting off of trade and financial links with the rest of the world will itself generate 'true development' has, after the end of the Cold War, virtually disappeared, except from the haunts of anarchists and radical environmentalists. The reasons for its intellectual decline are set out in the chapter by Alan Winters. Many of the arguments that have been used to defend regimes of heavy trade protection have been shown to be logically faulty over the years. Empirical studies have also shown that the results of heavy protection are very arbitrary and cannot be easily rationalized in terms of developmental goals. Further, the methods of protection adopted have given rise to problems of governance as a result of regulatory capture. Over fifty years, but particularly in the 1990s, informed opinion has swung in favour of increased openness to trade, and a strategy of treating such equity issues as arise by explicit exercises of redistribution. In recent years, it has become much more generally believed that expanding the opportunities for trade will accelerate the growth and development of a country.[4] At the same time, Alan Winters concedes that the academic proof positive of this central policy proposition remains elusive in terms both of the appropriate concept and measures of openness to trade, and of modelling the relation of trade openness to economic growth. Orthodox trade economists have plenty of work still to do, despite the fact that many policy makers have embraced their policy recommendations.

Nowadays, most debate centres on the terms on which countries should insert themselves into the global trade and finance network, and whether they possess the requisite expertise and bargaining power to achieve terms that are consistent with their future development goals. To some economists, the idea of industrial policy for development seems merely retrogression to the bad old days of import substitution. To many others, the East Asian economic miracle of the years 1965–97 demonstrates the value to economies genuinely seeking rapid development of strategies that include some means of protecting their infant industries. Such protection need not be by tariffs, but can be by means of industrial subsidies. For those of this persuasion, it is essential, however, that such subsidies be selective, temporary and explicitly conditional on export performance. It is therefore a key issue whether industrial policies for development are or are not permissible under the rules of the World Trade Organisation.

In Chapter 5, Alice Amsden's paper argues that such policy devices, or similar ones, are not wholly outlawed by the WTO. She argues that scope for industrial policy is given by rules that allow subsidies for the purposes of research and development, regional development and environmental conservation. The rules also provide for the imposition of safeguards against surges of imports and damage to the balance of payments. The main difficulty that appears to arise is linking the payment of subsidies to specific firm-level export targets, a device that was evidently crucial in the East Asian case in overcoming the political economy problem of regulatory capture. Given that WTO rules are subject to refinement by a process of adjudication of case law, it is still not possible to provide a definitive interpretation on this question. In any case, the uncertainty over this issue will ensure that it remains a central one for countries seriously interested in development in the new round of international trade negotiations agreed at Doha in November 2001.

The demise of the belief in autarchy as a path to development is a clear example of the shortening of the ideological spectrum that the ending of the Cold War has brought about. Another example is the new priority that is given to the maintenance of macroeconomic stability. That economists ever strongly advocated macroeconomic *instability* is something that I seriously doubt. However, it was commonplace for politicians in developing countries to take decisions that resulted in higher inflation and increased balance of payments deficits. They did so in the hope that their Cold War partners would bail them out of the consequent economic crises. Since that option is now much less available, many more politicians are themselves taking responsibility for the maintenance of macroeconomic stability, or creating conditions for other institutions to do so. The debate today centres, not on the desirability of the objective of stability, but on the means to such stability, and whether it is sufficient to ward off financial and economic crises.

Yet another casualty of the end of the Cold War in the realm of economic strategies is the idea that the national state can itself spearhead a modernization of the economy by means of setting up state-owned industries. Although in principle there are no economic reasons why such a strategy could not be made to work, in practice this strategy has lost much of its credibility. Politically, it has proved difficult for governments to maintain a hard budget constraint on state industries, and this has contributed to the swelling of the budget deficit and consequent acceleration of inflation. It has also proved hard to regulate the negative externalities of their operations. As a result, they have often been responsible for creating both macroeconomic instability and excessive environmental costs.

The state industry strategy has also lost support because state enterprise has proved less effective than private in mastering the art of absorbing the new technologies that, at any one time, are the heart of economic development. Carlota Perez explains in Chapter 6 how the displacement of one technology by a new one in the industrial countries alters the conditions under which technological absorption can take place in developing countries. Identifying, in a continuous dynamic of change, the window of opportunity for successful absorption of technology is a task that most governments in the developing world have not performed well. Now they are increasingly willing to create investment policy regimes that are attractive to private enterprise, whether domestic or foreign, so that it can take the lead in the task of technological upgrading, it is hoped with greater success.

The move towards freer trade, recognition of the imperative of macro stability and the promotion of the private sector to drive, through its capacity for technological absorption, the process of economic development – in these three respects, informed public opinion on economic policy has converged during the last ten years. It has increasingly supported liberal views of desirable economic policies in these areas. Opinion is by no means homogenous, but the range of difference has been significantly reduced. This is important because it has provided the basis on which developing countries can move towards meeting the international norms and standards that are preconditions of greater global economic integration.

However, narrowing of the range of economic opinion in the last ten years has not only been a drift in the direction of liberal economic policies, due to the withering away of extreme left viewpoints on policy. In equal measure, it has consisted of the increasing acceptance of propositions that during the Cold War were denied persistently by the celebrants of the marvels of the free market. Let me cite three examples of this contrary movement of ideas.

The notion that capitalism is an economic system that is highly vulnerable to damaging financial crises has long been resisted. Although Keynes produced a *General Theory* that explained how monetary factors could prevent an economy from functioning optimally, the Cold War period was one of increasingly successful attempts to discredit the Keynesian analysis. Free market economists did not care to acknowledge the vulnerability of the real economy, the economy of people's employment, income and saving, to malfunctions in the monetary sector. There have been plenty of such economists who have been willing to argue that complete freedom of financial markets, including capital markets, would produce the best of all economic worlds. From the early 1990s, however, dissenters warned of trouble ahead for developing countries from the importation of what Juan Somavia has called 'casino capitalism'. 'The fact is that capitalism is inherently unstable and it is particularly so in its early, infant stages,' according to John Kenneth Galbraith. As the Prime Minister of Singapore put it at UNCTAD X: 'Today, capitalism is everywhere triumphant ... and that may pose a challenge.' For countries that begin to integrate globally, rapid economic progress brings in its wake new insecurities.

The economic collapse of Chile in 1982, following the Chicago-inspired free market experiments of General Pinochet, led Carlos Diaz-Alejandro to coin the slogan: 'Goodbye, financial repression! Hello, financial crisis!' The subsequent twenty years have provided plentiful evidence of how prescient that slogan was.[5] The Asian financial crisis of 1997–9 highlighted the difficulties of successful exchange rate management in a world of liberalized capital accounts. Economists for many years modelled the exchange rate as being determined by macroeconomic fundamentals and their effects on the stock of domestic foreign exchange reserves. On this view, countries that maintained sound fundamentals could not suffer a successful speculative attack on their exchange rate. The Asian crisis showed that this reasoning was inadequate, and that other factors were at work – contagion effects on country reputation, and herding behaviour on the part of foreign investors. In the Asian financial crisis, the disruption resulting from badly executed financial liberalization became systemic in scope, including countries where the macroeconomic fundamentals were pretty sound.

That episode also revealed the sheer size of the financial flows that the industrial world can generate, and then withdraw, relative to the normal size of financial flows in developing countries. This disparity is evident in the figures quoted in Kwesi Botchwey's informative contribution on the performance and problems of financing economic development. The swift entry, and even swifter exit, of such massive flows made clear for all to see the havoc that can be unleashed on small and fragile financial systems that are open to such tidal waves of finance. Despite the commitment of the IMF to the complete liberalization of capital markets right up to (and even beyond) the hour of Asia's crisis, the same agency now says that it can see some virtues in certain types of capital controls. Repentance is always welcome, however late in coming.

At last, then, a more realistic evaluation of the limits of unrestricted capitalism is evident. The leaders of Asia told the Bangkok Conference of their perception of the increased volatility and systemic instability of international finance. At the conference, the leaders of Malaysia and Indonesia gave extremely forceful accounts of the travails of their peoples in the Asian financial crisis. Their message was that volatility of capital flows could not be effectively managed by means of the existing financial architecture. As Yilmaz Akyuz, UNCTAD's chief economist, put it:

> when policies falter in managing integration and regulating capital flows, there is no limit to the damage that international finance can inflict on an economy. It is true that control and regulation over such flows may reduce some of the benefits of participating in global markets. However, until systemic instability and risks are adequately dealt with through globalization ... the task of preventing such crises falls on governments in developing countries.

Once again, it is not global solutions that are to be feared, but the inadequacy of those that are currently on offer.

Facilitating positive processes of integration into the world economy must remain the goal of international economic policy. However, issues of sequencing are of the essence in approaching this goal, and the liberalization measures that are necessary to this end must be phased in a prudent and orderly manner. They must take account of specific local circumstances; they must be complemented by appropriate domestic policies and accompanied by institutional development and capacity building. Only then can they hope to succeed.

Free market economists traditionally have scorned the idea that producers of primary commodities, especially of agricultural commodities, labour under any special economic handicap. Yet, after fifty years of development, many of the poorer developing economies remain marginal because of their very narrow export base in primary commodities. Binswanger and Lutz point out in Chapter 8 that these producers cannot increase the demand for their products, and indicate how they are constrained in what they can export by the protective barriers that have surrounded, and to a lesser extent still surround, the agricultural producers of the developed countries. Since this clearly limits the possibilities of agricultural diversification, dependence on primary exports has been a difficult condition for most of them to escape from.

In the short run, the primary producers in the developing world are adversely affected by financial crises (such as affected Asia) only indirectly, as the price levels of primary commodities fall cyclically with the deflation of world demand. However, their longer-run development is jeopardized by the secular fall in the terms of trade of commodities *vis-à-vis* manufactures. Alf Maizels emphasizes in Chapter 9 that primary commodity prices have been historically depressed for the last twenty years, with no signs of improvement on the horizon. The long run downward trend of commodity prices is now increasingly recognized, even though the international community has turned its attention away from most of the special problems of commodity producers (chronic oversupply, price volatility, price cycles and the hedging of risk).

My third example of the belated recognition of inconvenient facts concerns the question of income distribution, and absolute poverty. Throughout the 1980s, the item 'poverty reduction' was entirely off the official international agenda. The excuse was that only once growth was achieved could matters of redistribution be addressed. The neoliberal agenda proposed the following line of causation: openness leads to growth, and growth then leads to poverty reduction. To reverse the sequence and to begin redistribution before growth was achieved was regarded by neoliberals as a naive and impractical suggestion.

In 1990, nevertheless, poverty was chosen as the subject for the World Bank *World Development Report*. When Mr Wolfensohn became president, he declared that the reduction of poverty was the bank's 'overriding objective'. At UNCTAD X, Michel Camdessus, the outgoing Executive Director of the International Monetary Fund, declared, 'there is a mutually reinforcing relationship between ... growth and the reduction of poverty and inequality'. Behind these political shifts, a new line of thinking has emerged in which the achievement of growth is taken to be conditional on efforts to reduce the degree of inequality and of vulnerability to risk. High inequality is seen as a deterrent to macroeconomic adjustment and high level of risk at the household and firm level discourages the economic actions, such as borrowing and investment, which would lead to growth.[6]

This is fully in line with the arguments of Frances Stewart in Chapter 10 of this volume. She cites numerous studies to the effect that a more equal income distribution is associated with faster growth. The reasons for this are both political and economic in nature. Politically, regimes that sustain or actively create inequality tend to rely on policies that will put the brakes on economic growth. Economically, reducing inequality has a variety of positive economic effects, such as reducing the fertility of populations, widening the market, and raising the productivity of labour. Our instincts of solidarity are not arbitrary, we may infer from this contribution, but are well grounded in economic reason.

I have argued that, while we have observed a movement of informed opinion towards the policies of economic liberalism, simultaneously we have witnessed a surprisingly frank acknowledgment in official quarters of the key unsolved problems of the capitalist economic order. These are its proneness to financial crisis, its failure to find remedies for the economic problems of peasant production and its recurring tendency to neglect the problem of poverty. In Hegelian terms, it is as if world society had to wait for the inadequate policies of state socialism to be finally discredited *before* it could permit itself to rediscover the enduring problems of capitalism that state socialism claimed to be capable of solving, but could not. All of these problems especially affect developing countries, and their resolution will not come about naturally, but only with selective and intelligent forms of government action. As experience shows us the limits of independent national action in the economic field, so the problem of constructing an improved global economic order impresses itself more powerfully.

The narrowing of the range of opinion in the last decade has come about by contraction of both ends of the ideological spectrum. What does this imply? To me, it suggests that the period from 1914 to 1990 was indeed, as the historian Eric Hobsbawm has called it, 'the age of extremes', and we have now lost the extremes. Should we feel a sense of regret at this diminution of our intellectual diversity? As an economist, I feel no sadness in dispensing with doctrines of economic policy that, as a matter of historical fact, never were economic at all in their origin, but were created in the heat of a geopolitical conflict now mercifully concluded. Rather, the opposite. As a person, I can understand a feeling of nostalgia for the simple world they offered, as a shelter to the mind when it tires of endless complexities and uncertainties. However, that shelter was illusory, and unavoidably scholars must learn to live, as we have increasingly since 1990, without resort to these doctrines of the political extremes. To say this is not to advocate the artificial restriction of academic debate. Issues of economic policy will always remain contested and, unless there is free scope for the exchange of economic ideas, for criticism and counter-criticism, our economic understanding will not make any further progress. I am merely recognizing the fact that, precisely under the influence of free criticism, the intellectually habitable terrain for economic policy making has shrunk.

I venture to suggest that one of the important ways in which critical thinking has caused the retreat of the ideological element in economics is by the renewal of interest in the moral foundations of market operations. As a result of much discussion and experiment, we are now increasingly aware that markets function better when underpinned by a morality that fosters general trust and reciprocity. Markets cannot operate well when they are dominated by the behaviour of opportunists, inside traders or players who freely break their contracts. Markets cannot operate well unless supported by governments that encourage a social, and indeed political, atmosphere of general trust and reciprocity. Governments cannot do that if they are dominated by the behaviour of the corrupt and greedy. And development itself is impossible unless both markets and governments function properly, that is, work together in a constructive partnership. Dani Rodrik put it well: 'The idea of the mixed economy is possibly the most valuable heritage that the twentieth century bequeaths to the twenty-first in the realm of economic policy.'[7]

Many aspects of the so-called 'failure of development' during the last fifty years can be readily explained, once we have these precepts in mind.

Economies do not develop just because they exist. Economic development has been historically exceptional, and not a general rule. It does not happen automatically in response to the fact that a country has fertile land or large deposits of mineral resources. It is more likely to happen where a particular kind of system or systems of human cooperation have evolved. The good functioning of markets and governments rests not only on habits of personal trust, but on habits of general and impersonal reciprocity of behaviour. This is the theme of the important contribution by Jean-Philippe Platteau, which also sounds a note of warning. Even if a process of social learning is spreading the required practices and norms of social cooperation more widely, the world cannot wait while this evolution takes place. Countries have to face the choices of globalization now, whether or not these norms are strongly entrenched in their culture. In consequence, some botched and painful attempts can be expected. In Chapter 12, Ippei Yamazawa discusses the Asian financial crisis as an example of a flawed integration. Then, building on the distinction between globalization and regionalization, he goes on to examine the extent to which regional organizations can facilitate the smoother integration of developing economies into the world economy.

As we look to the future, let us not forget the wise words spoken in Bangkok by the Indian Minister of Commerce and Industry, Murasoli Maran:[8] 'The end of socialism does not silence the cry of the poor, and out of the pain of poverty must be born new dreams of justice – a new world economic order.' The building of an international economic governance community that will respect the aspirations of all its members for sustainable development must rest on the same moral foundation as does sustainable development itself. The fundamental idea is once again that of generalized reciprocity. However, as Raul Prebisch emphasized when UNCTAD was established in 1964, the reciprocity of international economic relations must be real. It cannot be merely conventional. It cannot be formal only. It cannot be based on a nominal equality of countries that is belied in all the practices of negotiation, decision making and dispute settlement. Precisely because, so far, global integration has affected only a dozen developing countries, the economic world is still divided. In such a world, real reciprocity means taking account of the underlying asymmetry of economic structures. International economic governance based on real reciprocity still has to be constructed. That will be the new international order for which so many developing nations at UNCTAD X appealed.

Despite the intellectual convergence I have noted, the setting of international economic standards remains problematic. They will have to be negotiated between all the parties that subscribe to them in a democratic and transparent manner. The developed countries should not expect to be able to set international economic standards exclusively. And, once they are negotiated, the developed countries must be willing to be bound by them, even when they cut across their particular national interests. This is not well-established behaviour at the moment. Although the USA has expressed willingness to change practices that have been found to be in breach of its WTO obligations, it has also been willing to resort to tariffs, in the certain knowledge that the complaint, panel and appeal procedures are lengthy ones. All states on occasion try to put their own interests ahead of international norms, most of all hegemonic states that have long been used to having their own way and that can credibly threaten to change unilaterally the rules that do not suit them.

One of the clearest appeals made at UNCTAD X in Bangkok by the heads of state and government who spoke there was for a more inclusive and participatory decision-making process at the international level. What are the developing countries asking for? Three things that they seek above all are a mixture of substantive and procedural issues:

1. They want the massive barriers to be dismantled in relation to trade in agriculture, textiles and clothing and in the areas where tariff peaks and escalation still prevail, even after the implementation of the Uruguay Round Agreements. Although greater access to industrial countries' markets will not be enough to solve the problems of the least developed countries, it is crucial to securing the benefits of an open global trading system for the more advanced developing countries.
2. They want recognition for their efforts in promoting regional economic solidarity. Provided that these efforts are in the form of 'open regionalism', they can strengthen the move towards positive global economic integration.
3. They want existing international economic institutions to evolve so that they are capable of bridging the interests of both developed and developing countries. As the NGOs have emphasized, such institutions must be more pluralistic and participatory than they are today.

In the aftermath of the WTO Ministerial Meeting in Seattle, the prospects for progress in these three directions looked quite bleak. UNCTAD X provided the opportunity for a wide-ranging exchange of views on the issues surrounding globalization. In my view, it was instrumental in creating an improved atmosphere for negotiation, and in promoting greater mutual understanding on the complexities and policy choices of the globalization process. Some fruit from this was seen at the Doha Ministerial Meeting that launched a new negotiating round. However, a long agenda remains to be worked through in translating these better atmospherics into practical moves for institutional change at the international level, especially in the fields of trade and finance.

As the concluding chapter by Peter Evans stresses, there is a danger lurking in the drive towards a more broad-based system of international governance in the field of trade, finance and development. He regards the political foundations of the existing system, dominated as it is informally by the USA, as quite fragile. A strong push by the developing countries for greater participation in WTO decision making would be most likely, he suggests, to undermine its existing political support. The Bush Administration's retreat from multilateralism in international relations gives some credence to these fears. Yet, although it may be the less likely outcome, the successful adaptation of the institutions of international economic governance to a more multipolar world is still a possibility, and as such should be the star that the world statesmen of the new century steer by.

NOTES

1. This was the title of the WIDER (World Institute for Development Economics Research) Annual Lecture that he gave in Helsinki in January 1998. See Ha-Joon Chang (ed.), *Joseph Stiglitz and the World Bank. The Rebel Within*, London: Anthem Press, 2001, pp. 17–56.
2. The speech was given to OXFAM as the Gilbert Murray lecture in Oxford on 11 January 2000.
3. Michel Camdessus, 'The IMF at the Beginning of the Twenty-First Century: Can We Establish a Humanized Globalization?', *Global Governance*, 7 (4), pp. 363–70.
4. See Shahid Yusuf and Joseph E. Stiglitz, 'Development Issues: Settled and Open' in Gerald M. Meier and Joseph E. Stiglitz (eds), *Frontiers in Development Economics. The Future in Perspective*, Oxford, Oxford University Press, 2001, pp. 227–68.
5. See the empirical evidence of the association of financial liberalization and banking crises assembled by Asli Demirguc-Kunt and Enrica Detragiache, 'Financial Liberalization and Financial Fragility', in Boris Pleskovic and Joseph E. Stiglitz (eds), *Annual World Bank Conference on Development Economics 1998*, Washington, DC: World Bank, 1999, pp. 303–31.
6. Ravi Kanbur and David Vines, 'The World Bank and Poverty Reduction: Past, present and Future', in Christopher Gilbert and David Vines (eds), *The World Bank: Structure and Policies*, Cambridge: Cambridge University Press, 2000, pp. 87–107.
7. Dani Rodrik, 'Development Strategies for the Next Century', Santiago: ECLAC, 2001, pp. 1.
8. For a tribute to Mr Maran, see M. Naganathan, 'Murasoli Maran: an Intellectual Leader of the Dravidian Stock', in Vinanchi Arachi Jebamalai (ed.), *India's Time. Essays in Honour of Murasoli Maran*, Chennai: Kadiroli Publications, pp. 259–81.

2. The historical conflict of socialism and capitalism, and the post-socialist transformation

Bernard Chavance

ARGUMENTS FOR CAPITALISM AND SOCIALISM

Fundamental arguments by advocates of both capitalism and socialism were developed in the nineteenth century. The experience of the twentieth century led to an adaptation and a strengthening of these arguments. Advocates of capitalism, which is understood as a system based on private ownership, market allocation and entrepreneurship, have generally stressed the efficiency and rationality of the capitalist development process. In their view, private interests may spontaneously fall in line with the common good, and the population's standard of living may systematically be improved on a long-term basis through the virtues of competition. Distribution based on the market process is approximately fair, as individuals get, in principle, revenues proportional to their productive contributions. Hypothetical or existing socialism is considered economically irrational and inefficient as it destroys the institutional and spiritual bases of the 'good economy'. Moreover, it is contrary not only to economic, but also to political liberty.

Advocates of socialism, which is defined as a system based on social ownership and planned coordination of the economy, have often used similar normative criteria as their opponents, but with opposite conclusions about historical realities. They view capitalism as an irrational system resulting from market anarchy, which leads to high social waste and suffering (notably through crises and unemployment). It produces large inequalities and works in favour of a wealthy minority, both within capitalist societies and at the level of the capitalist world economy. Ideal or existing socialism, on the other hand, is seen as allowing consciously planned rational development, which does away with such capitalist flaws as recurring crises, waste and unemployment; it fosters social equality and may promote a higher form of liberty where a united society comes to master its own progress.

This sketch is, of course, a caricature, as both intellectual families included many differences, oppositions and evolutions. But the two families did exist and structured the ideas of the twentieth century. On both sides (see Table 2.1), we find a widely contrasting approach, as well as a distinction between the historical realities of the favoured system – that, admittedly, may have been full of concrete imperfections or mismanagement biases – and the ideal model that was deemed to give, by its very nature, a secure direction for future improvement (Chavance, 1994a).

So the systemic contest was founded on a similar set of proclaimed values or objectives: rationality, efficiency and equity on a general level, and modernization, growth and an improved living standard for the majority on a more concrete level. While the relative weight given to these values varied, as a whole they provided the normative standards of economic modernity.

Table 2.1 Contrasting views of the two systems based on similar values

The good system (capitalism or socialism)	The bad system (socialism or capitalism)
Rationality and overall efficiency	Irrationality and waste
Possibility of steady and long-term growth	Instability, endogenous fluctuations
Social justice, potentially realized	Unequal distribution of wealth and income, or power
Economic development and modernization for latecomers	Obstacles to genuine development, dependency *vis-à-vis* the great power(s)
Liberty ensured (individual or social)	True liberty denied

COMPARISON OF THE TWO SYSTEMS

General Similarities and Institutional Arrangements

Most interpretations of capitalism and socialism as economic systems were based on a model which emphasized their contrasting features (Steinberg, 1958). But on a general historical and theoretical level, there were important similarities, pointing to a kind of brotherhood, or even twin character of both families of system, that obtained throughout the process of their coevolution. Capitalism and socialism alike are highly diversified monetary and wage-labour systems, based on an extended division of labour within the economy and within large organizations. They both face the problem of finding sustainable forms or regimes of capital accumulation and income distribution. Coordination of the division of labour in a complex and monetary economy, and reproduction of the wage-labour nexus – that presupposes structural tensions in production and distribution – need to find proper and consistent institutional mediations. Such mediations would allow growth and development as conditions of systemic sustainability, and provide legitimacy for social domination (in a Weberian sense). As national economic systems represent complex configurations of numerous interdependent institutions – some designed and others evolved (and, most often, a combination of both design and evolution) – they are faced, in a dynamic perspective, with the contrasting necessity of coherence and stability, on one hand, and of flexibility and adaptability, on the other.

Some Qualifications

Conclusions based on the actual historical experiences of the national systems belonging to each of the two families seemed less sharp than in those delineated within the general contrasting models of each system. While some positive features of the preferred system seemed enhanced in particular periods or in specific countries, some flaws also became visible in different periods or countries. Significant regularities observed in countries belonging to each of the actually existing systemic families led to a comparative assessment where favourable, and adverse trends were mixed on both sides, making objective economic comparison more difficult (see Table 2.2).

MAIN PERIODS OF COEVOLUTION AND MUTUAL PERCEPTIONS

The Great Depression had a deep impact on both defenders and critics of capitalism. At the end of the 1940s, the memory of the 1930s, and the extension of socialist systems to a significant part of Europe and Asia, gave credence to the pessimistic or sober views of capitalism's future. Also the search for modernization and development by newly independent countries strengthened the attraction of the socialist model. Economically, the third quarter of the century was a kind of 'golden', or rather, 'silver' age for both systems, marked by significant overall growth and structural change in many countries belonging to each systemic family. The challenge of 'catching up', repeated by Khrushchev in 1961, was taken seriously by prominent Western leaders, and an emphasis on productivist criteria as a measure of success and a cult for growth were shared by both systems for the next decade.

Table 2.2   Two great historical systems

	Capitalism	Socialism
General commonalities	Division of labour, monetary-wage labour economies	
Political regime	Diverse (democratic or authoritarian)	Mono-party regime based on Marxist–Leninist ideology (dictatorship)
Dominant forms of ownership and coordination	Private ownership Market coordination	State ownership Vertical mediations in coordination
Type of structural disequilibrium	Surplus economy (demand-constrained system)	Shortage economy (resource-constrained system)
Dominant employment trend	Unemployment	Labour shortage
Accumulation regime	Diverse: extensive, intensive, mixed	Predominantly extensive
Stability of growth	Weak, important fluctuations, business cycles	Weak, important fluctuations, investment cycles
Stability of prices	Generally low	Generally high
Technological change	Generally fast, endogenous	Generally lagging, often imitative
Degree of social security for wage earners	Generally low, tendency for historical increase	Generally high
Income distribution	Unequal	Fairly equal (for official incomes)
Consumer gains from growth	Significant	Limited
Relationship of national economy with the international economy	Generally strong	Generally limited

The period apparently confirmed some of the virtues attributed by each ideological family to its preferred system. At the same time, the economic flaws imputed to both capitalism and socialism seemed to diminish during the period of high growth (the judgement was different as far as political and geopolitical trends were concerned). Actually, an optimistic theory of systemic convergence developed during that period. Macromanagement by the interventionist state and the extension of planning by giant firms, on one side, and the reduction of centralization and renewed interest in monetary and profit categories, on the other, were pointing, so it was argued, to a possible evolution of both systems towards an intermediate and similar 'industrial society'. But while some socialist countries managed to introduce positive economic reforms, most reformist experiences were disappointing or short-lived. Moreover, the political element in the institutional base of these systems was the ultimate obstacle to genuine adaptive reform (though China later represented an interesting exception).

Most tenets of the classical socialist system were gradually qualified for practical and theoretical reasons (Kornai, 1992) and advanced economic reforms reduced the contrast with the capitalist system. Central imperative planning based on physical targets, that allowed fast initial structural change, soon came to be viewed as engendering critical rigidities and obstacles to endogenous technological and organizational change. Attempts to reintroduce market coordination were made progressively, first as an 'instrument' for planning, later as a complement or corrective and, eventually, in advanced reformist countries such as Hungary, Poland and China during the 1980s, as a dominant mode when compared with traditional central planning. Market socialism, understood as an economy combining state ownership and market coordination, never managed (outside China) to become a credible alternative, let alone acceptable to most ruling nomenclatures. The crisis of the central planning alternative to market coordination (Brus and Laski, 1989) eventually led to the collapse of the notion of the superiority of social ownership over private ownership. Social ownership had been postulated as the necessary basis for ending competition and anarchy and as the condition for unified management of large national economies, based on the model of a huge enterprise extended to the whole society.

Thus most socialist reforms eventually failed in terms of durably improving the functioning and performance of the economy. By the end of the 1970s, the European and Soviet socialist economies were entering an era of 'stagnation' (to use Gorbachev's term), while the capitalist economies faced a new great crisis with the end of high and rather stable growth, the acceleration of inflation and the return of unemployment. Old critical arguments were revived, and uncertainty loomed on both sides. Each of the two competing and opposing systemic families was faced with a specific, endogenous and major adaptation crisis, with both crises interacting at the international level.

The 1980s marked the real turning point. In the West, the conservative shock started by Margaret Thatcher and Ronald Reagan accelerated the gradual shift away from the postwar Keynesian compromise and resulted in proposals of structural adjustment policies for developing countries. In the East, the structural crisis spread and lasted (with the exception of gradually reforming China), while the whole geopolitical edifice of Soviet hegemony started to crumble with Gorbachev's new policies. Between 1989 and 1991, the communist political regimes collapsed, resulting in an immediate dismantling of the systemic coherence of socialist economies. While it had been maturing in some socialist countries during the 1980s, the transition to capitalism proper began.

INSTITUTIONAL ARRANGEMENTS AND DEVELOPMENT STYLES

The objective of 'catching up and overtaking' capitalism played a central role in the formation and evolution of socialist systems, sometimes combined with a nationalist motivation, as in Asian regimes (Riskin, 1985). This objective was reiterated by Lenin, Stalin, Khrushchev and Mao Zedong. Most countries entered the socialist family from a low or intermediate level of economic development. Capitalism was conceived by Marxist–Leninist ideology as contrary to economic and social modernization and liberation in backward countries, while socialist institutions and systems were deemed to allow unfettered growth, structural change and welfare improvement.

The growth style in the initial phase was based on a specific disequilibrium strategy and stressed a list of priorities: industry over agriculture, heavy over light industry, and in general production over consumption (Nove, 1969). The strategy crystallized in institutions and behaviour of economic agents, which gradually became a rather inflexible development mode, manifestly resistant to subsequent reformist attempts to modify it (Chavance, 1994b). The building of new industrial structures was imitative of productive patterns typical of the previous period of capitalist industrialization. In the quarter century following World War II, the Fordist regime that came to prevail in the advanced capitalist world was very different, being based on a rather virtuous interaction between productivity growth, investment and the increase in mass production and consumption. The tensions that grew out of the relative success of these two models became manifest in the 1970s. The systemic families responded differently to their mounting structural crises.

The eventual failure of socialist economic systems was relative rather than absolute. Its significance is to be found in the standards that communist political regimes had set themselves for comparison with capitalism ('catching up and overtaking', in productivity, global production and consumption). Moreover, their final dismantling was not the result of economic factors alone, but of the interaction of the latter with geopolitical contradictions within the socialist sphere and on a world scale. The structural economic crisis of the 1980s was only the background of a process that was triggered by Gorbachev's reforms, and eventually by his decision not to use Soviet force and not to back repression in countries where protest movements against communist regimes were again developing. This economic background also explains that the very tendencies that Schumpeter (1942) saw as pointing to a decay of the capitalist system during the inter-war period were ironically at work during the last decade of East European socialist societies: for example, the 'crumbling walls', the 'devitalization of ownership', the growing criticism from intellectuals and the loss of confidence of the ruling class in its own system and its own future.

Change, Innovation and Adaptation

Systemic evolution in capitalism rests on permanent technological, organizational and institutional change. Such change proceeds sometimes incrementally and sometimes by rapid and wide-ranging shifts. The internal movement of the capitalist economy was stressed by Marx and Schumpeter alike, who shared the idea of the ambivalent effects of such perpetual change, that appeared as both creative and destructive (although they differed as to its causes and in their evaluation of the balance between creation and destruction). Competition between national economies and polities, and competition and social conflicts within capitalist nation-states, have been historically essential in this 'whirlwind of creative destruction'.

The creation of socialist systems appeared as a gigantic experiment in organizational and institutional innovation that met with significant initial success in achieving some important development targets set by communist regimes (other objectives, like consumption increases or popular participation, having early been deliberately sacrificed or postponed). However, their capacity to adapt to internal and external change eventually proved limited indeed when seen from a long-term perspective. A kind of systemic lock-in made itself increasingly felt, owing to the 'coherence of the classical system' (Kornai, 1992) and to the strong restraints set by the 'institutional base' (mono-party communist regime combined with domination of state ownership) on genuine technological, organizational and institutional adaptive change. These constraints were compounded by the limited sovereignty of countries within the Soviet-dominated sphere (Berend, 1996). We observe that only two socialist countries – Yugoslavia and China – went quite far in reforming their economies, but they had slipped out of the Soviet domain.

THE PROCESS OF TRANSFORMATION AND THE TRANSITION DOCTRINE

Post-socialist transformation started with the disintegration of the socialist institutional base. In Central Europe and in the Soviet Union this happened when the political pillar of the base collapsed – end of the mono-party regime (Kornai, 1998b) – while in Asia (China and Vietnam) post-socialist transformation gradually opened through the progressive erosion of the ownership pillar – end of domination of classical state property (Chavance, 2000). Transformation represents the shifting process whereby national economies move from the socialist to the capitalist family through widescale institutional and organizational change. It is like a passage from one systemic species to the other, within the common genre of monetary-wage labour systems. The ending of the process of coevolution of the two rival systemic families has far-ranging, but ambivalent, consequences for the remaining, and now unique, capitalist species. The arms race is over, but the pressure for accommodating social tensions within capitalist societies and within the world capitalist economy as a whole has been significantly reduced.

In the former socialist countries of Eastern Europe and the Soviet Union, the transformation process began under the auspices of a specific transition doctrine adopted by most new governments after the collapse of what remained of the communist ideologies, and under pressure from international organizations and Western states. Its main components were the prevalent neoliberal theories and the Washington Consensus. Stabilization, liberalization and privatization were presented as the main objectives for this unique historical experience. The highest priority was the fight against inflation, and speed was seen as essential for privatization. The 'shock therapy' applied in Poland gave a model for the objective of building a market economy within a short historical period (Balcerowicz, 1995). Macroeconomic stabilization would bring back growth, while liberalization and privatization would put the incentives right and stimulate the needed restructuring of productive capacities.

Depression and Other Surprises

As the process of transformation advanced, many unexpected developments took place. This was, so to speak, foreseeable, considering the scale and complexity of such an epoch-making change, but among these developments figured important surprises from the viewpoint of the transition doctrine. A severe crisis developed everywhere in Eastern Europe and the former Soviet Union: GDP plummeted, investment collapsed, industrial production fell, real wages decreased, inflation reached high levels and unemployment appeared and grew everywhere (Lavigne, 1999). During the same period, the gradually reforming socialist countries of Asia – China and Vietnam – following completely different methods than the transition doctrine would have implied, experienced high and prolonged growth. Numerous negative trends developed as a result of the post-socialist depression and transformation strains. A general rise in social inequalities and poverty (Kolodko, 1998) was reflected in demographic indicators. Criminality and corruption spread and the parallel economy expanded. Privatization proved more difficult than expected, and often had unforeseen effects: state ownership actually appeared to be somehow resilient, 'insider' privatization became widespread (Uvalic and Vaughan-Whitehead,

1997), complicated cross-ownership links developed, and no clear relationship emerged in the first decade between privatization and the multifaceted process of enterprise and industry restructuring (Estrin, 1998) (with the exception of foreign ownership, which in most cases concerned only a minority of former state enterprises).

In view of such a great number of surprises that soon became apparent in the first transformation period, and following controversies over policies implemented and their theoretical background, a qualified transition doctrine evolved in the second half of the 1990s. Such a doctrine partly admits to: an early neglect of institutions, especially of law and the role of the State; the importance of real growth as an objective that cannot result spontaneously from monetary stabilization alone; the significance of enterprise governance besides ownership changes; and the role of social dimensions of systemic transformation (World Bank, 1996,1997; Zecchini, 1997). These aspects had early been stressed by non-standard economic schools, especially institutionalist, Keynesian, Austrian and evolutionary authors of diverse backgrounds (for example, Murrell, 1992; Stark, 1992; Amsden *et al.*, 1994; Ellman, 1994; Nove, 1995; Eatwell *et al.*, 1995; Poznanski, 1995). But the latter faced their own surprises, in the form of the contrasting effects of shock therapy on Poland and the Russian Federation, the actual importance of changes in formal rules (legislation), the possibility of some types of holistic social engineering (Ellman, 1997), the general acceptance of transformation strains by the populations concerned and the frequent advocacy of gradualism as a veil for slowing down the exit process from socialism.

Nevertheless, a significant number of such *heterodox* analyses have been confirmed, particularly regarding: the role of path dependency and the heritage of the socialist past (Stark and Bruszt, 1998; Chavance and Magnin, 1997); the resilience of informal norms in social change (North, 1997a); the error of the monetary view of stabilization in neglecting the evolution of the real sphere (Delorme, 1996); the importance of the sector of newly created private enterprises; the comparative interest of the Chinese experience (Naughton, 1996); the role of institution building; and the necessity to transform and develop the State, as opposed to the neoliberal view of the minimal state.

The Asian crisis of 1997 and the Russian '*krach*' in 1998 accelerated a debate on the standard policies and theories, which had developed even within the Bretton Woods organizations (Stiglitz, 1998,1999). While acknowledging the positive trend in the evolution of the transition doctrine, its limits should be stressed, as the neoliberal core has not disappeared.

Diversity of Transformation Trajectories

A striking differentiation in national paths of systemic and developmental change was another surprise and puzzle for the transition doctrine, with its uniform initial strategy and its underlying notion of convergence towards an idealized normative model of the 'market economy'. While all post-socialist economies were obviously transiting to the capitalist family, such a change was appearing to be less deterministic and much more path-dependent than in the teleologist view of 'transition'.

At an intermediate level of abstraction between distinct national paths of change and the evolution of the whole post-socialist family, three distinct trajectories of transformation have occurred. In these trajectories, interdependent phenomena of political change, institutional shift, macroeconomic trends and social tendencies have generally reinforced each other and produced specific configuration of cumulative causation processes. Table 2.3 presents a stylized view of the three trajectories: Euro-centred social liberalism, dominant in Central Europe; depressive state crisis, typical of post-Soviet societies; and high growth gradualism, observed in Asian reforming economies. While some post-socialist countries are following an intermediate path between the first and second trajectories (as in the Balkans), the assessment of the three routes in the transition to capitalism seems fairly robust. Monocausal explanations, based on pre-socialist or socialist heritage, on initial forms of political change, on strategies and policies followed, on external influences or on cultural differences, all give a very partial account of the variety of transformation paths.

The numerous interdependent links of causality and feedback between the processes of change in the various spheres of society and economy that lay behind the diversity of national or regional trajectories point to the enormous complexity of systemic change. In such a process, all elements of the economic system, of the juridical sphere and of the political regime undergo profound transformations, while social differences are reshaped, cultural values are modified, and the international environment also changes. All these transformations take place in a concentrated historical period of about one decade, but their relative rhythms or temporalities differ. Traditional economic theory, based on equilibrium analysis, is poorly equipped to deal with such cumulative causation processes. Comparative institutional analysis, avoiding a reductionist, economistic approach, is needed to understand national, sectoral and local path-dependent processes of change.

At a more disaggregated level, significant and sometimes growing differences became apparent between national trajectories during the first transformation decade, even within the same group of countries (Chavance and Magnin, 1997, 1998; Elster *et al.*, 1998). The diversity of national and regional paths of change, leading to a significant variety of post-socialist emerging capitalisms (Magnin, 1999), illustrates the role of idiosyncratic and evolving institutional configurations that represent the very content of systemic change.

The historical background, initial conditions, but also systemic interdependence and specific national arrangements of institutions, explain why the same

Table 2.3 Stylized trajectories in the first decade of post-socialist transformation: a comparison

		Euro-centred social liberalism (Central Europe)	Depressive state crisis (former Soviet Union)	High growth gradualism (Asia: China, Vietnam)
Politics and the state	Mode of disaggregation of the institutional base (exit from socialism)	Sudden break (destruction of the political pillar)	Sudden break (destruction of the political pillar)	Gradual change (erosion of the ownership pillar, ideological accommodation)
	Political evolution	Democratic consolidation, alternating coalitions	Sham democracy	Authoritarianism (mono-party) with elements of informal pluralization
	Legitimacy of the state	Rather strong	Weak	Rather strong
	Administrative and tax capacity of the state	Rather strong	Weak	Rather strong
	Corruption, criminality	Extending, but still limited	High	Significant
	Regional differentiation	Limited (small countries)	Very high, tendency to fragmentation	High, but no fragmentation
Institutional and organizational changes	Institutional change (new formal rules, legislation)	Wide-scale and fast change; rules rather hard but unstable	Wide-scale and fast; soft rules, very unstable	Wide-scale but gradual; semi-hard rules but limited formalism
	Privatization of the economy (privatization of states' assets; extension of new private enterprises)	Fast, reasonably legitimate	Fast, very very low legitimacy	Gradual, no 'large-scale privatization' of state assets
	Emerging ownership forms	Multiple forms: insider ownership, investment funds, banks, state frequent cross-ownership, fuzzy property rights	Insider ownership, financial–industrial groups	Large expansion of 'non-state', but not strictly private, forms, fuzzy distinction between private and public ownership
	Organizational change	Strong expansion of private SMEs (often micro-enterprises), restructuring of former SOEs	Limited expansion of private SMEs, slow restructuring of former SOEs	Strong expansion of 'non-state' SMEs, slow restructuring of former SOEs
	Networks	Reshaped and tranformed in the new environment	Resilient, expanded role as a coordination mechanism	Reshaped, but significant role in emerging capitalist forms

Macroeconomic trends	Growth	Initial depression of about three years, followed by resumption of fragile but lasting growth	Prolonged depression (cumulative reduction of GDP by about 50%)	High and lasting growth
	Unemployment	Fast initial increase, stabilization near 'European' levels	Low registered unemployment (but actual level higher: 10–15%) and growing	High actual level
	Inflation	High initial surge in prices, followed by decreasing inflation rates, but still at relatively high levels	Prolonged mega-inflation followed by a decrease to unstable levels, high proportion of economic barter	Middle-range inflationary tendencies
	Opening to the international economy	Fast reorientation of trade to the West (mainly EU). Significant FBI in manufacturing, but concentrated in advanced countries	Foreign trade strongly affected by depression. Low level of FDI, concentrated in energy sector	Gradual but intensive opening, strong expansion of foreign trade, high level of FDI in manufacturing
Social tendencies	Inequality, poverty	Big increase in inequality and poverty in the early transformation, followed by a relative decline	Explosion in inequality, high level of poverty	Increase in inequality, reduction in absolute poverty
	Demography	Decline in fertility, increase in morbidity (also deterioration in HDI in most cases)	Decline in fertility, increase in morbidity, sharp increase in mortality, decline in life-expectancy (deterioration in HDI)	Increase in HDI
	Social protection for wage earners	Socialized (externalized from enterprises). Significant level of protection, but decreasing	Still partially internalized in large enterprises. Low level of protection	Internalized in large enterprises, gradual externalization. Low level of protection
	Relationship between political and economic elites	Differentiation	Strong overlapping	Overlapping, partial differentiation

Notes: SMEs: small and medium enterprises; SOEs: state-owned enterprises; FDI: foreign direct investment; HDI: human development index.

institutional reform or transfer, or a similar policy, can produce very different outcomes in different countries. Gradual reform, based on a dual price and planning system, led the Chinese economy to 'grow out of the plan' (Naughton, 1996), but it was an important factor in the disintegration of the Soviet economy under Gorbachev (Chavance, 1994a); fast 'large privatization' programmes produced dissimilar ownership and governance set-ups, as in the Czech Republic and the Russian Federation; macroeconomic shock therapy had contrasting consequences in Poland and the Russian Federation; the fate of bankruptcy laws differed among transforming economies; and the relationship between growth patterns and the evolution of distribution appeared quite diverse across countries and regions.

The variety of experiences explains why generalizations heard about 'transition' may often be falsified by different national counter-examples. No absolute laws about such a complex, multifaceted and controversial historical process are likely to be found, but a few tentative historical and theoretical lessons can be drawn.

SOME TENTATIVE LESSONS

Capitalism is the only modern monetary-wage labour system that has proved to be viable in the long run. Socialism, as an alternative system, has proved to be sustainable in terms of decades, but not beyond (Kornai, 1992). Its failure is patent, when judged according to the very objectives and values that were basic to its promoters and advocates, especially the aim of overtaking capitalism in terms of rationality, efficiency and welfare, and of eventually replacing it as a more progressive historical economic system. If socialism is interpreted as a substitute for capitalism in countries that had missed the first industrial revolution (as suggested by Robinson, 1960), the overall judgment is more mixed, but in a majority of instances (the Chinese being the exception, as already noted) the early reduction of the economic distance with capitalist countries at a similar initial level of development was followed by a growing gap during the last two or three decades of the systemic life cycle of socialist economies (Asselain, 1999).

Monetary-wage labour systems in general are confronted with permanent problems of evolution and change, resulting from tensions arising in the process of accumulation and development; these problems may or may not find temporary solutions through endogenous or imitative organizational and institutional change or innovation. Such problems become acute in periods of structural crises, and remain latent during relatively limited periods of stable and regulated growth. The family of national capitalist systems overcame three or four structural crises in the last two centuries, but the majority in the socialist family could not find a way out of their structural crises in the 1980s. A great crisis is essentially a crisis of *adaptation* for institutions and organizations, and this has meant, for the two systemic families during the twentieth century, an adaptation to their very process of coevolution.

The ambivalence in capitalist development analysed by great theoreticians has in general been confirmed by historical experience: positive and negative, creative and destructive, beneficial and detrimental features are combined in this system, and their relative weights have been changing at different times and in different national and international contexts. Some (but assuredly not all) systemic flaws of capitalism as an economic system identified by critical theories or social movements since the nineteenth century have been confirmed by history – mainly instability, unemployment and inequality. Keynes (1926), or Kornai (1998a) in the recent period, view capitalism in terms of inevitable dilemmas and necessary compromises between conflicting values. Actually, the most penetrating judgment about capitalism was made by Keynes, who combined the criterion of efficiency with a normative evaluation: 'For my part I think that capitalism, wisely managed, can probably be made more efficient for attaining economic ends than any alternative yet in sight, but that in itself is in many ways objectionable. Our problem is to work out a social organisa-tion which shall be as efficient as possible without offending our notions of a satisfactory way of life' (Keynes, 1926, p. 294). At the end of a century that allowed extraordinary progress and at the same time produced human destruc-tion and suffering on an unprecedented scale, such an attitude seems wiser than 'capitalist triumphalism' (Wiles, 1992), at a time when the challenge of socialism is definitively over.

Among general lessons is the importance of historical and contemporary diversity of national economic systems and trajectories within each great systemic family, and in the process of shifting from the socialist to the capitalist family (Chavance and Magnin, 1998). International and transnational relations have considerable influence, which has been obviously growing in the recent historical period. However, national institutional arrangements remain the decisive level where specific types of capitalism emerge and endure, as the state, politics and the wage-labour nexus all retain a national foundation (Boyer, 1999). Different configurations of capitalist economies coexist for long periods, new ones emerge, and no absolute convergence towards a hypothetical optimal (or suboptimal) type can be expected even in a period of 'globalization', where interdependencies between nation states are redefined on a world scale (Berger and Dore, 1996).

The search for universal, but often conflicting, values of modernity (liberty, equality, rationality, efficiency and solidarity) will continue. It will be a search for different types of capitalism embedded in various socio-historical contexts, and as a process of unending adaptive reforms, triggered by the continuous change 'from within', specific to capitalism as an economic system.

Market, State and Path Dependence

The end of socialist systems strengthened the notion of the 'market economy' central to the neoclassical tradition, as the accurate category to characterize modern developed systems. Such a view is based on the model of exchange, the figure of the real price, the concept of equilibrium and the notion of allocative efficiency; it stresses common elements or convergence between national economies, especially in the recent historical period; it defines the system by a coordination mode, namely the market (Boyer, 1997). But it is striking to observe that great economists or historians with different theories of capitalism – such as Marx, Schumpeter, Keynes, Polanyi (1944) and Braudel (1979) – have all contrasted capitalism as a concept to the real or normative representation of the market economy. In this view, production is given greater importance and the problem of change through tensions or conflicts is underlined; adaptive efficiency comes to the fore; the role of institutions and history is emphasized, the variety of national trajectories is questioned; and the system is defined by a monetary category – capital. Modern history confirms the greater relevance of such alternative approaches.

The remarkable contrast between the Russian trajectory of change and the Central European and Asian paths provides some theoretical lessons in the field of systemic transformation about the role of the state, path dependence and irreversibility. The cumulative weakening of the state's capacity and legitimacy in the Russian Federation was accelerated by the very rapid and corrupt privatization programme; by deliberate policies of drastically curtailing budget expenditure in a period of severe depression – leading to wage and payments arrears in the public sector, that undermined the whole tax system and accelerated the demonetization and fragmentation of the economy; by moves such as the 'loans-for-shares' operation in 1995–6, that reinforced the growing power of oligarchic financial–industrial–media groups over the government and the economy; and by the rapid liberalization of the financial markets in conditions of a fragile banking system and growing systemic risk (Sapir, 1998). A cumulative causation process emerged, where interdependent changes in formal and informal institutions and agents' behaviour produced a perverse lock-in that became typical of the post-Soviet trajectory. In Central Europe, on the other hand, many of the states managed to reshape and rebuild their capacities. This proved decisive in forming a fragile, but eventually positive, cumulative process of systemic change and growth (Sgard, 1997; Kolodko and Nuti, 1997). The role of democratic consolidation and the prospect of integration into the EU has obviously been instrumental here. The Chinese trajectory, however, where these factors are absent, also points to the decisive role of state capacity in the virtuous growth path that accompanied gradual and uneven institutional reforms over a period of two decades (as exemplified in the agricultural reforms, the open-door policy, the transitional dual-track regime in industry and the change in the fiscal system – Chavance, 2000).

Path dependence in post-socialist transformation signifies that the heritage of socialist institutions and behavioural patterns is still present in most societies, as institutional analyses have rightly shown; and it will remain so for some time to come. But the weight and the consequences of such a heritage are extremely diverse in different fields and in different societies, and they are evolving during the very process of systemic change. While inertia in informal rules often has been underestimated (North, 1997b), such rules have sometimes also changed very fast, for better or for worse, in given contexts. The dynamic interaction between changing formal and informal rules has thus appeared to be very complex and context-dependent, and the interactive learning processes of economic agents reveal many specific patterns in different sectors, regions and societies. The change of rules in general – institutional and organizational rules, constitutional and ordinary rules, and formal and informal rules – represents the essential content of systemic change, hence the decisive role of law and the state in the process. However, the relationship between emerging and evolving arrangements of interdependent rules and the overall process of economic and social development is very uneven, as can be seen from the variety of national trajectories already mentioned. Comparative institutional and systemic analysis remains the only way to address the question of diversity and draw some tentative lessons from history.

A decade of post-socialist transformation has represented a widescale historical experience, where theories and policies have been put to a test which has been, in many instances, cruel. The transformation process is not over, but it has already entered a new stage where it becomes directly part of the general challenge of redefining economic development in a globalizing and increasingly unequal world.

REFERENCES

Amsden, A., J. Kochanowicz and V. Taylor (1994), *The Market Meets its Match. Restructuring the Economies of Eastern Europe*, Cambridge, MA: Harvard University Press.

Asselain, J.C. (1999), 'Comment le capitalisme a remporté le conflit du siècle: le basculement des années 1956–1968', in: B. Chavance, E. Magnin, R. Motamed-Nejad and J. Sapir (eds) *Capitalisme et socialisme en perspective. Évolution et transformation des systèmes économiques*, Paris: La Découverte, 93–121.

Balcerowicz, L. (1995), *Socialism, Capitalism, Transformation*, Budapest: Central European University Press.

Berend, I. (1996). *Central and Eastern Europe 1944–1993. Detour from the Periphery to the Periphery*, Cambridge: Cambridge University Press.

Berger, S. and R. Dore (1996), *National Diversity and Global Capitalism*, Ithaca: Cornell University Press.

Boyer, R. (1997), 'The variety and unequal performance of really existing markets: Farewell to doctor Pangloss?', in J. Hollingsworth and R. Boyer (eds) *Contemporary Capitalism: The Embeddedness of Institutions*, Cambridge: Cambridge University Press, pp. 55–93.

Boyer, R. (1999), 'Le politique a l'ère de la mondialisation et de la finance: le point sur quelques recherches régulationnistes', *L 'Année de la régulation*: 13–75.

Braudel, F. (1979). *Civilisation matérielle, economie et capitalisme*, Paris: (3 vols) Armand Colin.

Brus, W. and K. Laski (1989), *From Marx to the Market. Socialism in Search of an Economic System*, Oxford: Clarendon Press.

Chavance, B. (1994a), *La fin des systèmes socialistes: crise, réforme, transformation*, Paris, L'Harmattan.

Chavance, B. (1994b). *The Transformation of Communist Systems. Economic Reforms since the 1950s* (translation of *Les réformes économiques à l'Est: de 1950 aux années 1990*, Paris: Nathan, 1992), Boulder, CO: Westview Press.

Chavance, B. (2000), 'The evolutionary path away from socialism: The Chinese experience', in E. Maskin and A. Simonovits (eds), *Planning, Shortage, and Transformation. Essays in Honor of Janos Kornai*, Cambridge, MA: MIT Press.

Chavance, B. and E. Magnin (1997), 'Emergence of path-dependent mixed economies in Central Europe', in A. Amin and J. Hausner (eds), *Beyond Market and Hierarchy. Interactive Governance and Social Complexity*, Cheltenham, UK and Lyme, US: Edward Elgar: pp. 196–232.

Chavance, B. and E. Magnin (1998), 'National trajectories of post-socialist transformation: Is there a convergence towards western capitalism?', *Prague Economic Papers*, VII (3): 227–37, September.

Delorme, R. (ed.) (1996). *A l'Est du nouveau. Changement institutional et transformation economique*, Paris: L'Harmattan.

Eatwell, J. et al. (1995). *Transformation and Integration. Shaping the Future of Central and Eastern Europe*, London: Institute for Public Policy Research.

Ellman, M. (1994), 'Transformation, depression and economics: Some lessons', *Journal of Comparative Economics*, 19(1): 1–21, August.

Ellman, M. (1997), 'The political economy of transformation', *Oxford Review of Economic Policy*, 13(2): 23–32, Summer.

Elster, J., C. Offe and U. Preuss (1998), *Institutional Design in Post-Communist Societies. Rebuilding the Ship at Sea*, Cambridge: Cambridge University Press.

Estrin, S. (1998), 'Privatization and restructuring in Central and Eastern Europe', in P. Boone, S. Gomulka and R. Layard (eds) *Emerging from Communism. Lessons from Russia, China and Eastern Europe*, Harvard, MIT Press, pp. 73–97.

Keynes, J.M. (1926), 'The end of laissez-faire', in *Essays in Persuasion, The Collected Writings of J.M. Keynes*, Vol. IX, London: Macmillan, 1972, pp. 272–94.

Kolodko, G. (1998), '*Nouveaux riches* vs *nouveauxpauvres*: Equity issues in policy-making in transition economies', *Emergo*, 5(2), 2–35, Spring.

Kolodko, G. and D. Nuti (1997), 'The Polish alternative. Old myths, hard facts and new strategies in the successful transformation of the Polish economy', WIDER, Helsinki.

Kornai, J. (1992), *The Socialist System. The Political Economy of Communism*, Oxford: Clarendon Press.

Kornai, J. (1998a), *Struggle and Hope. Essays on Stabilization and Reform in a Post-socialist Economy*, Cheltenham, UK, and Lyme, US: Edward Elgar.

Kornai, J. (1998b), *From Socialism to Capitalism : What is Meant by the 'Change of System'*, London: The Social Market Foundation.

Lavigne, M. (1999), *The Economics of Transition. From Socialist Economy to Market Economy*, 2nd edn, London, Houndsmills: Macmillan.

Magnin, M. (1999), *Les transformations économiques en Europe de l'Est depuis 1989*, Paris: Dunod.

Murrell, P. (1992), 'Conservative political philosophy and the strategy of transition', *Eastern European Politics and Societies*, 6(1): 3–16.

Naughton, B. (1996), *Growing Out of the Plan. Chinese Economic Reforms 1978–1993*, Cambridge: Cambridge University Press.

North, D. (1997a), 'The contribution of the new institutional economics to an understanding of the transition problem', *WIDER Annual Lectures*, 1, Helsinki: WIDER.

North, D. (1997b), 'Understanding economic change', in J. Nelson, C. Tilly and L. Walker (eds), *Transforming Post-Communist Practical Economies*, pp. 13–18.

Nove, A. (1969), *An Economic History of USSR*, Harmondsworth: Penguin.

Nove, A. (1995), 'Economics of transition: Some gaps and illusions', in B. Crawford (ed.), *Markets, States and Democracy*, Boulder, CO: Westview Press.

Polanyi, K. (1944), *The Great Transformation*, New York: Farrar and Rinehart.

Poznanski, K. (ed.) (1995), *The Evolutionary Transition to Capitalism*, Boulder, CO: Westview Press.

Riskin, C. (1985), *China's Political Economy. The Quest for Development since 1949*, Oxford: Oxford University Press.

Robinson, J. (1960), 'Marx, Marshall and Keynes', *Collected Economic Papers*, 2, Oxford: Basil Blackwell.

Sapir, J. (1998), *Le Krach russe*, Paris: La Découverte.

Schumpeter, J. (1942), *Capitalism, Socialism and Democracy*, New York: Harper.

Sgard, J. (1997), *Europe de l'Est: la transition économique*, Paris: Flammarion.

Stark, D. (1992), Path dependence and privatization strategies in East Central Europe', *Eastern European Politics and Societies*, 6(1): 17–53.

Stark, D. and L. Bruszt (1998), *Post-socialist Pathways. Transforming Politics and Property in East Central Europe*, Cambridge: Cambridge University Press.

Steinberg, F. (1958), *Le conflit du siècle. Capitalisme et socialisme à l'épreuve de l'histoire*, Paris: Seuil.

Stiglitz, J. (1998), 'More instruments and broader goals: Moving toward the post-Washington consensus', *WIDER Annual Lectures*, 3. Helsinki: WIDER.

Stiglitz, J. (1999), 'Whither reform? Ten years of the transition', World Bank, Annual Bank Conference on Development Economics, Washington, DC, April.

Uvalic, M. and D. Vaughan-Whitehead (eds) (1997), *Privatization Surprises in Transition Economies. Employee-ownership in Central and Eastern Europe*, Cheltenham, UK, and Lyme, US: Edward Elgar.

Wiles, P. (1992), 'Capitalist triumphalism in Eastern Europe, or the economics of transition: An interim report', in A. Clesse A and R. Tokes (eds) *Preventing a New*

East–West Divide. The Economic and Social Imperatives of the Future Europe, Baden-Baden: Nomos.

World Bank (1996), *From Plan to Market. World Development Report 1996*, Oxford: Oxford University Press.

World Bank (1997), *The State in a Changing World. World Development Report 1997*, Oxford: Oxford University Press.

Zecchini, S. (ed.) (1997), *Lessons from the Economic Transition: Central and Eastern Europe in the 1990s*, Dordrecht: Kluwer and OECD.

3. Globalization and development strategies

Deepak Nayyar

This chapter endeavours to situate the process of globalization in the wider context of development. In doing so, it explores the implications of globalization for development in retrospect and prospect. The main object, however, is to analyse the implications of globalization for strategies of development, if development is to bring about an improvement in the living conditions of people. The structure of the chapter is as follows. The first section sets out the essential meaning of development, in the light of the very uneven development experience and the fundamental change in thinking about development strategies over the past fifty years. The second section outlines the dimensions and characteristics of globalization in our times, to examine the economic factors, the political conjuncture and the intellectual rationale underlying globalization. The third section considers the development experience of the world economy during the last quarter of the twentieth century, the age of globalization, which suggests that the exclusion of countries and of people, attributable partly to the logic of markets, is a fact of life. The fourth section seeks to focus on the rules of the game for international economic transactions and explains how the process of globalization, combined with these asymmetrical rules, is bound to reduce degrees of freedom for developing countries in using economic policies to foster development. The fifth section argues that sensible strategies of development in a world of globalization should create economic space for the pursuit of national interests and development objectives. In this task there is a strategic role for the nation state, both in the national and in the international context, which is elaborated upon. The final section sets out correctives and interventions in national development strategies that would make for a more egalitarian development, which can only be introduced by the state because, unlike markets, governments are accountable to their people. It concludes that, as we enter the twenty-first century, the time has come to evolve a new consensus on development, in which the focus must shift from economies to people and from means to ends.

CONCEPTION OF DEVELOPMENT

There is a vast literature on economic development which is rich in terms of
range and depth, yet there is not enough clarity about the meaning of development. There are many different views. And perceptions have changed over
time. There is, however, an irreducible minimum which may be construed as
the essential meaning. Development must bring about an improvement in the
living conditions of people. It should, therefore, ensure the provision of basic
human needs for all: not just food and clothing but also shelter, health care and
education. This simple but powerful proposition is often forgotten in the pursuit
of material wealth and the conventional concerns of economics. The early
literature on development emphasized economic growth and capital accumulation at a macro level. The current literature on development emphasizes
economic efficiency and productivity increases at a micro level. Industrialization has always been seen as an essential attribute of development. The
emphasis has simply shifted from the pace of industrialization to the efficiency
of industrialization. The underlying presumption is that economic growth and
economic efficiency are not only necessary but also sufficient for bringing
about an improvement in the living conditions of people. From time to time,
dissenting voices questioned conventional wisdom about economic growth, or
increases in per capita income, as a measure of development, to suggest other
indicators of development, such as a reduction in poverty, inequality and unemployment, that would capture changes in the quality of life.[1] But these aspects
of development were largely ignored by mainstream economics, for it did not
make a distinction between means and ends. Economic growth and economic
efficiency, or for that matter industrialization, are means. It is development
which is an end. Thus growth and efficiency need to be combined with full
employment, poverty eradication, reduced inequality, human development and
a sustainable environment, to attain development. The purpose of development, after all, is to create a milieu that enables people, ordinary people, to
lead a good life.

In conventional terms, the world has made enormous economic progress
during the second half of the twentieth century. Over the past fifty years, world
GDP has multiplied tenfold while per capita income has trebled.[2] The growth
has been impressive even in the developing world, particularly when compared
with the underdevelopment and the stagnation in the colonial era during the
first half of the twentieth century. But such aggregates might conceal more than
they reveal. For development has been very uneven between countries and
within countries. The pattern of development has been such that it has led to an
increase in the economic distance between the industrialized world and much
of the developing world. It has also led to an increase in the economic distance
between the newly industrializing countries at one end and the least developed

countries at the other. At the same time, economic disparities between regions and between people within countries have registered an increase. In other words, many parts of the world and a significant proportion of its people have been largely excluded from development. This may be attributable to the logic of markets, which give to those who have and take away from those who have not, as the process of cumulative causation leads to market-driven virtuous circles and vicious circles. This may be the outcome of patterns of development where economic growth is uneven between regions and the distribution of its benefits is unequal between people, so that there is growing affluence for some combined with persistent poverty for many. This may be the consequence of strategies of development, as a similar economic performance in the aggregate could lead to egalitarian development in one situation, and growth which bypasses the majority of people in another situation.

Uneven development is not without consequences for people. Poverty, inequality and deprivation persist. And there is poverty everywhere. One-eighth of the people in the industrialized world are affected by, or live in, poverty. Almost one-third of the people in the developing world, an estimated 1.5 billion, live in poverty and experience absolute deprivation insofar as they cannot meet their basic human needs. The same number does not have access to clean water. As many as 840 million people suffer from malnutrition. More than 260 million children who should be in school are not. Nearly 340 million women are not expected to survive to the age of 40. And, as we enter the twenty-first century, more than 850 million adults remain illiterate. Most of them live in the developing world, but, in a functional sense, the number of illiterate people in the industrialized countries, at 100 million, is also large.[3]

It is clear that the development experience of the world economy since 1950 has been uneven and mixed. The attempts to analyse what turned out right and what went wrong have led to both diagnosis and prescription. This has, in turn, meant a fundamental change in thinking about development strategies.[4] In the post-colonial era, which began soon after the end of World War II, most under-developed countries adopted strategies of development which provided a sharp contrast with their past during the first half of the twentieth century. For one, there was a conscious attempt to limit the degree of openness and of integration with the world economy, in pursuit of a more autonomous development. For another, the state was assigned a strategic role in development, because the market, by itself, was not perceived as sufficient to meet the aspirations of latecomers to industrialization. Both represented points of departure from the colonial era which was characterized by open economies and unregulated markets. In the early 1950s, this approach also represented a consensus in thinking about the most appropriate strategy of industrialization. There were a few voices of dissent, but it was, in effect, the development consensus at the time. Forty years later, in the early 1990s, perceptions about development apparently arrived at the polar opposite. Most countries in the developing world, as also in the erstwhile socialist bloc, began to reshape their domestic economic policies so as to integrate much more with the world economy and to enlarge the role of the market *vis-à-vis* the state. This was partly a consequence of internal crisis situations in economy, polity and society. It was also significantly influenced by the profound transformation in the world economic and political situation. The widespread acceptance of this approach, it would seem, represented a new consensus in thinking about development. It came to be known as the Washington Consensus. There were many voices of dissent, yet it remained the dominant view, in part because it was propagated by the IMF and the World Bank, which exercised enormous influence on economies in crisis. This belief system was somewhat shaken by the financial crisis in Asia, but the Washington Consensus has also lost some of its lustre as development experience during the 1990s has belied expectations. Its prescriptions are now subjected to question.[5] And the questions have not come from the critics alone.[6]

In spite of the shift in paradigm from the development consensus of the 1950s to the Washington Consensus of the 1990s, the degree of openness *vis-à-vis* the world economy and the degree of intervention by the state in the market have remained the critical issues in the debate on development. The past fifty years have, of course, witnessed a complete swing of the pendulum in thinking about these issues. But the complexity of reality is not captured by either consensus. The reality, however, is clear. The exclusion of countries and of people from development has become much less acceptable with the passage of time. The proposition that economic growth, or economic efficiency, will ultimately improve the lot of the people is, obviously, far less credible fifty years on. The democratization of polities, even if it is much slower than the marketization of economies, has enhanced the importance of time in the quest for development. For almost three-quarters of the world's people now live in pluralistic societies with democratic regimes. And even authoritarian regimes need more legitimacy from their people. Poverty or austerity now for prosperity later is no longer an acceptable trade-off, for people who want development here and now. Clearly, the time has come to evolve a new consensus on development where the focus is on people rather than economies and on ends rather than means. For the welfare of humankind is the essence of development.

CONTOURS OF GLOBALIZATION

Globalization means different things to different people, and the word 'globalization' is used in two ways, which is a source of some confusion. It is used in a *positive* sense to *describe* a process of increasing integration into the world economy; it is used in a *normative* sense to *prescribe* a strategy of development based on a rapid integration with the world economy.

Even its characterization, however, is by no means uniform. It can be described, simply, as the expansion of economic activities across national boundaries. In this elementary sense, the world economy has experienced a progressive international economic integration since 1950. However, there has been a marked acceleration in this process of globalization during the last quarter of the twentieth century. There are three economic manifestations of this phenomenon – international trade, international investment and international finance – which also constitute its cutting edge. But there is much more to globalization. It refers to the expansion of economic transactions and the organization of economic activities across political boundaries of nation states. More precisely, it can be defined as a process associated with increasing economic openness, growing economic interdependence and deepening economic integration in the world economy.

Economic *openness* is not simply confined to trade flows, investment flows and financial flows. It also extends to flows of services, technology, information and ideas across national boundaries. But the cross-border movement of people is closely regulated and highly restricted. Economic *interdependence* is asymmetrical. There is a high degree of interdependence among countries in the industrialized world. There is considerable dependence of developing countries on the industrialized countries. There is much less interdependence among countries in the developing world. It is important to note that a situation of interdependence is one where the benefits of linking and costs of delinking are about the same for both partners; where such benefits and costs are unequal between partners, it implies a situation of dependence. Economic *integration* straddles national boundaries as liberalization has diluted the significance of borders in economic transactions. It is, in part, an integration of markets (for goods, services, technology, financial assets and even money) on the demand side and, in part, an integration of production (horizontal and vertical) on the supply side.

The gathering momentum of globalization has brought about profound changes in the world economy. It is worth highlighting the characteristics of these changes.[7] An increasing proportion of world output is entering into world trade, while an increasing proportion of world trade is made up of intra-firm trade. Between the early 1970s and the late 1990s, the share of world exports in world GDP rose from one-eighth to almost one-fifth.[8] The share of intra-firm trade in world trade which was one-fifth in the early 1970s rose to one-third in the early 1990s.[9] The significance of international investment flows also registered a rapid increase. Between 1980 and 1996, the stock of direct foreign investment in the world as a proportion of world output rose from less than 5 per cent to more than 10 per cent, while world direct foreign investment flows as a proportion of world gross fixed capital formation rose from 2 per cent to almost 6 per cent.[10] The growth in international finance has been explosive, so much so that, in terms of magnitudes, trade and investment are now dwarfed by finance. The expansion of international banking is phenomenal. The international market for financial assets has experienced a similar growth. And there is a growing international market for government bonds.[11] The size of international foreign exchange markets is staggering. Global foreign exchange transactions have soared from $60 billion per day in 1983 to $1500 billion per day in 1997.[12] By comparison, in 1997, world GDP was $82 billion per day and world exports were $16 billion per day, while the foreign exchange reserves of all central banks put together were $1550 billion.[13]

The origins of globalization need to be analysed in terms of the economic factors underlying the process and the political conjuncture which has enabled it to gather momentum.[14] The economic factors which have made globalization possible are the dismantling of barriers to international economic transactions, the development of enabling technologies and the transforming nature of industrial organization. The political hegemony characteristic of a unipolar world has strengthened this process, which is driven by the lure of profit and the threat of competition in the market.

Globalization has followed the sequence of deregulation in the world economy. Trade liberalization came first, which led to an unprecedented expansion of international trade beginning in the mid-1950s. The liberalization of regimes for foreign investment came next. And there was a surge in international investment which began in the late 1960s. Financial liberalization – the deregulation of the domestic financial sector and the introduction of convertibility on capital account – came last. This has been followed by the internationalization of finance at a phenomenal pace since the mid-1980s. The technological revolution in transport and communications has witnessed the advent of jet aircraft, computers and satellites. The synthesis of communications technology, which is concerned with the transmission of information, and computer technology, which is concerned with the processing of information, has created information technology, which is remarkable in both reach and speed. These technological developments have pushed aside geographical barriers. The time needed is a tiny fraction of what it was earlier. The cost incurred has come down just as sharply. New forms of industrial organization have also performed an important role. The emerging flexible production systems are exercising a strong influence on the strategy and behaviour of firms in the process of globalization. The nature of technical progress, the declining share of wages in production costs, or the increasing importance of proximity between producers and consumers, are constantly forcing firms to choose between trade and investment in their drive to expand activities across borders.

The politics of hegemony or dominance is conducive to the economics of globalization. The process of globalization, beginning in the early 1970s, has coincided with the political dominance of the United States as the superpower. This political dominance has grown stronger with the collapse of communism and with the triumph of capitalism. And the political conjuncture has transformed the concept of globalization into a 'virtual ideology' of our times. Dominance in the realm of politics is associated with an important attribute in the sphere of economics. For globalization requires a dominant economic power with a national currency which is accepted as the equivalent of international money: as a unit of account, a medium of exchange and a store of value. This role is being performed by the US dollar.

Economic theorizing often follows in the footsteps of political reality. It should come as no surprise, then, that recent years have witnessed the formulation of an intellectual rationale for globalization that is almost prescriptive. It is perceived as a means of ensuring not only efficiency and equity but also growth and development in the world economy. The analytical foundations of this world view are provided by the neoliberal model. Orthodox neoclassical economics suggests that intervention in markets is inefficient. Neoliberal political economy argues that governments are incapable of intervening efficiently. The essence of the neoliberal model, then, can be stated as follows. First, the government should be rolled back wherever possible so that it approximates to the ideal of a minimalist state. Second, the market is not only a substitute for the state but also the preferred alternative because it performs better. Third, resource allocation and resource utilization must be based on market prices which should conform as closely as possible to international prices. Fourth, national political objectives, domestic economic concerns or even national boundaries should not act as constraints.[15] In conformity with this world view, governments everywhere, particularly in the developing countries and the former communist countries, are being urged or pushed into a comprehensive agenda of privatization (to minimize the role of the state) and liberalization (of trade flows, capital flows and financial flows). It is suggested that such policy regimes would provide the foundations for a global economic system characterized by free trade, unrestricted capital mobility, open markets and harmonized institutions. And the ideologues believe that such globalization promises economic prosperity for countries that join the system and economic deprivation for countries that do not.[16] It needs to be stressed that this intertwined normative and prescriptive view of globalization is driven in part by ideology and in part by hope. It is not borne out by experience.

GLOBALIZATION, DEVELOPMENT AND EXCLUSION

The process of globalization in the world economy has brought about profound changes in the international context. It could have far reaching implications for development. The reality that has unfolded so far, however, belies the expectations of the ideologues. The development experience of the world economy from the early 1970s to the late 1990s, which could be termed the *age of globalization*, provides cause for concern, particularly when it is compared with the period from the late 1940s to the early 1970s, which has been described as the *golden age of capitalism*. Any such periodization is obviously arbitrary, but it serves an analytical purpose.[17]

Available evidence suggests that the past twenty five years have witnessed a divergence, rather than convergence, in levels of income between countries and between people. Economic inequalities have increased during the last quarter of a century as the income gap between rich and poor countries, between rich and poor people within countries, as also between the rich and the poor in the world's population, has widened.[18] And income distribution has worsened. The incidence of poverty increased in most countries of Latin America and sub-Saharan Africa during the 1980s and in much of Eastern Europe during the 1990s. Many countries in East Asia, Southeast Asia and South Asia, which experienced a steady decline in the incidence of poverty, constitute the exception. However, the recent financial meltdown and economic crisis in Southeast Asia has led to a marked deterioration in the situation. In the developing countries, employment creation in the organized sector continues to lag behind the growth in the labour force, so that an increasing proportion of workers are dependent upon low productivity and casual employment in the informal sector. Unemployment in the industrialized countries has increased substantially since the early 1970s and remained at high levels since then, except in the United States, while there has been almost no increase in the real wages of a significant proportion of the workforce in many industrialized countries. Inequality in terms of wages and incomes has registered an increase almost everywhere in the world. In most countries, the share of profits in income is higher, while the share of wages is lower than it was in the early 1980s. Over the same period, the rate of growth in the world economy has also registered a discernible slowdown. And the slower growth has been combined with greater instability. It would seem that, in some important respects, the world economy fared better in the golden age than it has in the age of globalization.

It is obviously not possible to attribute cause-and-effect simply to the coincidence in time. But it is possible to think of mechanisms through which globalization may have accentuated inequalities. Trade liberalization has led to a growing wage inequality between skilled and unskilled workers not only in industrialized countries but also in developing countries.[19] As a consequence of privatization and deregulation, capital has gained at the expense of labour, almost everywhere, for profit shares have risen while wage shares have fallen.[20] Structural reforms, which have cut tax rates and brought flexibility to labour markets, have reinforced this trend. The mobility of capital combined with the immobility of labour has changed the nature of the employment relationship and has reduced the bargaining power of trade unions. The object of managing inflation has been transformed into a near-obsession by the sensitivity of international financial markets, so that governments have been forced to adopt deflationary macroeconomic policies which have squeezed both growth and employment. The excess supply of labour has repressed real wages. Financial liberalization, which has meant a rapid expansion of public as well as private debt, has been associated with the emergence of a new rentier class. And the inevitable concentration in the ownership of financial assets has probably contributed to a worsening of income distribution.[21] Global competition has driven large international firms to consolidate market power through mergers and acquisitions, which has made market structures more oligopolistic than competitive. The competition for export markets and foreign investment, between countries, has intensified, in what is termed 'a race to the bottom', leading to an unequal distribution of gains from trade and investment.

Globalization has, indeed, created opportunities for some people and some countries that were not even dreamed of three decades ago. But it has also introduced new risks, if not threats, for many others. It has been associated with a deepening of poverty and an accentuation of inequalities. The distribution of benefits and costs is unequal. There are some winners: more in the industrialized world than in the developing world; there are many losers: numerous both in the industrialized world and in the developing world. It is, perhaps, necessary to identify, in broad categories, the winners and the losers.[22]

If we think of people, asset owners, profit earners, rentiers, the educated, the mobile and those with professional, managerial or technical skills are the winners, whereas the asset-less, wage earners, debtors, the uneducated, the immobile and the semi-skilled or the unskilled are the losers. If we think of firms, the large, international and global, risk takers and technology leaders are the winners, whereas the small, domestic and local, risk-averse and technology followers are the losers. If we think of economies, capital exporters, technology exporters, net lenders, those with a strong physical and human infrastructure, and those endowed with structural flexibilities are the winners, whereas capital importers, technology importers, net borrowers, those with a weak physical and human infrastructure, and those characterized by structural rigidities are the losers. It needs to be said that this classification is suggestive rather than definitive, for it paints a broad-brush picture of a more nuanced situation. But it does convey the simultaneous, yet asymmetrical, inclusion and exclusion that characterizes the process of globalization. It is not surprising, then, that the spread of globalization is uneven and limited both among people and across countries.

The process of globalization began in the early 1970s. The situation in the late 1990s, a quarter of a century later, reveals that the exclusion of people and of countries is a fact of life. Consider some evidence for 1997.[23] The share of the richest 20 per cent of the world's people, living in high income countries, in world GDP was 86 per cent, while that of the poorest 20 per cent of the world's people, living in low income countries, was a mere 1 per cent. The income gap between the richest 20 per cent and the poorest 20 per cent was as high as 74 to 1.[24] Similarly, the richest 20 per cent of the world's people in high income countries accounted for 82 per cent of world exports and 68 per cent of world direct foreign investment, whereas the poorest 20 per cent of the world's people in low income countries accounted for just 1 per cent of world exports, as also direct foreign investment. The richest 20 per cent of the world's people in high income countries used 74 per cent of world telephone lines and constituted 93 per cent of Internet users, while the poorest 20 per cent of the world's people used just 1.5 per cent of the telephone lines and constituted a negligible 0.2 per cent of the Internet users.

This sharp divide between rich and poor countries is no surprise. But the spread of globalization is just as uneven within the developing world. There are no more than a dozen developing countries which are an integral part of the process of globalization: Argentina, Brazil, Chile and Mexico in Latin America, and the Republic of Korea, Hong Kong, Singapore, Taiwan, China, Malaysia, Thailand and, to some extent, Indonesia in Asia. These countries account for 70 per cent of exports from the developing world, absorb almost 80 per cent of investment flows to the developing world and receive more than 90 per cent of portfolio investment flows to the developing world.[25] Sub-Saharan Africa, West Asia, Central Asia and South Asia are simply not in the picture, quite apart from many countries in Latin America, Asia and the Pacific which are left out altogether.

Joan Robinson once said: 'There is only one thing that is worse than being exploited by capitalists. And that is not being exploited by capitalists.' Much the same can be said about markets and globalization, which may not ensure prosperity for everyone but may, in fact, exclude a significant proportion of people. Markets exclude people as consumers or buyers if they do not have any incomes, or sufficient incomes, which can be translated into purchasing power. Such people are excluded from the consumption of goods and services which are sold in the market. This exclusion is attributable to a lack of *entitlements*.[26] Markets exclude people as producers or sellers if they have neither *assets* nor *capabilities*. People experience such exclusion if they do not have assets, physical or financial, which can be used (or sold) to yield an income in the form of rent, interest or profits. Even those without assets can enter the market as sellers, using their labour, if they have some capabilities.[27] Such capabilities which are acquired through education, training or experience are different from natural abilities which are endowed. But the distribution of capabilities may be just as unequal, if not more so. It is these capabilities which can, in turn, yield an income in the form of wages. Hence people without capabilities, the poor, who cannot find employment, are excluded. In fact even people with capabilities may be excluded from employment if there is no demand for their capabilities in the (labour) market. And, in the ultimate analysis, such capabilities are defined by the market. That is the problem.

Globalization has introduced a new dimension to the exclusion of people from development.[28] Exclusion is no longer simply about the inability to satisfy basic human needs in terms of food, clothing, shelter, health care and education for large numbers of people. It is much more complicated. For the consumption patterns and lifestyles of the rich associated with globalization have powerful demonstration effects. People everywhere, even the poor and the excluded, are exposed to these consumption possibility frontiers because the electronic media have spread the consumerist message far and wide. This creates both expectations and aspirations. But the simple fact of life is that those who do not have the incomes cannot buy goods and services in the market. Thus, when the paradise of consumerism is unattainable, which is the case for common people, it only creates frustration or alienation. The reaction of people who experience such exclusion differs. Some seek short cuts to the consumerist paradise through drugs, crime or violence. Some seek refuge in ethnic identities, cultural chauvinism or religious fundamentalism.[29] Such assertion of traditional or indigenous values is often the only thing that poor people can assert, for it brings an identity and meaning to their lives. Outcomes do not always take these extreme forms, but globalization inevitably tends to erode social stability.[30] Thus, economic integration with the world outside may accentuate social tensions or provoke social fragmentation within countries.

RULES OF THE GAME

The process of globalization has placed new players centre-stage. There are two main sets of economic players in this game: transnational corporations which dominate investment, production and trade in the world economy, and international banks or financial intermediaries which control the world of finance. It would seem that the present conjuncture represents the final frontier in the global reach of capitalism to organize production, trade, investment and finance on a world scale without any fetters except, of course, for tight controls on labour mobility. Transnational corporations and international banks or financial intermediaries wish to set the new rules of the game which would enable them to manage the risks associated with globalization. In this task, the nation states of the industrialized world provide the much needed political clout and support. The multilateral framework of the World Trade Organisation, the International Monetary Fund and the World Bank is, perhaps, the most important medium.

In a world of unequal partners, it is not surprising that the rules of the game are asymmetrical in terms of construct and inequitable in terms of outcome. The strong have the power to make the rules and the authority to implement the rules. In contrast, the weak can neither set nor invoke the rules. The problem, however, takes different forms.

First, there are different rules in different spheres. The rules of the game for the international trading system, being progressively set in the WTO, provide the most obvious example. There are striking asymmetries.[31] National boundaries should not matter for trade flows and capital flows but should be clearly demarcated for technology flows and labour flows. It follows that developing countries would provide access to their markets without a corresponding access to technology and would accept capital mobility without a corresponding provision for labour mobility. This implies more openness in some spheres but less openness in other spheres. The contrast between the free movement of capital and the unfree movement of labour across national boundaries lies at the heart of the inequality in the rules of the game.

Second, there are rules for some but not for others. In the WTO, for instance, major trading countries resort to a unilateral exercise of power, ignoring the rules, because small countries do not have the economic strength even if they have the legal right to retaliate. The conditions imposed by the IMF and the World Bank, however, provide the more appropriate example. There are no rules for surplus countries, or even deficit countries, in the industrialized world, which do not borrow from the multilateral financial institutions. But the IMF and the World Bank set rules for borrowers in the developing world and in the transitional economies. The conditionality is meant in principle to ensure repayment but in practice it imposes conditions to serve the interests of international banks which lend to the same countries. The Bretton Woods institutions, then, act as watchdogs for moneylenders in international capital markets. This has been so for some time. But there is more to it now. IMF programmes of stabilization and World Bank programmes of structural adjustment, in developing countries and in transitional economies, impose conditions that stipulate structural reform of policy regimes. The object is to increase the degree of openness and to reduce the role of the state in these economies so that market forces shape economic decisions. In this manner, the Bretton Woods institutions seek to harmonize policies and institutions across countries, which is in consonance with the needs of globalization.

Third, the agenda for new rules is partisan, but the unsaid is just as important as the said. The attempt to create a multilateral agreement on investment in the WTO, which seeks free access and national treatment for foreign investors with provisions to enforce commitments and obligations to foreign investors, provides the most obvious example. Surely, these rights of foreign investors must be matched by some obligations. Thus a discipline on restrictive business practices of transnational corporations, the importance of conformity with antitrust laws in home countries, or a level playing field for domestic firms in host countries, should also be in the picture.

The process of globalization, combined with these rules, is bound to reduce significantly the autonomy of developing countries in the formulation of economic policies in their pursuit of development. This is attributable, in part, to the asymmetrical rules and, in part, to the economic implications of globalization.

The existing (and prospective) rules of the WTO regime allow few exceptions and provide little flexibility to countries that are latecomers to industrialization. In comparison, there was more room for manoeuvre in the erstwhile GATT, *inter alia*, because of special and differential treatment for developing countries. The new regime is much stricter in terms of the law and the implementation. The rules on trade in the new regime will make the selective protection or strategic promotion of domestic firms *vis-à-vis* foreign competition much more difficult. The tight system for the protection of intellectual property rights might pre-empt or stifle the development of domestic technological capabilities. The possible multilateral agreement on investment, when it materializes, will almost certainly reduce the possibilities of strategic bargaining with transnational firms. Similarly, commitments on structural reform, an integral part of stabilization and adjustment programmes with the IMF and the World Bank, inevitably prescribe industrial deregulation, privatization, trade liberalization and financial deregulation. In sum, the new regime appears rule-based but the rules are not uniform. And it is not clear how or why this is better than discretion. For, taken together, such rules and conditions are bound to curb the use of industrial policy, technology policy, trade policy and financial policy as strategic forms of intervention to foster industrialization. It must be recognized that such state intervention was crucial for development in the success stories among late industrializers during the second half of the twentieth century.[32]

The constraints implicit in the economics of globalization are most vividly illustrated by the vulnerability associated with rapid or premature integration into international financial markets. This often begins with a reliance on portfolio investment, or capital flows that can be withdrawn on demand, to finance current account deficits in the balance of payments. An economy needs high interest rates together with a strong exchange rate regime to sustain portfolio investment, or other similar capital flows in terms of both profitability and confidence. This erodes the competitiveness of exports over time and enlarges the trade deficit. It is important to recognize the macroeconomic implications. Larger trade deficits and current account deficits require larger portfolio investment (or short-term capital) inflows which, beyond a certain point, undermine confidence and create adverse expectations even if the government keeps the exchange rate pegged. But when a stifling of exports does ultimately force an exchange rate depreciation, confidence may simply collapse and lead to capital flight. It is possible to think of many variations around this theme but the essential story line is similar.[33] And the outcome is the same when capital flight precipitates a currency crisis. These problems did indeed surface to begin with in Latin America and subsequently in Southeast and East Asia.[34] Russia and Brazil were the most recent casualties. The frequency and the intensity of such financial crises has only increased with the passage of time. And it is no coincidence that the most advanced among the developing countries, which are an integral part of globalization, have been ravaged by such crises.[35]

The problem is, in fact, even deeper and larger. Exchange rates can no longer be used as a strategic device to provide an entry into the world market for manufactured goods, just as interest rates can no longer be used as a strategic instrument for guiding the allocation of scarce investible resources in a market economy. What is more, countries which are integrated into the world financial system are constrained in using an autonomous management of demand to maintain levels of output and employment. Expansionary fiscal and monetary policies – large government deficits to stimulate aggregate demand or low interest rates to encourage domestic investment – can no longer be used because of an overwhelming fear that such measures could lead to speculative capital flight and a run on the national currency.

The lesson is clear. For developing countries, it would be prudent to reconsider the question of financial liberalization and wise to resist the pressures for capital account convertibility, because a premature integration into international financial markets is fraught with danger and can put development at risk.

THE STATE AND DEVELOPMENT IN THE CONTEXT OF GLOBALIZATION

As we enter the twenty-first century, the facts of life in the world economy are clear. Globalization is the name of the game from which no country wishes to be excluded. And not even large countries can afford to opt out. The choice, then, is between a market driven, passive, insertion into the world economy and a selective, strategic, integration into the world economy. The sensible choice would be to opt for the latter. But is it possible to contemplate correctives that would make this market-driven process more people-friendly so that the outcome is globalization with a human face? The object of such a design should be to provide more countries with opportunities to improve their development prospects and more people within these countries with opportunities to improve their living conditions.

Globalization has reduced the autonomy of the nation state in matters economic, if not political, but there remain degrees of freedom which must be exploited in the pursuit of development. The ideology of globalization seeks to harmonize not only policy regimes but also institutions, including the economic role of the state, across the world. This is a mistake because the role of the state in an economy depends on level of income and stage of development. The object of any sensible strategy of development in a world of liberalization and globalization should be to create economic space for the pursuit of national interests and development objectives. In this task, there is a strategic role for the nation state not only in the sphere of domestic economic policies but also in the arena of economic and political interaction with the outside world.[36] In the national context, the state must endeavour to create the preconditions for more equitable development, bargain with international capital to improve the distribution of gains from cross-border economic transactions, practise prudence in the macro management of the economy so as to reduce vulnerability, and intervene to minimize the social costs associated with globalization. In the international context, the state should attempt to reduce the asymmetries and the inequalities in the rules of the game and build strategic alliances among developing countries for this purpose.

Consider the national context. First, in countries that are latecomers to industrialization, the state must create the conditions for the development of industrial capitalism. In the earlier stages of industrialization, this means creating a physical infrastructure through government investment, investing in the development of human resources through education and catalysing institutional change, say, through agrarian reform. In the later stages of industrialization, this means using strategic industrial policy for the development of technological and managerial capabilities at a micro level, establishing institutions that would facilitate, regulate and govern the functioning of markets, and evolving strategic interventions interlinked across activities to guide the market in the pursuit of long-term development objectives. It must be emphasized that the benefits of integration with the world economy would accrue only to those countries which have laid these requisite foundations. Indeed, creating the preconditions and using strategic intervention are essential for internalizing (maximizing) the benefits and externalizing (minimizing) the costs of globalization.

Second, in the search for foreign investment, the state must resist the temptation of incentives and concessions. Indeed, wherever possible, the state must bargain with large international firms. Such an approach would not only improve the distribution of gains from economic transactions with transnational firms but also ensure that their activities are conducive to development. The reason is simple. Transnational corporations are in the business of profit while governments are in the business of development. For large countries, this means strategic negotiations in the sphere of trade and investment, say, to improve terms of trade, to obtain market access for exports, to facilitate transfer of technology or to establish manufacturing capacities in components or downstream activities. But this can only be done by governments and not by individuals or firms. For small countries, this means a conscious decision to opt out of 'a race to the bottom'. Hence governments must possess the minimal determination to stand firm or to negotiate, rather than to surrender from a perceived position of weakness or to give concessions without reciprocity in keeping with the rhetoric of unilateral liberalization.

Third, the state must ensure a prudent macro management of the economy, particularly in the sphere of government finances. This is so for two reasons. For one, it saves governments from being forced into stabilization and adjustment programmes that come with high conditionality which, in turn, reduces degrees of freedom in the pursuit of development objectives. For another, it reduces the vulnerability and the problems associated with a rapid integration into international financial markets through portfolio investment or capital account convertibility. The bottom line is that such prudence can enable a country to avoid some of the costs of integration through globalization and, at the same time, to capture some of the benefits by retaining the freedom to create the necessary conditions.

Fourth, from the perspective of social progress and human development, state intervention is an important means of minimizing the social costs or negative externalities associated with the process of globalization. It is possible to cite several examples: unbridled consumerism, industrial pollution, environmental degradation, sex tourism, lax labour laws and so on. The necessity for such intervention is greater in a developing country where poverty is widespread, environmental concerns are minimal and the rights of the citizens are not assured. And the process of globalization often relocates the production of goods and services, in whole or in part, to avoid laws and regulations in the industrialized world or the home countries of transnational corporations.

In the international context, nation states must endeavour to influence the rules of the game so that the outcome is more equitable. It need hardly be said that the nature of the solution depends upon the nature of the problem. Where there are different rules in different spheres, it is necessary to make the rules symmetrical across spheres. Where there are rules for some but not for others, it is necessary to ensure that the rules are uniformly applicable to all. Where the agenda for new rules is partisan, it is imperative to redress the balance in the agenda. But that is not all. Rules that are fair are necessary but not sufficient. For a game is not simply about rules. It is also about players. And, if one of the teams or one of the players does not have adequate training and preparation, it would simply be crushed by the other. In other words, the rules must be such that newcomers or latecomers to the game, say, the developing countries, are provided with the time and the space to learn so that they are competitive players rather than pushover opponents.

There is a clear need for greater symmetry in the rules of multilateral trading system embodied in the WTO. If developing countries provide access to their markets, it should be matched with some corresponding access to technology. If there is almost complete freedom for capital mobility, the draconian restrictions on labour mobility should at least be reduced. Similarly, the rules of the multilateral financial institutions, implicit in conditionalities of the IMF and the World Bank, which are applicable only to deficit countries or to borrowing countries, should be reshaped so that the standardized package of policies, which is inflexible, is not imposed on countries, irrespective of time and space, particularly where some of its elements are not consistent with national development objectives in the long-term.

In addition, the agenda for the new rules needs careful scrutiny for it is shaped by the interests of industrialized countries while the needs of development are largely neglected. For instance, if the proposed multilateral agreement on investment is so concerned about the rights of transnational corporations, some attention should also be paid to their possible obligations. In any case, such an agreement should not be lodged in the WTO. The issue of labour standards, of course, is simply not in the domain of the WTO. And, insofar as a game is not only about fair rules but also about competitive players, it is essential to reconsider the existing provisions of the unequal agreement on trade-related intellectual property rights (TRIPs), which was signed at a time when most governments and most people did not understand its economic implications. Such a reconsideration should endeavour to strike a balance between the interests of technology leaders and technology exporters in the industrialized world, which are the focus of attention, and the interests of technology followers and technology importers in the developing world, which are the object of neglect.

But that is not all. There are some spheres where there are no rules, such as international financial markets or cross-border movements of people, which are not even on the agenda. The time has come to introduce some rules that govern speculative financial flows constituted mostly by short-term capital movements, sensitive to exchange rates and interest rates, in search of capital gains. It is also perhaps necessary to think about a new international financial architecture in which a World Financial Authority would manage systemic risk associated with international financial liberalization, coordinate national action against market failure or abuse, and act as a regulator in international financial markets.[37] Similarly, it is worth contemplating a multilateral framework for consular practices and immigration laws that would govern cross-border movements of people, akin to multilateral frameworks that exist, or whose creation is sought, for the governance of national laws, or rules, about the movement of goods, services, technology, investment and information across national boundaries.[38] The essential object should be to create a transparent and non-discriminatory system, based on rules rather than discretion, for people who wish to move, temporarily or permanently, across borders.

In this context, it is important to stress that, for countries at vastly different levels of development, there should be some flexibility, instead of complete rigidity, in the application of uniform rules. For we should be concerned with the desirability of the outcomes and not with the procedural uniformity of rules. It is, in principle, possible to formulate general rules where application is a function of country-specific or time-specific circumstances, without resorting to exceptions. It implies a set of multilateral rules in which every country has the same rights but the obligations are a function of its level or stage of development.[39]

In sum, there is need to reduce asymmetries and inequalities in the rules of the game. How is this to be done? In the multilateral institutions, whether the WTO, the IMF or the World Bank, developing countries and transitional economies must ensure that their voices are heard. This is easier said than done, but groups of countries with mutual interests are more likely to be heard than single countries by themselves. For this purpose, it is essential to find common causes in a world where there are many conflicts and contradictions. There are two means of creating such country groupings: regional and subregional economic initiatives or strategic alliances between countries across regions. These must be based on a coincidence of mutual interests. Unless they constitute an integral part of the pursuit of national interest, such alliances or arrangements cannot sustain themselves, let alone provide a real solution. This is, perhaps, the most important lesson that we must learn from the failed quest for a new international economic order during the 1970s. An appeal to the enlightened self interest of the rich, which was the spirit of the North–South dialogue, or the rhetoric of solidarity among the poor, which was the spirit of South–South cooperation, cannot suffice. The impetus can only come from material interests in the sphere of economics and national interests in the realm of politics. There will always be conflict and contradiction. But there would be areas where it is possible to find common cause and accept trade-offs. Regional arrangements or strategic alliances among developing countries, which provide an institutional mechanism for this purpose, can also help in preventing a race to the bottom and in acquiring more bargaining power in the international context.

It needs to be said that governing globalization is, perhaps, just as important as reducing asymmetries in the rules. The momentum of globalization is such that the power of national governments is being reduced, through incursions into hitherto sovereign economic and political space, without a corresponding increase in effective international cooperation or supranational government which could regulate this market-driven process. In other words, national economies are much less governable while the global economy is largely ungoverned. In a world where the pursuit of self-interest by nations means uncoordinated action or non-cooperative behaviour, suboptimal solutions which leave everybody worse off are a likely outcome. International *public bads* such as environmental degradation, arms trade or drug traffic would increase, while international *public goods* such as a sustainable environment or world peace would decrease. Such outcomes can only be prevented through institutional mechanisms for cooperation. This requires more than rules. It needs a consensus as the regulation of public bads requires self-restraint from all countries, while the promotion of public goods requires a contribution from all countries. Global governance, then, is not so much about world government as it is about institutions and practices combined with rules that facilitate cooperation among sovereign nation-states.

DEVELOPMENT STRATEGIES IN THE NATIONAL CONTEXT

Markets and globalization have a logic of their own, which leads to inclusion for some and exclusion for others, or affluence for some and poverty for others. Given this reality, is it possible to think of correctives and interventions, in national development strategies, that would make for a more egalitarian economic development and a more broad based social development. The answer to this question can be contemplated in terms of two strategic approaches.[40] The first approach can be characterized as *proactive*. It should seek to develop mechanisms and policies to ensure that the benefits of development are widely shared. In turn, this requires an integration of social policy into the strategy of economic development. It also requires the creation of institutions to mediate between economic and social development. The object is to pre-empt exclusion. Such measures can be described as *correctives*. The second approach can be characterised as *reactive*. It should attempt to curb the degree of exclusion and, at the same time, provide social safety nets for those who are excluded. The object is to limit the adverse effects of exclusion. These measures can be described as *interventions*. It need hardly be stressed that there is a critical role for governments, in both spheres, particularly in the developing world.

The formulation of correctives requires careful design and implementation. The object should be to foster inclusion where markets exist and to create markets where they do not exist. The inclusion of poor people, where markets exist, requires the spread of education and an increase in social consumption. Human resource development, of course, is both a means and an end. And the role of governments is vital, particularly in primary education, adult literacy and vocational education, all of which would foster inclusion. Similarly, the development of a social infrastructure which provides the poor with access to shelter, health care, clean water or sanitation, and ensures a steady increase in social consumption, is almost entirely dependent on governments in the developing world. The creation of markets, where they are missing, requires a substantial investment in physical infrastructure, particularly in the rural areas and backward regions.[41] For example, roads which connect hinterlands to the world outside are essential for the creation of markets.[42] Governments must, therefore, find the resources for stepping up public investment in infrastructure, especially power, transport and communications. The withdrawal of governments from these sectors, in keeping with the ideology of marketization and globalization, is premature because sufficient private investment, whether domestic or foreign, is simply not forthcoming.

The integration of people who are excluded by markets into economy and society, requires one fundamental corrective. Such people must acquire either capabilities or assets which would provide them with access to the market as producers or sellers which, in turn, would yield an income so as to provide them access to the market as consumers or buyers. How can this be achieved?[43] First, there must be a systematic attempt to make the unemployed employable. This means creating capabilities through education or training. These capabilities must, of course, be related to the needs of the market. The object should be to create a market responsiveness in the supply of labour. Second, the creation of employment opportunities for the unemployed is imperative. This means economic policies that are employment-friendly and a strategy of development that is conducive to employment creation. The object should be to stimulate the demand for labour. Third, whenever possible, the poor should be provided with assets, so that they can enter the market as producers and earn an income on a sustainable basis. This is essential for those who have nothing to sell except their labour, but are not able to find employment. The obvious example is land reform which provides land for the rural poor who are landless.

The design and implementation of interventions is just as important. The object should be to ensure that markets do not accentuate exclusion. In this, too, the role of governments is crucial. For markets tend to widen disparities between regions and people, through a process of cumulative causation. Better

endowed regions experience a rapid growth. Like magnets they attract resources
and people from elsewhere until congestion or pollution halts the process. In
contrast, disadvantaged regions tend to lag behind. The same is true of poor
people or excluded groups who are disadvantaged because they do not have
sufficient income or assets, are not skilled or educated, and live in backward
regions. The extent of exclusion can be limited by providing public goods and
services for such regions, groups or people who are vulnerable, marginalized
and excluded. For the people who remain excluded despite such interventions,
it is essential to widen and strengthen safety nets such as anti-poverty
programmes or social security.[44]

It is clear that markets may exclude a significant proportion of people, particularly the poor, from the benefits of development, unless governments
regulate and complement markets so as to make them people-friendly. This
implies a crucial role for the state. The mood of the moment, however, is not
quite receptive to such ideas, for there is a disillusionment with the economic
role of the state. It now extends much beyond economists to politicians, opinion
makers and concerned citizens. And scepticism about the state runs deep. In
this milieu, there is a tendency to forget that markets are good servants but bad
masters and that the market is as much of a human institution as the state. It is
important to remember that success or failure of either is not exogenous but is
shaped in economy, polity and society. It is just as important to recognize that
the juxtaposition of government failure and market failure, or judgments about
which is worse, as if there is a choice to be made, is misleading because it
diverts us into a false debate.[45] Both market failure and government failure are
facts of life. For neither markets nor governments are, or can ever be, perfect.
Indeed, markets are invariably imperfect and governments are without exception
fallible. The important thing is to introduce corrective devices against both
market failure and government failure. In fact, as institutions, markets and governments can provide some mutual checks and balances *vis-à-vis* each other.

There can be no doubt, however, that it is necessary to redefine the economic
role of the state *vis-à-vis* the market. Such a redefinition should be based on
two basic propositions.[46] First, the state and the market cannot be substitutes
for each other but must complement each other. Second, the relationship
between the state and the market cannot be specified once-and-for-all in any
dogmatic manner, for the two institutions must adapt to one another in a cooperative mode over time. These propositions explain the difference between
success and failure at development. The real question is no longer about the
size of the state or the degree of state intervention. The question is now about
the nature of state intervention and the quality of the performance of the state.[47]

In contrast, the dominant ideology of our times seeks to create a world in
which the retreat of the state from the economy is matched only by the advance
of the market. Globalization, also, is a market-driven process. In the absence

of correctives, however, it may erode the social stability of institutions and the political legitimacy of governments in countries that are part of the process. Such correctives can only be introduced by the state and are, in fact, the responsibility of the state. The reason is simple: governments are accountable to their people, whereas markets are not accountable.

Even so, the changed international context attributable to globalization has important implications for strategies of development which must be recognized. An increase in the degree of openness of economies is inevitable, while the degrees of freedom for nation states are bound to be fewer. But it would be a mistake to consider this necessity as a virtue. Simplified prescriptions, which emphasize more openness and less intervention to advocate a rapid integration with world economy combined with a minimalist state that simply vacates space for the market, are not validated by either theory or history. Economic theory recognizes and economic history reveals the complexity of the development process. The degree of openness and the nature of intervention are strategic choices in the pursuit of development which cannot be defined and should not be prescribed irrespective of time and space, for they depend upon the stage of development and must change over time. And there can be no magic recipes in a world where economies are characterized by specificities in time and space. It is clear, however, that success at development needs an adaptive interaction between the state and the market.

It follows that the role of the state in the process of development will continue to be important for some time to come, even as the scope of the market increases through liberalization in the wider context of globalization.[48] Most would find this argument persuasive, yet many would doubt whether such a redefined economic role of the state is feasible in terms of politics. The willingness and the ability of the state to perform such a role depends on the nature of the state which, in turn, is shaped by the underlying politics. If we look at the world around us, it is obvious that states are not Plato's guardians. Thus governments do not always act in the interests of people at large. Indeed, governments are frequently sectarian in their actions as they seek to protect or to promote the interests of the classes, or groups, whom they represent. The state can be persuaded to act in the interests of its people only where political democracy exists, not just in form but in substance. For it is only democratic political systems, with supporting institutions and practices, that can provide checks and balances.[49] And it is possible for people to be at the centre of development, not only as its beneficiaries but also as the main actors, in a democracy which empowers people to participate in decisions that shape their lives.

As we enter the twenty-first century, it is time to reflect on a new agenda for development. In this reflection, the concern for efficiency must be balanced with a concern for equity, just as the concern for economic growth must be balanced with a concern for social progress. It is also time to evolve a new consensus on development, in which the focus is on people rather than economies. Such a consensus must be built on a sense of proportion which does not reopen old ideological battles in terms of either–or choices, and on a depth of understanding which recognizes the complexity and the diversity of development. This thinking should not be limited to the sphere of economics. It must extend to the realm of politics. For substantive democracy, which creates a political accountability of governments to the people, must be an integral part of the new agenda for, and the new consensus on, development. In such a world, ensuring decent living conditions for people, ordinary people, would naturally emerge as a fundamental objective. The distinction between ends and means would remain critical. And, in the pursuit of development, the importance of public action cannot be stressed enough. It must be an integral part of development strategies, which should not be forgotten in the enthusiasm for markets and globalization.

ACKNOWLEDGMENTS

I am grateful to Amit Bhaduri for helpful discussion and constructive suggestions. I would also like to thank Alice Amsden, Jacques Baudot, Hans Binswanger, Bernard Chavance, Mritiunjoy Mohanty, Siripurapu Rao, Rubens Ricupero, Ignacy Sachs, Shrirang Shukla, Frances Stewart and John Toye for comments and suggestions.

NOTES

1. See, for example, Baster (1972), Seers (1972) and Morris (1979). In recent years, this view has been put forward strongly by the UNDP in its *Human Development Reports*.
2. Cf. UNDP (1999, p. 25.
3. The evidence cited in this paragraph is obtained from UNDP (1999).
4. For an analysis of contending views about openness and intervention, see Nayyar (1997).
5. The critical literature on the subject is extensive. See, for example, Killick (1984), Cornia *et al.* (1987), Taylor (1988, 1993), Bhaduri (1992), Cooper (1992) and Bhaduri and Nayyar (1996).
6. See Stiglitz (1998).
7. For a detailed discussion, as also more evidence on these characteristics, see Nayyar (1995, 1997).
8. The export–GDP ratios are calculated from data on exports in UNCTAD, *Handbook of International Trade and Development Statistics* and United Nations, *Yearbook of National Accounts Statistics*, various issues.
9. UNCTAD (1994, p. 143).
10. UNCTAD (1998b, p. 385, 399).
11. For evidence on the expansion in international bank lending and the rapid growth in the international market for financial assets, including government bonds, see Nayyar (1995, 1997). See also UNDP (1999, p. 25).
12. Bank for International Settlements, *Survey of Foreign Exchange Market Activity*, Basle, various issues.

13. The value of world GDP and world exports in 1997, reported by the United Nations, has been converted into an average daily figure for the purpose of comparison. The figure on foreign exchange reserves of central banks is obtained from the IMF *Annual Report 1998*.
14. This outline of the underlying factors draws upon earlier work of the author. For a more detailed discussion, see Nayyar (1995). See also Oman (1994).
15. In this world, domestic economic concerns mesh with, and are subsumed in, the maximization of international economic welfare, and national political objectives melt away in the bargain.
16. See, for example, Sachs and Warner (1995).
17. The quarter-century that followed World War II was a period of unprecedented prosperity for the world economy. It has, therefore, been described as the *golden age of capitalism*. See, for example, Marglin and Schor (1990) as also Maddison (1982). The *age of globalization*, however, is not a phrase that has been used in the literature to describe the world economy during the last quarter of the twentieth century. It is suggested here by the author as this periodization facilitates comparison.
18. For supporting evidence, see UNCTAD (1997) and UNDP (1999). See also IMF (1997).
19. For evidence in support of this proposition, see UNCTAD (1997). In addition, see Wood (1994, 1997). Stewart (1999) also suggests that trade liberalization, (associated with globalization) provides an explanation for rising inequality and cites supporting evidence.
20. Some evidence on the increase in profit shares in industrialized countries and the decrease in wage shares in developing countries is reported in UNCTAD (1997). Stewart (1999) develops a similar argument that globalization may have led to an increase in inequality through an increase in returns to capital as compared with labour.
21. This argument is developed in UNCTAD (1997).
22. Cf. Streeten (1996), who draws up a balance sheet of globalization based on a rough approximation of what is good and what is bad.
23. The evidence cited in this paragraph is from UNDP (1999).
24. This income gap has widened over time. The ratio of the average GNP per capita in the poorest quintile of the world's population to the average GNP per capita in the richest quintile of the world's population rose from 1:31 in 1960 to 1:60 in 1990 and 1:74 in 1997. See UNCTAD (1997) and UNDP (1999).
25. See Nayyar (1995) and UNCTAD (1998b). This concentration of trade and investment flows in a small number of developing countries has increased sharply during the past two decades. It is worth noting that these twelve countries accounted for less than one-third of total exports from the developing world during the 1970s.
26. This term was first used by Sen (1981) in his work on poverty and famines.
27. In this chapter, I use the word *capabilities* to characterize the mix of natural talents, skills acquired through training, learning from experience and abilities or expertise based on education, embodied in a person, that enable him or her to use these (capabilities as a producer or worker) for which there is not only a price but also a demand in the market. It follows that even persons with capabilities may be excluded from employment if there is no demand for their capabilities in the market. It is essential to note that the same word, *capabilities*, has been used in a very different sense by Amartya Sen, who argues that the well-being of a person depends on what the person succeeds in *doing* with the commodities (and their characteristics) at his command. For example: food can provide nutrition for a healthy person but not for a person with a parasitic disease; or a bicycle can provide transport for an able-bodied person but not for a disabled person. Thus, for Sen (1985), *capabilities* characterize the combination of functionings a person can achieve, given his personal features (conversion of characteristics into functionings) and his command over commodities (entitlements).
28. The term *exclusion* has become part of the lexicon of economists recently, although it has been in the jargon of sociology and the vocabulary of politics in Europe for somewhat longer. The European Commission, for example, uses the phrase *social exclusion* to describe a situation, as also to focus on a process, which excludes individuals or groups from livelihoods and rights, thus depriving them of sources of well-being that have been assumed, if not taken for granted, in the industrialized countries. The essential point is that economic stratification is inevitable in market economies and societies, which systematically integrate

some and marginalize others to distribute the benefits of economic growth in ways which include some and exclude others. See Commission of the European Communities (1993). For an extensive discussion on social exclusion, ranging from conceptual issues through country studies to policy issues, see Rodgers *et al.* (1995).

29. This argument is developed by Streeten (1996) who also cites Benjamin Barber, *Jihad vs McWorld*, New York: Random House, 1995, on this issue.

30. The hypothesis that there are actual or potential sources of tension between global markets and social stability is developed, at some length, by Rodrik (1997).

31. The asymmetry in the rules of the game for the international trading system, emphasized here, is examined in Nayyar (1996).

32. For convincing expositions of this view, see Amsden (1989), Wade (1991) and Chang (1996).

33. Cf. Nayyar (1997).

34. For a systematic analysis of, and evidence on, financial crises in Southeast and East Asia, as also elsewhere, see UNCTAD (1998a).

35. The response of the multilateral financial institutions, in particular the IMF, to these financial crises was both inadequate and inappropriate. In some instances, the approach was counter-productive for it accentuated, rather than alleviated, the crises (cf. UNCTAD, 1998a). This experience exposed deep flaws in the international financial architecture.

36. For a more detailed analysis of the role of the state in a world of globalization, see Nayyar (1997). The discussion that follows in this section draws upon, and builds on, earlier work of the author.

37. The rationale for international regulation of global financial markets, possibly through such a World Financial Authority, is developed at some length by Eatwell and Taylor (2000).

38. For an elaboration of this idea, as also a more detailed discussion on its rationale, see Nayyar (2002).

39. It is possible to think of a weaker version of this formulation. The conditions under which countries can depart from, or even opt out of, multilateral rules can be specified. This would be the equivalent of an escape clause mechanism which is provided for in the WTO and also existed in the erstwhile GATT. For an articulation of this view, see Rodrik (1997).

40. Rodgers (1995) makes a distinction between two basic strategic alternatives – reactive and proactive – in a detailed discussion on the design of policy against exclusion. The implications of these alternatives for social integration are obviously different.

41. It is now widely accepted that substantial public investment in rural infrastructure was an important factor underlying the sharp decline in rural poverty in Indonesia between the mid-1970s and the early 1990s.

42. There is some evidence to suggest that *connectivity* provided by roads is critical in the inclusion of poor people and the integration of distant places into markets. In research on rural India, Bhalla (1997) has shown how economic activities have developed in clusters around arterial roads, running from the north to the south over long distances in the country, integrating rural settlements and small towns into the markets of faraway metropolitan cities.

43. In an analysis of development strategies that are likely to produce egalitarian outcomes, Stewart (1999) emphasizes similar factors: education and training, employment creation, asset distribution and government intervention.

44. In situations where exclusion takes the form of discrimination against identifiable social groups (say women, refugees or minorities) social legislation is necessary. But it may not be sufficient because it is difficult to implement and to enforce a law of equal opportunities. If such exclusion has a history, affirmative action in favour of vulnerable sections is inevitably needed to redress past discrimination. However, it is not possible to continue such affirmative action in perpetuity. In the ultimate analysis, therefore, it is the economic and political empowerment of these social groups that can end their exclusion. For this, political democracy is an imperative.

45. For a more detailed discussion, see Bhaduri and Nayyar (1996) and Nayyar (1997).

46. Cf. Bhaduri and Nayyar (1996).

47. For a discussion on the economic role of the state, see Stiglitz *et al.* (1989) and Killick (1990). See also Bhaduri and Nayyar (1996).

48. Economic historians tracing the evolutionary course of the market under early capitalism noted repeatedly that the market could become the organizing principle of capitalism only when it was embedded in the regulatory mechanism of the nation state. See, for instance, Polanyi (1944) who examined the complex interaction between state regulation and the growth of the market as an institution. This proposition is also borne out by the experience of countries that were latecomers to industrialization. For a discussion, see Bhaduri and Nayyar (1996). See also Wade (1991), Chang (1996) and Nayyar (1997).
49. This argument is developed, at some length, in Bhaduri and Nayyar (1996) and Nayyar (1998).

REFERENCES

Amsden, A. (1989), *Asia's Next Giant: South Korea and Late Industrialization*, New York: Oxford University Press.

Baster, N. (1972), 'Development Indicators', in N. Baster (ed.), *Measuring Development*, London: Frank Cass, pp. 1–20.

Bhaduri, A. (1992), 'Conventional Stabilization and the East European Transition', in S. Richter (ed.), *The Transition from Command to Market Economies in East–Central Europe*, San Francisco: Westview Press, pp. 13–32.

Bhaduri, A. and D. Nayyar (1996), *The Intelligent Person's Guide to Liberalization*, New Delhi: Penguin Books.

Bhalla, S. (1997), 'The Rise and Fall of Workforce Diversification Processes in Rural India', in G.K. Chadha and A.N. Sharma (eds), *Growth, Employment and Poverty: Change and Continuity in Rural India*, New Delhi: Vikas, pp. 145–83.

Chang, H. (1996), *The Political Economy of Industrial Policy*, London: Macmillan.

Commission of the European Communities (1993), *Towards a Europe of Solidarity: Intensifying the Fight against Social Exclusion and Fostering Integration*, Brussels: EC.

Cooper, R.N. (1992), *Economic Stabilization and Debt in Developing Countries*, Cambridge: MIT Press.

Cornia, G.A., R. Jolly and F. and Stewart (1987), *Adjustment with a Human Face*, Oxford: Clarendon Press.

Eatwell, J. and L. Taylor (2000), *Global Finance at Risk: The Case for International Regulation*, New York: The New Press.

International Monetary Fund (1997), *Globalization:Opportunities and Challenges, World Economic Outlook*, Washington, DC: IMF.

Killick, T. (1984), *The Quest for Economic Stabilization: The IMF and the Third World*, London: Overseas Development Institute.

Killick, T. (1990), *A Reaction Too Far: Economic Theory and the Role of the State in Developing Countries*, London: Overseas Development Institute.

Maddison, A. (1982), *Phases of Capitalist Development*, Oxford: Oxford University Press.

Marglin, S. and J. Schor (eds) (1990), *The Golden Age of Capitalism*, Oxford: Clarendon Press.

Morris, M.D. (1979), *Measuring the Conditions of the World's Poor*, Oxford: Pergamon Press.

Nayyar, D. (1995), 'Globalization: The Past in Our Present. Presidential Address to the Indian Economic Association', reprinted in *Indian Economic Journal*, 43(3), pp. 1–18.

Nayyar, D. (1996), 'Free Trade: Why, When and For Whom?', *Banca Nazionale del Lavoro Quarterly Review*, XLIX (198), pp. 333–50.

Nayyar, D. (1997), 'Themes in Trade and Industrialization', in D. Nayyar (ed.), *Trade and Industrialization*, New Delhi: Oxford University Press, pp. 1–42.

Nayyar, D. (1998), 'Economic Development and Political Democracy', *Economic and Political Weekly*, XXXIII (49), pp. 3121–31.

Nayyar, D. (2002), 'Cross-Border Movements of People', in D. Nayyar (ed.), *Governing Globalization: Issues and Institutions,* Oxford: Clarendon Press.

Oman, C. (1994), *Globalization and Regionalisation: The Challenge for Developing Countries*, Paris: OECD Development Centre.

Polanyi, K. (1944), *The Great Transformation*, New York: Holt, Rinehart and Winston.

Rodgers, G. (1995), 'The Design of Policy against Exclusion', in G. Rodgers, C. Gore and J.B. Figueiredo (eds), *Social Exclusion*.

Rodgers, G., C. Gore and J.B. Figueiredo (eds) (1995), *Social Exclusion: Rhetoric Reality Responses*, Geneva: ILO.

Rodrik, D. (1997), *Has Globalization Gone Too Far?*, Washington DC: Institute for International Economics.

Sachs, J. and A. Warner (1995), 'Economic Reform and the Process of Global Integration', *Brookings Papers on Economic Activity*, 1, pp. 1–118.

Seers, D. (1972), 'What are we Trying to Measure?', in N. Baster (ed.), *Measuring Development*, London: Frank Cass, pp. 21–36.

Sen, A.K. (1981), *Poverty and Famines: An Essay on Entitlement and Deprivation*, Oxford: Clarendon Press.

Sen, A.K. (1985), *Commodities and Capabilities*, Amsterdam: North-Holland.

Stewart, F. (1999), 'Income Distribution and Development', paper for UNCTAD X High-Level Roundtable, UNCTAD, Geneva.

Stiglitz, J.E. (1998), 'More Instruments and Broader Goals: Moving toward the Post-Washington Consensus', *WIDER Annual Lectures*, 2, Helsinki: WIDER.

Stiglitz, J.E. *et al*. (1989), *The Economic Role of the State*, Oxford: Basil Blackwell.

Streeten, P.P. (1996), 'Governance of the Global Economy', paper presented to a Conference on Globalization and Citizenship, 9–11 December, UNRISD, Geneva.

Taylor, L. (1988), *Varieties of Stabilization Experience: Towards Sensible Macroeconomics in the Third World*, Oxford: Clarendon Press.

Taylor, L. (1993), *The Rocky Road to Reform: Adjustment, Income Distribution and Growth in the Developing World*, Cambridge: MIT Press.

UNCTAD (1994), *World Investment Report 1994*, New York and Geneva: United Nations.

UNCTAD (1997), *Trade and Development Report 1997*, New York and Geneva: United Nations.

UNCTAD (1998a), *Trade and Development Report 1998*, New York and Geneva: United Nations.

UNCTAD (1998b), *World Investment Report 1998*, New York and Geneva: United Nations.

UNDP (1999), *Human Development Report 1999*, New York: Oxford University Press.

Wade, R. (1991), *Governing the Market: Economic Theory and the Role of the Government in East Asian Industrialization*, Princeton: Princeton University Press.

Wood, A. (1994), *North–South Trade, Employment and Inequality*, Oxford: Clarendon Press.

Wood, A. (1997), 'Openness and Wage Inequality in Developing Countries: The Latin American Challenge to East Asian Conventional Wisdom', *The World Bank Economic Review*, 11(1), pp. 33–57.

4. Trade policy as development policy: building on fifty years' experience

L. Alan Winters

INTRODUCTION[1]

International trade continues to be one of the main areas of policy controversy for developing countries. Some see protection from the cold winds of competition as an essential part of the early stages of development, while others see protection as creating, rather than curing, problems in developing economies. This debate has continued over the last fifty years and, although current thinking is closer to the liberal end of the spectrum than it used to be, controversy is very far from over.

The paper on which this chapter is based was written in response to an invitation from the UNCTAD Secretary-General to take a brief personal look at the course of thinking on trade policy since 1950, at the processes by which views have evolved and at the agenda for UNCTAD and similar organizations over the next decade or so. It is brief and personal and makes no pretence towards comprehensiveness. I stress the way in which more open policies have come to dominate import substitution in policy advice and urge that, in the future, openness and non-discrimination remain our watchwords. I concede, however, that the objective empirical evidence in favour of this view is not as strong as one might hope after fifty years of research. I base my advocacy of openness not only on arguments about economic efficiency and growth, but also on the belief that simple and open trade regimes offer a means of reducing governance problems in developing countries: they reduce the opportunities for discretionary policy, and hence for corruption and arbitrariness, and they offer a way of conserving skilled labour, in both public and private sectors, for the many other challenges of development such as education, efficient administration, entrepreneurship and research.

I argue that a key factor in the ascendancy of more open trade policies was measurement. The collection of data and their sensible presentation in the 1970s showed the parlous and indefensible state of most developing countries' trade regimes under import substitution. I also argue that our inability to measure and summarize trade regimes lies at the heart of our inability to prove conclusively that openness is good for economic growth. For the next decade, an UNCTAD that devises and produces effective measures of trade regimes would make a huge contribution and more than measure up to the complaints of its critics: 'An UNCTAD that measures, measures up!'

LOOKING BACK

In this section, I offer a stylized history of postwar thinking on trade policy, as summarized in Table 4.1. The aim is to identify both the trends in thinking about trade policy as development policy and the intellectual and experiential factors that lay behind them. I recognize that real life was both more complex and messier than my account, but I am trying, first, to be brief and, second, to highlight what I believe to be the major story-line behind these events. The major challenge of producing a historical account of policy thinking is to avoid a mere *ex post* rationalization of the trends. Economic research is so diverse that one can always find an intellectual precursor to any change in policy views, but that does not answer the question of whether the precursor was influential and, if it was, why it happened to be preferred among the alternatives available at that particular time. Thus I urge the reader not to take the history in too simplistic a cause-and-effect way. I have also added at the end of the section a few comments about the other forces that underpinned the major shifts in policy advice.

Throughout this chapter, I focus exclusively on developing countries' own trade policies. I do not deny that other countries' (specifically industrial countries') policies have some effect on growth and development; but they are not the main factor. Despite facing a more or less common trading environment, developing countries have had fundamentally different development experiences, from which I conclude that country-specific factors dominate. Once one recognizes that most countries are economically small, simple economic theory also suggests that countries' own trade policies dominate global factors in their development.[2]

The Story so far: Policy[3]

Table 4.1 distinguishes, perhaps a little arbitrarily, between theories of macro policy and those based on the economics of resource allocation. The former are the big issues, such as what fosters development, and deal quite explicitly with the whole economy. The latter encompass both macro- and microeconomic issues. They are macro to the extent that they draw on the fundamental insights of general equilibrium analysis. This is one of economists' unique con-

Table 4.1   A stylized history of postwar thinking on trade policy as development policy

Decade	Macro policy	Resource allocation
1950s	Import substitution Commodity pessimism and industrialization; infant economy protection; special and differential treatment; regionalism	Welfare economics of trade Second best
1960s and 1970s	Export promotion	General theory of distortions Infant industry arguments Costs of protection Effective protection
1980s	Outward orientation Getting prices right; fallacy of composition; costs of adjustment	Political economy of protection Rent seeking
1990s	Endogenous growth Theory and evidence; governance Economic geography	Trade and technology Poverty/income distribution

tributions to the policy-making process and an *indispensable* component of trade policy thinking because comparative advantage is a general equilibrium concept. Resource allocation economics also covers micro issues, however, such as optimal policy choice, and is the basis of the measurement of protection and its effects which, I shall argue below, underpinned the major advances in trade policy thinking.

In the beginning there were Smith and Ricardo; but by the 1950s, despite a number of brilliant disciples, such as Viner and Haberler, they were in eclipse. Several factors conspired to persuade economists that developing countries should manage their international trade very tightly. The apparent success of government intervention in the wartime economies and in Russia legitimized state management. Development was equated with industrialization, and industrialization was seen as an indivisible whole: one needed to advance over a wide range of industrial sectors simultaneously to have any chance of success, which called for considerable coordination. Further, the key to industrialization was investment, and since investment goods had to be imported from the industrialized countries, it was essential to conserve foreign exchange for that purpose. Primary commodity exports were not seen as a viable long-term source of foreign exchange because their demand prospects were limited and their terms of trade inexorably falling.

These views informed a fairly coherent policy position that import substitution (IS) was the route to development. Local industry was to be highly protected and there was a strong case for special and differential (S&D) treatment under GATT. Developing countries required both exemption from liberalization under GATT and enhanced access to industrial markets. Regional trading arrangements (RTAs) were another logical conclusion, for by increasing the size of the import-substitutes market they reduced the cost of the industrialization (Cooper and Massell, 1965).

The policy may have been internally coherent, but it was wrong. As time progressed, IS regimes became ever more arbitrary and distorted as governments tried to micromanage their economies. Moreover, IS was conspicuously unsuccessful in improving developing countries' trade, employment and poverty performances, and not obviously successful in stimulating economic growth. In addition, by the early 1970s, an alternative strategy based on promoting trade, rather than curtailing it, was beginning to show promise in the startling performance of the four tigers (the newly industrializing economies [NIEs] of Taiwan Province of China, the Republic of Korea, Hong Kong [China] and Singapore). I discuss briefly below what lay behind the success of these economies, but at the absolute minimum their experience showed that growth and industrialization were feasible without contemporaneous IS.[4]

A further, albeit slightly later, blow to the IS school was Balassa's (1981) demonstration that the more open NIEs weathered the oil shocks far better than did the more closed import substituters. This was a genuine surprise, for one of the previous claims for IS was that it offered some insulation from the excessive shocks in the world economy. Clearly, the open economies did face greater shocks, but apparently they were so much more flexible that they could withstand and recover from these better than the import substitutes could cope with their smaller shocks.

The factual attack on IS was influential but it depended on, and was supplemented by, an intellectual one. The critical contribution to trade and development theory, from research in the 1950s on resource allocation issues, was not the advances in the welfare analytics of international trade – for these largely reinforced the old arguments that trade was desirable in a static sense - but the theory of second-best (Lipsey and Lancaster, 1956). This offered cover for IS by using the liberalizers' own neoclassical tools to show that trade liberalization could not be guaranteed to be advantageous in an imperfect world. In the 1960s, however, second-best aspects of policy choice were refined into a general theory of distortions (based, for example, on Corden, 1957; Bhagwati and Ramaswami, 1963), which led to rankings of policies in which trade policy was almost always *n*th-best.

The apex of this literature from apractical point of view was, perhaps, Robert Baldwin's (1969) dissection of the infant industry argument, which left almost no respectable case for such protection at all. In addition, the dangers of casual second-best theorizing were realized, as in Harry Johnson's (1970) wise health warning that the application of second-best economics needs first-best economists, not its usual complement of third- and fourth-raters.

Even more important in the 1960s were advances in measurement. The theory of effective protection provided a pragmatic, if theoretically inelegant, measuring rod, and pioneers, such as Bela Balassa and Ian Little, showed that distortions could be identified and quantified. The result was startling in revealing not only the chaos of most developing countries' trade regimes but also the cross-country regularities in such chaos. These regularities largely rebutted the 'excuse' that IS was acceptable in principle but had been ruined in practice by incompetent administrators.

Initially, the NIEs' strategy was seen as one of export promotion (EP), which was contrasted with IS. However, it soon became obvious that no countries' net export incentives were as large as IS countries' anti-import distortions. Dispute raged, and still rages today, about whether this was because significant import restrictions were being offset by export incentives or because the policy stance was less interventionist overall. There is still, for example, disagreement about the interpretation of the East Asian experience.

Two forces led the balance of the normative argument in the 1980s, to shift (over the 1980s) from the use of export promotion tools towards the non-interventionist school, which is what I mean by outward orientation in Table 4.1. First, there was a broad-based swing in industrial country opinion away from government action and towards letting markets work. Ironically, at least at first, this was less evident in their trade policies than elsewhere – the 1980s saw increased numbers of voluntary export restraints (VERs), tighter Multi-Fibre Arrangement (MFA) restrictions, and more anti-dumping actions – but this did not prevent such opinion from covering trade policy when these countries offered development policy advice. Second, Krueger (1974) argued that implementing policy effectively was very difficult and that rent seeking could lead to efficiency losses far exceeding the traditional losses due to resource misallocation. Krueger's was an argument for preferring tariffs over quotas and other regulations, but it was soon realized that such difficulties afflicted all policy to some extent, and even the policy-making process. Increases in the complexity and extent of intervention seemed likely to lead directly to increases in the efficiency costs of implementation, in the probability of policy makers being captured[5] by special interests, and in the waste of resources devoted to directly unproductive activities. Thus, except where there was strong evidence to the contrary, simple, transparent and predictable policies looked best.

The World Bank's writings and advice illustrated this transition clearly over the 1980s, and it became one of the strongest advocates of the simple light-handed touch. The Bank did not undertake the fundamental research for this view, but was prominent in filling in the holes, providing measurement and thinking about its practical application. Again, measurement was critical, in which aspect the Bank was immeasurably helped by UNCTAD's pioneering work to record and categorize non-tariff barriers.

Trade liberalization featured in very many Bank (and eventually IMF) policy matrices, and since about 1987 there has been a significant reduction in trade distortions in developing countries. There have been many protests, however. Among the concerns expressed were that open borders would preclude developing countries from ever developing manufacturing sectors, that world markets could not absorb export growth from all developing countries at once, and that the costs of adjustment (political and economic) would be too large for the prospective gains.

The first of those worries is just old IS again, and while liberalization can lead to the loss of some protected manufacturing, the evidence of deindustrialization, still less of deleterious deindustrialization, is not great. The second is clearly a concern for some primary goods, but, as a general proposition, it neglects the fact that liberalizing countries are markets as well as suppliers. While there are likely to be adverse terms-of-trade spillovers if several similar countries liberalize together, these do not seem likely to offset the overall benefits of liberalization. Adjustment costs are a worry but one cannot put off change indefinitely. There is a case for some subtlety in the timing and sequencing of liberalization if the ultimate goal is wholly credible, but far too often delay undermines credibility, and sometimes ill-chosen transition paths worsen distortions for quite long periods.

The 'victory' for outward orientation in the policy debate challenged even its own advocates. Casual empiricism supported the position, but pure theory was agnostic. The intellectual challenge to IS had been essentially static, whereas the problem to be solved was dynamic. The need was to establish that 'openness leads to growth' as a robust, perhaps universal, prescription, and to explain why it worked. That is, economists and policy makers needed not only to address the comparative static benefits of openness but also to analyse the path towards the static gains and the genuinely dynamic benefits, if any.[6]

Theoretical work did not help very much. The new theories of 'endogenous growth', stressing learning, knowledge and human capital, opened up new dimensions to comparative advantage – learning versus producing – and new ways in which international specialization could generate economies of scale, by eliminating redundant research efforts. But their results were mostly very fragile and far from being applied in the real world. These results frequently suggested the possibility that some countries could lose from international trade, but since it was difficult to identify empirically when a country might fall into this last class, this analysis just did not help practical policy making. It is one thing to declare that trade policy should foster learning and the adoption of technology, but quite another to design a policy that actually does so.[7]

Empirical work to establish the growth benefits of openness looked more promising. Initially (in the late 1980s) there was some hesitancy about whether cross-section econometrics could deliver the necessary insight, but developments among growth empiricists swept this aside. Although the 'endogenous growth' theory was technically complex and subtle, its empirical implementation became heavily dominated by simple cross-section regression methods.[8] Over the early 1990s such studies, perhaps most famously by Sachs and Warner (1995), suggested, *prime facie*, that openness strongly enhanced growth. These results were always somewhat contentious, especially in their definitions of openness, but in policy debate they ruled supreme. Recently, however, Rodriguez and Rodrik (1999) have formalized some of the misgivings about this research stream and, as it were, re-established the old agnosticism. While there is no evidence that openness or trade liberalization is bad for growth, the case that they are good is not completely secure either.

Recent work on economic geography, for example Krugman (1995), has paralleled some of the uncertainties of the endogenous growth literature. The knowledge externalities of the latter are replaced by agglomeration externalities in the former, and the result is again that, within certain bounds, cumulative processes can occur and some countries can lose from trade. Geography is intellectually very attractive, as it deals with real-world phenomena, such as agglomeration and growth spurts, but it has not, I believe, yet produced any practical guidance on trade policy. One of the reasons is that its results depend critically on a generalized notion of trading costs, which we are currently quite unable to measure convincingly.

At the same time, as intellectual doubt has increased about whether openness is always beneficial at a country level, interest has also revived in whether it could hurt some people within a country. This was always known to be a possibility theoretically, but practically it had been neglected over the 1980s and early 1990s. Wood (1994) deserves most of the credit for reviving the issue.

The Lessons from History: Policy Making

History has definitely taught us one huge substantive lesson: closed and tightly managed economies do not prosper. A fair degree of openness, both in terms of policies and outcomes, seems to be more or less necessary for sustained economic development. History also, I believe, helps us to understand the process whereby broad trends in policy thinking evolve – an essential exercise if we wish to influence future policy (and understand why, on occasions, we fail to do so).

The above account comprises statements about stylized facts/perceptions of the world, actual facts (taking care that the two are usually distinguishable) and analytical advances. To elucidate the policy process, however, we need to add the incentives for the various actors involved. Policy is neither designed nor analysed by disinterested automatons, but by individuals who, even behaving by the strictest professional standards, have interests and opinions. These interests and opinions do not necessarily dominate hard evidence, but they do influence the research agenda and, in the areas that evidence does not determine for us, policy decisions.

As well as being based on a series of false premises about the world and about development, import substitution also received strong backing from two particular constituencies. First, World War II had allowed manufacturing to emerge in a number of peripheral economies, and they would undoubtedly have felt considerable pressure if the re-establishment of traditional manufacturing supplies had not been attenuated by protection. The importance of industrial elites in these countries made IS politically very powerful. Second, and more contentiously, planning was what official economists and bureaucrats knew how to do. They had little incentive to challenge conventional wisdom.[9]

Academic economists did not offer much of a challenge either. Of the several reasons advanced by Krueger for this, the most significant is their failure to operationalize either their positive or negative results. Thus, for example, it is hard to disagree that a positive dynamic externality provides a case for temporary intervention (for example, infant industry assistance). But to be useful we need tools to detect and quantify the externality and to know when it has run its course; that is, we need to know which infants will grow up healthy and repay their keep, and which to strangle at birth. Similarly, a major modality for trade theory research was to provide reasons why unrestrained trade based on comparative advantage was not guaranteed to be optimal. Although there was nothing wrong with that intellectually, these papers frequently gave succour to those intent on overruling comparative advantage for quite different reasons. It would have been better had their authors more carefully noted their arguments' limitations, delimited their areas of application, and spelt out *operational* conditions for identifying when their results were likely to be beneficial.

Perhaps unfortunately, academic criteria do not encourage either operationalization or modesty about the scope of applicability of results. Rather, the emphasis is on elegance and surprise. An example of the policy dangers inherent in these relativities is strategic trade policy, which was elegant, surprising, exciting and, at first, fun. Its applicability was never going to be particularly great – especially to developing countries – and after a few years its leading exponents (such as Paul Krugman and Avinash Dixit) abandoned it as a practical tool. However, it still fills lesser journals and figures in discussions with policy makers.

Parallel to operationalization is *measurement*. Measurement was, perhaps, the key antidote to IS, and this is a very important lesson. The economics profession undervalues measurement (measurers) relative to theory (theorists), and is weaker for that. I believe that the major barrier to understanding the links between openness and growth is the measurement one: our inability to characterize trade regimes adequately owing to failures in both data collection and analysis. One of the features of the cross-section literature referred to above is a tendency to treat openness as a dichotomous variable: you are either open or closed. In fact, however, while there is probably a threshold above which trade policy can be thought of as 'closed' (as with the Democratic People's Republic of Korea), and another below which such policy can be considered 'open' (such as Hong Kong, China), there is also a middle range in which 'openness' is ordinal or even cardinal. At present we are nowhere near being able to identify these thresholds or discuss degrees of openness satisfactorily.

One of the derivatives of the IS view was the case for special and differential treatment for developing countries under GATT. From relatively minor beginnings, this assumed a dynamic of its own over the 1950s and 1960s, in which offering export preferences to developing countries and releasing them from the various disciplines on import policy was driven by politics and rhetoric rather than economic analysis. GATT disciplines were seen as a cost to member governments, and waiving them was a simple and cheap way of purchasing developing country participation in GATT and the Western economic system. This dynamic was reinforced by the rivalry between GATT and UNCTAD, the latter of which turned degrees of bias in favour of developing countries into almost the only politically correct yardstick for measuring trade liberalization (see Finger, 1991). This experience reinforces two lessons, in my mind: first, you cannot divorce policy from politics, but the latter can emphasize and develop quite unimportant aspects of the former. Second, measurement is king. In this case, as Finger argues, the measurement was inappropriate, but its influence on the debate was undeniable.

Policy making has a good deal of inertia. I have already noted that IS was attractive to incumbent policy makers and it is evident from the record that it took a long time to overcome this effect. More recently, one might detect a similar effect in trade negotiations. The large trade bureaucracies built up to handle the Tokyo Round needed something to do over the early 1980s. They pressed for further trade talks and also helped make trade an issue in areas such as development policy. Since the Uruguay Round these bureaucracies have had a similar effect, as well as turning their hands to regional trade agreements. Geoff Raby, Australian Ambassador to the WTO, argues that this 'making work for idle hands' is a major factor behind regionalism in the 1990s. The lessons here are that policy messages are far more likely to succeed if there is a ready-made machine for implementing them, and that it is best to have useful things ready for bureaucracies to do.

LOOKING FORWARD

I want also to consider the future of trade and trade policy. In this section I pose five questions/issues that seem likely to be important over the next decade, and sketch some tentative answers where I have them. I conclude with some thoughts about what all this means for UNCTAD.

Five Key Policy Questions

Can we identify non-neutral interventions in international trade that accelerate development, and can we prevent their capture?

This question is carefully phrased: it is not 'are there' interventions, but can we 'identify' them. There are undoubtedly hundreds of individual cases where a one-off policy intervention would be beneficial, for example where protection would allow learning or training, or generate a terms-of-trade gain, or support a poor family while it learned new skills. But these opportunities are mostly far beyond our grasp for three sets of reasons.

First, we do not generally have the information required to identify the opportunity effectively. The difficulty is not usually in seeing that something is going wrong, but in saying why it is going wrong and in showing that trade and related interventions will cure it. For example, if the cost of training labour penalizes prospective manufacturing firms, will protection increase their incentive to train workers, or reduce it by increasing the rate at which new firms would enter the sector and bid labour away from the leader? Agricultural protection may raise prices, but it will not raise the return to agricultural labour or small farmers if the effect is wholly capitalized into land prices and rent. Moreover, it is important to realize that policy is relative. It is not only necessary to ask whether someone benefits from an intervention, but also whether they will benefit more than they might under an alternative policy, and whether they benefit more than the losers lose. Protecting car manufactures may help firms and workers in that sector, but consumers and other users (frequently other firms) will lose through higher prices, and other producers will lose via higher wages for skilled workers. Skilled workers in car manufacturing may generate some spillover effects on learning and on unskilled workers, but they might have generated even more had they remained in small-scale undistorted manufacturing service activity.

Second, the processes whereby interventions are translated into behaviour and outcomes often depend on quite subtle parameters, which are not amenable to observation, especially for hard-pressed developing country governments. This immediately puts the policy process at the mercy of interested parties. It is not only rank dishonesty that leads to capture but also an insidious process of information sharing and norm creation. Moreover, as I noted above (see note 5), capture is possible not only by the sector but by the policy-making bureaucracy as well. Recent years have seen a welcome surge of practical and academic interest in governance, and current opinion locates governance failure at the heart of the development challenge. Robust, simple and non-discretionary policies are far better than the opposite for encouraging clean administration, because they offer fewer opportunities for corruption and fewer distractions for the monitors. In addition, less distorting policies generally offer lower returns to corruption than do more distorting ones. From these perspectives, the advantages of a low uniform tariff over a high and finely graduated one seem huge.

Third, there are systematic aspects to intervention. Sufficient effort might overcome the information and the governance problems of an interventionist trade policy, but it is costly. Moreover, by signalling a willingness to intervene, one is encouraging petitions for interventions: the mere act of establishing the public and private institutions necessary to examine trade interventions objectively perpetrates a flow of requests for intervention that absorbs labour that would be better employed otherwise. Moreover, institutions cause inertia, so that the game continues even after the conditions that may once have justified it have changed – consider the European agricultural bureaucracy, for example. In other words, effective intervention, even if possible (which I doubt), is likely to be very costly and may just not be worth it.

These strictures about trade policy apply in some other areas of government as well, for example industrial policy, but they are not a case 'against government'. There are myriad tasks for government: health, education, infrastructure, legal structures, customs administration and so on. That these other tasks are so critical is yet a further reason why governments should eschew trade intervention.

Even in an account as brief as this, one cannot discuss trade policy and development without mentioning East Asia. The key exhibits are the Republic of Korea and Taiwan Province of China. They undoubtedly had intervention, although, as noted above, it was relatively neutral between exports and imports overall, and they clearly developed rapidly.[10] There were special features to their policy stances. For example, the focus on exports provided discipline to improve firms' competitiveness, a yardstick for policy and constraints on excessive distortion elsewhere in the economy; also the policy-making environment permitted the rapid correction of policy mistakes. These countries also had very strong performance in other policy areas such as education and infrastructure. It is interesting that Lee (1995) finds that trade interventions impeded productivity growth in the Republic of Korea (while tax intervention aided it). I am not sure we have really got to the bottom of the East Asian story yet, but I do think that experience elsewhere suggests that it is an Asian rather than a universal story.

It is sometimes argued that advocates of openness promote allocative efficiency at the expense of technical efficiency (for example, Nayyar, 1997). The evidence that openness directly boosts technical efficiency in middle-income countries is not particularly strong. However, its indirect effect is significant in terms of allowing efficient firms to expand, and policies which discourage firm turnover (such as tailor-made protection for incumbents) will reduce the rate of technical advance (Roberts and Tybout, 1996). Moreover, Bigsten *et al.* (1998) show that in low-income Africa technical efficiency in manufacturing is enhanced by openness.

Finally, it is necessary to ask whether optimal trade intervention varies by country. If one believes that development equates with manufacturing, one might argue for distinguishing by comparative advantage, because comparative advantage will lead some countries away from that sector. I do not believe this view, however. Small isolated economies, or those that are rich in resources or have high internal transactions costs, as in Africa, are unlikely to develop major manufacturing bases; however, some subsectors will still be open to them for local markets and, possibly, for particular export markets. Moreover, a decent living can be made outside manufacturing, as in New Zealand and Chile; and there is no evidence that a coddled manufacturing sector will improve on that living.

Another school of thought suggests distinguishing by stage of development, arguing that very poor countries need different stances in their policies on trade from other countries. This takes us to the second question.

Are there preconditions for benefiting from trade liberalization, and are there necessary concomitant policies?

My general answer to this question is that, while some conditions clearly help, there are no absolute preconditions. It is quite clear that trading infrastructure – hard and soft – greatly facilitates exporters and importers taking advantage of open borders. And if it is not in place, developing this infrastructure is, I believe, a necessary concomitant. But even if the infrastructure is not in place, liberalization is likely to open up some opportunities, and to postpone liberalization would be to forgo these opportunities. Only if the holes in the infrastructure are severely biased, so that trade will develop contrary to long-term comparative advantage (an unlikely condition), or if a slow start will irredeemably damage the political conditions for liberalization, would I suggest waiting.

The problem with most delays is that they cast doubt over the eventual policy reform itself and thus hinder, rather than assist, evolution towards an appropriate policy constellation. If one waits until everything is 'right' for trade reform, one waits indefinitely. Once the final destination is credibly established (by political action, possibly aided by bindings at WTO or commitments to the Bretton Woods institutions), my personal view is that transition periods can be quite long. Such gradualism would permit putting in place the various legal and institutional reforms that help to maximize the benefits of liberalization and the smoothing over of any cyclical hindrances to liberalization. The key condition, however, is that the eventual liberalization be quite assured. It is interesting that some trade reforms, which initially generated great resistance and could be negotiated only with recourse to long transition periods, have actually been speeded up once the adjustment has started: for example, the Kennedy Round and internal free trade in the European Economic Community. Presumably, once the destination is clear, economic actors prefer to get on with it.

The success of outward-oriented policies in East Asia followed periods of import substitution and was accompanied by huge steps in education and training. Are these preconditions or concomitants for trade liberalization? In East Asia, which has a strong comparative advantage in manufacturing, this portfolio of policies worked well, but that does not necessarily make it applicable to other countries.

Education is essential to development quite independently of trade policy, and hence is not really covered by this debate. The question of whether a preceding period of import substitution is necessary for trade liberalization to be successful is more complex, however. To one extent or another, nearly all countries have developed their export industries out of those already supplying domestic markets. Amsden (2001) argues eloquently that among industrial economies and those constituting her 'rest' (broadly speaking a set of well-established middle-income economies) only Switzerland and Hong Kong (China) used free trade as a catch-up strategy. And she lists an impressive number of cases in which exports have grown from domestic industries.

History has been unkind to us in resolving this dilemma, as import substitution was a more or less universal creed over the 1950s and 1960s. Thus, just as successful episodes have emerged from it, so have unsuccessful ones. Moreover, the practical issue is not so much whether exports grow out of domestic sales – they almost always do, for very few entrepreneurs set up purely exporting operations in new industries – but whether exports grow out of highly protected domestic sales. Amsden argues that the key difference between successful and unsuccessful industrialization strategies is the ability of governments to extract exports out of protected domestic industries.[11] I would argue that low levels of protection can help that process. I would also argue that an open low-income developing country is likely to have a real exchange rate so low that manufacturing will emerge to serve domestic markets from which, if comparative advantage dictates, exports can develop. Moreover, building up a manufacturing sector that will not have comparative advantage is not an obviously useful strategy. It creates lobbies for continuing protection and will have to undergo significant change when liberalization occurs. I argued above that industrialization and development are not synonymous, and so I am rather unsympathetic to building up this sector before liberalizing.

In very poor countries, trade taxes are an important source of revenue. Creating alternatives, including excise taxes, is a concomitant policy, but again I would not delay liberalizing until those alternatives are introduced. Nearly all protection structures can be reformed without loss of revenue if they switch non-tariff barriers (NTBs) into tariffs, unify rates (ideally to a single level) and abolish exceptions.

Is non-discrimination passé?

My answer here is unambiguously 'no'. Unilateral preferences, much beloved by UNCTAD and many developing country policy makers, have not, in general, been a success (Wang and Winters, 1998). In most goods the margins are small because industrial country tariffs are low. Where they are not small, the preferences are constrained either quantitatively (formally or informally) or by rules of origin. Where developing countries have comparative advantage, they frequently have no preferences at all; for example, the United States' general system of preferences (GSP) excludes clothing. In the few cases where preference margins are significant, they are no basis for investment and development because they are insecure. Focus on preferences teaches developing country negotiators to choose short-term quasi-rents rather than to focus on long-term needs, and opens them up to put pressure on unrelated issues such as labour standards.

I am similarly sceptical about regional trading arrangements (RTAs) for developing countries. There are undoubtedly cases where North–South arrangements have delivered benefits to developing countries, such as Portugal and, I believe, Mexico, but these have been cases of middle-income countries joining very close and much richer neighbours. For most developing countries, RTAs seem likely to be a distraction from devising suitable development policies based on the world market; they seem as likely to produce trade diversion as trade creation; and they seem unlikely to do anything for economic growth (see Winters, 1998; Vamvakidis, 1998). Regional trading arrangements can figure as a route to non-discriminatory trade liberalization, for example by creating coalitions for more general reforms. But research suggests that they are just as likely to thwart movements in that direction (Winters, 1999c).

The danger of the world splitting into a few trading blocs is not immediate, but neither is it completely absent. Such a development would be deleterious for developing countries, which would almost inevitably have to identify with one bloc or another. This would probably be costly in terms of trade diversion and the distortion of their production patterns to fit into the bloc overall. It would also have political costs, as dependence on a single metropolis would erode their bargaining power (McLaren, 1997).

What about vulnerable groups?

Trade policy is strongly redistributive, and almost any change is bound to create both winners and losers. We tend to forget that existing policy has already influenced current income distribution and to discuss reform in terms of those whom it hurts. There is undoubtedly a moral and political case for concern if policy change suddenly undercuts particular families, but it is important to ask whether the status quo is the correct benchmark for the long-term. Import substitution typically benefits urban capital owners, urban workers and bureaucrats, and some rebalancing in favour of other groups may well be desirable.

In the real world, the distributive consequences of trade reform can be quite subtle and surprising, depending on very particular details of local conditions. Winters (1999a, 1999b) discusses the various factors linking trade and poverty in more detail, and describes some field research from a project supported by the United Kingdom's Department for International Development (DFID). This suggested that trade and associated reforms in India and in countries in Africa have a capacity to help alleviate poverty by allowing the poor to sell their produce or their labour on better terms. It also suggested, however, that markets could collapse and disappear under certain circumstances, with serious consequences for poverty. An example was the way in which remote farmers in Zambia lost the ability to sell their maize when the state marketing board (which had cross-subsidized rural collection) was replaced by private trading firms. This suggested that reform should be accompanied by careful monitoring and remedial action to ensure that markets function competitively and efficiently when trade liberalization occurs.

The adverse effect of trade liberalization on poverty is sometimes advanced as a reason for not reforming. I do not accept this, although timing maybe something to consider in this light – for example, not liberalizing a labour-intensive sector in the middle of a slump. First, as I have hinted above, one needs to think hard about the *net effects* of reform on poverty and income distribution. Merely identifying some losers – even poor losers – is not sufficient to condemn a policy. Since trade reform usually stimulates growth, the usual case will be that liberalization will help the war on poverty.

The correct approach, then, is to think in terms of compensatory policies. Specific compensation in the form of trade adjustment assistance has been tried, not least in the United States, where it has had mixed success. It is probably not as effective as general anti-poverty compensation policies, such as public works and food-for-school programmes. These treat poverty directly and avoid the tortuous business of identifying whether a problem is due to trade reform or not. Also they are not generally particularly distortionary because they affect only people who have virtually no alternative. Poverty programmes can be very useful for alleviating poverty, and thus are certainly concomitants of trade liberalization, where poverty impacts might be a problem. They are not, however, suitable for addressing adverse shocks higher up the income distribution. There, general unemployment and training programmes are required.

It is not useful to pretend that no one gets hurt by trade reform. On the other hand, one clearly cannot allow reform programmes to become hostage to a few losers. The correct approach, it seems to me, lies in policies that ease adjustment in general, possibly supplemented by temporary trade reform-specific programmes if there is a widespread view that trade reform will throw up uniquely difficult problems.

Is trade policy critical to development?

Trade policy continues to be a real issue. There are undoubtedly other equally important policies for development, such as education, health, infrastructure and macroeconomic management, but a bad trade policy is likely to stymie development efforts. A very restrictive trade policy probably permits other policies to get further out of line (Krueger, 1990), and if trade policy is arbitrary and interventionist it poisons the whole government/business relationship.[12]

To refine the answer a little, the evidence is quite strong, if actually rather informal, that trade is important to development. The less secure link is whether trade policy matters for trade. At the extremes, it clearly does: consider the Democratic People's Republic of Korea, the EU's Common Agricultural Policy and so on. The issue is at what stage policy falls into the 'acceptable' range, and here, I believe, we are largely at sea because we cannot measure trade regimes adequately.

The problem is not only in collecting and summarizing information on formal barriers, but in capturing the subtler aspects, such as how reliably tariffs are collected, how frequently changes are made, how sensitive those changes are to lobbying and how accessible and distortionary safety valve protection is. Clarity, predictability and the absence of official discretion are probably just as important as whether the tariff is 5 per cent or 15 per cent.

Related to this is 'trade policy' in a broader sense, covering trade facilitation issues such as customs administration; and support services such as banking, insurance, communication and transport, and port efficiency. These are more difficult to reform than mere tariff rates, but are probably becoming more important as tariffs fall and global supply chains come to dominate production and trade. Moreover, these are the issues to which recent work on endogenous growth and economic geography relates industrial location and take-off. Interpreted in this way, trade policy moves right back to centre stage.

I conclude that trade policy is a real issue. Even if its traditional concerns are not sufficient to ensure development, getting them right is an important first step towards that goal, and an indication of serious intent on the other broader front. Reforming trade infrastructure will only be worth the effort if the traditional instruments are liberal enough to permit meaningful trade volumes and sufficient competition to ensure that lower trading costs get passed on to consumers.

LESSONS FOR UNCTAD: POLICY MAKING

Finally, I ask what does all this imply for UNCTAD and its trade activities? A dominant message from this chapter is the importance *of measurement*. This plays to a major strength of UNCTAD with its inventories of trade barriers in its Trade Analysis and Information System (TRAINS), and I would urge that this is the area for future focus. No other body has shown the ability to assemble trade policy data. The WTO has the means, but cannot divorce data collection from the negotiating/political aspect of its work, which makes it an extremely unreliable source of data for analysis.[13] UNCTAD can place itself at the centre of the whole of this debate by devoting resources to collecting, verifying and publishing trade policy and trade data.

Relatedly, UNCTAD should undertake and promote other agencies' and researchers' efforts to collect data on other trade frictions. These include regulatory restrictions in areas such as environment, procurement and services, as well as costs in the areas I identified under trade facilitation above. Again UNCTAD has a track record in some of this – for example, on environmental regulations and the World Bank–UNCTAD programme on Expansion in Foreign Direct Investment and Trade in Services (EFDITS) – but the need for additional information is almost unbounded. Moreover, there is scope for significant analytical work in devising appropriate measurement methods and analytical summaries for these data.

On policy, UNCTAD has perhaps become identified with a view sympathetic to trade intervention. Too often, however, this appears to be based on possibilities, or on refutations of the generalizations made elsewhere in favour of the market. Krueger's (1997) plea for operationalization is crucial here. We should stress the need to delineate the area over which a policy recommendation applies, with clear ways of identifying when we have moved outside the limits. Honest delineation will (on all sides) leave us with many grey areas where we just do not know what policy is appropriate, but a rush to colonize these areas with rhetoric is neither edifying for an international organization nor, ultimately, useful.

Related to this delineation is honesty about how well we understand our advice. International organizations and donors, not least my former employers, the World Bank, frequently talk about 'best practice'. For long-term objectives like development, this raises serious questions of how we know what is best. Some clarity on this would be welcome. Most of what we say will, at best, be provisional.

There is always a fear that, if policy advice is not bold, confident and comprehensive, it will just leave the field open for policy makers to pick-and-mix a pseudo-scientific justification for what they wanted to do anyway. Of course, it is for politicians/policy makers to decide; but if analysts are to avoid being misrepresented, we need to be more prepared than heretofore to point out the consequences, the surprising correlates (such as which firms benefit from a policy) and the false premises of actual policy. This runs the risk of conflict with governments, the 'owners' of international organizations. However, if the approach is applied even-handedly, most of the governments that resent comment on their own affairs will, nonetheless, accept it as a price for greater clarity on others' affairs.

NOTES

1. I am grateful to J. Michael Finger and Adrian Wood for comments on the outline of this chapter, and to colleagues on the Round Table on UNCTAD X for comments on an earlier draft. The chapter would doubtless have been better if I had accepted all their good advice. I am also grateful to Beatrice Harrison for logistical help.
2. In the World Bank I coined the acronym WYDIWYG (What you do is what you get) to remind people of this message.
3. This section draws on Anne Krueger's (1997) brilliant essay on much the same subject, which I strongly recommend to interested readers. Other recent accounts of the same material include Rodrik (1992), Nayyar (1997) and Bruton (1998).
4. Carlota Perez (2000) argues, in a very interesting paper prepared for the UNCTAD Round Table, that IS did not so much fail as become inappropriate. When the prevailing mass-production technologies were growing fast in the 1950s and 1960s, industrial country firms were pleased to export them to nascent developing country manufactures. As the technologies matured in the next decade, however, the search for efficiencies via factor costs and global sourcing turned export promotion into the successful paradigm. Interestingly, she doubts whether the information technologies of the turn of this century will ever provide IS opportunities. Hers is an attractive view, but it depends for its future usefulness on unproven regularities between successful technological revolutions. Also it is not informed by the chaos

that characterized IS regimes, which arose too rapidly and were too *ad hoc* to be explained solely by global changes.

5. Capture is the process by which regulators/policy makers come to identify with the sectors they are supposed to be regulating and thus begin to give undue weight to the direct interests of those sectors.

6. Economists generally think of growth in simple income terms, but other dimensions of growth, let alone development, are obviously also important. Fortunately, there is a fairly high positive correlation between the various dimensions. Moreover, to the extent that they conflict, the difficulty of making trade-offs owes more to disagreements about relative weights than to uncertainty about the technical relationships between the different factors.

7. My co-panellist, Deepak Nayyar, has offered a rather similar history to that in this section so far (Nayyar, 1997), but he sees it as a regrettable victory for a flawed doctrine rather than the painful struggle towards better policies.

8. The literature on 'convergence' was more sophisticated, but it has been less influential in trade policy circles than the simple growth models.

9. Carlota Perez also argues that IS suited industrial country firms: see note 4 above.

10. Hong Kong (China) and Singapore were more liberal initially, as were the second-wave economies, when they took off.

11. Relatedly, Roberts and Tybout (1996) show that export booms typically rely heavily on existing domestic firms starting to export.

12. Even if the parties concerned are hooked on the poison and do not realize it.

13. The data from WTO are reliable in themselves, and indeed the WTO criticizes UNCTAD's for being less so. The problem is that *access* to WTO data is unreliable.

REFERENCES

Amsden, A. (2001), *The Rise of the Rest: Late Industrialization outside the North Atlantic Region*, New York: Oxford University Press.

Balassa, B. (1981), 'The newly-industrializing developing countries after the oil crisis', *Weltwirtschaftliches Archiv*, 117(1): 142–94.

Baldwin. R.E. (1969), 'The case against infant industry protection', *Journal of Political Economy*, 77: 295–305.

Bhagwati, J.N. and V.K. Ramaswami (1963), 'Domestic distortions, tariffs and the theory of optimum subsidy', *Journal of Political Economy*, 72: 44–50.

Bigsten, A. *et al.* (1998), 'Exports and firm-level efficiency in the African manufacturing sector' (mimeo), Centre for Study of African Economies, Oxford University.

Bruton, H. (1998), 'A reconsideration of import substitution', *Journal of Economic Literature*, 36(2), June: 903–36.

Cooper, C.A. and Massell, B.F. (1965), 'Towards a general theory of customs unions for developing countries', *Journal of Political Economy*, 73: 461–76.

Corden, W.M. (1957), 'Tariffs, subsidies and the terms of trade', *Economica*, 24: 235–42.

Finger, J.M. (1991), 'Development economics and the GATT', in J. de Melo and A. Sapir (eds), *Trade Theory and Economic Reform*. Oxford: Basil Blackwell, pp. 203–23.

Johnson, H.G. (1970), 'The efficiency and welfare implications of international corporations', in I.A. McDougall and R. Snape (eds), *Studies in International Economics*, Amsterdam, North-Holland, pp. 83–103.

Krueger, A.O. (1974), 'The political economy of the rent-seeking society', *American Economic Review*, 64: 291–303.

Krueger, A.O. (1990), 'Asian trade and growth lessons', *American Economic Review: Papers and Proceedings*, 80: 108–112.

Krueger, A.O. (1997), 'Trade policy and economic development: How we learn', *American Economic Review*, 87: 1–22.

Krugman, P.R. (1995), *Development, Geography and Economic Theory*, Cambridge, MA: MIT Press.

Lee, J.W. (1995), 'Government interventions and productivity growth in Korean manufacturing industries', NBER Working Paper W5060, National Bureau of Economic Research, Cambridge, MA.

Lipsey, R.G. and K. Lancaster (1956), 'The general theory of second-best', *Review of Economic Studies*, 24: 11–32.

McLaren, J. (1997), 'Size, sunk costs, and Judge Bowker's objection to free trade', *American Economic Review*, 87: 400–20.

Nayyar, D. (1997), 'Themes in trade and industrialization', in D. Nayyar, *Trade and Industrialization*, Oxford: Oxford University Press, pp. 1–42.

Perez, C. (2000), 'Technological strategies for development in a context of paradigm change', paper prepared for the Round Table at UNCTAD X, Bangkok, February.

Roberts, M.J. and J.R. Tybout (1996), *Industrial Evolution in Developing Countries: Micro Patterns of Turnover, Productivity and Market Structure*, Oxford: Oxford University Press, for The World Bank.

Rodriguez, F. and Rodrik, D. (1999), 'Trade policy and economic growth: A skeptic's guide to the evidence', CEPR Discussion Paper no. 2143.

Rodrik, D. (1992), 'Closing the productivity gap: Does trade liberalisation really help?', in G. Helleiner (ed.), *Trade Policy, Industrialisation and Development: New Perspectives*, Oxford: Oxford University Press.

Sachs, J. and A. Warner (1995), 'Economic Reform and the Process of Global Integration', *Brookings Papers on Economic Activity*, 1: 1–95.

Vamvakidis, A. (1998), 'Regional trade agreements versus board liberalization: Which path leads to faster growth? Time-series evidence', IMF Working Paper no. 98/40, IMF, Washington DC.

Wang, Z.K. and L.A. Winters (1998), 'Africa's role in multilateral trade negotiations: Past and future', *Journal of African Economies*, 7 (Supplement 1), June: 1–33.

Winters, L.A. (1998), 'Assessing regional integration arrangements', in J. Burki, G. Perry and S. Calvo (eds), *Trade: Towards Open Regionalism*, Washington, DC: World Bank, pp. 51–68.

Winters, L.A. (1999a), 'Trade, trade policy and poverty: a framework for collecting and interpreting the evidence', paper prepared for the UK Department for International Development (mimeo), University of Sussex, Brighton, UK.

Winters, L.A. (1999b), 'Trade liberalisation and poverty', paper prepared for the UK Department for International Development (mimeo), University of Sussex, Brighton, UK.

Winters, L.A. (1999c), 'Regionalism versus Multilateralism', in R. Baldwin, D. Cohen, A. Sapir and A. Venables (eds), *Regional Integration*, Cambridge, MA: Cambridge University Press.

Wood, A. (1994), *North–South Trade, Employment and Inequality: Changing Fortunes in a Skill-Driven World*, Oxford, Clarendon Press.

014 L60 (Thailand, LDCs)
019 038
F13 024

5. Industrialization under new WTO law

Alice H. Amsden

INTRODUCTION

For nearly half a century after World War II, many countries which were outside the main orbit of world manufacturing nonetheless experienced rapid industrial expansion under old GATT law (see Table 5.1).[1] These, and other latecomers, are now confronted by the challenge of continuing to build their manufacturing sectors under a new trade regime. This new regime is allegedly more liberal than the previous one, which operated from the time of the Bretton Woods Agreement in 1944 to the formation of the WTO in 1994.

The challenge is indeed great because, historically, relatively high tariffs have accompanied major waves of industrialization: the first industrial revolution in the United Kingdom from about 1770 to 1830; the second industrial revolution in the North Atlantic from about 1873 to 1914; and 'late' industrialization from about 1950 to 1995. In broad terms, tariffs fluctuated in a downward direction from 1830 to 1873, and then went up again between 1873 and 1914, and still further up during the inter-war years (O'Brien, 1997). After World War II, tariffs were again high and then gradually diminished, first in the North Atlantic and then, in an even more desultory fashion, in latecomer countries.

This raises the question of how less industrialized countries, with only modest manufacturing experience, are to continue to move into mid-technology industries if the WTO forbids infant industry protection and subsidization. This chapter provides an answer to this question.

THE FLEXIBILITY OF WTO LAW

The WTO, like the GATT, enables members to protect themselves from two types of foreign import competition: competition from aggregate imports that destabilizes their balance of payments (Article XVIII), and competition that threatens their individual industries, owing either to an import surge (Article XIX on temporary safeguards) or to an unfair trade practice (Article VI on anti-dumping and countervailing duties). GATT placed no formal limits on the duration of safeguards, whereas the WTO limits their duration to eight years and improves their transparency.

Table 5.1 *Real annual average growth rates of GDP in manufacturing latecomer countries, 1960–95 (per cent)*

Country	1960–70	1970–80	1980–90	1990–95	1960–95
Argentina	5.4	0.9	–1.4	11.6	2.1
Brazil	8.0	9.0	0.15	25.2	8.5
Chile	9.4	1.8	2.9	10.4	5.5
China	n.a.	8.4	9.6	13.5	9.9
India	3.1	4.0	7.4	2.3	4.5
Indonesia	6.4	14.2	7.4	15.1	10.1
Korea, Republic of	17.7	16.0	12.0	10.9	14.6
Malaysia	10.9	11.8	9.5	19.8	12.0
Mexico	9.7	7.2	2.2	8.4	6.6
Taiwan Province of China	15.0	12.6	7.2	4.8	10.6
Thailand	9.1	10.1	9.6	13.2	10.1
Turkey	8.1	5.1	7.1	4.7	6.5
Prime 12: Mean	**9.7**	**9.1**	**6.8**	**11.7**	**9.0**
Egypt	4.8	9.7	n.a.	8.3	7.9
Tunisia	7.8	11.9	6.8	5.6	7.6
Pakistan	9.4	8.4	2.2	6.4	6.7
Philippines	6.7	7.0	1.1	9.5	6.6
Nigeria	9.1	14.8	–8.8	14.8	6.4
Venezuela	6.4	5.2	1.1	7.1	5.8
Colombia	5.7	5.7	3.0	9.1	5.7
Ecuador	4.9	9.6	0.5	11.7	5.7
Kenya	6.5	5.7	4.8	2.4	5.2
Honduras	4.5	5.7	3.0	3.4	4.9
Secondary Top 10[a]: Mean	**6.6**	**8.4**	**1.4**	**7.8**	**6.2**

Notes: Statistics for each column represent averages of real annual growth rates for all available years. An entry was labelled unavailable if growth rates were not available for seven out of ten possible years. Growth rates are calculated using inflation-adjusted current market prices. Comparability is not ensured because sometimes manufacturing includes some combination of mining, construction and/or utilities. The definition of manufacturing may also vary across countries depending on the coverage of firms below a minimum employment level.
[a] The average is for the period 1960–95.

Source: 1990–95 data adapted from UNIDO (1997) and earlier years. All other data adapted from World Bank (various); cited in Amsden (2001).

Under GATT, voluntary export restraints (VERs) were the premier safeguard. While they had been used most extensively by the North Atlantic economies of Europe, Canada and the United States, they had also been relied upon by 'the rest' to protect strategic industries.[2] The Republic of Korea, for example, used a form of VER to ban imports of cars and electronics from Japan, its most serious competitor. This 'agreement' (to which Japan was not even a consenting party) began to function in the 1980s and remained in effect until 1999 – long enough to allow these industries to build up their knowledge-based assets (Taiwan Province of China and mainland China were not GATT members, nor are they signatories to the WTO, and thus may protect these and other industries more openly; the electronics industry in Taiwan Province of China is a case in point). The new WTO bans VERs because they are discriminatory, that is, their effect varies by country. The advantage of eliminating VERs was that they were non-transparent. The disadvantage was that they served a useful purpose, and 'unless a superior means of serving that purpose is provided, then countries will find ways of their own to do it, and those ways are likely to be even worse' (Deardorff, 1994, p. 57).

As predicted, countries in 'the rest' have raised tariffs in lieu of using VERs or other cumbersome safeguards. Despite the fact that the level of tariffs fell after the Uruguay Round of trade negotiations, developing countries have bound many of their tariffs at fairly high levels (or have left them altogether unbound) as the starting point for their entry into the WTO (see Table 5.2). In the event of an import threat, they can raise their tariffs to these high levels and keep them there for at least eight years:

> While developing countries have committed to a significant increase in their tariff bindings in the Uruguay Round (albeit at levels generally well above currently applied rates), they are still unlikely to invoke Article XIX (on safeguards) because they have both the unfettered right to raise tariffs to their bound levels and virtual carte blanche authority to impose new tariffs or quotas for balance of payments reasons. (Schott, 1994, p. 113)

Raising tariffs in an emergency has become the recourse even of countries whose policy regime has been liberalized; for example, when a new 'free-trade' Mexico confronted stiff foreign competition in 1995, tariffs were increased from the prevailing rates of 20 per cent, or less, to 35 per cent on clothing, footwear and manufactured leather products on imports from non-preferential sources. *These sectors were already protected to a certain degree through anti-dumping duties and a relatively restrictive use of marking and origin requirements* (OECD, 1996a, p. 106).

Marking and origin requirements are forms of non-tariff measures (NTMs) that restrict trade. In the Uruguay Round of negotiations, however, 'achievements in the area of NTMs had been less than had been expected' (Raby, 1994).

Mexico' s affiliation to the North American Free Trade Agreement (NAFTA) is in itself a form of managed trade that violates orthodox free market principles. Members of free trade agreements can protect themselves against all other countries except one another and, unlike members of customs unions, they need not have common external tariffs. Of 100 or so regional trade agreements notified to the WTO since its inception, only one was approved by the end of 1999 (that between the Czech Republic and Slovakia). Others, such as NAFTA, were not forbidden; WTO members simply agreed not to take action on them.

Table 5.2   Tariffs before and after liberalization (pre- and post-Uruguay Round)

	Trade- weighted tariff averages	
	Pre-Uruguay Round	Post-Uruguay Round
Argentina	38.2	30.9
Brazil	40.7	27.0
Chile	34.9	24.9
India	71.4	32.4
Indonesia	20.4	36.9
Korea, Republic of	18.0	8.3
Malaysia	10.0	10.1
Mexico	46.1	33.7
Thailand	37.3	28.0
Turkey	25.1	22.3
European Union	5.7	3.6
Japan	3.9	1.7
United States	5.4	3.5

Note: The pre-Uruguay Round duties refer to 1994 bound duties or, for unbound tariff lines, to duties applicable as of September 1986. The post-Uruguay Round duties refer to the concessions listed in the schedules annexed to the Uruguay Round Protocol to the GATT (1994). As import statistics refer in general to 1988, trade-weighted duties using post-Uruguay Round import data may be slightly different. The data are preliminary and may be revised to reflect the final schedules annexed to the Final Act of the Uruguay Round, although, as of April 1999, no changes were registered, except for Thailand. The changes for Thailand appear above.

Source: GATT secretariat (1994), appendix tables 5 and 6, as cited in Hoda (1994).

Anti-dumping duties have emerged as another way to protect trade in an emergency, supposedly when competitors engage in 'dumping', or selling below costs. In the late 1980s, the United States, the European Union, Australia and Canada accounted for about four-fifths of all anti-dumping cases. However, by 1998 they accounted for barely one-third of the 225 cases opened in that year.

Instead, the developing countries became leaders in anti-dumping initiatives, especially India (which also maintains almost permanent import surcharges to protect its balance of payments), Brazil and Mexico. As other types of trade barriers decreased, anti-dumping suits rose in importance (data are from Row and Maw Ltd., London). Thus Argentina's steel industry, a showcase of restructuring, cut tariffs unilaterally to within a range of 0 per cent to a 'mere' 24 per cent. But when Brazilian steel started to flood the Argentine market in 1992, a tax on imports was 'temporarily' increased by almost fourfold (Toulan and Guillen, 1996).[3]

In response to US pressure, the Uruguay Round of negotiations was extended to trade in services, which included foreign investment. The results of the Uruguay Round on trade-related investment measures (TRIMs), however, were 'relatively modest' (Startup, 1994, p. 189).[4] As a consequence of limited agreement in the area of TRIMs, developing countries are able to maintain or even strengthen local content requirements. They can also retain trade balancing stipulations and the 100 per cent export requirement of export-processing zones, both of which are forms of export promotion. In 1995, for example, Brazil hammered out an agreement with the countries representing its major car assemblers, whereby all of them consented to export cars whose value equalled the imports of parts that components assemblers were bringing into Brazil. Countries that had notified the WTO of their local content and/or trade-balancing programmes under a new 1998 TRIMs Agreement include Argentina (automotive industry), Chile (automotive industry), India (pharmaceuticals and, in the case of 'dividend balancing', 22 consumer goods industries),[5] Indonesia (selected products), Mexico (automotive industry), Malaysia (automotive industry) and Thailand (selected products) (UNCTAD, 1998).

Thus safeguards of various sorts enable countries to buttress their balance of payments and sustain an industry under siege. Safeguards can also be used to protect an infant industry with eight years of protectionism virtually guaranteed. The major risk is that of triggering unilateral trade sanctions under Section 301 of the US Omnibus Trade Act, but not until a US industry is actually threatened by foreign competition are sanctions likely to be invoked (Low, 1993).

Subsidies also receive relatively permissive treatment under WTO law. They fall into three categories. Some are prohibited (for exports and for domestic, rather than imported, inputs); others are 'actionable' (they can be punished subject to proof of injury); and three are permissible (all heavily utilized in the North Atlantic). Permissible subsidies include those to promote R&D, regional development and environmentalism. Any high-tech industry, therefore, can receive unbounded subsidies for the purpose of strengthening science and technology. Export subsidies are also permissible for countries with per capita incomes equal to, or less than, $1000. As noted earlier, exports can be promoted indirectly through the establishment of science parks or export processing zones.

All in all, the liberal bark of the WTO appears to be worse than its bite, and 'neo-developmental states' in 'the rest' have taken advantage of this, where necessary.

PERFORMANCE STANDARDS

Here we may distinguish among latecomer countries, between those with prewar manufacturing experience that were generally successful in introducing reciprocal control mechanisms ('the rest') and those with negligible prewar manufacturing experience whose reciprocal control mechanisms, if any, were weak or malfunctioning ('the remainder').[6]

Given their absence of rich knowledge-based assets, countries in 'the remainder' may need to use subsidies in order to make mid-technology industries sufficiently profitable to attract enough resources to undertake a 'three-pronged' investment: in managerial and technological capabilities, in plants of minimum efficient scale, and in distribution networks (Chandler, 1990). Nevertheless, whereas subsidies continue to be sanctioned under WTO law, and may be a necessary condition for industrial expansion, they are not a sufficient condition. Countries must also allocate subsidies in a disciplined manner, under what may be called a 'reciprocal control mechanism'.

A control mechanism is a set of institutions that disciplines economic behaviour on the basis of a feedback of information that has been sensed and assessed.[7] The control mechanism of the North Atlantic countries revolved around the principle *of market competition*, which disciplined economic actors and allocated resources efficiently. The 'invisible hand' thus transformed the chaos and selfishness of free market forces into general well-being (Mandeville, 1714; repr. 1924). The control mechanism of 'the rest' revolved around the principle of *reciprocity*, which disciplined subsidy recipients and thereby minimized government failures. Subsidies were allocated to make manufacturing profitable – to convert money lenders into financiers and importers into industrialists – but did not become giveaways. Recipients of subsidies were subjected to monitorable performance standards that were redistributive in nature and result-oriented. The reciprocal control mechanism of 'the rest' thus transformed the inefficiency and venality associated with government intervention into collective good.

In the cotton textile industry, for example, the privilege of selling in the protected domestic market was made conditional on the fulfilment of export targets. Later, other industries had to match imports with an equivalent value of exports (or comply with some sort of 'trade-balancing' arrangement). In car assembly and consumer electronics, the right to sell locally under tariff protection was tied to the 'localization' of parts and components manufacture.

A condition for receiving the soft loans of development banks was the employment of non-familial professionals in responsible positions, such as chief financial officer and quality control engineer. Development bank credit for heavy industries committed borrowers to contributing their own capital (under debt–equity ratio requirements) and constructing plants of minimum efficient scale. In India, price controls in the pharmaceutical industry encouraged cost-saving innovation and exporting in exchange for loosely enforced foreign patent laws. In the Republic of Korea, a lucrative licence to establish a general trading company depended on exports meeting criteria related to value, geographical diversity and product complexity. As industries in 'the rest' were upscaled, performance standards increasingly pertained to research and development, as noted below. Chinese 'science and technology enterprises' were granted a special legal status in exchange for performance standards with respect to technically trained employment and new products in total sales. The best small firms in Taiwan Province of China were specially picked to locate in science parks which obliged them to spend a certain percentage of their sales on R&D and to employ advanced production techniques.

'The rest' rose, therefore, in conjunction with getting the control mechanism right. No matter what prices existed, whether as a consequence of market forces, technocratic choice or political intervention, they were taken as given by policy makers concerned with industrial expansion. Around existing prices a set of rules and institutions was constructed to attract resources into manufacturing and to make those resources conform to performance standards that were result-oriented.

DEVELOPMENT INSTITUTIONS: THE CASE OF THAILAND

We briefly review here the developmental institutions created by Thailand, a case of relative minimalism as far as government intervention is concerned (World Bank, 1993). A country overview, based on information from high-ranking government officials, gives some sense of the depth and breadth of controls in Thailand.[8]

Selection by Academic Merit

Thailand's control mechanism was managed by civil servants selected by academic merit, as a result of a 1932 political movement which had led to civil service reforms. The Thai civil service thus became very well-educated in a society where social status came to depend on higher education. In 1963, as much as one-third of Thai students studying abroad were government officials on leave of absence (Evers and Silcock, 1967). Thailand's Board of Investment (BOI), the overseer of industrial promotion, claimed that, until the 1990s, it had never faced a shortage of well-trained engineers, despite low school enrolments. In the early phase of industrialization, as most Thai manufacturing firms were first-generation family-owned enterprises, government officials tended to be better educated than private entrepreneurs.[9] Whatever the balance, the BOI attracted the brightest talents after World War II, as did elite bureaucracies in Meiji Japan and other countries in 'the rest' (Daito, 1986).

A permanent opposition to the developmental policies of the Thai civil service arose in the form of American-trained economists.[10] Officials in the BOI complained of constant criticism from the 'pure economists' in the Prime Minister's Office who 'misunderstood the real world'. Pure economists countercharged that private enterprise would have grown strong without BOI support, that power bred corruption, and that the BOI's methods of 'picking winners' were arbitrary. The BOI responded by appointing its critics as advisers.

Coverage

A very large number of investment projects in Thailand grew up under the BOI's wing. A survey of Thailand's big businesses in the 1990s estimated that around 70 per cent of the manufacturing firms belonging to the largest industrial groups had received benefits and had fulfilled performance standards under contract with the BOI (Suehiro, 1993). According to the BOI's own estimates, it was involved in about 90 per cent of Thailand's major manufacturing projects covering both the private and public sectors and foreign and local firms, with investments totalling around $14 billion by 1990. Given Thailand's thin industrial base and BOI's relatively small staff, any official with the BOI for 23 years (1968–1991) would know every major investor personally. In 1990, 70 per cent of the BOI's professional staff were engineers, and only 100 engineers were employed in total.

As it became clearer that manufacturing activity under the BOI's direction could generate profits, the government became more committed to industrialization. As such commitment from top political leaders strengthened, industrial promotion expanded and development flourished despite militarism and corruption. As one senior government official commented, 'Everyone was nervous that rapid growth would end', and success itself helped keep corruption in check, at least through the early fast-growth years.

Thailand's real annual average growth rate of manufacturing output jumped from 5.6 per cent in the pre-plan period before 1960 to 9.1 per cent in the period 1960–70, and 10.1 per cent in the period 1970–80. The share of manufacturing in GDP rose from 12.5 per cent in 1960 to 18.3 per cent in 1975. The BOI's pervasive influence thus went hand-in-hand with sustained manufacturing expansion (Amsden, 2001).

New Rules

The BOI gave mainly tax breaks, protection (in consultation with the Ministry of Finance), subsidized credit (reserved for national firms by a development bank, the Industrial Finance Corporation of Thailand), entry restrictions on other firms (in consultation with the Ministry of Industry) and special benefits for foreign firms (permission to own land and to import labour). These benefits were exchanged for performance standards related to export targets, local content requirements, debt–equity ratio ceilings, national ownership floors, operating scale minima, investment timetable obligations, regional location criteria and, eventually, product quality specifications and environmental rules. The government specifically promoted technology transfers from multinational firms by making the support of such firms contingent on their hiring local managers. The Foreigners' Occupation Control Law restricted the number of working visas issued to foreign personnel, thereby initiating the replacement of foreign managers and engineers with Thais.

In the 1960s, Thailand's corporate income tax was as high as 30 per cent and its import duties on inputs for finished manufactures were pervasive. Import duties had been a major source of government revenue since before the eighteenth century. Despite Thailand's reputation for 'openness', import duties around the time of the Third National Economic and Social Development Plan (1972–76) averaged 30–40 per cent, and 60 per cent on luxuries. In 1983 the average nominal tariff was 31 per cent in 'open' Thailand, compared with 24 per cent in 'fortress' Republic of Korea (James, 1987). Therefore the right to a reduction or exemption of import duties was a rich reward. To protect local industry, however, duty exemptions were only given for machinery and other inputs *not* made in Thailand (variants of this 'law' of similars existed throughout 'the rest', the first instance possibly dating back to the 1930s in Brazil). BOI staff argued that 'tax benefits under the Investment Promotion Law were the beginning of business prosperity in this country'.

All BOI projects followed the same procedure no matter who initiated them (missions abroad to court potential investors were usually BOI-initiated). Proposals were first subject to project analysis by engineers, who checked technical feasibility and capacity fit with related industries, and by economists, who checked conformance with policy criteria specified in five-year plans. Viable proposals were then sent to a Decision Committee, whose members were from the BOI and private industry. Proposals approved by this committee then went to a Privileges Committee, which reviewed the benefits package involved. As a way to reduce corruption, Decision Committee meetings on major projects were open to all concerned ministries, and approved projects, no matter what their size, had to have a detailed Return Statement indicating the rationale for their acceptance. After approval, inspectors monitored performance (for instance, they checked to see if specified technologies had been bought and machinery installed). On average, the BOI annually withdrew benefits from 7 per cent of its clients for non-compliance with agreed terms.

Performance standards attached to tax breaks were designed to create new capacity in targeted industries based on modern, as opposed to second-hand, equipment. Firms that expanded their own capacity through acquisition of an existing firm or extension of an existing plant facility did not qualify (although new plants of existing firms did qualify). Additional performance standards were negotiated when projects were being screened. In the case of pre-screened projects, performance criteria were laid down by the BOI. Cotton textile manufacturers, for example, had to export 50 per cent of their output after the first energy crisis in 1973 to qualify for new or continued support. This applied equally to foreign and national firms. Given this 50 per cent floor (which was determined after 'detailed study'), a textile firm would be selected for promotion depending on how competitive its proposal was in terms of the additional performance standards it promised.

In the case of guided projects, the BOI divided all industries into three classifications with varying benefits lasting for a finite duration. As economists criticized this procedure, the BOI resorted to a case-by-case decision rule. However, as this was unworkable, in 1977 the BOI went back to a three-way classification, but used new criteria to select the industries for the largest privileges, such as export intensity and regional location, rather than capital or labour intensity. On average, only 15 per cent of applications were rejected, but only companies that fitted BOI criteria tended to apply.

In the case of big projects, the BOI and potential clients engaged in intense bargaining. Major sticking points were the number of entrants to an industry that the BOI would promote (and the Ministry of Industry would license) and the amount of 'own-capital' the firms would supply (which influenced a firm's debt–equity ratio). In the case of coloured television picture tubes, for example, considerations of scale economy led the BOI to offer privileges to only one player. Players in big projects were selected in a transparent process involving all ministers with economic portfolios.

Response to Economic Disequilibria

At critical turning points before the 1990s (defined by exogenous shocks, big new projects or more foreign competition), the BOI responded by altering the scope and nature of support. Tariffs were the business of the Ministry of Finance, but a key section of a general tariff law gave the BOI power to impose surcharges on existing tariffs. When Thai industry faltered after the second energy crisis of 1979, 20 product groups were subjected to import surcharges ranging from 10 to 40 per cent on top of existing duties (Narongchai and Ajanant, 1983). Likewise, extraordinary measures were taken in order to build major industries. In the case of cars, one of the most problematic industries in the BOI's portfolio, from 1978 to 1990 the BOI banned imports of small cars (below 2400cc cylinders) and limited the number of brands and models of cars that could be assembled or produced locally. A diesel engine project related to motor vehicles, which received competitive bids from three Thai–Japanese joint ventures, typified the BOI's non-bureaucratic side. On the issue of number of entrants to produce diesel engines in Thailand, the BOI's technical staff 'fought hard' (in the words of a senior official) for a limit of one, at most two, but was overruled by the BOI's governing board, which wanted more competition and licensed 'no more than three firms'. On the issue of using Thailand's casting capacity to make engine blocks, the BOI supported local Thai casters against the Japanese claims of poor quality. In exchange, the BOI forced Thai casters to subcontract work to smaller Thai suppliers. Finally, with regard to exports, the BOI secured an export commitment from Japanese contenders (who had initially demanded export *restrictions)* by causing cutthroat bidding among them (Doner, 1991).

All the BOI's daring-cum-bureaucratism may have reflected 'culture' at work, but not necessarily Thai culture. Developmental bureaucracies throughout 'the rest' exhibited similar behaviour under conditions of economic disequilibria. The culture among all latecomers in the 1960s was 'getting the job done'. The problem by the year 2000 for latecomers trailing behind Thailand in manufacturing growth and industrial diversification is precisely the lack of a culture or vision to 'get the job done'. The constraint does not lie in the liberal machinery of the new 'global' world order, as exemplified by the WTO. This machinery sanctions the use of reciprocal performance standards in exchange for (legal) subsidies and trade protection, as examined earlier.

Three major types of performance standards may be distinguished for purposes of assessing their legality: first, techno-standards, which tie subsidies (typically, subsidized credit offered by development banks) to the professionalization of managerial practices; second, policy standards, which tie subsidies to the promotion of major national strategic priorities, such as maintaining price stability, increasing local content, raising the level of exports and not worsening income distribution; third, both types of performance standards, as they operate in the area of science and technology, which are designed to increase national skill formation and the generation of firm-specific knowledge-based assets. Possibly, the only performance standard restricted by WTO law concerns exporting, insofar as direct export subsidies can no longer be offered by WTO members. Indirect requirements to export, however, are possible in the form of trade-balancing requirements, for example, as noted earlier.

Given this permissiveness, we turn now to the issue of vision.

PROMOTING SCIENCE AND TECHNOLOGY

The principle of reciprocity has not died in 'the rest' with the liberalization of markets, the privatization of state enterprises and the deregulation of business. Instead, it has survived in the realm of science and technology, in the subset of countries in 'the rest' that have invested heavily in national skill formation and proprietary knowledge-based assets – let us call these countries 'the independents' (Amsden, 2001). Industrial development, through means that also strengthen science and technology, based on a reciprocal principle, presents a possible vision or culture to energize industrialization in secondary or tertiary latecomers in 'the remainder' countries (for the ten countries in 'the remainder' whose manufacturing sectors grew the fastest after World War II, see Table 5.1).

The principle of reciprocity slowly pervaded the policies of 'the independents' with respect to science and technology. The selection of firms for benefits in high-technology industries was typically transacted through public research institutes or science parks. Even when admission into such parks depended on a competitive process, picking winners was inherent in this process. Otherwise, given the benefits of locating in such parks, all firms would have wanted to operate in such a setting. To qualify for the benefits of a science park, a firm had to meet pre-screening criteria.[11] In Taiwan Province of China, for example, admission into Hsinchu Science Park depended on the evaluation of a committee that consisted of representatives from government, industry and academia. The major criterion for admission was the nature of the technology a firm was developing. Tainan Science Industrial Park (TSIP), approved by the legislature in 1995, was designed to attract firms in the microelectronics, precision machinery, semiconductor, agricultural and biotechnology industries. Benefits for TSIP companies included grants of up to 50 per cent of necessary funds from government programmes, tax exemptions and low interest loans, as well as special educational facilities. In exchange, companies seeking admission into TSIP had to meet criteria related to operating objectives, product technology, marketing strategy, pollution prevention and management (Tainan Science-Based Industrial Park, 1996).

In comparison with Europe, what appeared distinct about the science parks in Taiwan Province of China was their scope (measured in terms of sales and park employees) and the extent to which the neodevelopmental state made park benefits conditional on innovative behaviour. According to the Hsinchu Park Administration, 'An existing company would be asked to leave if it changed to labour-intensive operations and no longer met the evaluation criteria (which the Park Administration specified)' (Xue, 1997, pp. 750–51).

Taiwan Province of China promoted S&T through science parks and related government research institutes, as well as spin-offs from such institutes in the form of 'model factories' (such as United Microelectronics Corporation, which manufactures integrated circuits). The Republic of Korea promoted S&T by means of large national research projects. These expanded in the 1990s with a plan for Highly Advanced National Projects (HAN), or 'G7 projects' as Koreans called them, in recognition of their aim to propel their country into the ranks of the world's top group of seven countries (G7).[12] Both approaches involved the selection of firms for benefits. The science park administrations of Taiwan Province of China and the Republic of Korea's G7 Planning Committee selected projects according to the criterion of how well they advanced 'strategic industries', which were themselves selected at the highest political level of decision making. By involving large-scale projects, however, the Korean approach also tended to involve participation by big firms.

By the 1990s, China had also moved away from the defence-oriented national innovation systems of the United States and the former Soviet Union towards a firm-focused system that emphasized industrial competitiveness.[13] The transition had come in 1985, when the Central Committee of the Chinese Communist Party and the national State Council had decreed that 'economic construction should rely on science and technology', which was far richer in China than in equally poor developing countries, and 'science and technology research should serve the needs of economic development' (Lu, 1997, p. 17). To modernize S&T, China combined science parks and national R&D projects, tax breaks and subsidized credit, playing a large role in both. The Beijing city government, for example, established a leading-edge R&D testing zone dubbed 'Beijing's Silicon Valley', with exports in 1998 of $267 million (expected to reach $1 billion by 2000). 'In the enterprise zone, the Government adopted institutional devices nested in the taxation process and investment process that redistributed resources to strategic sectors.' (Lu, 1997). Target industries were given tax breaks, special loans from state banks with below-market interest rates, and permission to exceed normal debt–equity ratio ceilings (Lu, 1997, p. 234). On the other hand, the Chinese government also emphasized national R&D projects and the formation of 'science and technology enterprises' that were neither state-owned nor private. The State Planning Commission announced a policy to build approximately 100 national key laboratories (analogous to corporate central R&D laboratories) in selected fields of basic science in which Chinese capabilities already excelled. 'S&T enterprises' were spun-off by city, provincial or national governments to commercialize the knowledge of public labs (see, for example, the annual report of Stone Electronic Technology Ltd, one of China's most successful S&T enterprises). Although these enterprises were nominally independent, 'in granting S&T enterprises a special legal status, the government obliged them to meet certain requirements (analogous to performance standards under a reciprocal control mechanism). These requirements included the percentage of technology personnel, the percentage of sales contributed by new products, the percentage of products exported, the allocation of retained earnings, etc.' (Lu, 1997, p. 235). Thus, to a greater or less degree, the neodevelopmental state retained its conditionality-based form of subsidy allocation in the high-tech phase of industrial transformation.

CONCLUSION

Late industrializes may expect both discontinuity and continuity between GATT and WTO rules. The major difference between the two trade regimes from the viewpoint of late industrializers is the prohibition by the WTO of subsidies to exports. This prohibition terminates a very powerful developmental tool insofar as latecomers that made the transition from low-technology into mid-technology industries after World War II made exporting, with subsidies, a condition for operating in protected domestic markets. Exporting was a performance standard that contributed to efficiency and growth. Continuity characterizes the two trade regimes insofar as most preferential measures to protect infant industries and to diversify manufacturing industry are still permissible, as is the reciprocal control mechanism that the most successful latecomers used to ensure that subsidies to business were not given away for nothing.

WTO provisions related to science and technology enable developing countries to promote their mid-technology (and especially high-technology) industries through the medium of science parks and R&D national projects, as well as temporary and transparent barriers to imports. The major lesson from successful industrializers after World War II is that, whatever the instrument of promotion, to be successful it must be tied to a monitorable performance standard, and operate within a reciprocal control mechanism that disciplines all parties involved in industrial expansion. Given whatever prices exist as a consequence of market forces, technocratic decision making or political intervention, it is important to get the control mechanism right. Getting the control mechanism right, in conjunction with promoting science and technology, are twin pillars of a new industrial development strategy that may serve to energize still later industrializers.

NOTES

1. To avoid the bias introduced by different levels of manufacturing activity among countries in 1950, it would have been preferable to examine manufacturing output per worker. However, the requisite data are not available to make this calculation for a sufficient number of countries. Table 5.1 is meant to suggest the wide variety of countries, if only in terms of geography, whose manufacturing sectors have grown rapidly over the past fifty or so years.

2. 'The rest', or prime latecomers (as listed in Table 5.1), includes 12 economies, most of which have well-developed control mechanisms (the major exception being Argentina): Argentina, Brazil, Chile, China, Thailand, India, Indonesia, Malaysia, Mexico, Republic of Korea, Taiwan Province of China and Turkey.

3. The steel industry accounted for roughly 40 per cent of all anti-dumping cases in 1998 (data are from Row and Maw Ltd., London, 1999).

4. Trade-related aspects of intellectual property rights (TRIPs) were a whole other new area of regulation, designed to protect, rather than liberalize, access to proprietary know-how. The United States placed TRIPs on the WTO agenda: 'Just before the Uruguay Round an American *enquête* among industries cited intellectual property rights as the biggest problem when investing in other countries' (Knutrud, 1994, p. 193). The effect of TRIPs by the year 2000 is still unknown, but much feared by developing countries, especially those with large pharmaceutical industries, which circumvented patents to produce and deliver drugs locally at below-world prices (see Mourshed, 1999). There was also a movement afoot among North Atlantic members of WTO to regulate international business practices (Malaguti, 1998).

5. Dividend balancing stipulates that, during a period of seven years after the start of commercial production, the amount of dividend that a firm can repatriate must be covered by the firm's export earnings (UNCTAD, 1998, p. 58).

6. Economies comprising 'the rest' are identified in note 2; 'the remainder' includes secondary, tertiary and still later industrializers, few of which had substantial prewar manufacturing experience (Amsden, 2001).

7. The concept of a control mechanism was first applied to the animal and the machine, and adapted to cybernetics by a physicist (Wiener, 1948). It also became an integral part of modern corporate management techniques (Merchant, 1985). All control mechanisms share at least four elements: a *detector* or *sensor*, or a measuring device to identify what is happening in the process to be controlled; an *assessor*, or a device to determine the significance of what is happening (where significance is typically evaluated by comparing information on what *is* happening with a specified standard of what *should* happen); an *effector*, or a feedback device to alter behaviour, if necessary; and a *communications network*, or a device to transmit information between the detector and assessor and between the assessor and effector (Anthony and Govindarajan, 1995).

8. Information on Thailand is from interviews with Board of Investment officials, Bangkok: Deputy Secretary General Vanee Lertudumrikarn, July 1991 and August 1993; Deputy Secretary General Khun Chakchai, July 1991 and April 1996; and Deputy Secretary General Chakramon Phasukavanich, April 1996. Shorter quotations in the text from Board of Investment officials are from one or another of these people.

9. This contrasted with a more even incidence of university education in the public and private sectors in India, Brazil and Mexico, whose industries were more advanced than Thailand's in the late 1950s, and hence more managerial. For the private sector, see CEPAL (1963) for Latin America, and Agarwala (1986) for India. For the bureaucracies responsible for economic policy in Brazil, see Willis (1990). For country examples, see Ross Schneider (1998).

10. For a comparable situation in the Republic of Korea, see Amsden (1994).

11. 'Because of the attractive investment policies in Hsinchu Science Industrial Park, HSIP could easily be filled with companies from various kinds of industries. ... Should that happen, however, HSIP would simply become another industrial park or Export Processing Zone. It would not be able to achieve its main objective of developing high-tech industry. To prevent this from happening, the Park Administration (under the auspices of the National Science

Council) has played an active role as the "gatekeeper" to make sure that only firms which fit the target industry list are considered' (Xue, 1997, p. 750).

12. Four HAN projects fell into the product technology category: new agrochemicals; broadband integrated service digital networks; high definition television; and next-generation vehicle technology. Seven projects fell into the fundamental technology category: next-generation semiconductors; advanced materials for information, electronics and energy; advanced manufacturing systems; new functional bio-materials; environmental technology; new energy technology; and next-generation nuclear reactors. In addition to these projects, S&T in the Republic of Korea in the 1990s involved more centralized coordination (to avoid duplication by competing ministries), a 1997 law ('Special Law for the Promotion of S&T Innovation') to expedite R&D within a five-year period, and the internationalization of R&D activity (see Cho and Amsden, 1999; Cho and Kim, 1997; Kim and Yi, 1997; Lim, 1999; OECD, 1996b).

13. For the old system, see Wang (1993) and Saich (1989), who also discuss reforms in the 1980s.

REFERENCES

Agarwala, P.N. (1986), 'The development of managerial enterprises in India', in K. Kobayashi and H. Morikawa (eds), *Development of Managerial Enterprise*, Tokyo: University of Tokyo Press, pp. 235–57.

Amsden, A.H. (1994), 'The spectre of Anglo-Saxonization is haunting South Korea', in L.J. Cho and Y.H. Kim (eds), *Korea's Political Economy: An Institutional Perspective*, Boulder, CO: Westview, pp. 87–125.

Amsden, A.H. (2001), *The Rise of the Rest: Challenges to the West from Late-industrializing Economies*, Oxford: Oxford University Press.

Anthony, R.N. and V. Govindarajan (1995), *Management Control Systems*, Chicago: Irwin.

CEPAL (1963), 'El empresario industrial en America Latina', document prepared for the CEPAL Executive Secretariat, Santiago, Chile.

Chandler, A.D. (1990), *Scale and Scope. The Dynamics of Industrial Capitalism*, Cambridge, MA: Harvard University Press.

Cho, H.D. and A.H. Amsden (1999), *Government Husbandry and Control Mechanism for the Promotion of High-Tech Development*, Cambridge, MA: MIT, Materials Science Laboratory.

Cho, H.H. and J.S. Kim (1997), 'Transition of the government role in research and development in developing countries: R&D and human capital', *International Journal of Technology Management, Special Issue on R&D Management*, 13(7/8): 729–3.

Daito, E. (1986), 'Recruitment and training of middle managers in Japan, 1900–1930', in K. Kobayashi and H. Morikawa (eds), *Development of Managerial Enterprise*, Tokyo: University of Tokyo Press, pp. 151–79.

Deardorff, A.V. (1994), 'Market access', *The New World Trading System: Readings*, Paris: Organization for Economic Cooperation and Development, pp. 57–63.

Doner, R.F. (1991), *Driving a Bargain: Automobile Industrialization and Japanese Firms in Southeast Asia*, Berkeley and Los Angeles: University of California Press.

Evers, H.D. and T.H. Silcock (1967), 'Elites and selection', (ed.), *Thailand: Social and Economic Studies in Development*, in T.H. Silcock, Durham N.C.: Australian National University Press in association with Duke University Press, pp. 84–104.

Hoda, A. (1994), 'Trade liberalisation', *The New World Trading System: Readings*, Paris: Organization for Economic Cooperation and Development, pp. 41–56.

James, W.E. (1987), *Asian Development: Economic Success and Policy Lessons*, Madison, WI: University of Wisconsin Press (for the International Center for Economic Growth).

Kim, L. and G. Yi (1997), 'The dynamics of R&D in industrial development: Lessons from the Korean experience', *Industry and Innovation*, 4(2): 167–82.

Knutrud, L.H. (1994), 'TRIPs in the Uruguay Round', *The New World Trading System: Readings*. Paris: Organization for Economic Cooperation and Development, pp. 193–5.

Lim, Y. (1999), *Public Policy for Upgrading Industrial Technology in Korea*, Boston: MIT Press.

Low, P. (1993), *The GATT and US Trade Policy*, New York, Twentieth Century Fund Press.

Lu, Q. (1997), *Innovation and Organization: The Rise of New Science and Technology Enterprises in China*, Cambridge, MA: Harvard University Press.

Malaguti, M.C. (1998), 'Restrictive business practices in international trade and the role of the World Trade Organization', *Journal of World Trade*, 32(3): 117–52.

Mandeville, B. (1714, repr. 1924), *The Fable of the Bees: or, Private Vices, Public Benefits*, London: Oxford University Press.

Merchant, K. (1985), *Control in Business Organizations*, Marshfield MA: Pitman.

Mourshed, M. (1999), 'Technology transfer dynamics: Lessons from the Egyptian and Indian pharmaceutical industries', *Urban Studies and Planning*, Cambridge, MA: MIT.

Narongchai, A. and J. Ajanant (1983), *Manufacturing Protection in Thailand: Issue and Empirical Studies*, Canberra: ASEAN–Australia Joint Research Project.

O'Brien, P.K. (1997), 'Intercontinental trade and the development of the third world since the industrial revolution', *Journal of World History*, 8(1): 75–133.

OECD (1996a), *Trade Liberalization Policies in Mexico*, Paris: Organization for Economic Cooperation and Development.

OECD (1996b), *Reviews of National Science and Technology Policy: Korea*, Paris: Organization for Economic Cooperation and Development.

Raby, D. (1994), 'Introduction', *The New World Trading System: Readings*, Paris, Organization for Economic Cooperation and Development.

Ross Schneider, B. (1998), 'Elusive synergy: Business–Government relations and development', *Comparative Politics*, October: 101–22.

Saich, T. (1989), 'Reforms of China's Science and Technology Organizational System', in D. Simon and M. Goldman (eds), *Science and Technology in Post-Mao China*, Cambridge: Cambridge University Press, pp. 69–88.

Schott, J.J. (1994), 'Safeguards', in *The New World Trading System: Readings*, Paris: Organization for Economic Cooperation and Development, pp. 113–16.

Startup, J. (1994), 'An Agenda for International Investment', in *The New World Trading System: Readings*, Paris: Organization for Economic Cooperation and Development, pp. 189–92.

Suehiro, A. (1993), 'Capitalist development in postwar Thailand: Commercial bankers, industrial elite, and agribusiness groups', in R. McVey (ed.), *Southeast Asian Capitalists*, Ithaca NY: Southeast Asia Program, Cornell University Press, pp. 35–63.

Tainan Science-Based Industrial Park (1996), 'Prospectus', Tainan, Taiwan Province of China, Tainan Science-Based Industrial Park.

Toulan, O. and M. Guillen (1996), *Internationalization: Lessons from Mendoza*, Cambridge and Mendoza: CIT/MIT.

UNCTAD (1998), *World Investment Report*, Geneva and New York: United Nations.

UNIDO (1997), *International Yearbook of Industrial Statistics*, Vienna: Edward Elgar Publishing Limited.

Wang, Y.F. (1993), *China's Science and Technology Policy: 1949–1989*, Aldershot: Avebury.

Wiener, N. (1948), *Cybernetics: Or Control and Communication in the Animal and Machine*, New York: John Wiley.

Willis, E.J. (1990), *The Politicized Bureaucracy: Regimes, Presidents and Economic Policy in Brazil*, Boston, MA: Boston College.

World Bank (1993), *East Asian Miracle: Economic Growth and Public Policy*, New York: Oxford University Press.

World Bank (various), *World Tables*, Washington, DC: World Bank.

Xue, L. (1997), 'Promoting industrial R&D and high-tech development through science parks: The Taiwan experience and its implications for developing countries', *International Journal of Technology Management, Special Issue of R&D Management*, 13(7/8): 744–61.

6. Technological change and opportunities for development as a moving target

Carlota Perez

TECHNICAL CHANGE AND DEVELOPMENT

Technology has usually been treated as a specialized area in development policies, dealt with by separate institutions. Yet, as this chapter aims to show, technology is much more than an ingredient in development strategies; it is a conditioning element of their viability.

Development opportunities are a moving target. Any serious observer of the development achievements from the late 1950s to the late 1970s will have recognized that import substitution strategies applied by one country after another led to gradual and significant advances. There was, in fact, increasing hope for continued success in the mid-1970s, when the combination of 'industrial redeployment' and export promotion was showing and promising further and deeper advances. The subsequent failure and deterioration of the protected, subsidized model in most countries that tried to continue with it has swung the pendulum towards a complete denial of the achievements of such a model, and opened the way for upholding free markets as the only way to succeed in development, though proof of this is yet to come.

We argue here that windows of opportunity for development appear and change as successive technological revolutions are deployed in the advanced countries. Transfer of technology and of production facilities is only willingly undertaken if it promises mutual benefits. The reason why import substitution strategies were successful at the time was that they represented a positive-sum game for maturing industries in the developed world that faced technological constriction and market saturation. The advent of the information revolution radically changed such conditions, and created different viable options.

This interpretation examines development strategies from a different angle, which we believe to be particularly useful for the challenges of globalization and the 'Information Age'. The chapter first reviews how technologies evolve in order to understand the conditions that generate development opportunities and to identify their nature. It then approaches the question of development as one of learning to benefit from such changing opportunities. This is illustrated with an overview of the successive development models of the last fifty years and a look at the challenges posed by the next stage of concentration of power in the global economy. Finally, some of the institutional requirements for coping with the new 'flexible networks paradigm' are examined.

PRODUCT CYCLES, DEVELOPMENT AND CHANGING BARRIERS TO ENTRY

The role of imported technologies as stepping-stones to industrialization is a historically well recognized fact, on the basis of the experiences of the United States and of successive European countries in the nineteenth and early twentieth centuries. More recently, this role has been confirmed by the rapid emergence of Japan as a front-rank country and by the surge in development of the four 'dragons' in Asia. Their success has been clearly associated with the absorption of technology from the more advanced countries, and with their own efforts to adopt, adapt, modify and gradually master the technical know-how involved (Freeman, 1987; Amsden, 1989). Yet, during the same recent period, many more countries have had little success while making apparently similar attempts to use imported technology for development. In fact, many countries, and whole regions, such as Africa and most of South America, seem to have lost much of the ground gained (Mytelka, 1989; Katz *et al.*, 1996).

The causes of these different results lie partly in the particular policies applied and partly in the specific conditions of the countries in question. Even more profoundly, they are rooted in the nature of the windows of opportunity created by technological evolution in the core countries and in the capacity to take advantage of them, whether consciously or intuitively. We need, therefore, to draw on the abundant literature on how technologies evolve and diffuse.

The Product Life Cycle and the Geographic Outspreading of Technologies

One of the earlier attempts to deal with technological opportunities for developing countries was made by Hirsch (1965). Examining the behaviour of the traditional electronics industry in terms of the product cycle, he showed how advantages shifted in favour of the less developed countries as technologies approached maturity. Louis T. Wells (1972) graphically summarized the process, by examining the United States, in his review of the product cycle literature (Figure 6.1).

This outward migration from the country of origin to other advanced countries, and from there to the less advanced, revealed one of the processes behind Leontief s surprising finding that US exports had a higher labour content than its imports (Leontief, 1953). This paradoxical situation of the technological leader at the time was thus associated with the changing characteristics of evolving technologies. In the early phases, technologies are likely to be more labour-intensive – they are higher users of relatively costly knowledge-intensive labour[1] than when they approach maturity and begin to use highly mechanized and automated processes.

As technologies mature, there are forces *pushing* them further and further out towards the periphery where, presumably, there are complementary forces *pulling* such technologies in order to unleash development processes. Although this applies mainly to consumer goods and to certain basic capital goods, it covers a wide enough range for it to serve as a starting point for our discussion.

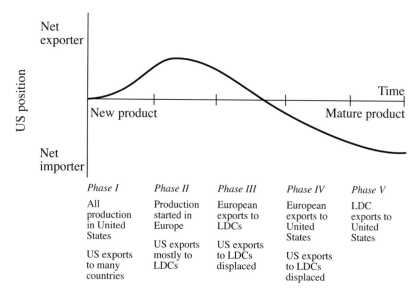

Source: Wells (1972, p. 15).

Figure 6.1   The geographic outspreading of technologies as they mature

Mature Technologies are not enough for Catching up[2]

Ironically, the advantage shifts to capital-poor countries when products become more capital-intensive. By then, tasks have been so routinized, as shown in phase four of the graphs in Figure 6.2(a),[3] that managers are not required to have much previous knowledge or be highly experienced, while unskilled labour can be utilized. In addition, as technology and markets mature, comparative costs become a determining advantage.

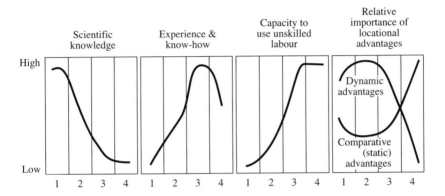

Source: Based on Perez and Soete (1988) and Hirsch (1967).

Figure 6.2(a)   Changing requirements for entry as technologies evolve to maturity

Can a process of catching up be based on mature technologies? It is very difficult for several reasons. As shown in Figure 6.2(b), mature technologies reach a point where they have minimal potential for profit making; they face stagnating markets and have almost no space left for improvements in productivity. Thus, in general, entering at maturity is expensive, not very profitable and not very promising. Nevertheless, it is probably the best starting point for creating a basic industrialization platform, generating learning capabilities and setting up the main infrastructure and other externalities needed to support development.

However, catching up involves a dynamic development process, fuelled by local innovation and growing markets. This requires as early an entry as is feasible; surprisingly enough, apart from the mature phase of technologies, the other moment when weaker players confront surmountable barriers is not in phases two or three but rather in phase one. This happens to be the most promising entry point, since, as indicated in Figure 6.2(b), potential profits are high, there is ample space for market and productivity growth, and investment costs are relatively low. Even R&D investment can often be lower than that of the original innovator.

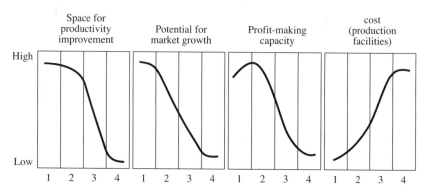

Source: Based on Gerschenkron (1962), Cundiff *et al.* (1973), Kotler (1980) and Dosi (1982).

Figure 6.2(b)   Changing potential of technologies as they evolve to maturity

One would think, however, that only firms in advanced countries would possess the high degree of knowledge required in this phase, as shown in Figure 6.2(a). Nevertheless, when new products are part of the early stages of a technological revolution, the knowledge involved is usually publicly available (in universities or elsewhere). The recent example of Silicon Valley, and of the thousands of successful imitators locally and worldwide, serves to illustrate the phenomenon. In those cases, required previous experience is also low, and having it could even be a hindrance because, as will be discussed later, technological revolutions bring with them new managerial models, making the old ones obsolete.

The other constraining factor is context-related. Dynamic advantages and externalities of various sorts, especially physical, social and technological infrastructures, as well as competent and demanding local clients, are important complements for success with new technologies. These elements can be built up by entering mature technologies, engaging in intense learning processes and investing in improving the social and economic environment.

Could one then design a strategy for accumulating technological and social capabilities on the basis of mature technologies and then using this platform for entering new, dynamic, ones? Such possibilities are strongly dependent on the peculiar windows of opportunity created by successive technological revolutions. Developing countries wishing to design viable strategies can benefit from a thorough understanding of the evolution of technologies in the advanced countries. The following section is an overview of the characteristic patterns of such evolution.

TECHNOLOGIES, SYSTEMS, REVOLUTIONS AND PARADIGMS

The evolution of technologies is a complex process; technologies are interconnected in systems, which are interwoven and interdependent, both among themselves and with the physical, social and institutional environment.

A great deal of learning is gradual and incremental. However, there is no inevitable progression towards an ever more advanced – and ever more unattainable – frontier; there are important discontinuities that become breaches permitting latecomers to leap forward. These take the form of technological revolutions, which create major shifts in the direction of technical change. They provide the means for modernizing most activities at the cost of abandoning many of the previously accumulated managerial skills and part of the previous equipment with its associated expertise. The revolutionary new technologies provide entirely fresh opportunities for learning and catching up; and the interplay of continuous and discontinuous changes explains why and how windows of opportunity for development change over time.

Technological Trajectories and Accumulated Experience

Despite their individual specific variations, many technologies tend to follow a similar sequence in the rate and direction of change and in improvement, from initial innovation to maturity, which very roughly coincides with the evolution of their markets, from introduction to saturation (Abernathy and Utterback, 1975; Dosi, 1982; Sahal, 1985).[4] Figure 6.3(a) represents the typical trajectory of a technology.

After a radical innovation gives birth to a new product that is capable of creating a new industry, there is an initial period of further innovation and optimization, leading to the acceptance of the product in the appropriate market segment. Soon the interaction with the market determines the direction of improvements, often defining a dominant design (Arthur, 1989; David, 1985); from then on, as markets grow, there are successive incremental innovations to improve the quality of the product, the productivity of the process and the market position of the producers. Eventually, maturity is reached, when further investment in innovation brings diminishing returns. Depending on the significance of the product, the whole process can take a few years or several decades. In this latter case, 'improvements' usually involve successive models.

After the early innovations, those who are developing the technology acquire advantages, not only through patents but also, and perhaps more importantly, through accumulated experience with product, process and markets. This confines the relevant knowledge and know-how within the firms and its

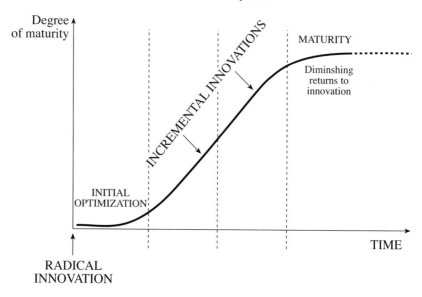

Source: Based on Dosi (1982, 1988) and Wolf (1912).

Figure 6.3(a)   The evolution of a technology technological trajectory

suppliers, making it less and less accessible to entrants. Furthermore, this experience gradually increases the speed with which innovations can be adopted, so that the later ones are very rapidly incorporated, making it difficult for lagging followers to catch up. Figure 6.3(b) illustrates this phenomenon using the case of the car.

Technology Systems and the Construction of Social Capabilities

Individual technologies do not grow in isolation but, rather, are interconnected in systems, building upon each other and taking advantage of what their predecessors created within the system, in terms of experience, suppliers, consumer learning and externalities (Freeman *et al.*, 1982). The evolution of technology systems follows a trajectory essentially similar to that of single products (Figure 6.3(a)). The series of new *products* would be the 'incremental improvements' to the system. In the first two phases, there are many truly major products with a long life-cycle; thereafter, their numbers and importance tend to diminish, until the last ones are minor and short-lived (as in Figure 6.3(b)).

Figure 6.4 presents a stylized example of the system of home electrical appliances, which begins with refrigerators, washing machines and vacuum

Percentage of output
incorporating innovations

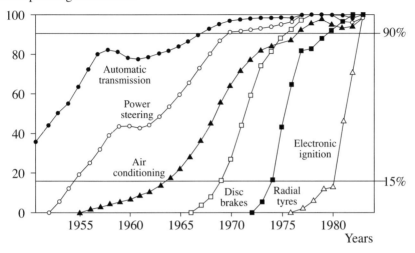

Source: Jutila and Jutila (1986) cited in Grubler (1990, p. 155).

Figure 6.3(b)   The diffusion of successive technologies in the US car industry

cleaners, and then grows with a series of new products and successive models
of the early ones. They all tend to reach maturity together with the introduction
of the last minor innovations, such as with electric can-openers and carving
knives. The figure also indicates how systems become rooted in particular territories through the growing network of parts and service suppliers, and the
gradual construction of the regulatory framework and other institutional facili-
tators. This growing interplay of 'hard and soft' elements is part of what
Abramovitz (1986) meant when he criticized the notion of development as
simply the accumulation of capital and labour and when he emphasized the
need for accumulating *social* capability. It is also related to the notion of national
or regional 'systems of innovation', formed by the interacting agents (Freeman,
1987; Lundvall, 1988, 1992).

The need to form these complex webs of mutually supporting activities and
institutions explains some of the limitations involved in development based
on the transfer of already mature technologies. It also strengthens the case of
those who recommend building upon the existing traditions, local capabilities
and knowledge of each specific territory (Porter, 1990). Finally, it shows the
type of effort required for supporting the survival of pioneering firms in
developing countries.

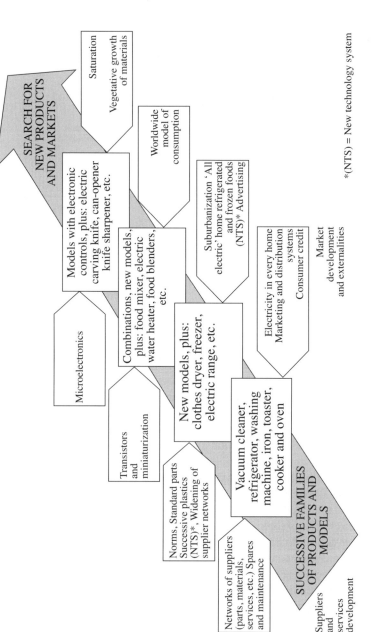

Figure 6.4 Coevolution of a technology system and its environment: home electrical appliances

SEARCH FOR
NEW PRODUCTS
AND MARKETS

Saturation

Vegetative growth
of materials

Models with electronic
controls, plus: electric
carving knife, can-opener
knife sharpener, etc.

Worldwide
model of
consumption

Microelectronics

Combinations, new models,
plus: food mixer, electric
water heater, food blenders,
etc.

Suburbanization 'All
electric' home refrigerated
and frozen foods
(NTS)* Advertising

Transistors
and
miniaturization

New models, plus:
clothes dryer, freezer,
electric range, etc.

Electricity in every home
Marketing and distribution
systems
Consumer credit

Market
development
and externalities

Norms, Standard parts
Successive plastics
(NTS)*, Widening of
supplier networks

Vacuum cleaner,
refrigerator, washing
machine, iron, toaster,
cooker and oven

Networks of suppliers
(parts, materials,
services, etc.) Spares
and maintenance

SUCCESSIVE FAMILIES
OF PRODUCTS AND
MODELS

Suppliers
and
services
development

*(NTS) = New technology system

Technological Revolutions and the Interconnection of Systems

Each technological revolution is a cluster of technology systems, which gradually create conditions for the appearance of further systems, all following similar principles and benefiting from the same externalities. Figures 6.5(a) and 6.5(b) sketch two such explosions of new technologies: the mass production revolution with its successive systems, crystallizing around 1910 and reaching maturity in the 1960s and 1970s, and the information revolution, diffusing since the 1970s.

This process of upstream and downstream multiplication of innovations and technology systems represents the massive growth potential involved in each technological revolution. It is like the opening of a vast new territory for innovation, expansion and growth. The early innovations mark the 'discovery', while the full 'occupation' falls within the maturity and exhaustion phase.

Again, Figures 6.3(a) and 6.3(b), stretching the 'time' dimension, can be roughly seen as representing the life trajectory of a technological revolution, where the 'improvements' are the successive new technology systems. Many major systems appear in the early growth period, and fewer and less significant ones as maturity is approached.

Technoeconomic Paradigms and the Rejuvenation of All Activities

The existing mature industries, however, do not just stagnate or passively cohabit with the new ones. Each technological revolution provides generically pervasive technologies and new organizational practices resulting in a significant increase in the potential productivity of most existing activities. The principles behind this process are gradually articulated into an ideal best-practice model, which we have proposed to call a 'technological style' or a 'technoeconomic paradigm' (Perez, 1983, 1985).[5] The result is a gradual rejuvenation of the whole productive structure, so that modernized mature industries can again behave like 'new' ones.

This is one reason why those who expressed hopes in the 'North–South Dialogue' of the late 1970s for the transfer of 'old' industries to the developing world were disappointed. Since the 1980s, one industry after another has been modernized. Even the very traditional clothing industry has been upgraded, segmented and put on an innovative path (Hoffman and Rush, 1988; Mytelka, 1991).

A Paradigm Shift as a Change in Managerial 'Common Sense'

The technoeconomic paradigm articulates the technical and organizational model for taking best advantage of the potential of the technological revolution.

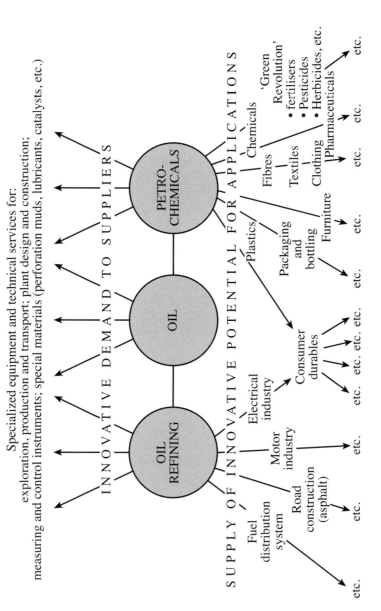

Figure 6.5(a)   *The mass production revolution as a growing network of technology systems from the 1910s*

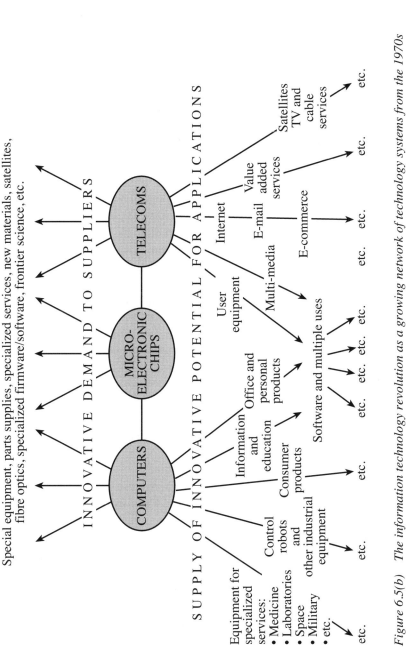

Figure 6.5(b)   *The information technology revolution as a growing network of technology systems from the 1970s*

111

It provides a new set of 'common sense' principles guiding the decision-making processes of entrepreneurs, innovators, managers, engineers and investors towards maximum efficiency and effectiveness in new and old activities. For those who had been successful with the previous paradigm the adoption of a new one can be devastating. Apart from requiring the abandonment of hard-earned experience, it feels as if the world were turned upside down (Peters, 1989; Coriat, 1991). Figure 6.6 illustrates how the shift from the mass production paradigm to the flexible networks model transforms management criteria in all activities, from product choice and design, through organizational structures, to forms of operation and personnel relations.

Phenomena such as globalization and the trend towards political decentralization are also strongly related to the change of paradigm, to the new possibilities it offers and to the most effective way of taking advantage of them. Thus the Schumpeterian description of technological revolutions as processes of 'creative destruction' can be seen to apply beyond the economy to politics and institutions. The process of change is not easy; the transition to the new practices can take two or three decades. But in the long-run the new paradigm becomes common sense, to the point of being considered natural and normal.

Newcomers, or those who had not been very successful with the previous paradigm, can redirect their efforts towards learning the new practices, while the established leaders are 'unlearning' much of the old and adopting the new. Much of the experience and considerable amounts of investment become obsolete and need to be replaced. This is a painful and prolonged process and newcomers may have some advantages, which can be reinforced by early investment in infrastructures and adoption of adequate facilitating institutions.

DEVELOPMENT AS LEARNING TO TAKE ADVANTAGE OF CHANGING OPPORTUNITIES

The picture we have been trying to paint, with the widest of brush strokes, is one of technological evolution as characterized by continuities and discontinuities rooted in the nature of competition in the capitalist system. On a micro level, each radical innovation represents a discontinuity followed by continued evolution, until the constriction of the space for increasing productivity and profits gives rise to other radical innovations. On the macro level, technological revolutions erupt in the economic system, bringing whole constellations of new products, technologies and industries. These major discontinuities induce great surges of growth, which swell initially in the core countries, gradually encompass and rejuvenate most of the previously existing industries and finally

MASS PRODUCTION MODEL
Age of oil and motor cars

FLEXIBLE NETWORKS MODEL
Age of information technology

	MASS PRODUCTION MODEL		FLEXIBLE NETWORKS MODEL
INPUTS and VALUE	ENERGY AND MATERIALS INTENSITY In products, processes, transport, etc. TANGIBLE PRODUCTS	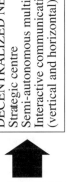	INFORMATION & KNOWLEDGE INTENSITY Materials and energy saving INTANGIBLE VALUE and SERVICES
PRODUCTS and MARKETS	STANDARDIZED PRODUCTS MASS MARKET		DIVERSIFIED ADAPTABLE PRODUCTS HIGHLY SEGMENTED MARKETS From high volume basic to narrow niches
OPERATION	'ONE BEST WAY' The optimal routine as a goal		CONTINUOUS IMPROVEMENT Change as the main routine
STRUCTURES	CENTRALIZED ORGANIZATIONS Hierarchical pyramids Functional compartments Rigid communications channels		DECENTRALIZED NETWORKS Strategic centre Semi-autonomous multifunctional units Interactive communications (vertical and horizontal)
PERSONNEL	HUMAN RESOURCES Labour as a cost Training as an expected externality		HUMAN CAPITAL Labour as an asset Training as an investment

Figure 6.6 A change in technological and managerial 'common sense'

spread out towards the periphery, while another great surge takes shape and erupts in the core.

Developing countries are thus running after a moving target. It not only moves constantly ahead but it also shifts direction about every half century. Ruling out autarchy as an option, development would be about learning to play this constantly shifting game, which is also a power game. Could this be another version of dependency theory? It certainly involves a notion of North–South centre–periphery complementarity. At the same time, however, it presents the possibility of breaking the vicious circle of underdevelopment through appropriate policies. Followers who understand the game and play it well might find a way of leaping forward and catching up. The favourable conditions for such an outcome would occur during the periods of paradigm shift.

Paradigm Transitions as Double Technological Opportunities

For twenty years or more, during the transition, there is a coexistence of old and new technologies. The bulk of already mature technologies of the previous paradigm is stretching, suffering from constriction of productivity and markets, and spreading out geographically to survive, while the new ones are exploding, flourishing and growing at high rates with huge profit margins. This leads to centrifugal trends, where the rich, modern and successful get richer, and the poor and weak get poorer. Yet, paradoxically, it is at this period, with the worst social and economic conditions, that the best opportunities appear.

This period of paradigm transition provides the simultaneous opening of the two widest windows of opportunity: phase one of the new technologies, and phase four of the old (Figure 6.7). We argued earlier that, although mature products can serve to achieve growth for a while, they are not capable of fuelling a process of catching up, because they have basically exhausted their innovation space. During paradigm transitions, however, there is a powerful opportunity to leap forward. The new generic technologies and organizational principles can be used to modernize and rejuvenate mature technologies (and even old traditional ones), as with the car and other industries in Japan, shipbuilding and steel in the Republic of Korea (Shin, 1992), surgical instruments in Pakistan (Nadvi and Schmitz, 1999), fresh flower exports in Colombia and fresh salmon in Chile (for these and other examples, see ECLAC, 1990).

It is also possible to try a direct entry into the new industries, as many firms in the developing world did in microelectronic products and software, during this transition. The challenge is to survive phases two and three successfully. Many early shining stars disappeared in the process. As we have seen, staying in the race demands growing support from the environment, constant innovation, intensive investment and probably very skilful manoeuvring in terms of markets and alliances, for example memory chips in the Republic of Korea, disk drives in Singapore, Asian computer clones, and other successes – although each had particular conditions.

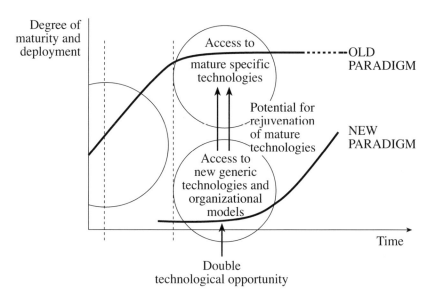

Figure 6.7   The transition as the best opportunity to leap forward

In this specific transition, a very strong third possibility appeared in the context of globalization. In contrast with the way the industries of the mass production paradigm deployed nationally first, before moving internationally, many industries in this paradigm have operated globally from phase one. This has opened the possibility of participating in global networks in many different ways and with varied arrangements (Hobday, 1995; Radosevic, 1999). It has also made it possible to produce locally for global trading companies, either as single firms or through cooperating clusters (Schmitz and Knorringa, 1999; Schmitz and Nadvi, 1999; see also IDS Collective Efficiency Research Project).

'Dancing with Wolves'[6] or the Issue of Power Structures

An understanding of the conditions of access to technology is not complete without addressing the question of power structures. In fact, changing barriers to entry are closely related to the levels and forms of competition and concentration in the industry in question. The nature of each phase marks the behaviour of the firms involved and gradually modifies their focus and their interests.

Table 6.1 provides a stylized summary of the changing patterns of competition and power structures, which can typify evolving industries, their technologies and markets. It also indicates the 'width' of the window of opportunity in each phase and the conditions demanded of aspiring entrants, be they dependent (that is, joining the strategy of owner firms) or autonomous firms acting as direct challengers in the market. Obviously, such a schematic attempt cannot account for all cases. Nor is it within the scope of this chapter to discuss the necessary variations and subtleties. The table can, however, serve as a basic framework for making a few important points.

- Since there are always products and industries going through the various phases, it is important to be informed and aware of the stage of evolution of the technologies and of the patterns of competition, in order to assess the interests and strengths of possible partners or competitors. This allows the evaluation of a firm's assets and possibilities, and improves decision-making and negotiating tactics.
- However, the stage of deployment of the technological revolution also matters. Since technological revolutions lead to the coevolution of many successive systems, during the early period there tend to be many new important technologies in phases one and two, whereas in later periods there is a predominance of technologies approaching maturity (phases three and four) until they overlap in the next transition. So individual windows of opportunity are strongly shaped by the wider context. This affects both entrepreneurial and national strategies.
- Finally, the choice of dependent or 'autonomous' entry is very much determined by a firm's conditions. But it also demands a good understanding of the evolving power structures, in order to identify the present and future interests of the incumbents. The weaker the player, the more important it is to learn to dance with the powerful 'wolves' (and even to distinguish between wolves and how to attract them).

Of course, not all technologies are open to negotiation; sometimes, real success may lead to confrontation and zero-sum games. What should be avoided is negotiating mutual benefit arrangements as if they were confrontations. Failure to identify the interests and needs of the prospective partners risks aiming at the wrong target, and is likely to waste the value of one's assets.

Historically, rapid growth and economic development, whether catching up from behind or forging ahead to the front ranks, have usually occurred as a result of successful processes of *technological* development (Lall, 1992; Bell and Pavitt, 1993; Reinert, 1994; Freeman, 1994; von Tunzelmann, 1995). These have usually been based on playing *successive positive-sum games* with those ahead, and being prepared to change the game as the context and the structures evolve.

Table 6.1 Changing competition patterns and power structures facing aspiring entrants as technologies evolve, stylized summary

	Phase in the Life Trajectory of the Product and its Technology			
	1. Introduction	2. Early growth	3. Late growth	4. Maturity
Focus: competitive factors Competition and power	Product quality test of market Many challengers, uncertain outcome	Process efficiency access to market Industry taking shape; firms growing and battling for markets; emerging leaders	Scale and market power Drive for concentration; giant complex structures; oligopolies, cartels, etc.	Diminishing costs Financial power looking for profitable outlets and stretching solutions
		Dependent entry		
Window 'SIZE'	NARROW	VERY NARROW	WIDENING	VERY WIDE
Basis for dependent entry	Comparative or dynamic advantages, complementary assets	Interesting market competence as supplier or advantageous access to resources or markets	Significant market existing or created externalities or other sources of profit propping	Comparative cost advantages, access to finance, learning capabilities
Character of dependent or allied entry (usually initiated by the owner)	Alliances; mutual benefit negotiations for sharing complementary capabilities and/or assets (to strengthen competitive potential)	As supplier or commercial representative	As part of the structure (as supplier, producer, distributor or in whatever role fits the power and expansion strategy of the owner firm)	Production agreements or joint ventures in mutual benefit negotiations (transfer of mature technologies and of market access)
		Autonomous entry		
Window 'SIZE'	WIDE	NARROW	VERY NARROW	WIDENING
Basis for attempting entry	Knowledge: capacity to imitate and innovate (without violating patents); local know-how for creating a special niche	Knowledge plus experience in process technology and markets (brand names or privileged access to markets important)	Experience, financial muscle and market control; comparative cost advantages, learning capabilities, copying capacity	Comparative cost advantages, learning capabilities, copying capacity
Character of autonomous entry (initiated by the challenger)	'Free' competition for market acceptance, possibly for dominant design; patents often important	Aggressive competition for growing and profitable markets; possible alliances	Takeover or exclusion of previous weaker players, possible cartels	Compete with other low-cost entrants; buy (or copy) mature technology and 'know-how' or make rejuvenating innovations

PAST EXPERIENCE AND THE NEXT WINDOW

Looking back at the recent history of the developing world and the various
strategies applied, we can recognize how, consciously or intuitively, something
akin to positive-sum games was constructed between the interests of advanced
country firms and those of developing countries. An analysis of this experience
can help us look ahead with more informed criteria for the future. Nevertheless,
as always happens with the lessons of history, it is crucial to distinguish between
recurrence and uniqueness. There are patterns of change that recur in each
paradigm, yet each paradigm is basically unique and must be analysed with its
peculiar features.

Inventing and Reinventing Development Strategies

In the 1950s, the modern era of conscious 'third world' state involvement in the
industrialization process began in earnest. It was a time when an increasing
number of mass production industries were in their third phase: seeking
extended markets, pursuing economies of scale, forming oligopolies and
opening international outlets. Import-substituting industrialization (ISI),
subsidized and protected behind tariff barriers, became a positive-sum game.
The international companies multiplied their markets by exporting much greater
quantities of 'unassembled' parts to their affiliates abroad, which, in addition,
had higher profit margins; these 'screwdriver assembly' plants provided a
learning context for management and workers in the developing countries. The
resulting demand for roads, ports, transport, electricity, water and communications stimulated modernization and fostered the growth of many
complementary capabilities.

By the mid-1960s, limitations of the ISI strategy began to surface in some of
the countries, at the same time as many products and industries in the advanced
world were reaching phase four. Transfer of technology and export promotion
came to be seen as new mutually beneficial policies. It began with the transfer
of mature technologies to national governments, combined with local capital and
production for re-export from low-cost labour locations. By the 1970s, transnational corporations (TNCs) were engaged in 'redeployment' generating a
significant flow of exports to the advanced world. 'Miracles' in Brazil and the
Republic of Korea and 'export processing zones' in many countries made it
seem as if a new international economic order was emerging. The 'North–South
Dialogue' became the place where such hopes were negotiated.

By the early 1980s, the scene had changed again. Many products of the microelectronics revolution which had erupted in the early 1970s were reaching phase
two. The Japanese had rejuvenated the car industry and their new organizational paradigm was radically transforming its competitors in the United States

(Altshuler *et al.*, 1984) and Europe. 'Stagflation' accompanied maturity in most of the old industries in the advanced world, export markets began to shrink and the debt crisis set in. A new strategy had to be designed.

However, most of Latin America failed to adapt, and lived through the aptly designated 'lost decade'. The 'four tigers' in Asia, on the other hand, took the leap forward by capturing market after market from behind and at the edges of the fast growing revolutionary industries. They also rejuvenated mature technologies with modern practices and joined the networks of global firms as original equipment manufacture (OEM) suppliers of parts and components. The intense learning, and the emphasis on human capital and on the active absorption of technology which was behind these achievements, cannot be overstated (Amsden, 1989, ch. 9; Pavit and Bell, 1992). This was in sharp contrast to the much more passive 'transfer of technology' practices still common in most Latin American and African countries, as well as in the rest of Asia during that period. Figure 6.8 presents a summary of the way in which development strategies from the 1950s adapted to the windows of opportunity created by the evolving paradigm.

The 1990s were marked by the structuring of emerging industries and the widespread modernization of existing ones. As one industry after another reached phase two, the fierce competition for market positioning set in. The construction of global corporations and global markets, the battle to set the dominant design and other standards, the weaving of complex webs of collaboration on a worldwide scale, the strengthening of the market power of brands, the search for locational advantages, both dynamic and static, the interest in adapting products to specific market segments, the tendency to 'outsource' and other connected phenomena have created a wide range of possibilities depending on the conditions and disposition of the players.

Developing country experiments have been extremely varied both in practice and in results. They ranged from the modern '*maquiladoras*' (free trade zones) and OEM contracts, through various joint ventures and alliances to the fiercely competitive independent Asian firms (Hobday, 1994). There has also been a flourishing growth of interconnected local clusters in specific industries (such as Indian software) with export market successes. During this period, the 'four tigers' moved another step forward, setting up production in other countries of Southeast Asia and China. The successful strategies have generally implied *learning to live with globalization*.

Each of the previous successive strategies has had advantages and disadvantages, benefits and harmful effects. Some countries have made big leaps, and others small ones or none at all; some have maintained the advances gained, others have lost them and fallen back. Some of the setbacks maybe due to sticking to policies when they were no longer effective. Admittedly, the overall results are discouraging. This can lead to disillusion or to recognizing the

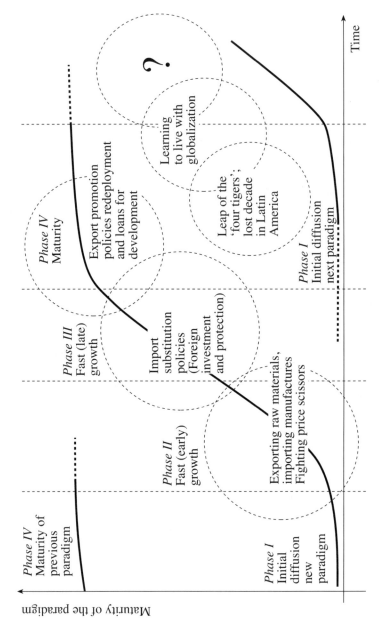

Figure 6.8 Successive development strategies along the phases of successive paradigms

extreme difficulty involved in bridging the chasm and the need for a deeper understanding of the issues.

Confronting the Next Stage

The new century will sooner or later see the creation of conditions for the full deployment of the wealth-creating potential of the Information Age.

The 1990s were a decade of experimentation everywhere – inside and outside global firms, in countries, regions, cities and localities, in the economy, in governments and other institutions, and in various levels of society. As a result, the 'common sense' of the flexible systems paradigm has spread widely and is becoming the normal way of seeing and doing things; many industries are reaching phase three of their trajectories. Agreements, mergers, acquisitions, takeovers and other arrangements are likely to lead to the worldwide concentration of each industry in a few mega-firms or a few global alliances (Chesnais, 1988,1992; Bressand, 1990; Klepper and Kenneth, 1994; Castells, 1996). Furthermore, the growing power of intermediation, through control of access to clients, could be leading to a modern version of the old 'trading companies' based on the power of information and telecommunications (Bressand and Kalypso, 1989; Kanellou, 1999). These giant firms might become huge global 'umbrellas' encompassing worldwide diversity, covering all segments – from the luxury and speciality niches to the cheapest standard product or service – purchasing and selling across the planet and locating each activity wherever advantages are greater.

For the developing world, the next stage may be a very complex period of adaptation to the new emerging power structures. For firms, localities, regions and countries, learning to play positive-sum games with these giants may be the nature of the next window of opportunity. Attempting local or regional networks, either independently or by connecting with global networks, could still be a possibility based on very specific local advantages. Of course, those countries and firms that have accumulated capabilities in technology, organization, marketing and negotiation will be much better placed for locating themselves favourably under the 'umbrellas' or, audaciously, outside them. Cooperation between firms, regions or countries can strengthen the bargaining power of both strong and weak actors and agents.

We are suggesting, then, that the design of successful strategies requires assessing the conditions and accumulated capabilities of the country, region, firm or network in question, in order to take advantage of the next (not the previous) window of opportunity, while recognizing, adopting and adapting the potential and the features of the relevant paradigm. The last section will review some of the implications of these features.

APPROACHING DEVELOPMENT UNDER THE PRESENT PARADIGM

Accelerated growth of firms, localities or countries depends on the availability of *a rich technological potential* and *an appropriate form of organization* to take advantage of it. Whatever the point of departure, and whatever the goal to pursue, success in these times is likely to hinge on how deeply the logic of the new paradigm is absorbed and creatively adopted and adapted at all levels of society.

The earlier centralized pyramids of mass production effectively served firms and Governments, universities and hospitals, and private and public organizations of all sorts. For more than two decades now, modern firms – global or local – have been profoundly restructuring and rapidly learning the advantages of networks and of learning organizations (Nonaka, 1994; Senge, 1990; Lundvall, 1997; see also DRUID project website). The time has come for governments to experiment in the same direction. Below, we touch upon some aspects of the necessary transformation.

Technology at the Core of Development Strategies

It is widely recognized that the Japanese surge ahead involved exercises in technological foresight to collectively signal the path ahead, and intense learning, training and innovating efforts (Peck and Goto, 1981; Irvine and Martin, 1985). The advance of the 'four tigers' from behind also involved widespread education and learning (Ernst *et al.*, 1998). Furthermore, successful global firms have redesigned their structures and practices to favour continuous learning and improvement. Knowledge management (Nonaka, 1995; Burton-Jones, 1999; Lamoreaux *et al.*, 1999) is becoming a key concern: not only do such firms organize regular training at all levels; some have even set up their own 'universities' (Wiggenhorn, 1990).

For a developing country to believe that significant advances are possible without equivalent efforts is an illusion. There is no short-cut to development without people's mastery of technology, in the simple sense, of social, technical and economic know-how. This was blurred by the peculiar conditions of import substitution policies, which for a time made it possible for many countries to achieve impressive growth performance by investing in mature plant and equipment, without intensive learning efforts.

In this particular paradigm, developing capacity to handle information and knowledge for innovation is more central than ever. Perhaps the most relevant meaning of the expression 'knowledge society' (Castells, 1996; Mansell and Wehn, 1998) is the creation of conditions for access to and use of information by all members of society. Therefore strengthening the individual and social learning capacities for wealth creation becomes an essential way of enhancing development potential. Consequently technology must be at the core – not at the edge – of development policies. In practical terms, this implies a different way of conceiving strategies, and demands a complete rethinking of both the education and training systems and of science and technology policies.

Educational reform needs to upgrade and update the technical contents and, perhaps mainly, effect a radical transformation in the methods, goals and tools to make them compatible and relevant for the future (Perez, 1992; ECLAC/UNESCO, 1992). It must allow students to take responsibility for their own process; emphasize 'learning to learn' and 'learning to change'; encourage creative teamwork and learning to formulate problems and evaluate alternative solutions; find ways of giving access to Internet and computers; and provide conditions for acquiring the ability to ask questions and process information. These skills are becoming the basis for participating in the modern workplace, where firms face a constantly changing environment with continuous improve-ment practices. They also enable individuals and groups to manage the growth of their own wealth-creating capabilities, as employees or entrepreneurs, and provide the necessary organizational abilities for improving their communities and organizations, as group members or as leaders.

The other crucial transformation regards the science and technology (S&T) system, which was created by most developing countries as a set of government institutions in charge of technological development. Experience showed that the use of these capabilities for actual innovation in production was very low. Given the mature technologies with which most industries worked, there was little capacity to absorb the results of these laboratory technologists. The ensuing frustration when trying to build the university–industry 'bridge' led most research technologists to become adjuncts of the scientific community and to adopt their methods, timescales, values and attitudes.

In the new context, it is necessary to move in two directions: invest sub-stantially in research for the future and steer technology towards the direct and immediate improvement of the production networks and of the quality of life. This move from a 'supply-push' S&T system to an interactive network with producers has warranted the term National System of Innovation (NSI – Freeman, 1987; Lundvall, 1988) defined by Freeman (1995) as 'the network of institutions in the public and private sectors whose activities and interactions initiate, import, modify and diffuse new technologies'. This assumes the NSI to be a social rather than a governmental construction. It includes the environ-ment in which innovativeness is stimulated and supported; the quality of the links between suppliers, producers and users; the education and training system; diverse public and private organizations facilitating technical change; the laws, regulations and even the ideas and attitudes towards technology and change (Arocena, 1997).

Reinventing the 'Strong' State[7]

It should by now be clear that the markets versus state debate is unsuitable for dealing with the concrete problems discussed here. Both are needed, but redefined and in a new combination. In any case, after the discussion above, it is clear that, for a lagging country, a successful development strategy under the logic of this paradigm, and especially in the face of global mega-firms, is bound to require vast cooperation among firms and between them and the state at various levels. Although the size and complexity of the task require a strong state, the all-powerful 'national state', as it developed after World War II, needs to be redefined and reinvented, probably along lines similar to those applied by modern global corporations.

Nobody believes that the central management of a giant corporation becomes weak when it decentralizes and gives high autonomy and decision-making power to its product, plant or market managers across the world. Computers and telecommunications have made it possible to exercise strong leadership over a vast and growing structure made up of semi-autonomous units, following strategic guidelines. Interactive information channels make it possible to monitor and control highly complex networks with strongly differentiated components.

The new shape of the needed strong 'public sector' can imitate those networks. As in the past, once technology helps define the optimal shape of organizations, it can be applied effectively, even without the technology. This, in turn, prepares the terrain for the incorporation of modern technology when required. The central national state can exercise its leadership by inducing the convergent actions of the various social actors towards a commonly agreed general direction of change. It can play a crucial role as 'intermediary' between the growing global or supraregional levels and the increasingly autonomous regional, local and even parish or community levels.

There is also a process of 'diffusion of power' (Strange, 1996). Networks of private interests, units of civil society, global firms, communications media, organized interest groups, non-governmental organizations, and others, are increasing the diversity of development agents and their interlinkages, nationally and globally. The capacity of the national state must serve as 'broker' within the country and between the various supranational and subnational levels for promoting and negotiating a fair game for all. It could exercise more effective authority if it acted as consensus builder among the various players with real power to influence the course of events.

Thinking Global, Acting Local

The new seat of the proactive development state is, in our view, the *local* government. The old 'central plan' idea of promoting a set of national industries to generate the wealth to fund social advance needs to be reconsidered. Obviously, each country must have some important activities, strongly connected to world markets and keeping up with the technological frontier so as to propel growth and produce the necessary foreign exchange. However, the time and the conditions are ripe to abandon the illusion of a 'trickle down effect' and move towards the direct involvement of the whole population in wealth-creating activities.

The capacity of the present paradigm for a variety of products and scales, its power to increase the quality and efficiency of all sectors and activities and, most of all, its accessibility to all human beings enabling them to learn how to constantly improve themselves, their work and their environment, make it possible to envisage a more comprehensive form of development.

There are already many examples of local governments identifying the 'vocation' of the community, promoting consensus, involving local and foreign firms, banks, the education systems and other actors to promote development projects (Tendler, 1997; Gabor, 1991; The Illinois Coalition, 1999). There are also local networks of small- and medium-sized firms collaborating in business and technology for the export markets (Nadvi and Schmitz, 1999). The study of interaction in these 'clusters' has suggested the term 'local systems of innovation' (Cassiolato and Lastres, 1999), although in our view it would be more appropriate to call them 'territorial networks of innovativeness'.

There is also the incredibly successful experience of specialized banks giving 'microcredits' to help men and women in urban and rural areas to set up income-generating activities (Otero and Rhyne, 1994). This is gradually breaking the myth of 'jobs' as the only way to improve the quality of life of whole populations by moving towards multiple forms of individual or collective entrepreneurship. In order to address the plight of rural communities, the old pro-urban and pro-manufacturing biases will need to be abandoned (Fieldhouse, 1986, p. 152; Mytelka, 1989) and local governments empowered with the resources and technical support to address directly the issue of improving local living standards. These 'localized' activities can often connect as suppliers with the networks of global corporations or become part of the support network of the big exporting activities of the country.

Modernity and Values

Of course these are political decisions, but the actual choices are not always clear. Historically, in every paradigm transition, the usual definitions of 'left' and 'right' become confused. Each of the groupings suffers an internal divide between those that stick to the old ways of reaching their goals and those that embrace the potential of the new paradigm and gear it to their ends (Figure 6.9).

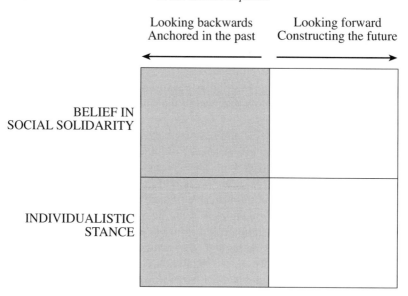

Looking backwards   Looking forward
Anchored in the past   Constructing the future

BELIEF IN
SOCIAL SOLIDARITY

INDIVIDUALISTIC
STANCE

Figure 6.9   A simple location matrix

In the previous transition, between the two world wars, the homogenizing 'social' character of the emerging paradigm of mass production was so strong that even Nazism called itself National Socialism. Equally, the strong role of a centralized state was so crucial that government intervention in the economy along Keynesian lines – so fiercely opposed in the 1920s and 1930s – was fully adopted after World War II, even in the most liberal nations. Unfortunately for those convinced of the need for social solidarity, neoliberalism is the only consistent programme that has embraced the present paradigm. Though there are thousands of isolated experiments with forward-looking practices, such as participatory democracy and local consensus building, we have yet to see a coherent experience or proposal that can serve as a modern alternative to pure markets. Without it, in our view, there may be world growth, but there is probably little hope of a widespread surge in development.

NOTES

1. Hirsch (1965, 1967), Vernon (1966) and recently von Tunzelmann and Anderson (1999).
2. Based on Perez and Soete (1988).
3. Phase four can be roughly understood to encompass phases IV and V in Figure 6.1.
4. For text books on management, see Cundiff *et al.* (1973) and Kotler (1980). For a comprehensive overview, see Coombs *et al.* (1987) and Dosi (1988). For a complete interpretation of

the relationship between technology, economics and policy, see Freeman's (1974) classic on the economics of innovation, or the updated version of Freeman and Soete (1997).
5. The term is meant to serve as an umbrella concept connecting to the notion of 'technological paradigms' proposed by Dosi (1982) to refer to the trajectories of individual technologies.
6. Used in a similar sense by Mytelka (1994).
7. See Reinert (1999), Wade (1990), Osborne and Gaebler (1993).

REFERENCES

Abernathy, W. and J. Utterback (1975), 'A dynamic model of process and product innovation', *Omega*, 3(6): 639–56.

Abramovitz, M. (1986), 'Catching up, forging ahead and falling behind', *Journal of Economic History*, 46: 385–406.

Altshuler, A. *et al.* (1984), *The Future of the Automobile: The Report of MIT's International Automobile Program*, Cambridge, MA: MIT Press.

Amsden, A. (1989). *Asia's Next Giant. South Korea and Late Industrialization*, Oxford: Oxford University Press.

Arocena, R. (1997), *¿Que piensa la gente de la innovacion, la competitividad, la cienciay elfuturo?* Montevideo: Trilce.

Arthur, B. (1989), 'Competing technologies, increasing returns and lock-in by historical events', *The Economic Journal*, 99: 116–31 (reproduced in Freeman (ed.), 1990, pp. 374–89).

Bell, M. and K. Pavitt (1993), 'Technological accumulation and industrial growth: Contrast between developed and developing countries', *Industrial and Corporate Change*, 2(2): 157–211.

Bressand, A. (1990), 'Electronics cartels in the making?', *Transatlantic Perspectives*, 21: 3–6.

Bressand, A. and N. Kalypso (eds) (1989). *Strategic Trends in Services: An Inquiry into the Global Service Economy*, New York: Harper and Row.

Burton-Jones, A. (1999), *Knowledge Capitalism: Business, Work and Learning in the New Economy*, Oxford: Oxford University Press.

Cassiolato, J. and H. Lastres (eds) (1999), *Globalização & Inovação Localizada. Experiencias de Sistemas Locals no Mercosul*, Brasilia: Institute Brasileiro de Informacao em Ciencia e Tecnologia (IBICT).

Castells, M. (1996), *The Information Age: Economy, Society and Culture (Volume I). The rise of the Network Society*, Maiden and Oxford: Blackwell.

Chesnais, F. (1988), 'Multinational enterprises and the international diffusion of technology', in Dosi *et al.* (eds), pp. 496–527.

Chesnais, F. (1992), 'National systems of innovation, foreign direct investment and the operations of multinational enterprises', in Lundvall (ed), 1992, pp. 265–95.

Coombs, R., P. Saviotri and V. Walsh (1987), *Economics and Technological Change*, Basingstoke and London: Macmillan Educational.

Coriat, B. (1991). *Penser a l'envers*, Paris: Christian Bourgeois Editeur.

Cundiff, E. *et al.* (1973), *Fundamentals of Modern Marketing*, Englewood Cliffs, New Jersey: Prentice-Hall.

David, P. (1985). Clio and the economics of QWERTY', *AEA Papers and Proceedings*, 75(2): 332–7.

Dosi, G. (1982), 'Technical paradigms and technological trajectories: A suggested interpretation of the determinants of technical change', *Research Policy*, 11(3): 147–62.

Dosi, G. (1988), 'Sources, procedures and microeconomic effects of innovation', *Journal of Economic Literature*, XXVI: 1120–117, September (reproduced in Freeman (ed., 1990, pp. 107–58).

Dosi, G. *et al.* (eds) (1988), *Technical Change and Economic Theory*, London: Pinter; New York: Columbia University Press.

DRUID (Danish Research Unit on Industrial Dynamics), *The Firm as a Learning Organization*, (website: *http://www.business.auc.dk/druid*).

ECLAC (1990), 'Changing Production Patterns with Social Equity', United Nations publication, sales no. E.90.II.G.6, Santiago de Chile.

ECLAC/UNESCO (1992), 'Education and Knowledge: Basic Pillars of Changing Production Patterns with Equity', United Nations publication, LC/G.1702 (SES 24/4). Santiago de Chile, April.

Ernst, D., T. Ganiatsos and L. Mytelka (eds) (1998), *Technological Capabilities and Export Success in Asia*, London: Routledge.

Fagerberg J., B. Verspagen and N. von Tunzelman (eds) (1994), *The Dynamics of Technology, Trade and Growth*, Aldershot, UK and Brookfield, US: Elgar.

Fieldhouse, D. (1986). *Economic Decolonisation and Arrested Development*, London: George Allen.

Freeman, C. (1974), *The Economics of Industrial Innovation*, Harmondsworth: Penguin Books.

Freeman, C. (1987), *Technology Policy and Economic Performance, Lessons From Japan*, London and New York: Pinter Publishers.

Freeman, C. (ed.) (1990), *The Economics of Innovation, an Elgar Reference Collection*, Aldershot, UK and Brookfield, US: Edward Elgar.

Freeman, C. (1994), 'Technological revolutions and catching up: ICT and the NICs', in J. Fagerberg *et al.* (eds), pp. 198–221.

Freeman, C. (1995), 'The national system of innovation in historical perspective', *Cambridge Journal of Economics*, 19(1): 1–19.

Freeman, C. and C. Pérez (1988), 'Structural crises of adjustment: Business cycles and investment behavior', in: Dosi *et al.* (eds), pp. 38–66.

Freeman, C. and L. Soete (1997), *The Economics of Industrial Innovation* (3rd edn), London: Pinter.

Freeman, C., J. Clark and L. Soete (1982), *Unemployment and Technical Innovation. A Study of Long Waves and Economic Development*, London: Frances Pinter.

Gabor, A. (1991), 'Rochester focuses: A community's core competence', *Harvard Business Review*, July–August.

Gerschenkron, A. (1962), *Economic Backwardness in Historical Perspective*, Cambridge, MA: Harvard University Press.

Grubler, A. (1990), *The Rise and Fall of Infrastructures. Dynamics of Evolution and Technological Change in Transport*, Heidelberg: Physica-Verlag.

Hirsch, S (1965), 'The United States electronic industry in international trade', *National Institute Economic Review*, 34: 92–107.

Hirsch, S. (1967), *Location of Industry and International Competitiveness*, Oxford: Clarendon Press.

Hobday, M. (1994), 'Export-led technology development in the four dragons: The case of electronics', *Development and Change*, 25(2): 333–61.

Hobday, M. (1995), *Innovation in East Asia: The Challenge to Japan*, Aldershot, UK and Brookfield, US: Edward Elgar.

Hoffman, K. and H. Rush (1988), *Microelectronics and the Clothing Industry*, New York: Praeger.

IDS Collective Efficiency Research Project (website: *http://www.ids.ac.uk/ids/ global/coleff.html*).

Irvine, J. and B. Martin (1985), *Foresight in Science Policy: Picking the Winners*, London: Pinter.

Kanellou, D. (1999), 'Cyberhopes and Cyberrealities: ICTs and Intermediaries in Travel and Tourism' (unpublished PhD thesis), Roskilde, Denmark, Institute of Economics, Roskilde University Centre.

Katz, J. *et al.* (1996), 'Estabilizacion macroeconomica', *Reforma estructuraly comportamiento industrial: Estructura y funcionamiento del sector manufacturero en los años 90*, Buenos Aires: Alianza.

Klepper, S. and S. Kenneth (1994), 'Technological Change and Industry Shakeouts', paper presented at the Fifth Conference of the International Joseph A. Schumpeter Society, Münster, Germany, August.

Kotler, P. (1980). *Principles of Marketing*, Englewood Cliffs, NJ: Prentice-Hall.

Lall, S. (1992), 'Technical capabilities and Industrialisation', *World Development*, 20(2): 161–86.

Lamoreaux, N. *et al.* (eds) (1999), *Learning by Doing in Markets, Firms and Countries*, Chicago: National Bureau of Economic Research, University of Chicago Press.

Leontief, W. (1953), 'Domestic production and foreign trade: The American capital position re-examined', *Proceedings of the American Philosophical Society*, 97; reproduced in *Input–Output*, Oxford: Oxford University Press, 1966, 5, pp. 68–99.

Lundvall, B.-A. (1988), 'Innovation as an interactive process: From user–producer interaction to the national system of innovation', in Dosi *et al.* (eds), pp. 349–69.

Lundvall, B.-A. (1992), *National Systems of Innovation: Towards a Theory of Innovation and Interactive Learning*, London: Pinter Publishers.

Lundvall, B.-A. (1997), 'Information technology in the learning economy: Challenges for development strategies', *Communications and Strategies*, 28: 177–92.

Mansell, R. and U. Wehn (eds) (1998), Knowledge Societies: *Information Technology for Sustainable Development*, Oxford: Oxford University Press.

Mytelka, L. (1989), 'The unfulfilled promise of African industrialization', *African Studies Review*, 32(3): 77–137.

Mytelka, L. (1991), 'New models of competition in the textile and clothing industry', in J. Niosi (ed.), *Technology and National Competitiveness*, Montreal: McGill University Press.

Mytelka, K. (1994), 'South-south co-operation in a global perspective', Paris: OECD.

Mytelka, K. (1999), 'The cutting edge: Collective efficiency and international competitiveness in Pakistan', Oxford Development Studies, 27(1): 81–107.

Nadvi, K. and H. Schmitz (eds) (1999), 'Industrial clusters in developing countries', *World Development* (Special Issue), 27(9).

Nonaka, I. (1994), 'Dynamic theory of organisational knowledge creation', *Organizational Sciences*, 5(1): 15–37, February.

Nonaka, I. (1995), 'The knowledge-creating company: How Japanese companies create the dynamics of innovation', *Harvard Business Review*: 97, November–December.

Osborne, D. and T. Gaebler (1993), *Reinventing Government: How the Entrepreneurial Spirit is Transforming the Public Sector*, New York: Plume Penguin.

Otero, M. and E. Rhyne (eds) (1994). *The New World of Microenterprise Finance. Building Healthy Financial Institutions for the Poor*, West Hartford, CT: Kumarian Press.

Pavitt, K. and M. Bell (1992), 'National capacities for technological accumulation: Evidence and implications for developing countries', World Bank Annual Conference on Development Economies, Washington, DC, April–May.

Peck, J. and A. Goto (1981), 'Technological and economic growth: The case of Japan', *Research Policy*, 10: 222–43.

Perez, C. (1983), 'Structural change and the assimilation of new technologies in the economic and social systems', *Futures*, 15(5): 357–75.

Perez, C. (1985), 'Microelectronics, long waves and world structural change: New perspectives for developing countries', *World Development*, 13(3): 441–63.

Perez, C. (1992), 'New technological model and higher education: A view from the changing world of work', in G. Lopez-Ospina (ed), *Challenges and Options: Specific Proposals* (vol. 2). Caracas: UNESCO, pp. 23–49.

Perez, C. and L. Soete (1988), 'Catching up in technology: Entry barriers and windows of opportunity', in Dosi *et al.* (eds), pp. 458–78.

Peters, T. (1989), *Thriving on Chaos: Handbook for a Management Revolution*, London: Pan Books, Macmillan.

Porter, M. (1990), *The Competitive Advantage of Nations*, New York: The Free Press.

Radosevic, S. (1999), *International Technology Transfer and Catch-up in Economic Development*, Cheltenham, UK and Northampton, MA: Edward Elgar.

Reinert, E. (1994), 'Catching-up from way behind. A third world perspective on first world history', in Fagerberg *et al.* (eds), pp. 168–97.

Reinert, E. (1999), 'The role of the state in economic growth', *Journal of Economic Studies*, 4.

Sahal, D. (1985), 'Technological guideposts and innovation avenues', *Research Policy*, 14(2): 61–2.

Schmitz, H. and P. Knorringa (1999), 'Learning from Global Buyers', IDS Working paper 100, Institute of Development Studies, University of Sussex.

Schmitz, H. and K. Nadvi (1999), 'Clustering and industrialization: Introduction', *World Development*, 27(9): 1503–14.

Senge, P. (1990), *The Fifth Discipline*, New York: Doubleday.

Shin, J.-S. (1992), 'Catching up and Technological Progress in Late-industrializing Countries', Mphil dissertation, Cambridge University.

Strange, S. (1996), *The Retreat of The State. The Diffusion of Power in The World Economy*, Cambridge: Cambridge University Press.

Tendler, J. (1997), *Good Government in the Tropics*, Baltimore: Johns Hopkins University Press.

The Illinois Coalition (1999), 'Technology and jobs agenda. A vision and plan for technology-based economic development in Illinois', (website: *www.ilcoalition. org/tja.htm*).

Vernon, R. (1966), 'International investment and international trade in the product cycle', *Quarterly Journal of Economics*, 80: 190–207.

Von Tunzelmann, N. (1995), *Technology and Industrial Progress. The Foundations of Economic Growth*, Aldershot, UK and Brookfield, US: Edward Elgar.

Von Tunzelmann, N. and E. Anderson (1999), 'Technologies and Skills in Long-Run Perspective' (mimeo), SPRU, University of Sussex.

Wade, R. (1990), *Governing the Market: Economic Theory of Government in East Asia Industrialization*, Princeton: Princeton University Press.

Wells, L. (1972), 'International trade: The product life cycle approach', in L. Wells (ed.), *The Product Life Cycle and International Trade*, Boston: Division of Research, Graduate School of Business Administration, Harvard University Press, pp. 3–33.

Wiggenhorn, W. (1990), 'Motorola U: When training becomes an education', *Harvard Business Review*, 68(4) July–August.

Wolf, J. (1912). *Die Volkswirtschaft der Gegenwart und Zukunft*, (A. Deichertsche Verlags-buchandlung).

(LDCs)

016
F32
F34
F21
019

7. Financing for development: current trends and issues for the future

Kwesi Botchwey

INTRODUCTION

The 1997 Asian financial crisis spawned a vigorous debate about the weaknesses in the international financial system and a frantic search for remedies. The debate was, for the most part, concentrated on problems caused by the volatility of short-term capital flows and, in particular, on ways, not only of managing crises once they break out, but also of anticipating and preventing them in the future. At a general level, these issues are no doubt important for all countries, including even those in low-income regions of the world that are as yet marginalized from the growing universe of private capital flows. While the recent financial crisis affected the entire world economy, its effects were much more trenchant for the developing countries as a whole than for the developed ones. The GDP growth of the developing countries as a group fell in the immediate wake of the crisis to less than 2 per cent, as they suffered the combined effects of a slowdown in world import demand, a deterioration in the terms of trade and a decline in capital inflows. Net financial flows to developing markets from international markets fell sharply from about $136 billion in 1997 to $72 billion in 1998 (WorldBank/IBRD, 1999, p. 24). Flows to the relatively better performing low-income countries, which in recent years have begun to improve their access to capital financing, also fell, from $6 billion in 1997 to $5 billion in 1998. For sub-Saharan Africa (SSA) and South Asia, net equity flows reportedly fell to almost zero from their levels in 1997 (World Bank/IBRD, 1999). Thus the issues in the debate on crisis prevention and resolution in a new financial architecture are important for all countries, but even more so for the developing countries as a whole. There are lessons to be learned from these recent experiences – especially by the so-called 'emerging market' group of countries in the developing world – notably concerning the dangers of large and rapid accumulation of foreign debt, particularly from short-term loans, and the use of such capital for speculative investment. An equally important lesson that these countries must heed is the crucial importance of overall macroeconomic stability and the proper management of financial sector reforms and capital account liberalization in national development.

However, there can be no denying that the financial architecture debate has mostly failed to address, or even to recognize, the most pressing problem that the low-income countries face, namely the availability of development finance, especially long-term finance. The insistence that this issue be addressed and concrete mechanisms included in the new financial architecture better to secure the flow of development finance to the most needy regions of the world is often met with barely disguised bemusement, or polite silence at best, in these debates.[1]

Sub-Saharan Africa's peculiar circumstances serve to put the matter in perspective. For the non-oil-producing countries in the region, excluding South Africa, by far the largest proportion of all international flows through the 1990s has come from concessional loans and grants, about three-quarters of which have been offset by terms-of-trade losses, thanks to the extreme dependence of these countries on a narrow range of primary commodity exports. To compound matters, they also suffer from a high amount of capital flight and, by 1997, their external debt stock had risen to a level equivalent to over 80 per cent of their combined GDP. Yet, just to achieve the poverty reduction target set by the international community of halving poverty by the year 2015, these countries will have to sustain, for over a generation or more, a rate of real GDP growth of about 8 per cent by some estimates, implying financing needs that obviously go well beyond domestic resource mobilization possibilities. For these countries, and for most of the developing countries, therefore, the issue is clearly not how to deal with the problems of short-term capital volatility, for they attract precious little of it in the first place. About 90 per cent of all private capital flows in the 1990s (loans, bonds, portfolio equity flows and foreign direct investment – FDI) has gone to the middle-income countries. The issue is how to improve their access to more varied and secure sources of development finance, and end their precarious dependence on official development assistance (ODA). Although IDA-12, the World Bank's soft loans arm, was recently replenished successfully, net concessional assistance to developing countries (mostly in sub-Saharan Africa and South Asia) fell slightly in 1998 compared to 1997, and it pales into insignificance compared to the $190 billion put together in rescue packages for the crisis-stricken countries.[2]

This chapter reviews the lessons learned from international experience with development finance from the particular perspective of the low-income, mostly sub-Saharan African countries, whose growth and stability depends most critically on the availability of external, long-term development finance. The first section looks at the determinants, evolution and concentration of international capital flows, while the second section reviews the current trends and issues in the evolution of ODA. The third section argues the case for debt relief as development finance and reviews the Heavily Indebted Poor Countries (HIPC) Initiative of the World Bank and IMF in its post-Cologne form and terms, with particular regard to country eligibility and resource additionality. The fourth section draws lessons from the current trends in the evolution of the various constituents of development finance, and recommends actions at the country, regional and international levels to improve the outlook for such finance.

THE EVOLUTION AND CONCENTRATION OF INTERNATIONAL CAPITAL FLOWS

Private Capital Flows

The 1990s have witnessed a phenomenal increase in the level of private flows from international capital markets to developing countries and a consequent shift in the composition of capital flows going to these countries. In 1990, of the net long-term resource flows of just over $100 billion, official flows accounted for about 57 per cent. By 1996, before the onset of the Asian crisis, net resource flows had rocketed to $338 billion, of which $299 billion came from private sources. To be sure, these numbers do not capture the whole story of financial transactions between the developing countries and international capital markets. Among other things, they do not take account of capital outflows, which, by some estimates, were quite considerable in the 1990s, especially in the wake of the 1997 Asian crisis. Nevertheless, they mark a distinctive trend in the growth and composition of capital flows to developing countries, underscoring the much-diminished importance of ODA. The most remarkable increase has been in the subcomponent of FDI flows to developing countries, which grew from a mere $24.5 billion in 1990 to over $163 billion in 1997, and accounted mainly for the huge increase in average annual flows of global FDI in recent times. The share of global FDI flows going to developing countries rose from 18 per cent in the mid-1980s to an estimated 42 per cent in 1998 (World Bank/IBRD, 1999, p. 48, Fig. 3). A number of factors account for this, among them policy liberalization, regional integration and technological changes in transport and communications.

The surge in private capital flows to the developing countries helped to fuel the belief that the development financing needs of all developing countries could be met by the normal working of the market. A closer examination of the underlying trends shaping this market, however, suggests that such optimism is misplaced, as these large flows have been concentrated in a handful of countries, namely the so-called 'emerging market' group of countries in East

Trade and development

Asia and Latin America, as well as South Africa. The middle-income countries have accounted for over 90 per cent of capital market financing during the 1990s. Moreover, although flows from capital market financing to low-income countries have been rising in recent years, they too are concentrated in a handful of these countries. For instance, of the total private capital flows of about $4.7 billion in 1998, India alone accounted for 70 per cent.

The picture is not much different for FDI, which, on balance, has been far more important for developing countries, especially low-income countries, than capital market flows. Although FDI flows to developing countries have grown the fastest, as we have already noted, and have become more diversified in their country destination, they too have been highly concentrated in a few countries. Ten middle-income countries accounted for about 70 per cent of FDI flows to developing countries in the 1992–8 period, while middle-income countries as a group accounted for over 90 per cent, compared to 6–7 per cent for the low-income countries. There is a further differentiation in the country destination of FDI flows going to the low-income countries. The vast bulk of these flows has tended to go to the mineral and oil exporters among them. For the period 1990–7, FDI accounted for about 68 per cent of total long-term capital flows to low-income mineral producers, compared to under 29 per cent for others (Table 7.1).

Table 7.1   Share of FDI in long-term private flows to developing countries, 1990–98 (per cent)

Country or country group	1990	1991	1992	1993	1994	1995	1996	1997	1998[a]
Middle-income	59.0	57.0	46.2	39.9	50.3	51.6	44.8	54.2	68.2
Excluding China	63.1	56.8	44.3	29.8	40.8	42.5	36.4	49.1	62.1
Top 10 countries	50.2	54.4	44.8	39.6	58.4	57.9	50.5	59.0	72.8
Excluding China	52.9	53.5	41.5	24.4	45.8	44.5	38.3	52.6	65.2
China	43.0	58.2	52.4	69.5	76.1	82.0	80.2	72.8	89.4
Low-income non-oil exporters									
Mineral producers	78.5	81.6	59.5	69.7	51.3	63.8	66.0	76.6	n.a.
Others	–3.3	32.5	21.3	17.0	19.2	50.5	48.0	46.8	n.a.
Low- and middle-income									
oil exporters	**	82.6	209.7	67.1	64.2	69.5	74.7	95.4	n.a.

Notes:
[a] = Preliminary, ** = large negative number (caused by negative total net flows).

Source: World Bank/IBRD (1999, p. 52).

Although there is reason to believe that the medium- to long-term prospects for international market flows to the developing countries are good, the prospects for the low-income countries may not be quite as sanguine, as transaction costs (particularly in sub-Saharan Africa) tend to be high and risk perceptions often exaggerated.

The picture that emerges from the above analysis is one of rising flows of capital market financing and FBI to an increasingly diverse, but still concentrated, subgroup of countries in the developing world. It is therefore necessary, in the light of these trends, to classify the developing countries into at least three categories:

- the emerging market countries, mostly the middle-income countries in East Asia, Latin America and South Africa. This group will include: Argentina, Brazil, Chile, China, Malaysia, Mexico, South Africa, Thailand and Venezuela;
- the oil and mineral exporting countries among the low-income countries, mainly in sub-Saharan Africa and South Asia;
- the so-called 'high performing' countries among the low-income countries, mainly in sub-Saharan Africa and South Asia. India would be easily the dominant country in this group.

Foreign Direct Investment

As already discussed, FBI flows – as with capital market flows – which have been the fastest-growing component of long-term flows to developing countries as a whole and which, in the estimation of most analysts, are likely to remain the main source of foreign finance to developing countries over the long-term, will, in the final analysis, depend on the growth and stability of the world economy. Moreover, it is important to note that the factors that have been shown in recent studies to be associated with the rapid growth in FDI in the 1990s, including the policy environment, high growth rates, low transaction costs and market size, are not particularly strong in the low-income countries, which have thus far been minor players in the world of FDI flows.

EVOLVING TRENDS IN OFFICIAL DEVELOPMENT FINANCE

Official development finance, comprising grants and long-term concessional and non-concessional loans from bilateral and multilateral sources, is the other source of development finance to developing countries. It was indeed a major source of such finance throughout the 1970s and 1980s, when it constituted more than half the total resource flows to developing countries. Even at the start of the 1990s, official flows made up a larger proportion of these resource flows (Table 7.2). However, from a peak in 1991, when they reached about $63 billion, net official long-term flows have declined both in absolute terms and as a percentage of total resource flows to developing countries, falling from about half at the beginning of the 1990s to just over a fifth of total resource flows in 1998. To be sure, some of this decline is attributable to currency values and classification factors (World Bank/IBRD, 1999, p. 70). But even after correcting for these factors, the decline in net flows of ODA in real terms has been significant, with only four countries – Denmark, the Netherlands, Norway and Sweden – exceeding the UN target for ODA of 0.7 per cent of GNP. The decline has been particularly marked in the G7 countries.

Apart from the decline in the levels of ODA, there are other important trends that affect its role as a source of development finance. First, the share of ODA directed to emergency and relief work has risen, as has the share going to the administration of aid programmes in the donor countries themselves. Secondly, although the proportion of tied aid in total development assistance has reportedly fallen from a peak of about 50 per cent in 1979 to an estimated 20 per cent in 1996, it is still significant in terms of its impact on cost effectiveness. Some estimates suggest that aid tying increases the cost of supplies by between 10 to 30 per cent (World Bank/IBRD, 1999, p. 73).

Table 7.2   Long-term flows to developing countries, 1990–98 ($ billion)

	1990	1991	1992	1993	1994	1995	1996	1997	1998[a]
Net long-term resource flows	100.8	123.1	152.3	220.2	223.6	254.9	308.1	338.1	275.0
Official flows	56.9	62.6	54.0	53.3	45.5	53.4	32.2	39.1	47.9
Private flows	43.9	60.5	98.3	167.0	178.1	201.5	275.9	299.0	227.1
International capital markets *	19.4	26.2	52.2	100.0	89.6	96.1	149.5	135.5	72.1
Foreign direct investment	24.5	34.4	46.1	67.0	88.5	105.4	126.4	163.4	155.0

Notes: Although the Republic of Korea is a newly industrializing country, it is included in the developing country aggregate since it is a borrower from the World Bank.
[a] = preliminary, [b] = bonds, loans, and portfolio equity flows.

Source: World Bank/IBRD (1999, p. 14).

Even so, the evidence of recent cross-country economic analysis confirms the rather self-evident view that aid not only promotes growth in countries where the policy environment is good, but also 'crowds in' private investment and improves investor perceptions of risk. The World Bank cites the cross-country studies suggesting that an increase in aid of 1 per cent of GDP in the recipient country increases private investment by an additional 1.9 per cent of GDP in countries with good policies (World Bank, 1998). At the same time, the policy environment has improved markedly in the vast majority of countries in South Asia and sub-Saharan Africa. According to the World Bank's suggested criteria of growth, inflation and trade openness, policy performance in both sub-Saharan Africa and South Asia is better now than at any time in the previous quarter-century.

It is therefore rather ironic that ODA should be experiencing a steady decline even as conditions are improving for its greater effectiveness. The prospects for a reversal of this trend are at best mixed. While a small number of countries increased their ODA budgets in 1998, it has been significantly reduced in Japan, which has been the largest donor in recent years. Fiscal constraints and the need to reduce deficits (in compliance with criteria set in the Maastricht Treaty for EU member states, for example) have been cited, and will probably continue to exercise a restraining influence on future aid flows, although recent experiences with international resource mobilization suggest that these constraints can be overcome with amazing speed when the stability of the international financial system is threatened! In the light of these experiences, it is probably true to say that the radical shift in strategic interests on the part of the leading industrialized countries following the end of the Cold War is the most credible explanation for the downward trend in ODA, and may very well also determine future trends.

The low-income countries are a particularly capital-scarce group among the developing countries. They must import capital from the developed countries (and use it efficiently) even as they improve the environment for domestic resource mobilization through increased savings, which have tended to closely match investment rates.[3] Indeed, their need to reduce reliance on foreign savings is widely recognized. Such an effort is being made in sub-Saharan Africa, for instance, with some impressive results (see Table 7.3). At the same time, it is also recognized that, in the near term, these efforts will continue to be constrained by low levels of income. In these countries, therefore, and especially in sub-Saharan Africa, capital scarcity has been filled largely by ODA, the outlook for which is not promising, as discussed in the preceding section. Given the limited prospects for a significant and sustained upturn in the level of ODA flows, the future of the low-income countries depends on their ability to attract larger flows of FDI, the dynamics of which have also been examined above. Increased reliance on FDI will not only enable them to avoid a worsening of their debt burden, it will also, it is hoped, improve their access to technology and management expertise. We now turn to the issue of debt relief for the low-income countries, both as a way of improving their ability to attract FDI and also as a way of providing them with additional and predictable financing for development.

Table 7.3   International comparison of savings and investment

	1990	1991	1992	1993	1994	1995	1996	1997ᵃ	1990–4	1995–7
Investment										
Sub-Saharan Africa	16.2	17.1	16.9	16.4	17.5	18.2	17.7	17.4	16.8	17.8
Western hemisphere	20.2	19.7	20.5	20.3	20.4	20.0	20.4	21.0	20.2	20.5
Asia (excluding Japan)	30.1	30.3	30.8	34.6	34.0	34.6	35.5	34.3	32.0	34.8
Newly industrializing										
countries of Asia	31.1	32.1	31.7	31.0	32.3	32.3	32.1	31.0	21.0	20.9
Advanced economies	22.1	21.4	20.7	20.1	20.6	20.7	20.8	21.1	21.0	20.9
Private investment										
Sub-Saharan Africa	11.8	12.8	13.1	11.3	12.3	13.2	11.7	11.7	12.3	12.2
Western hemisphere	—	14.3	15.6	15.8	15.4	15.0	15.7	16.2	15.3	15.6
Asia (excluding Japan)	18.2	18.5	18.4	18.4	19.2	20.4	20.9	21.0	18.5	20.8
Newly industrializing										
countries of Asia	24.1	24.8	24.6	23.8	24.3	25.3	25.1	24.5	24.3	25.0
Advanced economies	18.1	17.4	16.6	15.9	16.6	16.8	16.9	17.2	16.9	17.0
Domestic savings										
Sub-Saharan Africa	18.4	17.6	15.6	15.9	16.6	16.7	17.4	17.0	16.8	17.0
Western hemisphere	20.1	18.5	17.8	16.9	17.5	18.0	18.6	18.0	16.8	17.0
Asia (excluding Japan)	29.2	30.0	30.0	31.9	33.0	33.2	33.9	32.2	33.6	32.6
Newly industrializing										
countries of Asia	34.4	34.2	33.3	33.3	33.0	33.2	32.4	32.2	33.6	32.6
Advanced economies	21.5	21.2	20.2	19.7	20.2	20.8	21.0	21.2	20.6	21.0

Note: ᵃ = preliminary.

Source: IMF, African Department and World Economic Outlook databases (various years); Fisher *et al.* (1998).

DEBT RELIEF AS DEVELOPMENT FINANCE

Ever since the HIPC Initiative was launched in 1996, it has become the framework and the operational instrument for negotiations and for the provision of debt relief to debt-burdened developing countries. A reduction in the debt stock through this initiative would promote growth by attracting more investment, especially FDI. At the same time, resources freed through relief from debt servicing would help finance larger investment spending by government, provided the cost of the scheme is not financed by a diversion of current or existing ODA resources.

Under the original HIPC Initiative, eligible countries qualified for debt relief once they went through two stages of three years each. In the first three years, a country seeking relief would establish a track record of good performance in its implementation of a structural adjustment programme prescribed by the Enhanced Structural Adjustment Facility (ESAF) of the International Monetary Fund (IMF). In return, its Paris Club creditors would commit themselves to rescheduling debt service payments so as to achieve a roughly 67 per cent reduction in the net present value (NPV) of eligible debt (this essentially meant a Naples-terms rescheduling), while non-Paris Club members would provide comparable relief.

At the end of the first three-year period, the country would reach a 'decision point' when it would be decided whether it would be given HIPC debt relief if the Naples-terms reduction it had obtained failed to reduce its debt burden to a sustainable level. The country would then begin a second three-year period, also requiring an ESAF-supported programme, during which time the Paris Club creditors would provide additional debt service relief up to 80 per cent in NPV terms (Lyons terms), with the non-Paris Club members also providing relief. A so-called 'completion point' would be reached at the end of the second three-year stage, when the creditors would reduce the country's debt burden to a sustainable level (a debt-to-exports ratio of 200–250 per cent in NPV terms), implying up to 80 per cent stock relief in NPV terms.

The changes in the HIPC arrangements agreed at the recent meeting of the G7 in Cologne (hereafter referred to as the Cologne Initiative) made important modifications to the original proposals, which would improve them in at least four ways: first, by accelerating the pace of debt relief through the provision of interim relief before the 'completion point'; secondly, by allowing countries to advance the 'completion point' by accelerating the pace of policy reforms; thirdly, by broadening country eligibility through changes in the sustainability thresholds. Finally, the Cologne Initiative also sought to link debt relief to poverty alleviation.

However, even with these improvements, the Cologne Initiative still suffers from three major pitfalls that erode the potential of the HIPC Initiative to become an important stimulus for development finance: (i) it applies an inappropriate criterion for determining the ability of the HIPCs to pay their debts; (ii) it misses the fact that these countries need large transfers from the rest of the world and that, for the most part, they pay their debts at the cost of investments in physical infrastructure and human capital; and (iii) the current mechanisms for easing the debt burdens of these countries leave them with marginally positive net resource flows that are grossly inadequate to meet urgent social expenditures; moreover, they are unstable and unpredictable, making long-term strategic planning impossible.[4]

The Capacity to Service Debt

The original HIPC Initiative determined a country's ability to pay based on its ratio of debt to exports, when in fact its capacity to service debt depends more on its fiscal position. Although 'fiscal sustainability' is by no means a trouble-free concept,[5] it nevertheless provides a better measure of debt-servicing capacity, since not all export receipts accrue to the country's budget from which debt service payments must be made.

Indeed, it would seem that the world already recognizes that these countries simply cannot service their debts. Under current arrangements, a proportion of debt service due is rescheduled either formally through negotiation, or informally through a build-up in arrears. The substantial portion that is paid is, in fact, financed from new loans and grants from bilateral sources. In general, the HIPCs receive net resource transfers that are just marginally positive. In 1997, these net resource transfers amounted to less than $10 per head in the HIPCs. As Figure 7.1 shows, for the years 1996 and 1997, net resource transfers were negative for all loans for the HIPCs as a group; that is, they paid more in interest and amortization than they received in new loans. New grants, however, exceeded the negative net transfers from loans, thereby making the overall net resource transfer positive; in effect, grants and loans together exceeded interest plus amortization. Net resource transfers from the rest of the world to the HIPCs – that is, grants plus new loans minus debt servicing – have been positive throughout the 1990s, but, as Figure 7.1 shows, they have been on the decline as new loans have declined in relation to debt servicing, while grants have remained more or less unchanged in nominal terms. Net transfers have fallen from a peak of about $10 billion in the mid-1990s to about $6 billion in 1998.

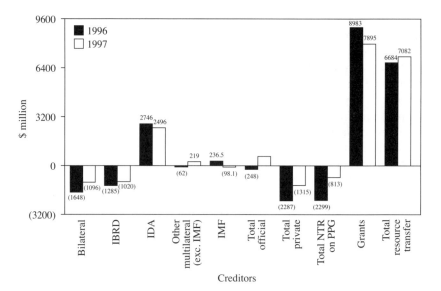

Source: Sachs *et al.* (1999).

Figure 7.1   Net debt transfers to HIPCs, 1996–97, by category of creditor

Moreover, the process by which these burdensome debt service payments are financed through new loans and grants is rather unstable, and the net resource transfers are highly volatile and unpredictable (see Tables 7A.1, 7A.2 and 7A.3). Malawi, for instance, saw its net resource transfers fall dramatically in a two-year period, from 129 per cent of revenues in 1995 to 48 per cent of revenues in 1997. In contrast, a write-off of debt servicing on public and publicly guaranteed debt, with bilateral loans and grants remaining unchanged at current levels, would result in positive net resource flows of some $5 billion a year to the HIPCs,[6] compared to net flows of long-term debt of $4.8 billion and net FBI of $4.0 billion to these countries in 1998. Thus the case that is being made by some academics and NGOs, notably Jubilee 2000, for more generous relief than is envisaged under the Cologne Initiative is particularly strong.

However, in a development that is very much a sign of the times, it is worth noting that even the original HIPC Initiative was never fully financed, and it is therefore reasonable to expect that there would be difficulties with financing the Cologne Initiative, let alone proposals for a complete write-off of outstanding debt for all or the poorest of the HIPCs.

Total costs of the original HIPC Initiative were estimated at $12.5 billion in 1998 NPV terms,[7] and of the Cologne Initiative at about $27.4 billion.[8] Costs are based on a proportional basis, or burden-sharing principle. Under the Cologne Initiative, the costs for bilateral and multilateral creditors are estimated to be about equal, with multilateral costs being roughly doubled. Estimated costs by creditor group are broken down in Table 7.4.

Judging from these orders of magnitude, and also from the recent record of international resource mobilization for bail-out operations and for humanitarian relief in the wake of the Kosovo crisis, it is clear that the question of HIPC financing is largely a matter of political will. The total cost of some $40 billion is, after all, about a fifth of the resources that were mobilized in the space of a few months for bail-out operations for a handful of countries as a result of the Asian crisis. Indeed, the speed with which the G7 has mobilized a consensus to revise the terms of the original HIPC Initiative proves the point. However, for the Initiative to be truly effective in providing HIPCs with fresh budgetary resources – estimated by the IMF to be about 2 per cent of GDP – the financing will have to come from genuinely additional sources, along with a commitment by the bilateral donors to continue to provide ODA. But funding difficulties still remain, among them the unevenness of creditor country exposure, with a disproportionate burden falling on Japan and France. It is also worth noting that Japan's decision to make countries, notably Ghana, choose between HIPC relief and continued Japanese concessional assistance is a most unfortunate development.[9]

Table 7.4   Costs of HIPC Initiative by creditor group (including retroactive assistance, $ billion)

Creditor group	Original HIPC	Cologne
Bilateral and commercial creditors	6.3	14.2
Paris Club	5.2	11.5
Other government bilateral	1.0	1.7
Commercial	0.1	0.9
Multilateral creditors	6.2	13.3
World Bank	2.4	5.1
IMF	1.2	2.3
African Development Bank & Fund	1.0	2.0
Inter-American Development Bank	0.5	1.0
Other	1.3	2.9
Total	12.5	27.4
Memorandum:		
Total cost for all 41 countries		
(including Liberia, Somalia and Sudan)	19.0	36.1

Note: Items fo not necessarily add up to the total owing to rounding.

Source: HIPC documents (IDA/SecM99–187/2, 12 May 1999 and EBS/99/52, 12 May 1999) and IMF staff estimates.

Africa's Special Circumstances

Of all the regions of the world, sub-Saharan Africa faces the most daunting development challenge in the new millennium. According to the World Bank's latest estimates, output per head (without South Africa, which accounts for about 40 per cent of the region's output) was lower than South Asia's. Sub-Saharan Africa also has the largest 'poverty gap' and, arguably, the highest levels of income inequality. Although Africa shares these grim indicators with South Asia, there is a growing belief that development prospects for South Asia are more hopeful than for sub-Saharan Africa (see, for instance, Qureshi, 1997).

Understandably, therefore, much attention has been focused on the region's development prospects in recent discussions on development cooperation, and also in academic literature. Attempts have been made over the years to estimate the development finance needs of the region, some of them under the auspices of the United Nations,[10] and others by international financial institutions (EGA, 1993; ADB, 1995). Most recently, fresh attempts have been made to estimate the level of development financing that would be required to achieve the development targets set by the international community, including that of reducing poverty by half by the year 2015. However, none of these exercises is free from methodological and other technical problems. One recent critique has focused, for instance, on the use of the incremental capital output ratio (ICOR) for these estimates (Easterly, 1997). Nevertheless, these calculations offer broad indications of Africa's resource needs, and, provided their limitations are understood, they can be useful points of departure in measuring the depth of the crisis in development finance.

One such recent study, by Amoako and Ali (1998), based on ICORs and domestic savings and investment rates that the authors consider reasonable, estimates external financing requirements that far exceed what would be considered within the realm of possibility, given current trends. For 1998, for instance, they estimate development financing requirements for sub-Saharan Africa alone of $82.4 billion.[11]

LESSONS AND A MINIMUM AGENDA FOR ACTION

While in recent years international capital markets have surged and become by far the most significant source of development finance to developing countries, even in the wake of the Asian crisis, market access has been highly concentrated in a narrow group of middle-income countries. Flows to low-income countries have been rising in recent years, but these too are concentrated in a narrow range of countries, with India alone accounting for the bulk of these flows. Overall, capital market financing has been less important than FDI, but it too has been characterized by a high degree of concentration among oil and mineral-exporting low-income countries.

Many low-income countries in both South Asia and sub-Saharan Africa have undertaken important policy reforms and have begun to achieve high levels of growth, in some cases backed by a rising share of investment in total output. But even for these fast growing countries with a good policy environment, the recent levels of growth are unlikely to be sustained without significant flows of external finance, especially private finance.

The mobilization of additional resources to help sustain high levels of growth where they have already been attained, and to accelerate growth in other cases, will require action both in the domestic policy arena and at the international level. Important domestic policy issues include export expansion, diversification and competitiveness. Much has been written about the need for further policy reform to improve the macroeconomic and governance environment. This is important not only for attracting foreign investment but also for reducing the extent of capital flight, which, by all indications, is higher than in other regions of the world (see Table 7.5). In addition, a lot can be done at the regional

Table 7.5   Estimates of capital outflows

Source	Region/country	Data covered	Amount
Chang et al., 1997	Sub-Saharan Africa	Cumulative 1971–90	80 per cent of 1990 GDP
	Middle East and North Africa	Cumulative 1971–90	90 per cent of 1990 GDP
Schineller, 1997	Latin America	Average 1978–993	1.4 per cent of GNP per year
	Asia	Average 1978–93	0.8 per cent of GNP per year
Claessens, 1997	All developing countries	Average 1971–92	$20 billion per year
Collier et al., 1998	East Asia	Flow in 1997	$80 billion
	Sub-Saharan Africa	Cumulative to 1990	39 per cent of private wealth
Institute of International Finance, 1998	All emerging markets	Flow in 1997	$161 billion
World Bank, 1993	All developing countries	Cumulative to 1991	30 per cent of GDP
	East Asia	Cumulative to 1991	20 per cent of GDP
	Sub-Saharan Africa	Cumulative to 1991	90 per cent of GDP
Lopez, 1998	Mexico	Cumulative 1973–91	$27 billion
Pinheiro, 1998	Brazil	Cumulative 1986–94	$25 billion
Tikhomirov, 1997	Russian Federation	Cumulative 1991–95	$60 billion
Loukine, 1998	Russian Federation	1991–95	$125 billion

Source: World Bank/IBRD (1999, p. 25).

level to bolster the macroeconomic environment and improve investor perceptions of risk. Promoting the image of the sub-Saharan region as an emerging market, for instance, would be a good way of improving prospects for attracting investments in equity portfolios. There are more than 13 functioning stock markets in the SSA region, with a total capitalization of over $309 billion and a turnover of $21 billion as at end-December 1995. The markets have great potential but are fragmented, and have, on average, low levels of capitalization. The World Bank estimates that, between 1970 and 1993 Africa's loss of market share in current prices amounted to an annual loss of some $68 billion (equivalent to 21 per cent of GDP). For non-oil producing African countries (excluding South Africa), for instance, the World Bank estimates that the cumulative terms-of-trade losses since the early 1970s represent about 120 per cent of GDP.

In the domain of international action, the crucial issue of debt relief (which we have discussed in the preceding sections) and the important issue of trade access, especially for textiles and clothing, need to be addressed. The successful resolution of developing country trade issues within the framework of the WTO is, like debt relief, an important aspect of the development finance debate.

CONCLUSION

There has been phenomenal growth in prosperity since the end of World War II. A number of developing countries, mainly in Asia, have made unprecedented strides in eradicating poverty. Some of these gains have suffered significant erosion in the wake of the recent crisis, and even with the faster than anticipated recovery that is taking place in the crisis-hit countries, a return to pre-crisis peaks of growth will take time. At the same time, the recent improvements in the policy environment in many low-income countries, and their efforts at achieving faster growth through integration in the world economy, are in danger of being throttled by the limited availability and undue concentration of development finance. The low-income countries themselves have the primary responsibility for pursuing domestic policies aimed at boosting domestic competitiveness. These include policies in the areas of exchange rate management, trade and technology. But conscious efforts are required at the international level, not just to boost the outlook for and effectiveness of aid, but also to create new instruments for the mobilization and channelling of long-term development finance to the low-income countries. It is important that these efforts also include action to improve developing country access to the markets of the developed countries, and to their products of science and technology. Above all, the reform of the international financial architecture should include contingency financing arrangements for compensating the low-income countries with limited access to capital market financing for income losses arising from the global effects of international crises. They have a decidedly better claim to compensation than the large international banks and hedge funds that benefit from bail-out operations. There should be a special focus on sub-Saharan Africa in future discussions on development finance for reasons of its exceptional capital scarcity and relatively weak prospects for rapid integration in the growing world of foreign private capital flows.

NOTES

1. In the economics profession itself, the business of estimating financing gaps according to the Harrod–Domar growth model has long gone out of fashion. Only its ghost still lurks. See Table 2 in Fisher *et al.* (1998) for investment rates.
2. Within the space of a few months, August–December 1998, the international community pledged this sum in support of Brazil, Indonesia, the Republic of Korea, the Russian Federation and Thailand. The amount does not include the $30 billion pledged by Japan in support of the East Asian countries (see World Bank/IBRD, 1999, pp. 91–2).
3. For investment rates, see Fisher *et al.* (1998, Table 2).
4. This critique is based on a study by Sachs *et al.* (1999).
5. It is difficult to apply where, for instance, a country's fiscal position depends, to a significant extent, on foreign grants.
6. This would be half the gross bilateral ODA disbursements to sub-Saharan Africa in 1996, for instance.
7. Excluding Liberia, Somalia and Sudan. With these countries included, total costs were estimated at about $19 billion.
8. Without Liberia, Somalia and Sudan. With these countries included, the costs would increase to $36 billion.
9. Ghana has in fact opted out of the HIPC Initiative for this reason, although it is by no means clear that this is in its best long-term interest.
10. For example, the United Nations Programme of Action for African Economic Recovery and Development (UNPAAERD) in 1986 and the United Nations New Agenda for the Development of Africa in the 1990s (UNNADAF).
11. This compares with net official development finance of about $48 billion for that year to all developing countries.

BIBLIOGRAPHY

ADB (1995), *African Development Report*, Abidjan: African Development Bank.

Amoako, K.Y. and A.A.G. Ali (1998), 'Financing development in Africa: Some exploratory results', (mimeo), African Economic Research Consortium (AERC), Collaborative Research Project on the Transition from Aid Dependency.

Collier, P. and W. Gunning (1997), 'Explaining economic performance', University of Oxford, Centre for the Study of African Economies.

Easterly, W. (1997), 'The ghost of financing gap: How the Harrod–Domar growth model still haunts development economists', policy research paper no. 1807, Washington, DC, World Bank.

EGA (1993). *Strategies for Financial Resource Mobilization for Africa's Development in the 1990s,* E/ECA/CM.19/5, Addis Ababa: Economic Commission for Africa.

Elbadawi, I., B. Ndulu and N. Ndungu (1996), 'Debt overhang and economic growth in sub-Saharan Africa', in Z. Igbal and R. Kanbur (eds), *External Finance for Low Income Countries*, Washington, DC: IMF.

Fisher, S. *et al.* (1998), 'Africa: Is this the turning point?', *IMF Paper on Policy Analysis and Assessment*, Washington, DC: International Monetary Fund.

Qureshi, M. (1997), 'Persistent poverty in developing countries', opening address at the Conference on International Peace and Security, The Aspen Institute, Broadway, United Kingdom, 2 December.

Sachs, J. *et al.* (1999), 'Implementing debt relief for the HIPCs', policy paper 2 (mimeo), Center for International Development, Harvard University, August.

World Bank (1998), *Bank Policy Research Report, Assessing Aid: What Works and What Doesn't, and Why*, New York: Oxford University Press.

World Bank/IBRD (1999), *Global Development Finance: Analysis and Summary Tables*, Washington, DC: World Bank/International Bank for Reconstruction and Development.

World Bank *et al.* (2000), *Can Africa Claim the 21st Century?*, Washington, DC: World Bank.

ANNEXE

Table 7A.1   *Debt servicing actually paid as percentage of total government*
             revenue

	1992	1993	1994	1995	1996	1997	Standard deviation
Angola	−5	−2	−5	−27	−27	−29	13
Guinea	−21	−22	−27	−43	−28	−35	8
Guinea-Bissau	−26	−14	−24	−46	−32	−22	11
Guyana	−73	−53	−56	−52	−42	—	11
Honduras	−57	−55	−71	−69	−75	−50	10
Madagascar	−34	−26	−26	−21	−23	−62	15
Malawi	−27	−20	−30	−39	−21	−19	8
Mali	−15	−21	−35	−24	−27	−19	7
Mauritania	−34	−54	−43	−44	−35	−36	8
Mozambique	−28	−41	−47	−58	−44	−24	13
Nicaragua	−16	−24	−41	−53	−38	−49	14
Niger	−11	−35	−36	−19	−18	—	11
São Tomé and Principe	−24	−21	−37	−24	−48	−86	25
Senegal	−16	−11	−39	−36	−36	−30	11
Uganda	−66	−65	−40	−25	−24	−28	20
United Republic of Tanzania	−42	−35	−27	−28	−27	−15	9
Zambia	−58	−69	−55	−379	−36	−33	135
Average	−33	−33	−38	−58	−34	−36	

Source: Sachs *et al.* (1999).

Table 7A.2   Net transfers on debt actually paid as percentage of total government revenue

	1992	1993	1994	1995	1996	1997	Standard deviation
Benin	21	26	47	22	25	2	14
Burkina Faso	32	33	44	34	21	13	11
Burundi	48	25	7	4	3	–8	20
Central African Republic	25	43	60	18	23	–8	23
Chad	117	48	127	68	91	57	32
Equatorial Guinea	34	37	23	1	–5	—	19
Ethiopia	21	40	14	7	–2	—	16
Guinea	32	56	25	7	8	27	18
Guinea-Bissau	143	80	73	27	61	66	38
Guyana	–13	–6	–29	–24	2	—	13
Honduras	17	38	–14	–24	–27	19	27
Kenya	–3	–6	–20	–1	–9	—	8
Lao People's Democratic Republic	34	31	21	32	68	40	16
Madagascar	9	16	8	13	22	36	11
Mali	32	6	31	43	17	18	13
Mauritania	26	24	26	9	19	–0.1	11
Mozambique	71	26	52	28	54	50	17
Nicaragua	42	–4	35	–0.5	4	–21	24
Niger	30	27	58	2	18	—	20
São Tomé and Principe	248	156	195	169	141	–15	88
Togo	8	–4	30	17	19	—	13
Uganda	123	108	47	28	24	23	45
United Republic of Tanzania	45	7	13	5	–2	18	16
Average	50	35	38	21	25	19	

Source: Sachs *et al.* (1999).

Table 7A.3   Net resource transfers as percentage of total government revenue

	1992	1993	1994	1995	1996	1997	Standard deviation
Angola	17	19	12	31	–13	–15	19
Benin	84	74	103	72	62	42	21
Burkina Faso	91	97	148	121	97	79	25
Burundi	130	93	153	133	121	69	30
Central African Republic	98	133	213	121	205	85	54
Chad	211	151	326	203	204	143	66
Côte d'Ivoire	7	11	66	20	9	–15	27
Equatorial Guinea	103	82	74	57	35	—	26
Ethiopia	99	112	74	50	31	—	34
Ghana	53	50	34	34	23	20	14
Guinea	87	101	71	65	46	55	20
Guinea-Bissau	254	208	242	186	223	189	28
Lao People's Democratic Republic	73	69	64	81	125	88	22
Madagascar	84	84	77	75	81	200	49
Malawi	106	87	118	129	78	48	29
Mali	85	53	119	102	68	73	24
Mauritania	70	99	80	62	74	53	16
Mozambique	348	252	304	316	205	178	67
Nicaragua	118	38	72	78	119	13	42
Niger	133	149	326	127	121	—	87
São Tomé and Principe	498	386	540	494	435	214	118
Senegal	42	39	86	48	36	35	19
Togo	47	37	92	80	53	–	23
Uganda	328	218	133	102	80	74	99
United Republic of Tanzania	171	139	100	63	43	61	50
Zambia	95	78	35	48	37	36	25
Average	132	110	141	111	100	78	

Source: Sachs *et al*. (1999).

151 - 68

(global)

Q17
F13
O19
O15

8. Agricultural trade barriers, trade negotiations, and the interests of developing countries

Hans Binswanger and Ernst Lutz[1]

More than two-thirds of the poor in the developing world live in rural areas. The poverty there is not only wider spread, it is deeper, as measured by income and by nutritional status. Ironically, hunger prevails in areas that grow food.

A poverty reduction strategy, in taking advantage of opportunities for rural–urban migration, needs to address directly how to improve and sustain the livelihoods of rural people – where they live. Rural growth is necessary for rural poverty reduction. It is not enough, however, as Brazil dramatically shows.[2] Growth must generate employment on farms and in the rural non-farm sector to be widely shared. This outcome is more likely where family farms dominate, rather than large, capital-intensive commercial farms.

Stewart, in Chapter 10 of the present volume, investigates how to achieve widely shared rural growth. This chapter focuses on the demand-side conditions required to fuel the engine of rural growth – the agricultural sector. It is true, with economic development, that the share of agriculture in the rural economy declines in favor of rural non-farm activities, but those activities can only rarely be the driving force for rural growth. The reason? Most non-farm activities in villages and rural towns are linked to agriculture through forward, backward and consumer-demand linkages. The demand to fuel their growth must thus come from agricultural growth.

Of particular importance in this are the consumer-demand linkages. Higher agricultural profits and labour incomes stimulate the local production of labour-intensive consumer goods, services and construction activities. So, under most circumstances, agricultural demand growth is a necessary condition for rural non-farm growth and for rural growth in general.[3] But we all know that the demand for basic staple food is inelastic with respect to income and to prices. That is why rural regions cannot generate sustained growth rates in agricultural demand unless they trade with cities, neighbouring countries and the rest of the world.

Two facts: world trade in agricultural and agroindustrial products has grown more slowly than general trade, and developing countries have not been able to capture as large a share of trade growth in agriculture as in industry. This has constrained agricultural growth and diversification in the developing world. The slower growth of agricultural trade, and the difficulties of developing countries in conquering a share of that growth, are not surprising. Both developed and developing countries erected massive barriers to agricultural trade over the course of the twentieth century. Their joint negative impact on agricultural growth rates in the developing world is a major reason for the slow progress in rural development and rural poverty reduction over the last half-century. That is why the World Bank's rural development strategy states:

> Without improved demand for developing countries' agricultural products, the agri-cultural growth needed to generate employment and reduce poverty in rural areas will not come about. Therefore, the World Bank Group will actively promote greater access to OECD country markets for the agricultural and agro-industrial products of its client countries, and support actions in the WTO to achieve this objective. (World Bank, 1997, p. 61)

Over the past fifteen years or so, developing countries have significantly reduced the anti-agricultural barriers of their policy regimes, but the developed countries' agricultural policy reforms and the last round of the GATT negoti-ation made only a very modest start in dismantling barriers to agricultural and agroindustrial trade. That is why the constraints on agricultural trade continue to inflict enormous welfare losses on the developing world – losses that exceed those from restrictions in the textile trade. (They also continue to inflict equally large welfare losses on the developed countries.)

A key question is whether the agricultural growth rate in developing countries can rise fast enough for agriculture to be a major engine of rural development and poverty reduction. Can the barriers to international trade for agriculture and agroindustrial products be reduced far enough and fast enough for a poverty reduction strategy for rural areas of the developing world to be based primarily on agricultural growth and rural non-farm activities rather than social programmes and safety nets?

In looking at policy constraints on agricultural demand growth, much has been said about the counter-productive interventions and barriers put in place by developing countries themselves. A lot of progress has been made in dis-mantling these interventions. Many interventions remain, however, and second-generation agricultural policy reforms are needed. But the main focus here is on the constraints that developed countries impose on agricultural trade, and on the prospects of reducing them in the current round of WTO negotiations.

TRADE AS THE ENGINE FOR GROWTH AND POVERTY REDUCTION

The share of total developing country exports in world exports increased from 19 per cent in 1973 to 28 per cent in 1980 (partly owing to high oil prices) and remained stable at 22 to 23 per cent thereafter. From 1985 to 1995, the Asian share increased from 10 per cent to 15 per cent, while the African share dropped from about 4 per cent to about 2 per cent (WTO, 1996). The Middle Eastern countries also lost about half their market share, while Latin America largely held its ground.

Agricultural trade has been lagging significantly behind trade in manufactured products. World trade in all manufactured products expanded at 5.8 per cent from 1985 to 1994, with agricultural trade growing at only 1.8 per cent during the same period. One of the reasons for this difference is the high agricultural protection in industrial and developing countries.

The share of developing country agricultural exports in total world agricultural exports has been decreasing steadily over time from 40 per cent in 1961 to 27 per cent in 1990. It increased to 30 per cent in 1996 as a result of temporarily higher commodity prices. Of all the major developing country regions, only East Asia and the Pacific increased their market share, while all other regions lost shares. The loss of Africa is particularly striking, decreasing from 8.6 per cent in 1961 to 3.0 per cent in 1996.

The change in shares of agricultural exports in world exports over time reflects mainly different growth rates in volume terms: for the period 1973–96, agricultural exports of OECD countries expanded at 3.2 per cent, whereas developing countries agricultural exports grew at 2.7 per cent. East Asia and Pacific countries achieved 4.2 per cent growth per annum, while African countries only reached 0.3 per cent. Manufactured exports of developing countries did much better than agricultural exports, steadily increasing from 7 per cent of world manufactured exports in 1973 to 20 per cent in 1995. Those exports now account for more than 62 per cent of total developing country exports (WTO, 1996).

Why have developing countries failed to keep or increase their share in world agricultural exports? Aside from protectionism including export subsidies in industrial nations, there may have been a limited response in developing countries to trade opportunities. That is why the World Bank actively encourages policy and institutional reforms in developing countries to create a more favourable incentive framework so that developing countries can benefit more from international trading opportunities.

There are many good examples of developing countries that have succeeded in developing a strong market position in selected export products, particularly non-traditional ones. Brazil has done very well in sugar, soybeans and orange juice. Thailand, in addition to its traditionally strong position in rice, has developed other export products like cassava. Bangladesh developed shrimp exports from a very small base to a major export industry. Kenya's non-traditional exports (fresh fruits, vegetables and flowers) are doing well, and Tanzania has increased its cashew nut exports significantly during the last decade. A good example of a successful country is also Chile, where reliability in quality, timeliness of delivery and other contractual conditions have contributed to a strong market position. Chile may be somewhat exceptional because it has strong technical capacities to stay at the forefront and anticipate developments in the phytosanitary and other areas. It also can afford to support and defend its position in trade disputes, whereas others may need technical assistance from the international community.

International trade has been one of the important engines of growth for industrial and developing countries. Agricultural trade can be equally important for growth of the agricultural sector, inducing non-farm employment and thus stimulating the whole rural economy. Aggregate agricultural exports are a robust explanatory variable for agricultural growth (Scandizzo, 1998).[4] In short, the agricultural sectors of countries with outward-looking policies and small distortions of their incentive frameworks benefited from international trade in agricultural commodities.

Adding value to locally grown agricultural products is one of the keys to an agriculture-led industrialization strategy. Hindering this potential today is tariff escalation in industrial countries: that is, increasing tariff rates with the degree of processing. This hurts the developing countries and must be reduced. In addition, developing countries need to pursue prudent development strategies conducive to efficient local processing.[5]

LOSSES FROM AGRICULTURAL TRADE AND POLICY, GAINS FROM LIBERALIZATION: WHO ARE THE LOSERS?

OECD agricultural protection still harms developing countries. According to Anderson and others (2000), the farm policies of OECD countries – even after the reforms under the Uruguay Round have been taken into account – cause annual welfare losses of $11.6 billion for developing countries (Table 8.1). That is more than the losses that developing countries incur due to OECD countries' import restrictions on textiles and clothing (9.0 billion).

The real income gains to households in poor countries from OECD agricultural policy reform would thus be sizable. The average net gains would range from $1 per capita in South Asia to $4 in Southeast Asia, $6 in sub-Saharan Africa and $30 in Latin America (Anderson *et. al.*, 1999a and b). The average producer household in the major developing country regions would gain, but consumer households with a food deficit would lose. Furthermore, the gains for producers would exceed any losses for consumers. They would also have dynamic multiplier effects for the rural areas and developing economies, so that consumers should also benefit in the longer run.

OECD countries themselves are incurring very large welfare losses from their own distortionary policies – $110.5 billion a year (Table 8.1). The main losers are the large numbers of consumers, who pay higher prices for food products than they otherwise would, for such commodities as milk, sugar and bananas. The main gainers are the relatively small groups of producers, who will mount the strongest opposition to the needed liberalization. Because OECD consumers would gain more than producers would lose, consumers could, in principle, compensate producers for their losses and still be better off. It seems therefore that ways should be found in OECD countries to develop compensation mechanisms so that producers do not oppose liberalization.

Agricultural trade reform would increase world food prices and would hurt low-income food-importing countries, especially their poorest consumers. This elicits much anxiety. But the expected price increases are not large, amounting to 4–6 per cent for wheat, rice and coarse grains (Valdes and Zietz, 1995), and many of these commodities show a downward trend in real prices over time. In addition, the terms of trade losses under the Uruguay Round tended to be relatively small – in only a few countries did the estimated welfare change constitute more than 1 per cent of GDP. And the least developed countries had the option to remove domestic barriers, allowing them to convert the small loss into a net gain (Ingco, 1997).

Concerns existed about the possible impact of the Uruguay Round on poor countries. These were recognized by the ministers at the Marrakech Meeting. They made a Ministerial Decision on 'Measures Concerning the Possible Negative Effects of the Reform Programme on Least-Developed and Net Food-Importing Developing Countries'. The intent of the Decision was to make sure that food aid could continue to meet the needs of developing countries. Rather than set quantitative targets, the Decision encouraged activities under the Food Aid Convention. But whether the Decision had any noticeable effect on the assistance to developing countries is unclear. Shipments amounted to 9.7 million tons a year from 1990/91 to 1994/95 and to 6.1 million tons a year from 1995/96 to 1997/98 (Tangermann and Josling, 1999). The new Food Aid Convention (effective 1 July 1999) reduced the minimum annual contributions of cereals to 4.9 million tons.[6]

Another chief worry was that agricultural trade liberalization would remove the ability of countries to deal with external price shocks. But, the freer world

Table 8.1   Sectoral and regional contributions to the economic welfare gains from completely removing trade barriers globally, post-Uruguay Round, 2005

(a) In 1995 US$ billions

Liberalizing region	Benefiting region	Agriculture and food	Other primary	textiles & clothing	Other manufactures	Total
	High income	110.5	–0.0	–5.7	–8.1	96.6
High income	Low income	11.6	0.1	9.0	22.3	43.1
	Total	122.1	0.0	3.3	14.2	139.7
	High income	11.2	0.2	10.5	27.7	49.6
Low income	Low income	31.4	2.5	3.6	27.6	65.1
	Total	42.6	2.7	14.1	55.3	114.7
	High income	121.7	0.1	4.8	19.6	146.2
All countries	Low income	43.0	2.7	12.6	49.9	108.1
	Total	164.7	2.8	17.4	69.5	254.3

(b) In percentage of total global gains

Liberalizing region:	Benefiting region	Agriculture and food	Other Primary	textiles & clothing	Other manufactures	Total
	High income	43.4	0.0	–2.3	–3.2	38.0
High income	Low income	4.6	0.1	3.5	8.8	16.9
	Total	48.0	0.1	1.2	5.6	54.9
	High income	4.4	0.1	4.1	10.9	19.5
Low income	Low income	12.3	1.0	1.4	10.9	25.6
	Total	16.7	1.1	5.5	21.8	45.1
	High income	47.9	0.1	1.9	7.7	57.5
All countries	Low income	16.9	1.0	4.9	19.6	42.5
	Total	64.8	1.1	6.8	27.3	100.0

Note: No account is taken in these calculations of the welfare effects of environmental changes associated with trade liberalization, which could be positive or negative, depending in part on how environmental policies are adjusted following trade reforms.

Source: Provisional GTAP modelling results: in final form in Anderson *et al.* (2000).

trade is, the less volatile world food prices become, since surpluses and deficits can be evened out more easily when there are more trading partners with different climatic conditions for growing food crops (Bale and Lutz, 1979; Zwart and Blandford, 1989).[7] And, aside from the scarcity of financial and other resources, there are hardly any constraints from the WTO side for least developed food-deficit countries to deal with the issue of national food supplies.

The policy positions by industrial countries on development and trade often conflict. Pronouncements are made on aiding the poorest and aid is given, but trade policies substantially negate the assistance provided. In 1998, official grant aid from DAC (Development Assistance Committee of the OECD) member countries and multilateral agencies amounted to $5.4 billion, and export credits were $4.0 billion![8] Thus, the costs of industrial country agricultural protectionism on developing countries are larger than the official grant aid and (net) export credits combined.

These issues are being discussed internally in the EU, particularly in the Directorate for Development (DG8). And they are debated in connection with the renewal of the Lomé Convention. Also of great importance is the future direction of the Common Agriculture Policy (CAP) on the expected expansion of the EU into Eastern Europe. Budget pressures will not permit extending an unrevised CAP to countries in Eastern Europe because this would mean a large expansion in subsidies. Even at lower internal EU prices, the central and eastern European nations joining the EU would be expected to expand their production so that the degree of self-sufficiency of the EU as a whole would not change much, if at all.

Put differently, developing countries can expect limited future opportunities for expanding their exports to the EU. They would, however, benefit from a reduction or outright ban on export subsidies. Without such subsidies, the EU would have to set internal prices somewhat lower so that it would be less likely to have surpluses; that is, it would have to achieve slightly less self-sufficiency. More important, the disruptions of the international market from surplus disposal of the EU would be reduced, especially in periods of low world prices, as in the second half of the 1990s.

A new form of non-tariff protectionism is becoming more common: keeping out imports of a good produced with production processes not permitted in the country: call it 'production process protectionism'. The motive for banning a production process is usually articulated on environmental or social grounds. Examples include attempts to keep out products produced using biotechnology ('genetically modified organisms'), certain pesticides, types of fishing nets, forest management practices, poultry or livestock production facilities that are judged not to protect the welfare of the animals, and labour practices (child and prison labour). We hope these issues will not hinder the current round of negotiations from making progress on the large unfinished agenda.

WHAT HAS THE URUGUAY ROUND ACHIEVED FOR AGRICULTURAL TRADE?

Agricultural trade has had a long history of exceptional treatment in GATT. Although non-tariff barriers have been prohibited for non-agricultural goods, quantitative restrictions were permitted by GATT for agriculture under certain circumstances. Over time these circumstances were broadened, allowing the use of quotas, variable levies and other protective measures in almost every country. There was also protection by ordinary tariffs, but these were bound for only 55 per cent of the products in developed countries and only 18 per cent in developing countries (Hathaway and Ingco, 1996).

In export competition, agriculture also got special treatment under GATT rules. Whereas export subsidies are prohibited for industrial products, they were allowed in agriculture 'as long as the country using them did not gain more than an equitable share of the world market' (Article XVI: 3). In practice, the equitable share concept proved useless, subverting GATT discipline over the use of export subsidies for agricultural products. So most countries in the OECD used (and continue to use) them, causing world market prices to be lower than otherwise, and harming producers in exporting countries with a true comparative advantage but without support from government subsidies. Export subsidies are also the key means for disposing of surpluses in industrial countries, produced inefficiently at high cost. They are thus a tool for rich countries to prop up their protectionist agricultural policies.

The Uruguay Round did bring agriculture under some multilateral discipline and agree to a partial, gradual liberalization. Behind this progress was the possibility of measuring agricultural protection and support much better (because of replacing quotas with tariffs) and thus of comparing countries' intervention policies and agreeing on verifiable cuts in interventions.[9] These measures revealed far greater barriers to trade in agricultural goods than in industrial goods.

Given agriculture's previous exclusion from GATT, perhaps more was achieved than could have been expected at the beginning of the Uruguay Round, but the results and associated benefits for farmers in developing countries have been modest (International Agricultural Trade Research Consortium, 1997). Under the Agriculture Agreement in the Uruguay Round, tariffs are to be reduced by 36 per cent by 2001 in the industrial countries, and 24 per cent by 2005 for developing economies.[10] The parties also agreed to limit domestic and export subsidies. Developed countries must reduce by 36 per cent the value of direct export subsidies from their 1986–90 base and cut the quantity of subsidized exports by 21 per cent over six years. For developing countries, the required reductions are two-thirds of those applying to developed countries, and the implementation period is extended to ten years. No reductions in export subsidies (where they exist) are required for the least developed countries. One problem with this part of the agreement has been that unused export subsidies can be carried over from one year to the next and shifted between commodities.

On domestic subsidies the Agreement acknowledged for the first time that domestic agricultural policies can, if income transfers are linked to the volume of production, distort trade. The Agreement categorized (in 'boxes') domestic agricultural policy measures by how much they distort trade. It bound the magnitude of trade-distorting subsidies, required reductions in this support relative to that in a base period, and encouraged their replacement with direct payments fully 'decoupled' from the volume of production.[11]

Unfortunately, the agreement to reduce trade-distorting agricultural support bound and cut only the aggregate support to the agricultural sector, rather than requiring uniform cuts in support afforded all commodities. As a result, the support to some politically powerful commodities rose relative to that for other commodities. There was almost no progress in reducing subsidies to sugar and dairy – two of the most politically powerful agricultural interests in high-income countries. These continuing barriers to production and trade ('peaks') need to be reduced more than proportionately in the next round.

Although the United States and the European Union did not make cuts in their internal support in the Uruguay Round, the negotiating process pushed both to reduce their subsidies and shift significant portions to direct payments decoupled from the volume of production ('blue-box' exceptions).[12] Under the agreement developed countries had to convert all non-tariff barriers into bound tariffs. The problem is that developed and developing countries often chose to bind their tariffs at rates higher than the actual tariff equivalents. This 'dirty' tariffication provides little, if any, reduction in protection – it only makes protection more transparent (Hoekman and Anderson, 1999).

Final bindings for the EU for 2000 are almost two-thirds higher than the actual tariff equivalents for 1989–93 (Anderson *et al.*, 1999 a and b) and for the United States more than three quarters higher (Ingco, 1995). Binding tariffs at such a high level allows countries to set the actual tariff below that level and to vary it to stabilize the domestic market in much the same way the EU has done with its system of variable levies – even after 1995 (Tangermann, 1999). This implies little, if any, actual benefit from replacing non-tariff barriers with tariffs. It also implies little, if any, reduction in the price fluctuations in international food markets, which tariffication was expected to deliver.[13]

Until all countries' internal prices are relinked to world markets, world prices will continue to be much more volatile than is desirable. With the decoupling in US and EU agricultural price supports, neither is accumulating much in the way of public stocks of commodities, which previously stabilized world markets. The Uruguay Round Agreement provided for the first time a minimum of market access, another seemingly important objective. All countries were obliged to ensure that imports make up at least 5 per cent of a good's consumption by the end of the transition period. Minimum access is being provided under 'tariff quotas', considerably undermined, however, by state trading agencies with monopoly power and exclusive rights (Ingco and Ng, 1998).

The Agreement on Agriculture recognized that 'the long-term objective of substantial progressive reductions in support and protection resulting in fundamental reform is an *ongoing process*' (emphasis added). And it committed the signatories to reopen the negotiations by the end of 1999 to carry forward liberalization embarked on in the Uruguay Round (Croome, 1998). The Seattle Meeting failed to start the process. It is now under way but not expected to make much progress until after the US presidential elections.

The Agreement on the Application of Sanitary and Phytosanitary Measures, linked with the Agreement on Agriculture, recognizes the right of governments to take measures to ensure food safety and to protect animal and plant health. It requires that such measures be applied only to the extent necessary to these ends and that they be based and maintained on scientific principles and scientific evidence. But, first, the SPS measures were not developed as part of the WTO process and left out the developing countries. Second, the measures are input-based (for example, one must have stainless steel up to a height of 2 metres on all walls) rather than on the quality of the end product (for example, level of *E. coli* bacteria must be less than some limit). Third, there is the issue that in some cases environmental concerns are used to serve protectionist ends. Fourth, even when the scientific basis of the restriction is sound, many developing countries have difficulties knowing what the applicable standards to their exports are and how to meet them. This causes problems for many countries, such as to Burkina Faso for meats, Kenya for fresh fruits and vegetables, and Papua New Guinea for canned tuna, respectively (Croome, 1998).[14] And finally, the cost of meeting legitimate SPS standards is large: Finger and Shuler (1999) estimated that meeting SPS requirements plus custom and intellectual property reform would cost a country some US$150 million, which is more than the development budget of many of the least developed countries. Developing countries need help in this area. There is an important role here for UNCTAD, FAO, the World Bank and others, with technical assistance as well as with financial assistance for upgrading facilities to meet the requirements (Krueger, 1999).[15]

The Uruguay Round introduced important differences in the obligation of developed and developing countries in agriculture, with special exemptions for the 48 least developed countries. The least developed countries can have bindings of tariffs rather than tariff equivalents. They are allowed lower rates of reductions in tariffs and domestic support. They have delayed tariffication for rice. They can use investment and input subsidies for low-income producers. They can subsidize low-income consumers. They can subsidize marketing and transport. And they can prohibit exports unless they are net exporters. The least developed countries are exempt from commitments to reduce tariffs. So, contrary to popular assertions, the exemptions imply that there are almost no binding constraints in WTO rules on the ability of the least developed countries to intervene in their agricultural trade – or to subsidize and otherwise promote their agricultural sectors.

WHAT SHOULD THE AGRICULTURAL AGENDA BE FOR THE FORTHCOMING WTO NEGOTIATIONS?

The Uruguay Round has been very important in putting agricultural trade on the agenda and starting the liberalization process. But a large unfinished agenda remains. For example, even if the Uruguay Round is fully implemented and China and Taiwan have joined the WTO by 2005, the agriculture and food processing sector will still have twice the average tariffs of textiles and clothing – and nearly four times those for other manufactures (Anderson and others, 1999). That makes it all the more important to adopt a bolder agenda for the current round, from which developing countries have much to gain.[16] One problem is that they have different perceived interests, and that could make it difficult to agree on a common agenda. Latin America, Chile, Argentina, Brazil and Uruguay belong to the Cairns Group, favouring deeper trade liberalization and strongly opposing export subsidies. Meanwhile, the English-speaking Caribbean countries, still pressing for trade preferences, are rather uncommitted to a more open trade regime for their economies.[17]

Although not homogeneous, the developing countries have a common interest in strengthening the system, given their limited bargaining power compared to the United States, the European Union or Japan. It is in their interest to participate in defining the agenda, and in the current round's substantive negotiations (Valdes, 1998; Tangermann and Josling, 1999).

Reform of domestic and trade policies in agriculture is the single most important agenda for developing countries in the forthcoming trade negotiations.[18] Negotiating agricultural trade demands trained policy analysts and negotiators. Given the limited capacity in developing countries, it is difficult for developing countries to face these challenges and to take advantage of opportunities. It is one of the important roles of international agencies to assist the developing countries in building local capacities. The new round of negotiations must seek the following:

- *to outlaw farm export subsidies*: nothing less than a ban on farm export subsidies is needed to bring agriculture into line with non-farm products under the GATT. Credit subsidies need to be quantified and included in the export subsidies;
- *to reduce domestic producer subsidies further*: this will involve binding aggregate support levels as well as support for individual commodities, outlawing carryovers of 'savings' from year to year, and cutting high peaks;
- *to increase access under tariff quotas* significantly from the current 5 per cent of consumption;

- *to get the level and dispersion of bound tariffs on agricultural imports of high-income countries down substantially* – say, to the applied average tariff rates for manufactured goods. As in domestic support, the high 'peaks' should be cut more than proportionately. This is important since the process of tariffication under the Uruguay Round may have actually increased the dispersion of tariff levels.[19]

A reduction in the dispersion of tariffs would benefit agro-processing industries in developing countries now hindered by 'tariff escalation' in industrial nations. Raw materials face low tariffs, but the rates increase with the degree of processing. That provides high rates of effective protection to value-adding industries in importing countries and hinders exporting countries from generating more employment, value-added and export revenue through processing their raw materials prior to exporting them. Developing countries may not have a comparative advantage processing all their raw materials, but tariff escalation by industrial countries clearly hinders development in this high-potential area and gives processing firms in rich countries an unfair advantage.

Although OECD countries would themselves benefit greatly from reducing or abolishing their high agricultural protection, they may not be willing to do so without some reciprocal changes in developing countries – say, in liberalized investment and competition policies. So, to allow for 'give-and-take' in the current round, and to liberalize access of processed and unprocessed agricultural commodities from developing countries in industrial economies, the negotiations may need to include new trade issues of interest to the rich countries. That is why developing countries, in terms of their negotiating strategy, should agree to include such other agenda items as services, intellectual property rights and manufactured products.

One question for developing countries is whether to preserve or expand preferential treatment by individual industrial countries (or country blocs) or to concentrate on obtaining tariff reductions from industrial countries that are applicable to all economies. Under the generalized system of preferences (GSP), agricultural products have not been important elements. Temperate zone agricultural products have been largely excluded from preferential treatment or received it only within tight quotas, and for unprocessed tropical products (except sugar); the generally applicable developed country tariffs are zero or relatively low anyway (Tangermann and Josling, 1999). But the developing countries should, if they can, keep what they got – for example, by having these preferences 'bound' in the current round.

Preferences under the Lomé Convention for the ACP countries have also been unimportant in the aggregate. They may have been significant for individual countries and for such commodities as sugar, bananas and beef, but it has been very inefficient to transfer aid in this form. For example, for bananas alone, it costs consumers in the EU about US$2 billion a year, while only US$150 million reaches its target (Borrell, 1999). One reason for the inefficiency is that, when the quota is fully utilized, a quota rent accrues, and so far the EU has given this rent to EU firms, thus limiting the potential benefit to ACP (African, Caribbean and Pacific) countries. There also are many uncertainties about the future benefits under the Convention.[20]

For sugar, the EU and the United States grant quota-restricted access to their highly protected markets. Producers in those countries as well as some exporting countries gain, while consumers in industrial countries and efficient producers lose. The overall losses of the highly distorted sugar policies amount to an estimated US$6.3 billion annually (Borrell and Pearce, 1999). The small net transfer in aid via the quotas should not be used as an excuse for not liberalizing the sugar markets during the current round.

If the new round could reduce agricultural tariffs by, say 40 or more per cent across the board, preferences would become less important and would cease to be relevant once trade is free. That is why developing countries should not rely on negotiations for special preferences, but should instead use their limited negotiating resources and limited leverage to focus on reducing most-favored-nation tariffs (applicable to all countries) and removing industrial country export subsidies.

WHAT IS THE UNFINISHED AGENDA FOR AGRICULTURAL REFORM IN THE DEVELOPING COUNTRIES?

Developing countries have to continue removing domestic policy distortions across the board. Benefits would amount to US$31.4 billions (Table 8.1). These reforms would counter the anti-agricultural and anti-rural bias in the trade regime. They would also open trade among developing countries, a good potential source of demand for their agricultural sectors. Distortions in need of reform have often included high protection of manufactured goods and services, overvalued exchange rates and direct taxation of agriculture (Schiff and Valdes, 1992, dated but still relevant). Removing them would improve the allocation of resources and increase investment and profitability in agriculture. And removing them in all goods markets could bring gains to developing economies of $65.1 billion a year (Table 8.1). Other desirable policy moves include the following:

- entry and arbitrage barriers, if significant, should be brought down to move towards regulatory regimes more supportive of growth and development;

- state trading entities should lose the exclusive right to import and export
  – and to control domestic supply and distribution of agricultural commodities;
- government should be more proactive in promoting export diversification away from a limited set of unprocessed primary commodities
  (McCalla and Valdes, 1999). They could fund part of the cost of
  searching for new markets, because the private sector would underinvest
  in this, given the public good nature of this activity and the associated
  'free-rider' situation;
- opening trade would increase the number of processing technologies –
  and expand the productivity and value added of agricultural products
  beyond the bounds of traditional agriculture. But success in this depends
  on good management to ensure tune-coordinated sales contracts,
  temporary storage and quality controls in all phases of the product cycle.

The new round of trade negotiations might cover trade-impeding measures
of domestic regulatory regimes, including subsidies, state trading, export
controls, competition law, procurement practices, and setting and enforcing
product standards. But even if it does not, unilateral, domestic regulatory reform
in agriculture would pay off in many countries.[21]

ASSISTING DEVELOPING COUNTRIES IN AGRICULTURAL TRADE

As UNCTAD seeks to place itself and decide which functions to take the
lead in, it could perhaps operate as the OECD does, but serving developing
country interests by building local capacity, providing a discussion forum for
these countries on trade and related issues, maintaining trade-related databases
and providing information, undertaking high-quality analyses, providing
technical assistance in norms and standards and in dispute settlement,
advocating better market access in industrial countries, and helping to build
coalitions and achieve common developing country positions in multilateral
trade negotiations.

It seems sensible that UNCTAD define its functions and its work programme
in partnership with WTO, FAO, the IMF and the World Bank. These organizations and other possible partners should, if they have not already done so,
agree on who takes the lead for what and on how to coordinate their efforts
most efficiently.

NOTES

1. The authors are grateful for useful comments, suggestions, and other assistance by members of the Rural Sector Board, and by many individuals including Kym Anderson, Malcolm Bale, David Cieslikovski, Gershon Feder, Bernard Hoekman, Don Larson, Will Martin, Milla McLachlan, Constantine Michalopoulos, Don Mitchell, Frank Plessmann, William Prince, Sudhir Shetty, Anna Strutt, Bob Thompson, Alberto Valdes, and Patrick Verissimo. The views expressed are their own and do not necessarily reflect those of the World Bank.

2. Between 1950 and 1987 the Brazilian economy grew at an average annual rate of 6.7 per cent. Agricultural output grew less rapidly, at an annual rate of 4.4 per cent, while agricultural employment grew only at 0.9 per cent (World Bank, 1990). The share of people living in urban areas rose from 68 per cent in 1980 to 75 per cent in 1991 (World Bank, 1995), but the massive rural–urban migration was unable to compensate for the absence of rural employment growth. While urban poverty (headcount index) in 1991 was 10.8 per cent for urban areas, it stood at 32.1 per cent for rural areas.

3. Of course, rural development should exploit other sources of growth whenever possible. Other sectors which sometimes fuel rural growth independent of agricultural growth are tourism, mining and handicrafts. They can be quite important for specific regions. However, for countries as a whole they are rarely sufficiently important in quantitative terms to make up for the absence of agricultural growth. Handicrafts in particular suffer from very serious demand-side constraints. There are also some notable exceptions where industrialization in sectors independent of agriculture has helped transform rural areas, such as the village and township industries of China, and rural industrialization in the province of Taiwan. These cases benefited from extremely high population densities in the rural areas affected. In China, moreover, the village and township industries are often near dynamic urban centres with adequate infrastructure, rather than in remote, marginal areas.

4. The composition of the exports is also important: Some primary commodities are under pressure from weak markets, and countries specializing in their production and exports may not gain as much or even lose in terms of demand-led growth as countries with more diversified products do (Scandizzo, 1998).

5. This does not mean banning raw material exports (such as logs) altogether, which can increase smuggling and induces inefficient production (such as of furniture). It may mean some initial protection of local industry by giving it a cost advantage (such as by an export tax), but such protection should later be gradually reduced.

6. One problem with food aid that should be noted is the tendency for shipments to increase when prices are low and to contract when prices are higher and when the needs in low-income developing countries may also be higher.

7. Note also that different trade restrictions, or combinations thereof, have different levels of exporting domestically generated instability to the world market.

8. Overall official development assistance from OECD/DAC members and the multilateral development agencies, which includes grants, export credits and loans, increased by $3.2 billion to a total of $51.5 billion (OECD, 1999). This represented 0.23 per cent of the combined GNP of the member countries. The crisis in confidence in emerging markets, which started in Asia in 1997, and later affected Russia and Latin America, led to a sharp fall in net private flows to developing countries and transition economies, from $242.5 billion in 1997 to $100.2 billion in 1998. Since the fall in total private flows was many times greater than the rise in official flows, the total net resource flows to these countries fell by over 40 per cent, from $325 billion to $181 billion (OECD, 1999).

9. See also the chapter by Winters in the present volume, which makes a passionate plea for further improvements in measurement.

10. The Food and Agriculture Organization (FAO) has provided developing countries with assistance in implementing the Uruguay Round agreement, such as with the production of manuals and technical assistance. The World Bank has organized joint workshops with FAO, such as the one in Santiago, Chile, November 1995 (FAO/World Bank, 1997), and in Katmandu, May 1996 (World Bank/FAO, 1999).

11. The Agreement acknowledged that there are many legitimate public goods functions of government in agriculture (listed in the 'green box') and suggested no restriction on them.
12. The 'blue box' comprises US and EU direct payments to farmers who restrict their output or at least some inputs. These were granted exemption from challenge under the Blair House agreement to move the Uruguay Round talks forward. In the next round, the 'blue box' should be eliminated.
13. The reason is that, the more stable domestic prices are kept, the more domestic instability is exported onto the world market.
14. At a workshop in San Jose, Costa Rica, 26–7 August 1999, which the World Bank helped organize, it was noted that most developing countries are working towards developing their own food safety strategies, particularly in response to opportunities and challenges presented by the SPS agreement. However, there is still a lack of priority setting in the sector with regard to investments, for example, in export versus domestic products or niche market products versus staples. Most countries still have poor institutional arrangements for addressing agricultural health and food safety, with too many agencies and not enough coordination among them. There is also poor enforcement of existing regulations. In addition, most systems are still heavily biased towards the public sector.
15. As one specific action, the World Bank will continue to assist with the organization of regional workshops to discuss these issues as well as with consultations during the negotiations.
16. Dynamic gains tend to be even larger than the calculated static gains.
17. The World Bank, in collaboration with FAO, WTO and various regional organizations has been assisting developing countries by organizing seminars, such as a workshop in Chile, 23–6 November 1998, or in Geneva, 19–20 September 1999. The key objectives were to stimulate wide ranging discussions on agricultural trade issues in the context of the WTO negotiations.
18. For detailed discussions of the agricultural trade agenda from the viewpoint of developing countries, see Tangermann and Josling (1999) and Anderson *et al.* (1999b).
19. This is because the Uruguay Round provided for a simple unweighted average reduction of 36 per cent, with a minimum cut of 15 per cent for each tariff. Thus many countries cut tariffs on important commodities by the minimum and make bigger percentage cuts on items of lesser domestic sensitivity.
20. It has been ruled that the Lomé Convention is not in accordance with WTO rules. A waiver was granted, but it needs to be renewed annually, thus putting pressure on the EU to bring the Agreement or its successor into conformity with WTO rules. A WTO dispute settlement panel also ruled that quantitative restrictions by the EU for bananas were violating the rules.
21. In addition to reforms, and for broad-based development to take place, there is of course also a need for improved financial intermediation, and infrastructure investments in transport, storage facilities and communications networks.

REFERENCES

Anderson, Kym, Erwidodo and Merlinda Ingco (1999b), 'Integrating Agriculture into the WTO: The Next Phase', paper prepared for the World Bank's Conference on Developing Countries and the Millennium Round, Council Room, WTO Secretariat, Centre William Rappard, Geneva, 19–20 September.
Anderson, Kym, Bernard Hoekman and Anna Strutt (1999a), 'Agriculture and the WTO: Next Steps', revision of a paper presented at the Second Annual Conference on Global Economic Analysis, Avernaes Conference Centre, Helnaes, Denmark, 20–22 June.
Anderson, K., J. Francois, T. Hertel, B. Hoekman and W. Martin (2000), *Benefits from Trade Reform in the new Millennium*, London: Centre for Economic Policy Research.
Bale, Malcolm and Ernst Lutz (1979), 'The Effects of Trade Intervention on International Price Instability', *American Journal of Agricultural Economics*, 61 (August): 512–16.

Borrell, Brent (1999), 'Bananas: Straightening Out Bent Ideas on Trade as Aid', paper presented at the World Bank Conference on 'Agriculture and the New Trade Agenda: Interests and Options in the WTO 2000 Negotiations', Geneva, 1–2 October.

Borrell, Brent and David Pearce (1999), 'Sugar: The Taste of Trade Liberalization', paper presented at the World Bank Conference on 'Agriculture and the New Trade Agenda: Interests and Options in the WTO 2000 Negotiations', Geneva, 1–2 October.

Croome, John (1998), 'The Present Outlook for Trade Negotiations in the World Trade Organization', Policy Research Working Paper no. 1992, Development Research Group, The World Bank, Washington, DC.

FAO Regional Office for Latin America and the Caribbean and World Bank (1997), *Implementing the Uruguay Agreement in Latin America: The Case of Agriculture*, edited by Jose Luis Cordeu, Alberto Valdes and Francisca Silva, Santiago: FAO.

Finger, J. Michael and Philip Shuler (1999), 'Implementation of the Uruguay Round Commitments: The Development Challenge', paper presented at the World Bank Conference on 'Agriculture and the New Trade Agenda: Interests and Options in the WTO 2000 Negotiations', Geneva, 1–2 October.

Hathaway, Dale and Merlinda Ingco (1996), 'Agricultural liberalization and the Uruguay Round', in *The Uruguay Round and the developing countries*, Will Martin and L. Alan Winters (eds), Washington, DC: Cambridge University Press for The World Bank.

Hoekman, Bernard and Kym Anderson (1999), 'Developing Countries and the New Trade Agenda', Policy Research Working Paper no. 2125, Development Research Group, The World Bank, Washington, DC.

Ingco, Merlinda (1995), 'Agricultural Trade Liberalization in the Uruguay Round: One Step Forward, One Step Back?', supplementary paper prepared for a World Bank Conference on the Uruguay Round and the Developing Countries, Washington, DC, 26–7 January.

Ingco, Merlinda (1997), 'Has Agricultural Trade Liberalization Improved Welfare in the Least-Developed Countries? Yes', Policy Research Working Paper no. 1748, International Trade Division, International Economics Department, The World Bank, Washington, DC.

Ingco, Merlinda and Francis Ng (1998), 'Distortionary Effects of State Trading in Agriculture: Issues for the Next Round of Multilateral Trade Negotiations', Policy Research Working Paper no. 1915, Development Research Group, The World Bank, Washington, DC.

International Agricultural Trade Research Consortium (1997), 'Bringing Agriculture into GATT: Implementation of the Uruguay Round Agreement on Agriculture and Issues for the Next Round of Agricultural Negotiations'.

Krueger, Ann O. (1999), 'Developing Countries and the Next Round of Multilateral Trade Negotiations', Policy Research Paper no. 2118. Development Research Group, The World Bank, Washington, DC.

McCalla, Alex and Alberto Valdes (1999), 'Diversification and International Trade', in G.H. Peters and Joachim von Braun (eds), *Food Security, Diversification, and Resource Management: Refocusing the Role of Agriculture? Proceedings of the 23rd International Conference of Agricultural Economists*, Aldershot: Ashgate, pp. 113–25.

OECD (1999), 'Financial Flows to Developing Countries in 1998: Rise in Aid; Sharp Fall in Private Flows', News Release, Paris, 10 June.

Scandizzo, Pasquale L. (1998), 'Growth, trade, and agriculture: An investigative survey', FAO Economic and Social Development Paper no. 143, FAO, Rome.

Schiff, Maurice and Alberto Valdes (1992), 'The Political Economy of Agricultural Pricing', in *A Synthesis on the Economics of Developing Countries, World Bank Comparative Study*, vol. 4, Baltimore: Johns Hopkins University Press.

Tangermann, Stefan (1999), 'The European Union Perspective on Agricultural Trade Liberalization in the WTO', paper presented at the University of Guelph, February.

Tangermann, Stefan and Tim Josling (1999), 'The Interests of Developing Countries in the Next Round of WTO Agricultural Negotiations', paper prepared for the UNCTAD Workshop on Developing a Proactive and Coherent Trade Agenda for African Countries, Pretoria, 29 June to 2 July.

Valdes, Alberto (1998), 'Implementing the Uruguay Round on Agriculture and Issues for the Next Round: A Developing Country Perspective', PSIO Occasional Paper; WTO Series no. 10, The Graduate Institute of International Studies, Geneva.

Valdes, Alberto and Joachim Zietz (1995), 'Distortions in World Food Markets in the Wake of GATT: Evidence and Policy Implications', *World Development*, 23(6): 913–26.

World Bank (1990), 'Brazil: Agricultural Sector Review: Policies and Prospects', Washington, DC.

World Bank (1995), 'Brazil: A Poverty Assessment', Report no. 14323-BR, Washington, DC.

World Bank (1997), 'Rural Development: From Vision to Action; A Sector Strategy', Environmentally and Socially Sustainable Development Studies and Monograph Series 12, World Bank, Washington, DC.

World Bank and FAO (1999), *Implications of the Uruguay Round Agreement for South Asia: The Case of Agriculture*, edited by Benoit Blarel, Garry Pursell and Alberto Valdes, New Dehli: Allied Publishers.

World Trade Organization (1996), 'Participation of Developing Countries in World Trade: Overview of Major Trends and Underlying Factors', Note by the Secretariat.

Zwart, Anthony and David Blandford (1989), 'Market Intervention and International Price Stability', *American Journal of Agricultural Economics*, 71(2) (May): 379–86.

9.   Economic dependence on commodities

Alfred Maizels

THE ROLE OF THE COMMODITY SECTOR

The great majority of the population in developing countries depends, for its welfare and livelihood, on the production and export of primary commodities.[1] A strong commodity sector is thus crucial for the progress, both economic and social, of the commodity-exporting developing countries. There are two ways in which this sector could promote economic and social development in these countries: by providing an increasing volume of food and raw materials to support domestic industrialization and economic growth; and/or by earning foreign exchange from commodity exports to finance the imports of capital goods and other essentials for domestic development. The relatively small size of domestic markets has caused almost all such commodity-dependent countries to follow the latter route. As a result, their economic development has been determined, to a large extent, by changes in world commodity markets. This dependent relationship has proved to be a major handicap in the efforts of the commodity-exporting countries to promote their economic and social development.

Several aspects of this handicap can be distinguished, reflecting the inelasticities of supply and demand operating in world commodity markets. The first is the tendency to deterioration in the long-term 'commodity terms of trade' (that is, a decline in the prices of commodities exported by developing countries relative to the prices of manufactures which they import from developed countries). This tendency is, to a large extent, the result of the low income-elasticity of demand for primary commodities in the developed countries, so that their real income growth has been accompanied by relatively little growth in demand for these commodities. For many commodities exported by developing countries, there has also been substantial substitution by synthetic materials over the past two decades, while a shift away from traditional 'heavy' industries, such as iron and steel, has also limited the rate of expansion in demand for natural raw materials. Second, low price elasticities of supply for many commodities mean that, following a rise in price, supply can be increased only after a time lag; however, efforts to expand supply are often self-defeating, since increased supply, when combined with inelastic demand, results in lower prices and reduced export earnings. This process gives rise to a sequence of multi-year price cycles.

The third consequence of low demand and supply elasticities in many commodity markets is the persistence of large short-term fluctuations in prices. Such price fluctuations inject substantial uncertainty into expectations about future sales and profitability, and are thus likely to limit the volume of investment in new productive assets in the commodity sector.

Countries heavily dependent on commodities that are exposed to wide short-term swings in prices for the bulk of their export earnings are generally acknowledged to experience additional constraints on their economic development. Fluctuations in export earnings result in fluctuations in domestic incomes (including multiplier effects on non-export sectors) and in domestic savings, as well as in government revenue (often largely dependent on taxes on export sector earnings) and, as mentioned earlier, they tend to affect adversely the level of investment in productive assets. High export instability can also increase the general climate of business uncertainty, and can lead to capital flight if savers prefer to invest abroad. Alternatively, private investment may be channelled into domestic projects yielding short-term profits rather than into more risky ventures, even though the latter may reflect the country's comparative advantage.

The various difficulties confronting developing countries in coping with the low elasticities of demand for commodities are accentuated by the structural characteristics of commodity supply. Most developing countries are small- or medium-sized producers, none of which can influence world prices by varying their own supplies. There is thus an in-built incentive for such countries to expand their exports since, other things being equal, this will result in higher export earnings. But if many such countries expand their exports simultaneously, this will result in lower prices and reduced export earnings for all of them. This underlying conflict of interest has become a significant element in the commodity problems developing countries have faced over the past two decades.

PHASES OF POSTWAR DEVELOPMENTS IN WORLD COMMODITY MARKETS

Two main phases can be distinguished in the working of world commodity markets since the mid-1950s. The first, lasting until 1980, was dominated by large short-term price fluctuations for a wide range of commodities exported by developing countries, with resultant fluctuations in these countries' export earnings. The 1970s had been a decade of successive 'shocks' to world commodity markets, beginning with a sharp increase in petroleum prices in 1973–4, which brought on fears of a more general rise in commodity prices, while a succession of shortages of some commodities (such as sugar and coffee) in particular years resulted in exceptionally large price swings. During that decade, the trend of real commodity prices was gently upward.

A major change occurred, however, after 1980, when the dominant feature of the commodity markets was a drastic general fall in real commodity prices, which have remained at depressed levels ever since.[2] By the end of the 1980s, the commodity price recession was more severe, and considerably more prolonged, than that of the Great Depression of the 1930s. From 1990 to 1997, there was no significant trend, upwards or downwards, in the commodity terms of trade, but there was a further sharp deterioration during the following two years as a result of the Asian financial crisis and the consequent depreciation of the currencies of the major Asian economies.[3]

The immediate cause of the fall in commodity prices in the early 1980s was the imposition of restrictive monetary policies in the main industrial countries in order to reduce inflationary pressures. This resulted in a marked slowdown in their economic growth rates, and in a sharp contraction of the growth in demand for raw materials. Since then, their growth rates have remained low by postwar standards, which is one reason why commodity prices have failed to show any substantial recovery.

The other main reason for the failure of commodity prices to recover is that the volume of commodity exports from developing countries rose rapidly, by over 40 per cent, from 1980 to 1990. With prices depressed, it would seem perverse for supply to expand at all, but a new factor came into play. A foreign exchange squeeze – largely a result of the earlier collapse in world commodity prices – together with the high interest charges on foreign debt and the virtual cessation of new commercial loans until the early 1990s, put pressure on commodity-exporting countries to expand exports. At the same time, loans from the IMF were usually accompanied by strict conditionality, including currency devaluation aimed at promoting exports.

Commodity prices in real terms have now been at historically depressed levels for two decades. One result has been that commodity-exporting countries have suffered large terms-of-trade losses over this period. The rate of loss has risen sharply, from about $5 billion a year for the period 1981–5 to almost $55 billion a year for the period 1989–91. Total terms-of-trade loss from 1980 to 1992 was about $350 billion,[4] with a considerably greater cumulative loss since then. This terms-of-trade loss was a major factor in the rise of their foreign debt as these commodity exporters strove to maintain a minimum of essential imports. Moreover, the burden of the commodity price recession has fallen disproportionately on sub-Saharan Africa, the poorest developing region, and the least able to make the necessary structural adjustments.

PHASES OF POSTWAR INTERNATIONAL COMMODITY POLICY[5]

In the early postwar period, trade policy was based essentially on free market principles and on non-discrimination, as set out in the Havana Charter of 1948. The Charter recognized that trade in some commodities may be affected by special difficulties, and approved the use of international commodity agreements (ICAs) to prevent or alleviate such difficulties only if 'adjustments between production and consumption cannot be effected by normal market forces alone as rapidly as the circumstances require'. The Charter principles were accepted by ECOSOC (The Economic and Social Council of the United Nations) in 1947 and a number of price stabilization agreements (for coffee, sugar, tin and wheat) were concluded under United Nations auspices.

A new phase of international commodity policy began with the first UNCTAD Conference (1964) when, for the first time, trade policy in general, and commodity policy in particular, were linked directly to the development needs of third world countries. A comprehensive strategy for strengthening the commodity sector of the economies of developing countries, in the form of an Integrated Programme for Commodities (IPC) was approved by UNCTAD IV in 1976. This programme envisaged the negotiation of price stabilization agreements on a range of commodities of export interest to developing countries on the basis of common general objectives and within a common time frame, with the aims of avoiding excessive price fluctuations, and achieving price levels remunerative to producers and equitable to consumers.[6] The IPC resolution also called for the negotiation of a Common Fund as a central financing facility for the whole programme.

There followed a series of intensive consultations and negotiations over a period of years, but the results were very limited, with only one new ICA – that for natural rubber – being concluded. Moreover, the Common Fund, which was established after several years of difficult negotiations, was a much weaker instrument for achieving price stabilization than had been envisaged in the original proposal. The original idea had been for a fund with substantial capital of its own, able to borrow additional funds if necessary, and providing an assured source of financing for the stock operations of existing, or new, ICAs. The Common Fund agreement of 1980, however, provided that it would be financed by associated ICAs, though it had the power to borrow additional funds from capital markets as required.

This reversal of the relationship originally envisaged between the Common Fund and the associated ICAs implied that the central role of the fund, in providing financial support for the price stabilization operations of ICAs, now depended on the success of the negotiations to establish new price-stabilizing

ICAs, or to renew old ones. The failure of these negotiations meant that the Common Fund could not function as envisaged.

By the end of the 1980s, all the then existing agreements, except that for natural rubber, had either collapsed or abandoned their price-stabilizing functions. The 1990s thus opened with no effective market-stabilizing mechanisms in place and, moreover, no consensus between developed and developing countries on the need for such mechanisms. It is, perhaps, ironic that this impasse in international commodity policy, which continued throughout the 1990s, began just as the dominant feature of world commodity markets changed (as explained in the previous section) from excessive short-term price volatility to a sharp downward trend in real commodity prices. If anything, commodity-exporting countries needed greater support, not less, from the international community during this period.

In considering the reasons for the present impasse, it must be recognized that there were undoubtedly a number of technical weaknesses in the various ICAs, which adversely affected their smooth operation and, at times, caused a breakdown.[7] However, from the early 1980s, the major weakness was that none of these agreements was equipped to cope with the downward trend in prices of unprecedented magnitude and duration. This situation inevitably resulted in a sharp conflict of views between exporting and importing countries as to the correct interpretation of the objectives of price stabilization. The exporters generally argued that an agreement should defend the agreed 'floor' price so as to protect their decreasing export earnings. The importers, on the other hand, insisted that, in a period of falling prices, the agreed price range had to be adjusted downwards in line with market trends.

This stance of the importing countries conformed with their more general view that regulation of the international commodity markets was an unnecessary interference with the free play of market forces, which would result in a misallocation of productive resources. Though this view was not generally accepted by exporting countries, the collapse of most of the existing price-stabilizing ICAs by the early 1990s allowed that free market influences to prevail in practice.

THE NEED FOR A NEW INTERNATIONAL COMMODITY STRATEGY

The focus on free market influences, and the absence of any new initiative in favour of appropriate intergovernmental market regulation, has not, however, succeeded in restoring the real export earnings of the commodity-dependent countries to anywhere near their level of two decades ago. On the contrary, these earnings appear likely to remain depressed for many years to come.[8] In the absence of a new initiative to strengthen the commodity sector of these countries, a 'solution' to this problem will eventually be achieved by a contraction, or even a cessation, of commodity production in small or poor high-cost countries. This will involve a further contraction in real incomes, which will add to the existing deflationary forces in the world economy.

A continuation of recent trends would indeed be very damaging for the majority of developing countries. It would limit their growth potential and undermine their efforts at domestic policy reform, debt restructuring and external resource mobilization. While the low-income and least developed countries would suffer the most, many other developing countries, including the recently industrializing ones, would also experience significant losses. Moreover, in the absence of a positive international commodity strategy, commodity prices and commodity export earnings of developing countries will continue to experience substantial degrees of instability.

As a result of these various factors, the debt burden of the commodity-exporting countries can be expected to remain high in relation to their export earnings, resulting in continuing pressure to expand exports to assist in meeting their debt service obligations. For many such countries, the interrelationship between exports and the foreign debt is likely to create a 'low-income trap', since depressed export prices have been, and remain, a major reason for the rise in their foreign debt. At the same time, the higher level of debt demands an expansion in export supply to service that debt, a process which further intensifies the depressive forces on world commodity markets.

If world commodity markets are left to the 'free play of market forces', while much high-cost agriculture in developed countries – even after the Uruguay Round – continues to be subsidized, the underlying problem of the downward trend in real prices of commodities exported by developing countries is likely to persist. Indeed, over the short-term, the downward trend might even be reinforced as the result of the working of the 'low-income trap' already mentioned. The commodity sector of developing countries' economies has been seriously weakened, while the retreat from the use of ICAs has removed an important 'safety net' which could have supported the real export earnings of commodity-dependent countries during the commodity price recession of the 1980s.

Developed countries, as well as developing ones, can be seriously harmed by large swings in commodity prices. Sudden and sharp price increases, for example, by causing a deterioration in the balance of payments of importing developed countries, and an increase in their inflationary pressures, can result in more restrictive monetary policies, thus adversely affecting their domestic growth rates. More generally, the continuing instability in commodity markets is likely, as already argued, to inhibit investment in productive capacity in the commodity sector and, to this extent, it would limit the future growth potential of the world economy.

The commodity problems of developing countries have received little, if any, attention in international forums for almost two decades. It now seems high time for this issue to be given serious consideration by the international community. The essential elements of a new international commodity strategy are discussed in some detail in the following sections, drawing on the lessons of the recent past.

RAISING DEPRESSED LEVELS OF COMMODITY PRICES

Supply Management

Since the prolonged period of depressed prices has become the dominant feature of world markets for the commodity exports of developing countries, an effective international commodity strategy needs to pay special attention to this problem. The objective here should be to devise effective measures to raise depressed prices to more 'normal' levels in a manner that would be acceptable to commodity-importing countries as fair and reasonable. Since depressed price levels reflect the persistence of excess supplies, the logical remedy would be some form of supply management.

Supply management is not, of course, a new idea. Buffer stocks and export quotas, as used in past ICAs, are themselves a form of supply management, as are arrangements designed to reduce or eliminate excessive stocks 'overhanging' a particular market. Several developed countries, too, have operated domestic 'set aside' programmes to reduce productive capacity for particular farm products in market surplus; while in cases of chronic overcapacity, developed country governments have, on occasion, encouraged the major firms involved to reach informal arrangements to reduce capacity.

A practical programme of supply management to reduce excess supply, and to bring a better medium-term balance into the market, would need to be based on detailed assessments of trends in world demand for, and supply of, each of the major commodities experiencing persistently depressed prices, the related trends in world stocks, and the expected future price trends, so as to determine the need for supply management in particular cases.

The appropriate form of any supply management scheme would need to address the underlying cause of price depression. A large stock overhang, for example, would require some form of stock retention by producers for, presumably, the limited period during which stocks fall to more normal levels. Such a scheme could be based on national stocks, subject to international coordination.[9] Where the problem is a faster growth of commodity supply than of commodity demand, an alternative policy could be based on export quotas, provided steps are taken to avoid the difficulties that arose in the operation of past export quota schemes.

Yet another alternative, for certain commodities, might be a uniform *ad valorem* export tax levied on shipments from the main producing countries. This would have the advantage of not altering the relative competitive position of the various producing countries, while acting to raise export prices generally. However, the export tax route would not be suitable for commodities having low short-term price elasticities of supply,[10] or where there is a large domestic market for the commodity.[11]

Supply management, in whatever form, is not, however, a panacea for dealing with the underlying long-term causes, of which depressed price levels are symptoms. Rather, it is to be viewed as an instrument for reducing serious market imbalances in the short- or medium-term. Over the long term, other measures would need to be considered to adjust the economic structures of commodity-dependent countries to world market trends. The two issues discussed below are particularly relevant in this context.

Diversification

Since the persistence of depressed levels of prices reflects a situation of chronic oversupply, a longer-term solution must be sought by diversification of the economies of commodity-dependent countries away from the production of the commodities concerned. Diversification, both within the commodity sector – into the production of non-traditional items with growing markets, or into the processing of commodities – and in manufacturing and service activities, has progressed in many developing countries over recent decades. But almost all such diversification has occurred in the larger countries, which have more extensive economic infrastructures, higher levels of labour and technical skills and better access to financial sources than the small or poor countries, especially those exporting commodities in structural surplus. Such low-income countries find considerable difficulty in attracting private foreign investment or loans from commercial banks, while loans from the international financial institutions have generally been concentrated in the larger countries.

The low-income commodity exporters would appear to need much greater technical assistance than hitherto provided to help them identify and formulate diversification projects which could attract adequate external financial support. Without such support, countries exporting commodities in persistent surplus will not be able to finance the necessary structural adjustments to their economies. In this context, the present efforts of the World Bank and of the regional development banks to promote economic diversification in low-income countries will need to be expanded.

A shift towards the processing of many commodities in developing countries has been limited in past years by the escalation of import duty rates according to the degree of processing which has been applied by developed countries. Though the GATT Uruguay Round made some progress in reducing this duty escalation, higher duty rates applicable at higher stages of processing may still discourage commodity-dependent countries from diversifying into the processing stages of production for a number of commodities so as to benefit from added value.[12]

The forthcoming WTO Round of trade negotiations would appear to be an appropriate occasion for substantial reductions in the various import barriers to commodity trade, including trade in processed commodities, with a view to extending the global market for the commodity exports of developing countries, and to promoting needed diversification of their economies. Some new inter-agency forum might also be considered to bring together experts in the problems of particular commodity markets, or of countries about to diversify, to ensure that their diversification programmes, when taken together, are not likely to result in lower export revenues from some commodities or for some exporting countries.

Making Natural Materials more Competitive with Synthetics

Many natural raw materials exported by developing countries have been displaced by synthetics or by other materials produced in developed countries, resulting in persistent oversupply and depressed levels of prices for the natural product. The most promising longer-term remedial policy is likely to be a well-designed and adequately financed programme of research and development to improve the technical qualities, and thus the competitive position, of all the major natural raw materials.

Producers of cotton and wool have already followed this approach, and have retained their competitive position by technical improvements justifying their sale as quality fibres. It should be possible, with appropriate research and development projects, to improve the technical characteristics of each of the principal natural materials exported by developing countries in a similar way. This is an area in which the Common Fund for Commodities has a special responsibility through its Second Account.[13] From 1991 to 1 May 1999, the Common Fund had approved 74 individual commodity projects with a total funding of some $220 million, about half the amount being financed by the Common Fund. Of these, 33 projects related to nine different natural raw materials, with a total of $43.4 million in Common Fund commitments, plus approximately the same in co-financing and counterpart funds.[14] This represents an annual average commitment of \$11–12 million for commodity development measures for the natural materials covered. Though this is an impressive start to what is necessarily a long-term programme, it may, none the less, be too small in scale to have a significant impact on the overall competitive positions of natural and synthetic materials in world markets.[15] Donor governments may therefore need to consider ways in which funding for Common Fund development projects could be substantially increased.

MINIMIZING MULTI-YEAR PRICE CYCLES

As mentioned earlier, some important commodity exports of developing countries have traditionally been subject to sharp price cycles, which arise when there is a multi-year delay in the adjustment of production to shifts in demand (and thus in world prices). This phenomenon is most marked for the tropical tree crops – cocoa, coffee and tea – though certain other commodities may also be affected.

The issue first came to the fore in the negotiations for a fifth International Cocoa Agreement (1993). Previous Agreements for cocoa had relied on a buffer stock plus export quotas, or on a buffer stock alone, to correct temporary or short-term market imbalances. However, the consensus among countries participating in the 1993 negotiations was that international cooperation on cocoa should address the longer-term problem of price cycles, and not concentrate on short-term price stabilization. This was a radical departure, not only from the earlier cocoa Agreements, but also from all other international commodity agreements, since none of the latter had distinguished between short-term price fluctuations and multi-year price cycles. This in itself had caused difficulties in the operation of various agreements, since the nature of the problem, and the appropriate remedial mechanisms, are quite different in the two cases.

Under the 1993 Cocoa Agreement, two main committees have been established under the International Cocoa Council. After the Council makes annual reviews and six-year forecasts of the world cocoa market, the Production Committee decides what adjustments to future production levels would be necessary to maintain a balanced market. This enables producers to make informed decisions about their individual production plans. The Consumption Committee examines consumption trends and problems in each country, and proposes actions to increase consumption, particularly in low-consuming countries.[16] It is expected that countries will collectively plan their production more effectively, while consumption will be stimulated as necessary, thus reducing the severity of the price cycle.

This new approach to commodity price problems is still at an early stage, and there is, no doubt, room for improvement in the mechanisms used. One major problem so far seems to be how best to improve the six-year forecasts, but these will become more reliable if proposals to conduct surveys of cocoa tree stocks in the main producing countries go ahead. The general approach of the 1993 Cocoa Agreement does, none the less, appear to be an important innovation in the mechanisms of international commodity policy and, moreover, operates within the framework of a producer/consumer agreement. Producers and consumers of other commodities with a significant supply lag could usefully consider emulating this approach.

MINIMIZING SHORT-TERM FLUCTUATIONS IN COMMODITY PRICES OR REDUCING THEIR ADVERSE EFFECTS ON DEVELOPING COUNTRIES

Though the dominant feature of international commodity markets since 1980 has been a generally depressed level of prices for a number of important commodity exports of developing countries, short-term price instability has remained high. The degree of instability has been greatest for sugar, reflecting the residual nature of the free market for that commodity, and the substantial annual variations in exports of subsidized sugar from the EU in recent years, as well as in exports from developing countries. High short-term price instability was also found in the markets for rice, most vegetable oils, jute and certain non-ferrous metals, of which copper is the most important.

Unregulated commodity markets tend to exhibit significant short-term price instability, making such markets inefficient mechanisms for optimal resource allocation, since prices in unstable markets cannot reliably indicate the relative profitability of alternative lines of investment in the production of different commodities. High price instability of a country's commodity exports would therefore tend to favour investment (for example in financial assets) for short-term gain, whereas low price instability would tend to favour long-term investment in productive assets. The constraints on economic development arising from excessive short-term instability of commodity export prices would be accentuated by the consequential variability in imports of capital goods and intermediate products into commodity-dependent countries.

International Buffer Stocks

The traditional approach to the problem of excessive commodity price instability has been the use of international buffer stocks and/or export quotas within the framework of an ICA. However, even if the degree of price instability were substantially reduced by such mechanisms, the export earnings of individual commodity-exporting countries could still exhibit large short-term fluctuations if the volume of their commodity exports was also subject to unduly large variations. An adequate system of compensatory finance for temporary shortfalls in commodity export earnings would, therefore, be an essential complement to the price stabilizing function of an ICA. Unfortunately, for many of the past ICAs using buffer stocks, these were not adequately funded, while the availability of compensatory financing, especially during the 1980s, represented only a small proportion of the export shortfalls experienced by commodity-dependent countries.

The failure of the various ICAs to defend the agreed 'floor' prices during the 1980s (as mentioned earlier), was no doubt one important reason for disillusionment among many commodity-exporting countries with this approach. More recent examples are the withdrawal in the course of 1999 of both Malaysia and Thailand from the ICA for natural rubber for the same reason. As already explained, the defence of a price 'floor', or the raising of depressed levels of prices, is a different problem from that of excessive short-term price fluctuations, and therefore requires different remedial measures.

If the ICA approach is ever resuscitated, the objective of short-term price stabilization should be explicitly separated from that of price raising, while the agreed price range would need to be market-related. Moreover, any new international buffer stocks would need to be adequately funded and supported by an adequate system of compensatory financing. Such a system should be conditional, in appropriate cases, on recipient countries taking measures to reduce short-term fluctuations in the volume of their commodity exports.

Risk Management

An alternative approach to minimizing the adverse effects of excessive short-term fluctuation in prices of commodity exports from developing countries has been strongly advocated by the World Bank since the late 1980s, namely the use of commodity-linked financial instruments to hedge against future price risks. This issue was considered at UNCTAD VIII in 1992, which recommended that, 'as far as possible, market-risk instruments should be used to alleviate the consequences of short-term variations in prices'. Since 1989, the World Bank has put much effort into training commodity traders in various developing countries on the use of these financial instruments. In addition, the remit for the Common Fund for Commodities was extended in 1995 to include, *inter alia*, 'the enhancement of commodity market risk management and commodity trade financing'.

Nevertheless, it would seem unlikely that these relatively sophisticated financial instruments, which include futures contracts and derivatives, options and swaps, will come into general use by commodity producers and traders in developing countries for many years to come. Particularly for peasant producers and small trading firms, the need to keep in constant touch with market trends, and the possibility of having to meet unexpected margin calls, are likely to limit their use of such financial instruments.

Now that there is a full decade of experience with the market risk management approach, the time may be ripe for a review of its scope, efficacy and cost. Such a review could show, for example, the problems that have arisen, and the measures taken to meet them; the degree to which commodity exports from developing countries are now covered by market risk instruments; the magnitude of the reduction in the short-term fluctuation in prices received by commodity producers and exporters using these instruments; and the magnitude of the reduction, if any, in the short-term fluctuation in export revenue of the commodity-exporting countries.

The role of market risk financial instruments in a new and comprehensive international commodity policy may also merit closer consideration. While the widespread use of such instruments would reduce individual commercial risks, this would not by itself reduce the degree of price instability in world commodity markets. Commodity price instability interacts with instability in world financial markets and thus tends to accentuate the instability of the global economic system. A system of adequately funded international buffer stocks, by contrast, would act as an important stabilizing element in the global economy.[17]

PROTECTING THE NATURAL ENVIRONMENT

It is generally acknowledged that the global economy is far from achieving a sustainable process of development in the sense of being able to meet present needs without compromising the ability of future generations to meet their own needs. Particularly over the past fifty years, global economic activity has resulted not only in growth in real incomes but also in serious environmental depletion and degradation. The principal underlying cause of continuing environmental damage has been that market processes do not reflect environmental costs and benefits. In many cases, the hidden environmental costs in the commodity sector are passed on to the general population, for example through polluted air or water supplies, or to taxpayers through the cost of land reclamation after mining has ended.

Governments therefore need to devise mechanisms, where these do not at present exist, to internalize the environmental costs of economic activities, particularly for those which have adverse environmental effects. Such mechanisms could include, for example, taxes on the production of items harmful to the environment, or the removal or reduction of existing subsidies on inputs, such as fertilizers and pesticides, which also have harmful effects. Conversely, financial incentives could be introduced for environmentally friendly activities.

It is now generally accepted that poverty in developing countries is a major cause of environmental damage (for example to forests). Poverty alleviation policies should thus help to meet environmental goals in many developing countries, with consequent benefits for developed countries also. Equally, some changes in developed countries' policies, such as reductions in existing trade barriers, would help to raise the commodity export earnings of developing countries, thus providing more resources and more flexibility for these countries to deal with problems of economic and social development, including poverty and environmental issues. Increased capital inflows, by assisting economic growth in developing countries, could also contribute to the attainment of environmental objectives. To the extent that supply management for commodities in excess supply can improve depressed levels of commodity prices, it could also be expected to reduce the pressure on environmental resources.

A number of natural products exported by developing countries have environmental advantages over their synthetic competitors. The world market for environmentally friendly natural products could be significantly expanded if developing countries took steps to promote the environmental attractiveness of their natural commodity exports.

CONCLUSION

The main points that arise from the above discussion of the problems of commodity-dependent countries are the following.

1. A high dependence on exports of primary commodities has been a major handicap to the efforts of developing countries, and particularly of the poorest among them, to promote their economic and social progress.
2. Since 1980, the dominant feature of world commodity markets has been their persistently depressed price levels, with consequent large terms-of-trade losses for commodity-exporting countries. These losses have played a major part in the rise in their foreign debts and the decline in their growth rates and in their standards of living. The low-income and least developed countries have been worst affected.
3. Over this period, also, international action to strengthen the commodity sector of developing countries' economies has been marginal or non-existent.
4. There is now a strong case for a new international initiative to deal effectively with the commodity issue in all its aspects. This should be a cooperative effort by developing and developed countries in the longer-term interests of both. Such cooperative action, to be fully effective, should

include both free-market instruments and selected forms of market intervention, where appropriate, in dealing with specific commodity problems.

5. The various pricing problems facing commodity-dependent countries must not be conflated. Short-, medium- and long-term pricing problems have distinct causes and require distinct remedial policies.

6. A new initiative in the commodities field should give priority to raising the present depressed levels of prices of the major commodities exported by developing countries. Supply management measures would be needed to reduce excessive stocks 'overhanging' a commodity market, combined, as appropriate, with measures to promote diversification away from commodities in persistent oversupply, or with additional measures to improve the technical characteristics of natural materials in competition with synthetics or other substitutes. Developed countries could support a new initiative on these lines by negotiating substantial reductions, and eventual elimination, of the various barriers to commodity imports, including tariff escalation on processed commodities from developing countries.

7. For commodities whose markets are subject to multi-year price cycles, consideration should be given to adopting the type of production management now being developed for cocoa. Where the main problem continues to be excessive short-term price fluctuations, the use of risk-management techniques will, no doubt, spread more widely, though it seems unlikely that they will come into general use by commodity producers and traders in developing countries for many years to come. There is, thus, a case for instituting, as soon as practicable, a detailed review of the scope, efficacy and cost of this approach, which could be used to minimize the adverse effects of excessive short-term price fluctuations of the commodity exports of developing countries.

8. Governments need to devise mechanisms, where these do not at present exist, to internalize the environmental costs of economic activities. Poverty alleviation policies in developing countries should also help to meet environmental goals. These countries could expand their export market if they took steps to promote the environmental attractiveness of their natural commodity exports.

NOTES

1. In this chapter, the terms 'commodities' and 'primary commodities' are used interchangeably, and exclude petroleum, which is best treated as a special case.

2. Over the decade of the 1980s the fall in real commodity prices was some 45 per cent, if the fall in real commodity prices is deflated by the United Nations Index of unit values of manufactures exported by developed countries, or about 35 per cent, if an index of commodity export unit values is used instead of the commodity price index.

3. The UNCTAD index of free market commodity prices fell by 11 per cent between the first halves of 1997 and 1998, and by a further 17 per cent between the first halves of 1998 and 1999 (UNCTAD, 1999).
4. Maizels *et al.* (1997).
5. A more detailed discussion of postwar international commodity policies can be found in Maizels (1992, pp. 101–55).
6. The IPC resolution also specified a number of longer-term objectives, including improvement in market access, diversification of production and improved competitiveness of natural products competing with synthetics.
7. For example, setting the price ranges to be defended at levels inconsistent with market trends, and allocating insufficient funds to finance buffer stock operations.
8. Recent estimates by the World Bank (1998/99, p. 24) put the level of real commodity prices in the year 2007 at 16 per cent below the 1998 average, almost all of the decline being due to a projected rise of 17 per cent in the unit value of manufactures exported by the G8 countries.
9. An international buffer stock, as used in many past commodity agreements, is more suitable for reducing short-term price fluctuations.
10. There is an inverse relationship between the export tax rate required to yield a given rate of increase in export revenue and the short-term price elasticity of supply, so that as the latter approaches zero the required tax rate rises sharply, for a given demand elasticity.
11. An export tax is likely to divert supplies from export to the domestic market in this case.
12. This point is also made in the chapter by Binswanger and Lutz in the present volume.
13. The Agreement establishing the Common Fund for Commodities (1980) specified that commodity development measures under its Second Account 'shall include research and development, productivity improvements, marketing and measures designed to assist ... vertical diversification' (Art. 18.3(*a*)).
14. Common Fund for Commodities (1999).
15. The commitment of $11–12 million a year represents only about 0.02 per cent of the approximately $50 billion of annual exports of natural raw materials from developing countries in the mid-1990s. By contrast, research and development expenditures by the large synthetic materials enterprises of developed countries are often above 5 per cent of the value of production.
16. UNCTAD (1993).
17. This stabilizing influence of international buffer stocks was strongly emphasized by J.M. Keynes (1942) in his famous wartime proposals for the postwar international economic and financial institutions.

REFERENCES

Common Fund for Commodities (1999), 'Notes on the common fund for commodities', Amsterdam, 2 June.
Keynes, J.M. (1942), 'The international regulation of primary products', reprinted in D. Moggridge (ed.) (1980), *Collected Writings of John Maynard Keynes*, London: Macmillan and Cambridge University Press.
Maizels, A. (1992), *Commodities in Crisis*, Oxford: Clarendon Press.
Maizels, A., R. Bacon and G. Mavrotas (1997), *Commodity Supply Management by Producing Countries*, Oxford: Clarendon Press.
UNCTAD (1993). *Fifth International Cocoa Agreement, 1993*, Geneva: United Nations.
UNCTAD (1999), *Monthly Commodity Price Bulletin*, XIX/7, Geneva: United Nations.
World Bank (1998/99). *Global Economic Prospects and the Developing Countries*, Washington, DC: World Bank, p. 24.

10. Income distribution and development

Frances Stewart

INTRODUCTION[1]

The distribution of income within a society is of enormous importance. It influences the cohesion of the society and, for any given level of GDP, determines its poverty level. Some relatively high-income economies have very unequal income distribution, with the result that there are large cleavages in society and high levels of poverty, as in Brazil. Other countries with more equal income distribution have less poverty and there is a sense of fairness within the society which makes for political stability, as in Costa Rica. The sensitivity of poverty to growth depends on a country's income distribution; for example, a 1 per cent growth rate of GDP leads to a 0.21 per cent reduction in poverty in Zambia, if distribution is unchanged, compared with a 3.4 per cent reduction in Malaysia (Sen, 1995). There is also considerable evidence that the distribution of income has a significant influence on the rate of growth, with more equal societies growing faster than less equal ones. Moreover, the average health status of a society depends on its income distribution, so that countries with more unequal distributions experience lower life expectancy.[2] An equitable distribution of income, as well as the achievement of social goals, are, therefore, essential aspects of development, over and above economic growth.

This chapter aims to explore the connections between income distribution and economic growth, and to identify some policy conclusions emerging from the analysis. There have been many investigations of the relationship between income distribution and development, starting with a classic paper by Kuznets, who argued that income distribution was generally relatively equal at low levels of income in the early stages of development, became more unequal as development proceeded, and finally a reverse move took place so that income distribution became more equal again as countries approached the levels of incomes of the developed countries. The work of Kuznets, and others, was based on the finding of correlations between levels and growth of per capita income and income distribution. Behind these correlations lie two possible types of causality: first, how growth affects the distribution of income; and secondly, how distribution affects growth. Both will be investigated, before exploring recent trends in income distribution.

The chapter is organized as follows: section I considers some important definitional issues; section II reviews findings on the ways in which growth affects income distribution; section III looks at the reverse causality, that is, how income distribution affects growth; section IV discusses growth strategies which are likely to generate more equal income distribution; section V reviews recent trends in income distribution; section VI explores wider dimensions of inequality extending beyond pre-tax private incomes, to encompass the incidence of taxation and expenditure, and some indicators of inequalities in capabilities; section VII discusses horizontal (or group) inequalities; section VIII briefly reviews changes in global income distribution; and, finally, section IX concludes.

I   SOME IMPORTANT DEFINITION ISSUES

Key issues concern distribution of what, among whom and within which unit.

Distribution of what? In almost all discourse, the focus is on the distribution of current monetary (or private) income – normally pre-tax and subsidy but sometimes post-tax and subsidy. Even within the 'income' paradigm of welfare, one needs to extend this to include future income (for example, by adding current asset distribution). But alternative approaches to well-being suggest the need for concern with one, other, or all of the following: the distribution of social income (that is, goods and services provided by the state) as well as private income; distribution of capabilities or functionings, of basic needs goods and services, or of human development achievements.[3] A broader approach to distribution is needed, whether it is a matter of assessing distribution in a society from the perspective of well-being, or from that of investment (that is, the impact of current distribution on growth). For example, inequality in access to education, which is acute in many societies, is a major influence on future household income, and may also affect the rate of growth, since in many occupations those deprived of education are unlikely to be as productive as the educated. Inequality in access to health services can be much more important than inequality in private incomes, since life itself may depend upon it. Nonetheless, most of the literature focuses on the distribution of private incomes.

In addition to household income distribution, there is the question *of functional* income distribution, that is, the distribution between profits, wages, rents and so on. This indeed was the 'great' question which Ricardo focused on. Functional distribution is important because it is a major determinant of household distribution, as well as being a determinant of savings, accumulation and growth, yet it is virtually ignored in most current empirical, and much theoretical, work (see, for example, reviews by Kanbur and Lustig, 1999; Kanbur, 1998).

Distribution among whom? The appropriate level of analysis depends on why the information is needed. If the aim is to assess well-being, and an individualistic approach to well-being is adopted (as with utilitarian and capability approaches) then the individual is the appropriate level. But many of the data are collected at a household level, as it is difficult to get information at the level of the individual. Frequently, household and individual information is used interchangeably, but there has been some effort to correct household data, in order to translate them into information about individuals, for example, by allowing for intra-household distribution (and sometimes correcting income to allow for the needs of people of different ages or genders within the household).

However, for some important aspects of well-being, the relevant distribution is that among *groups*, not individuals, such as distribution of income between groups of different ethnicities, religions, regions or races. We term this type of distribution *horizontal*, to differentiate it from the normal *vertical* measures of distribution among households or individuals. Horizontal distribution is one of the major causes of conflict between groups. It can also be directly relevant to individual well-being, where people identify strongly with the group to which they perceive themselves as belonging. For other purposes, such as for North–South negotiations, the appropriate measure of inequality may be average differences among nations.

Distribution within which unit? Another issue is the *unit* within which inequality is assessed. Conventionally, this unit is the *nation*, the obvious rationale being that this is the major policy-making unit. But some policies are made at the local level, so that the local administrative unit would be the relevant one. For purposes of aid and other international policies, the global level is appropriate, and, for intraregional policies, distribution within the region.

In practice, almost all the literature relates to *private income distribution among individuals within a nation*, thereby excluding many important issues. Much of this chapter will do likewise, but will return to some of the broader definitions at the end.

II   HOW GROWTH AFFECTS DISTRIBUTION

As noted earlier, in 1955 Kuznets famously propounded the view that there is an inverted 'U' curve relating levels of per capita income to income distribution, with income distribution first becoming more unequal, and at a later stage more equal, as per capita incomes rise. Kuznets derived this from cross-country evidence. Historical work on the changing income distribution in industrialized countries also provided supporting evidence (Paukert, 1973). But it should be noted that the Kuznets' work relates to *levels* of income per capita, not to the *growth* rate. Moreover, further work on the Kuznets curve has found the relationship weak, as it is dependent on the precise functional form adopted (for example, Anand and Kanbur, 1993a; Deininger and Squire, 1998). Bourguignon concludes: 'If there is any parabolic relationship between income inequality and GDP per capita across countries ... it is probably very weak and unstable over time [and] longitudinal data ... seem to suggest that there is much freedom in the way distribution in a given country may change over time' (Bourguignon, 1995, p. 47). Deininger and Squire (1998) also find 'virtually no support' for the Kuznets hypothesis. However, there is no uniform agreement on this. Several investigations have found some support for the Kuznets hypothesis (for example, Oswang, 1994; Ali, 1998; Milanovic, 1994; Fishlow, 1995).

Despite its fragile empirical foundations, made even more so by the recent increase in inequality in developed countries, the Kuznets curve has been widely accepted, and sometimes used as an excuse for taking no action on income distribution, on the assumption that the natural laws represented by Kuznets will unavoidably be realized. It may, of course, be that there are 'natural laws' leading to a Kuznets relationship in a laissez-faire development process, but these can be countered by policy which explains the many exceptions to the curve. It is in this spirit that it is worth briefly surveying the explanations that have been put forward for the Kuznets relationship.

First, in the case of a dualistic economy, with a low-productivity, more egalitarian agrarian sector, and a high productivity, less egalitarian industrial sector, development causes a sectoral shift to occur. Consequently, inequality rises, both because of the differences in average incomes between the sectors and because people are shifting from a more to a less egalitarian sector. But when the whole economy becomes part of the modern industrial sector, the inequality arising from the between-sector differences disappears, and when full employment is reached, income inequality within the modern sector also diminishes. This explanation, termed the 'Kuznets process', was developed into a formal model by Anand and Kanbur (1993b).

Another explanation, derived from the Lewis growth model, is that productivity and income growth is confined to the modern sector, where the profit share rises as the sector expands, while in the stagnant traditional sector incomes remain low (and may even fall as population growth occurs), so that between-sector inequality rises, as does within-sector inequality in the modern sector.

A third explanation attributes the process to an initially unequal distribution of assets, which contributes to rising inequality, as those with more assets also accumulate more; but, eventually, the rate of return to capital falls and the unequalizing effect of capital is offset by an equalizing effect arising from labour incomes.

Empirical work on growth (as against levels) of per capita income shows *no* relationship between growth rates and inequality (Ahluwalia, 1976); and recent work confirms this (Bruno *et al.*, 1995; UNCTAD, 1997). Histories of individual countries show that in some countries (such as Brazil) income distribution has worsened over time and in others it has improved (for example in Indonesia in the 1970s). In fact we can observe countries in each of the four possible quadrants representing combinations of growth and changes in income distribution, as shown in Table 10.1.

The conclusion, then, is that growth is 'distribution-neutral', that is, it does not necessarily lead to either a worsening or an improvement in income distribution, and may be consistent with either. Structural factors and policy stances determine countries' experiences.

Table 10.1   Growth and distribution in different economies

	High growth	Low growth
Distribution worsening	Brazil (1960s to early 1990s) Pakistan (1970–85) China (1980s) Thailand (1970s and 1980s) Botswana (1970s)	Post-Soviet Russia; most eastern European countries (1980s) Mexico (1980s) Kenya (1980s) Ethiopia (1980s) Guatemala (1970s and 1980s)
Distribution improving	Indonesia (1973–93) Malaysia (1970–90) Taiwan (1950–80) Republic of Korea (1950–80) Mauritius (1980s and 1990s)	Sri Lanka (1960–70) Cuba (1980s) Colombia (1980s) Morocco (1970–84) Trinidad and Tobago (1970s and 1980s)

Source: Demery *et al.* (1995); Chu *et al.* (1999).

III   HOW INCOME DISTRIBUTION AFFECTS ECONOMIC GROWTH

In the 1950s it was assumed that more unequal income distribution led to higher growth, via higher savings, and possibly incentive effects (for example, Galenson and Leibenstein, 1955).[4] Higher savings propensities associated with more unequal income distribution were variously attributed to the effect of a rising profit share (more, or only, savings out of profits, as assumed by Marx, Kaldor and Lewis) or of more unequal household income distribution (with a Keynesian consumption function). The early choice-of-technique literature (Dobb, 1956–7; Sen, 1968) argued that more capital-intensive techniques should be chosen to maximize surplus and reinvestible funds. From this, the view emerged that countries should grow first and redistribute later. This view was challenged, for example, by Adelman and Morris (1973), who argued that more equal initial income distribution would lead to higher growth.

Recent literature has supported Adelman and Morris; empirical work shows that countries with more equal income distribution have higher growth (Alesina and Perotti, 1994a; Persson and Tabellini, 1994; and many others[5]). Owing to data constraints, most work involves cross-country regressions. There are especially severe data problems in the area of income distribution, as under-declaration of income is common for obvious reasons.[6] Here too the robustness of the findings has been questioned, both by Fishlow (1995), who finds no statistically significant evidence of a relationship between growth and equality, when a dummy variable is introduced for Latin America, and by Forbes (2000), who controls for time-invariant country-specific effects and finds that when this is done more inequality is associated with higher growth subsequently. But investigations over time in developed countries have confirmed the relationship between greater equality and higher growth (for example, Panizza, 1999, who investigated growth performance in states in the United States from 1920). The large number of studies finding some relationship between more equality and higher growth gives some confidence in the existence of a positive relationship between equality and economic growth.

A variety of mechanisms have been suggested to explain the positive relationship between income distribution and economic growth. One type of mechanism relates to the political economy of more or less equal societies, suggesting that high inequality translates into growth-impeding factors as a result of political developments. For example:

1. It is argued that higher inequality leads to more political instability, more uncertainty, less investment and lower growth (Alesina and Perotti, 1994a; Bertola, 1993; Perotti, 1993; Persson and Tabellini, 1994).
2. It is suggested that higher inequality leads to populist redistributive tax policies, more disincentive effects and lower growth (Alesina and Rodrik, 1994; Persson and Tabellini, 1994).
3. Higher inequality gives a disproportionate influence to rich groups which lobby for preferential tax treatment, leading to overinvestment in certain areas and reducing growth (Bruno *et al.*, 1995).

Other explanations relate to the economic effects of higher equality/inequality:

4. Higher equality of land ownership leads to more labour input, and higher land productivity (for example, Lipton, 1993). There is abundant evidence that more equal land distribution is associated with higher agricultural productivity as well as more equally distributed rural incomes, and in rural economies this accounts for a significant proportion of total incomes.
5. Higher equality reduces poverty, and leads to more human development (nutrition, education and health), with a more productive workforce, more innovation and so on. (Birdsall *et al.*, 1995; Ranis *et al.*, 2000).
6. Higher equality in asset distribution leads to a more even access to credit and information, and more opportunities for the poor to make productive investments (Galor and Zeria, 1993; Deininger and Squire, 1998).
7. Higher equality leads to larger domestic markets, greater exploitation of economies of scale and hence more industrialization and growth (Murphy *et al.*, 1989).
8. Higher inequality, on the other hand, leads to higher fertility, since those who are poor and less educated have larger families, and this in turn reduces growth (Benabou, 1996; Khoo and Dennis, 1999; Bloom *et al.*, 1998).

These are all hypotheses, none of which have been thoroughly tested. The political economy explanations mostly rest on an assumption about the behaviour of the 'median voter', which is not relevant in non-democratic societies. Moreover, the statistical evidence supporting the positive relationship between more equality and higher growth appears to apply to non-democratic countries, not democratic ones, according to Deininger and Squire (1998). In addition, the model assumes that more inequality leads to higher government spending, when in fact the reverse appears to be true (Benabou, 1996). The 'human development' explanation, that is, that more equality leads to more education, better nutrition and health, and hence more productive people (see 5. above) is much better supported. There is considerable evidence that a more equal income distribution leads to a greater spread and level of education, as well as improved health and nutrition, and that this in turn brings about higher growth (Birdsall and Sabot, 1994; Ranis *et al.*, 2000). However, this does not seem to be the whole story, as empirical work has found that greater equality has an independent positive impact on growth, in addition to the impact via education levels (Birdsall and Sabot, 1994; Bourguignon, 1995).

Whatever the mechanisms – still subject to investigation – there is broad agreement on the empirical evidence, showing that more equality is associated with higher economic growth. Moreover, the order of magnitude of the effect is quite high. For example, Bourguignon estimates that a change of one standard deviation in inequality is responsible for half a percentage point of additional growth.

Taking the findings of sections II and III together would seem to point to a fairly optimistic conclusion, namely, that more egalitarian income distribution is better for growth, and that cross-country evidence shows that growth neither increases nor decreases inequality in any systematic way. Since more equal income distribution is desirable as an intrinsic part of the development agenda, as a mechanism for reducing poverty and enhancing human development, *and* as instrumental to growth, the agenda should be to identify which *types* of growth are more likely to improve income distribution and which policies would help bring about egalitarian patterns of growth.

IV   EGALITARIAN PATTERNS OF GROWTH

The distribution of income is the outcome of complex economic processes. Individuals' incomes depend on their incomes from assets and from their own current activities. Income from assets is a function of asset ownership and the rate of return on assets; and income from current activities depends, similarly, on quantity of, and returns to, employment (or self-employment), the returns to employment normally being a function of the individual's level of education and skills. For an economy as a whole, income distribution then depends on asset distribution, distribution of human capital, and returns on each. It is thus not surprising that we observe a large range of income distribution across countries: contrast, for example, Brazil, where 48 per cent of the income goes to the top 10 per cent of the population, and just 0.8 per cent of total income goes to the bottom 10 per cent, with India, where 25 per cent of the income goes to the top 10 per cent of the population, and 4.1 per cent to the bottom 10 per cent. This way of looking at income distribution indicates one rather obvious point: a large part of any particular distribution is determined by factors inherited from the past – in particular, the stock and distribution of capital (monetary, physical and human). Hence, unless there is very radical action involving asset redistribution (as was taken in Taiwan; and the Republic of Korea in the 1950s) or the destruction or flight of human capital (as in Cambodia), we should not expect large changes in income distribution in shortish periods of time.

Statistical investigation shows the importance of asset distribution. For example, education has been estimated to account for 10–20 per cent of observed inequality (Fishlow, 1995); Bourguignon and Morrisson estimate that inequality in land distribution accounts for 17 per cent of income inequality; they also show that the abundance of mineral resources in a country is associated with higher inequality (Bourguignon and Morrisson, 1990).

Aside from asset redistribution, changes in income distribution depend on changes in the amount and returns to current activities, that is to say, employment of different types of labour, and returns to that employment. The poor are invariably among those with low earnings. Some work for long hours but at very low rates of remuneration, and others have little or no employment. Some combination of low hours of work and low remuneration is normally found in the agriculture sector, in the informal urban economy and among some unskilled jobs in the formal sector. From this perspective, growth strategies likely to improve the earnings of the poor, and hence improve income distribution, include those which raise returns to agriculture, increase the availability of unskilled work and extend basic education.

This analysis and cross-country comparisons suggest the following factors are likely to lead to more egalitarian growth:

- agrarian-focused strategies, especially those also favouring rural industrialization;
- employment-intensive strategies (export-led, and/or supported by labour-intensive employment schemes);
- high levels of and widespread education;
- asset redistribution. This is important, not only for the immediate impact on income from assets, but also because it influences the rest of the development strategy in a variety of ways; for example, more equality leads to more widely spread education, and it may lead to mass markets for labour-intensive consumer goods rather than élite goods. The consequent political economy tends to favour more pro-poor economic decisions;
- government policies towards structuring the market, so that education, training and asset accumulation are directed towards deprived groups.

Examples of each of these approaches are presented briefly below.

Agrarian-focused Strategies

Considering that in the poorest countries a majority of the population works in agriculture, that the rural sector is typically poorer than the urban one, and that the percentage of the labour force in agriculture generally exceeds the share of agriculture in GDP, increasing the productivity of the rural sector should clearly promote more equitable growth. Indeed, Lipton saw 'urban bias' as the major source of poverty in developing countries (Lipton, 1977).

A wide range of strategies would tend to promote agrarian-focused growth. These include reducing macroeconomic biases against agriculture, which almost always arise as countries attempt to promote industrialization; introducing land reform; improving access to extension services, market information and input and output markets for smallholders; developing rural infrastructure; and promoting agricultural diversification and the non-farm rural sector (for example, through agro-processing, which has forward and backward linkages, and can employ those with little or no land).

One study estimated that in Pakistan, in the absence of government price interventions, farm incomes from the five major crops would have been 40 per cent higher over the 1983–87 period (Dorosh and Valdes, 1990). The effect of the price interventions for the five major crops translated into a transfer out of agriculture of 25 per cent of GDP in the 1978–87 period. In contrast, Taiwan had relatively moderate macro bias against agriculture, strong and egalitarian agricultural growth and high levels of rural industrialization (Burmeister *et al.*, 1999).

Most countries that have done well in agriculture have taxed the sector moderately and provided strong support for it. For example, in Malaysia, in the 1970s, total commodity taxation was relatively low at 19 per cent of value of output, while government spending in direct support of agriculture was 10 per cent of the sector's value added. Malaysia had an agricultural growth rate of 5 per cent per year. By contrast, in the same decade, Ghana taxed agricultural commodities at over 60 per cent and spent only 3 per cent of value added on support; its farm output fell by more than 1 per cent per year. Similarly, Latin America taxed agriculture much more heavily than East Asia (directly and via an overvalued exchange rate) and the growth in agricultural output and productivity was substantially lower (Schiff and Valdes, 1992).

Rural industrialization also tends to improve income distribution. This is more likely to be dynamic where agricultural output is rising fast, so that there are strong agriculture/non-agriculture linkages; such linkages can also be promoted by government support for rural infrastructure and credit, and are likely to be stronger where land distribution is more egalitarian (Ranis and Stewart, 1987). Decomposition of the factors accounting for the increase in equality in Taiwan Province of China over the 1960s has shown that an important element was rising household incomes from non-agricultural sources (Fei *et al.*, 1979).

A study in Bangladesh showed the strong impact of investment in rural infrastructure on rural incomes. A comparison between villages which had benefited from greater provision of infrastructure and those that had not found a one-third increase in average household incomes among the beneficiary villages. Crop income grew by 24 per cent, wage income by 92 per cent, and livestock/fishery income by 78 per cent, all benefiting the poor. Non-farm businesses increased by 17 per cent, which benefited both the non-poor and the poor via improved non-farm employment opportunities (World Bank, 1990).

Employment-intensive Strategies

Quite sharp differences can be observed in the employment intensity of output increases. For example, the employment elasticity with respect to output growth was estimated at *plus* 0.5 in East and Southeast Asia (1971–92), compared with *minus* 0.5 in Latin America. Within Asia, it was higher in some places (+0.7 in Indonesia), and lower elsewhere (for the 1980s, +0.3 in India, negative in the Philippines).[7] In general, more rapid growth in employment is likely to be associated with more egalitarian income distribution.

These differences are due partly to the output mix between and within sectors, and partly to choice of technique. Rapid expansion of labour-intensive exports, observed in many Asian countries, contributes to fast growth in employment. Policies which support this, and also favour more labour-intensive techniques (for example, by not subsidizing capital and by securing more credit for small enterprises) promote employment intensity (Stewart, 1987). Trade liberalization may increase labour-intensive exports in countries with abundant labour, but only if infrastructure is adequate and the labour has at least minimal education (Wood, 1994). In economies where the dominant export is minerals or plantation agricultural crops, trade liberalization can worsen income distribution.

Employment schemes can also contribute: for example, the Maharashtra Employment Scheme and the very extensive employment schemes in Chile in the early 1980s, and in Bangladesh in the 1970s.

Education

According to Thompson (1998), 'Considering the high payoff from investment in human capital, the unequal distribution of education opportunities is often a more important determinant of the skewed income distribution than is the skewed access to land.' Higher (primary and secondary) school enrolment rates tend to be associated with lower inequality. On the basis of cross-country analysis, Bourguignon and Morrisson estimate that a 1 per cent increase in the share of the labour force having at least secondary education increases the share of income received by the bottom 40 per cent by 6 per cent, and that received by the bottom 60 per cent by 15 per cent (Bourguignon and Morrisson, 1990). One more recent study (Behrman, 1993) finds that those with no schooling have a 56 per cent probability of being among the poorest 20 per cent, while those with university training have only a 4 per cent chance. In Brazil, an average 25-year-old in the top decile has an average of 11 years of education, while one in the bottom decile has just two years of education (IADB, 1999).

A study of Latin America in the 1980s found that about a quarter of the inequality among workers' incomes was due to differences in educational levels

(Psacharopoulos *et al.*, 1996). Education benefits the rural as well as the urban population: educated farmers are more likely to adopt new technologies and obtain higher returns on land (shown by studies in Malaysia, the Republic of Korea and Thailand). Chou and Lau (1987) show that in Thailand one additional year of schooling adds about 2.5 per cent to farm output. Even in the informal sector, there seem to be high returns to education. Returns were estimated to be as high as 33 per cent for women self-employed in the retail textile sector in Peru, and 14 per cent for post-primary educated men in the service sector (World Bank, 1990).

Educational access and expenditure is often distributed very unevenly. Adult literacy varies from over 80 per cent in East Asia to as little as 13 per cent in Niger, and only 36 per cent in Pakistan. Zambia spent nearly a quarter of its educational budget on tertiary education, with an estimated enrolment rate of 2 per cent in 1980, while Bangladesh spent 8 per cent with an enrolment rate of 3 per cent, and the Republic of Korea also spent 8 per cent, but with a much greater enrolment rate of 48 per cent.

Increasing educational access improves both equity and efficiency, and can make other reforms more effective, such as those aimed at promoting agricultural growth or labour-intensive exports.

Asset Redistribution

A more egalitarian asset distribution not only contributes to more equality in income distribution directly, but also contributes indirectly by increasing the employment intensity of output in both agriculture and non-agriculture, and strengthening domestic linkages (that is, the demands that agriculture generates for non-agriculture, and the demands that the formal sector generates for the products of the informal sector (Ranis and Stewart, 1987, 1993, 1999)). More equal distribution of land also raises output; Deininger and Squire (1997) show that a difference of one standard deviation in the initial Gini coefficient for land is associated with income gains of 0.5 per cent for the population as a whole, with gains of 1 per cent for the poorest 20 per cent and 0.9 per cent for the poorest 40 per cent.

A comparison between Vietnam and Bangladesh provides an illustration: in Vietnam, land distribution is much more egalitarian and there is much less landlessness; Vietnam has experienced an agricultural growth rate of 5 per cent per annum, compared with a rate of 2 per cent in Bangladesh over the past decade (Ahmed and Goletti, 1998).

Land reform has been very effective in some economies (for example, Taiwan Province of China and the Republic of Korea, and also Egypt in the 1960s), but political obstacles are often severe. In quite a number of countries, even though reforms have been only partially implemented, substantial land redistribution has been achieved (Powelson, 1984; Lipton, 1993). Moreover, even the more limited reforms generate some improvements in rural income distribution (El-Ghonemy, 1990; Besley and Burgess, 1998). There is a strong case for making land reform a high priority in strategies to improve equity and growth.

With industrialization, land distribution is becoming of lesser aggregate significance, while the distribution of industrial and financial assets is of growing importance. The public ownership of such assets previously represented a way of moderating asset inequality, but this is no longer regarded as a policy option. In highly unequal societies, as in South Africa, more direct policies to tackle asset inequalities are needed. Wealth and inheritance taxation is one option.

The distribution of credit influences accumulation and the distribution of assets. In general, formal-sector credit tends to be biased against the low-income groups because of their lack of collateral, while informal sources are extremely expensive. Surveys of the informal sector generally report that less than 1 per cent have access to formal-sector credit (see, for example, surveys quoted in IADB, 1999; Anderson, 1982; Stewart *et al.*, 1990). The self-employed and employees of micro enterprises are generally among the lower-income groups; for example, in Latin America it is estimated that these enterprises account for 30–40 per cent of low-income earners. New lending mechanisms, such as the group lending procedures of the Grameen Bank, can help to redirect credit to low-income groups.

Structuring the Market

This describes a set of policies directed towards ensuring that particular deprived groups get favoured access to assets, including education, in a market economy. A range of policies can be used to this effect; for example, employment regulations that require enterprises to employ a certain proportion of a target group, such as those introduced as part of the Africanization policies of many newly independent African states. Restrictions can also be directed towards educational institutions (as in the positive discrimination policies in the United States), towards banks, in the distribution of government expenditure, and so on.

The Malaysian New Economic Policy is an example of comprehensive policies to structure the market. In Malaysia in 1970, the majority population (the Malays or Bumiputra) were economically the most disadvantaged section, with an average household income 40 per cent less than that of the ethnic Chinese. A New Economic Policy (NEP) was introduced, designed to improve the economic position of the Malays. Targets were defined: 95 per cent of new lands were to be settled on Malays; at least 30 per cent of the equity of all public companies was to be owned by Malays; educational quotas in public institutions were specified in line with population shares; credit policies favoured Malays, both through credit allocations and more favourable interest rates.

The policy was a success from many perspectives. The employment share of Malays in manufacturing rose from 26 per cent to 41 per cent between 1967 and 1987, with their share in professional and technical employment rising from 47 per cent to 56 per cent; the share of ownership in public companies rose from 4.3 per cent in 1971 to 19.4 per cent in 1988; their proportion of university enrolment rose from 12 per cent in 1969 to 61.8 per cent in 1988. The income gap between Malays and other groups was almost eliminated. The success of the structured market in Malaysia in meeting its own objectives (narrowing gaps between Malays and others) was achieved without undermining growth, while income distribution improved. Malaysia's growth rate over the period was one of the fastest in the world, at 6.3 per cent per annum during the period 1960–89, while there was a marked improvement in income distribution, with the share of income of the bottom 40 per cent rising from 11 per cent in 1970 to 14 per cent in 1987, and the share of the top 10 per cent falling from 41 per cent to 35 per cent over the same period.

To some extent these strategies for achieving more egalitarian growth are complements, and to some extent, substitutes. Thus extending education will make land reform more effective, but it can also contribute to greater equality in the absence of land reform. A structured market generally would improve income distribution so long as the target groups for improved access are relatively deprived, but it would probably also contribute to greater efficiency only if accompanied by supportive policies towards education and employment. The appropriate strategy depends partly on the initial conditions in the country concerned, including resource availability, distribution of assets and particular weaknesses. For example, in resource-rich areas, labour-intensive strategies may not be feasible, and therefore emphasis would need to be placed on investment in human resources, innovation and upgrading technology, so as to improve international competitiveness and generate jobs in the export sector. This is the strategy advocated for Latin America by ECLAC in its integrated approach towards improving social equity through changing production patterns (ECLAC, 1992). However, it seems unlikely that this strategy alone would markedly improve income distribution without also tackling the gross inequalities in assets prevalent in many countries in the region.

The political feasibility of the alternative approaches, their economic desirability and their probable impact on income distribution and development are likely to vary according to the prevailing conditions, so any policy suggestions need to be country specific. From this perspective it is instructive to go back to the set of countries (shown in Table 10.1) that combined growth with improved income distribution, and identify the policy mix each adopted.

The adoption of the combinations of strategies shown in Table 10.2 explains why these countries succeeded in achieving egalitarian growth. But one needs also to analyse the underlying political economy to understand why the

*Table 10.2   Policies adopted by economies combining growth and improved
            income distribution*

Countries combining growth and improved income distribution	Prime features of policy mix	Growth rate, GNP per capita, 1975–95	Gini coefficient, recent date
Taiwan Province of China	Land reform; agricultural focus; rural industrialization; labour-intensive exports; education	6.7	0.29
Republic of Korea	Land reform; education; labour-intensive exports	7.0	0.35
Indonesia	Labour-intensive exports; agricultural growth	5.1	0.32
Malaysia	Structured market; education; labour-intensive exports	4.4	0.48
Mauritius	Education; labour-intensive exports	4.2	0.37

Source: UNDP (1999), World Bank, *World Development Indicators 1997*; Chu *et al.* (1999).

governments of these countries chose to follow such strategies, while others
did not. Our knowledge in this area is still rather limited, but a superficial
analysis of the countries in question provides a few pointers: the Republic of
Korea and Taiwan both undertook effective land reform to counter the perceived
threats from the Democratic People's Republic of Korea and mainland China,
respectively. For the same reason, both were anxious to promote economic
growth, and saw investment in human resources as their opportunity, since they
lacked natural resources. Both were strongly influenced by the United States
because of their history and geopolitical position, and were encouraged to switch
from import substitution to an outward orientation at an early stage. Malaysia's
strategy was more home-grown. It was inspired by the political imperative of
improving the relative position of the majority Malays, and of sustaining
economic growth to compete with its close neighbour, Singapore. The
Indonesian government was also partly motivated by the desire to promote local
entrepreneurs relative to the Chinese, and partly by the objective of cementing
the fissiparous tendencies by spreading education and health services throughout
the country. The government of Mauritius believed it was imperative to replace

its dominant export, sugar, which had poor prospects, and therefore promoted education and the immigration of textiles entrepreneurs from Hong Kong and from elsewhere, in order to achieve this.

V   RECENT TRENDS IN INCOME DISTRIBUTION

Earlier sections have shown the desirability of more equal income distribution, and also suggested ways of achieving this by adopting particular growth strategies, which would be especially effective when combined with asset redistribution or structured markets. The political realism of these strategies is shown by the large number of examples where they (or elements of them) have been put into effect. But this rather optimistic conclusion is countered by recent trends in income distribution.

While the direction of changes has been mixed, in the majority of countries inequality rose in the 1980s and 1990s: among developed countries, inequality rose in fifteen and fell in only one country during this period; among countries in transition, inequality rose sharply in every country; in Latin America it rose in eight out of thirteen countries, falling in just three; and in Asia it rose in seven out of ten cases. Only in Africa, where the data are incomplete, did the falls in inequality match the rises (see Table 10.3), and here it has been suggested that this may have been a matter of 'levelling down' (for example, in the Côte d'Ivoire; see UNCTAD, 1997). This rather uniform movement towards greater inequality is perfectly consistent with the finding that the rate of growth does not affect income distribution: the rises in inequality in recent years have affected high- and low-growth countries equally.

Table 10.3   Changing income distribution, 1980s to 1990s

	No. of countries with rising inequality	No. of countries with falling inequality	No. of countries with no change in distribution
OECD	15	1	2
Eastern Europe and CIS	11	0	0
Latin America	8	3	2
Asia	7	3	0
Africa	3	3	1

Source: UNDP (1999), Stewart and Berry (1999), Morley (1995).

It is essential to explore why inequality has been rising, if we are to determine whether a pro-equality agenda is possible in the current world situation, and how. The context in which the rise in inequality occurred was one of increased marketization, liberalization and globalization, and rapid information-intensive technological change, all of which affected most countries in the world in one way or another. It seems likely that each of these broad changes contributed to the rising inequality. Clearly, since we are dealing with a mass of heterogeneous countries, different specific reasons applied in different situations.

Deconstruction of the change in income distribution shows that the increased inequality was generally due, in part, to increased inequality in wage and salary earnings and, in part, to a rise in the profit share and a fall in the wage share, increasing the proportion of income arising from the ownership of assets, which is invariably distributed more unequally than work income. In the OECD countries, earnings inequality worsened in most countries (Gottschalk and Smeeding, 1997). This also occurred in most transition countries, but here the fall in wage share played a more important role (Cornia, 1996). A study of changing wage dispersion from the late 1970s to the late 1980s showed a rise in the majority of developing countries, in eight out of nine countries in Latin America, three out of five in Africa and six out of ten in Asia (van der Hoeven, 1999; see also Berry, 1997; Robbins, 1995, 1996; Láchler, 1997). Specific reasons put forward to explain rising inequality include the following.

Freer International Trade

Following the Stolper–Samuelson theorem, one might expect inequality to *decrease* with trade liberalization in labour-surplus developing economies, as employment and the share of wages rise because of the expansion of exports of labour-intensive manufactures. Indeed, this seems to have been a characteristic of the countries that combined growth with improved equity over the longer period, as just noted. In resource-rich areas, however, tradables are not labour-intensive; moreover, in import-substituting economies, import liberalization can undermine the wage-earning class (Taylor and Krugman, 1978; Berry, 1997; Roemer and Guherty, 1997). For example, studies in Chile and Mexico found that openness increased the wage gap between skilled and unskilled labour (Beyer *et al.*, 1999; Ghiara, 1999). In some primary producing areas (African economies largely), trade liberalization may reduce the income share of urban workers and may raise incomes of peasant farmers, who generally have lower incomes than urban workers. But rising differentiation within rural areas can offset this income-equalizing effect.

A number of studies have shown that trade liberalization has not benefited unskilled labour in developing countries in any straightforward way (Davis, 1996). Earnings dispersion has tended to increase with more trade liberalization; empirical work has shown that land- and capital-intensive countries have a less equal income distribution, while skill-intensive countries have more equal income distribution (Wood, 1995; Freeman and Katz, 1995; Spilimbergo *et al.*, 1999).

Freer international trade might be expected to worsen income distribution in labour-scarce countries (that is, the developed countries), where production of labour-intensive goods is undermined by competition from cheap labour in developing countries. This does seem to explain some of the deterioration in income distribution in developed countries, but the extent is open to debate; for example, Wood (1994) attributes one-third to one-half of the deterioration to this, and others, such as Learner (1995), point to technology change as a major factor.

Technology Change

The rapid pace of technology change has raised the demand for skilled labour, leading to rising income differentials among workers in both developed and developing countries (Learner, 1995; Láchler, 1997; Robbins, 1995,1996; Berman *et al.*, 1997). The effect is likely to be particularly acute in developed countries which specialize in technology-intensive goods and services. But it seems also to be felt by intermediate-stage economies which have moved on from unskilled labour-intensive products (for example, Mexico, Taiwan). Evidence from Bangladesh shows that new varieties of seed contributed to a rise in rural inequality (Rahman, 1999).

The Abolition or Erosion of the Minimum Wage

This also seems to be an element increasing inequality in some countries. The question of the impact of minimum wages on income distribution and poverty is a controversial one: neoclassical theory suggests a rise in the minimum wage should reduce employment, and this could offset the impact of any rise on poverty. But Keynesian (and other) accounts of the determination of employment challenge this conclusion. A study of changes in inequality in Latin America in the 1980s found that the real minimum wage fell in almost every case where inequality worsened and rose in the three cases where inequality lessened. They concluded that 'real minimum wages may have an equalizing effect on the income distribution' (World Bank, 1993, p. 26).[8] The rise in wage inequality in the United States has also largely been explained by the decrease in the minimum wage (Teulings, 1998; DiNardo *et al.*, 1996). Lustig and McCleod (1996) find that higher minimum wages are associated with lower poverty in developing countries, though they also lead to higher unemployment. Some evidence suggests higher minimum wages have a negative impact on employment (for example, Neumark and Wascher, 1991; Rama, 1996; Abowd *et al.*, 1999); some suggest they lead to a switch from the formal sector to informal employment (Jones, 1998); while other studies show that a rise in minimum wages is associated with no change or even a *rise* in employment (for example, Card *et al.*, 1994; Dickens *et al.*, 1994; Card and Krueger, 1994). While, evidently, many firms disobey minimum wage regulations – especially in developing countries – in general, the coincidence of eroding minimum wages with worsening wage dispersion in numerous countries supports the view that minimum wages can improve income distribution. However, clearly the level of the minimum wage needs to be calculated carefully in line with the economic conditions of the country.[9]

Transition from Communism to Capitalism

Rising inequality in Eastern Europe and the former Soviet Union has been 'one of the biggest and fastest increases ever recorded', according to Milonavic (1998), with an average increase in the Gini coefficient of between 0.25 and 0.28 to between 0.35 and 0.38 in less than ten years. This is explained by a peeling away of the factors which previously assured a high degree of equality, including privatization of assets, reduced restrictions on earnings differentials and a rising share of income from self-employment (including the black market) (Milanovic, 1998; Cornia, 1996).

Changing Functional Income Distribution

The functional income distribution (that is, the shares of factors of production) is an important determinant of household distribution, since household incomes depend on the returns on the various assets they possess (including their labour), as well as their quantity. Since the upper income groups own most financial and physical assets, they are likely to gain relatively when the share of profits rises and the share of wage income falls. For example, in Brazil, an extreme example of an unequal society, the lowest decile of households receives 0.8 per cent of non-labour income, compared with 47.2 per cent for the top decile (IADB, 1999). The rather limited evidence suggests that the share of wages fell, and that of profits rose, in the majority of countries over this period. In developed countries, the profit share in manufacturing rose in ten out of twelve countries from 1979 to 1989, the exceptions being Norway and Japan, and the biggest rises in profits took place in Australia, Belgium, Sweden and the United Kingdom (Glyn, 1992). Comparisons between the periods 1985–92 and 1975–80 show that among developing countries the share of wages in manufacturing fell in five Latin American countries and rose in three, with the biggest falls being in Mexico, Colombia and Venezuela; among Asian economies, it fell in four and rose in six, with big falls in Pakistan and Sri Lanka; and in Africa and the Mediterranean it fell in seven and rose in one, with the largest falls in

Ghana and Turkey (UNCTAD, 1997). There was thus a broad coincidence between changes in the functional distribution and changes in the household income distribution, suggesting that the former is partly responsible for the latter. One then needs to explain why the functional distribution has changed in this way. It is not possible to do this here in any depth, but the process of globalization and liberalization, and possibly the new technologies creating Schumpeterian profits, seem likely factors.

Globalization

Globalization in general can be expected to increase returns to capital, especially in the context of a rapid reduction in restrictions on capital movements while restrictions on the movements of unskilled labour are maintained. In developed countries, capital-intensive processes gain through trade specialization, and capital owners gain by their ability to export capital; in capital-importing countries, liberalization alone should decrease returns to capital, as the 'supply' of capital rises relative to labour, but this maybe offset by privatization, reduced regulation and so on, all of which tend to raise the gross returns to capital, as well as changes in the tax system favouring capital, which tend to raise the net returns. Globalization has decreased the bargaining power of labour and increased the power of capital, because capital (and goods) can move around the world relatively freely, while there are severe restrictions on the movement of labour, especially unskilled labour. Consequently, labour is discouraged from bargaining in case it frightens off capital and thus reduces employment. This may explain why there has been a worldwide decline in Trade Union membership (van der Hoeven, 1999).

VI WIDENING THE DIMENSIONS OF INEQUALITY: IMPLICATIONS

At the beginning of the chapter we pointed to the need to consider a broader set of indicators than simply pre-tax private household income, to which most of the previous discussion was related. A first requirement is to look at intra-household income distribution; secondly, post-tax income distribution; thirdly, the impact of state transfers (pensions and so on); fourthly, to include social income (that is, publicly provided goods and services), which is an extremely important component of human well-being. Finally, it would be desirable to examine the distribution of more direct measures of well-being, such as health, nutrition and even happiness. This chapter does not go far in these directions, but points to some ways in which extending the indicators may alter the conclusions.

Intra-household Income Distribution

Uneven distribution of income within the household (by gender and age) greatly increases overall inequality among individuals; for example, one study suggests that allowing for intra-household income distribution increases income inequality by 30–40 per cent (Haddad and Kanbur, 1990). (However, because the needs of people of different gender and age differ, it is difficult to determine what an equal distribution would look like.) Policies to counter inequality should include policies directed at correcting household inequality, for example, by improving female educational and earning opportunities.

Post-tax Income Distribution

Numerous studies of the progressivity, or otherwise, of tax systems have come to differing conclusions, partly because of differences in methodology. On balance, there appears to be mild progressiveness in many tax systems, with very few cases in which post-tax income distribution is more unequal than pre-tax income. For example, Shah and Whalley (1990, 1991), surveying seven tax incidence studies in developing countries, showed that mostly the tax systems were mildly progressive. A more recent survey of studies in developing countries found that thirteen out of thirty-six cases were progressive, seven were proportional and seven were regressive, with income tax being almost invariably progressive (Chu *et al.*, 1999). But it seems that on balance the progressiveness of tax systems has been falling, with a declining proportion of income tax (Chu *et al.*, 1999; Atkinson, 1999) and there has been a tendency for rates of individual and corporation income tax to decline. However, some developing countries, including Jamaica, Turkey and Indonesia, managed to reduce inequality significantly through the tax system (Chu *et al.*, 1999).

State Transfers

These include pensions and other state benefits, such as unemployment or disability benefits, which, in principle, can be substantial. Transfers are large and generally redistributive in many developed countries. But they are typically small, with less clear distributional implications, in developing countries because benefits are often largely confined to the relatively privileged formal sector workers. In Latin America, such systems have been shown to be regressive in some cases (Mesa-Largo, 1983). However, when appropriately designed, they can be highly redistributive (for example, means-tested widows' pensions and disability pensions introduced in Tamil Nadu: see Guhan, 1992; Drèze and Chen, 1995; Drèze and Sen, 1991).

Social Income

Most government expenditure is progressive compared with pre-tax incomes.[10] Despite the fact that a substantial proportion of benefits from social expenditure invariably goes to upper-income groups, expenditure on health and education is almost always progressive (that is, more equally distributed than pre-tax incomes): thirty-one out of 55 studies show that government education expenditure is progressive, and thirty out of thirty-eight studies show health expenditure is progressive. But there is considerable diversity among countries. For example, in Guinea the bottom fifth of households receives 5 per cent of school expenditure and the top fifth receives 44 per cent, while in Costa Rica, the bottom fifth receives 18 per cent and the top fifth 20 per cent; the poorest fifth of the population receives 4 per cent of total health expenditures in Guinea, compared with 30 per cent in Costa Rica (Castro-Leal *et al.*, quoted in Mehrotra *et al.*, 1999). As is well known, expenditure on primary education is most progressive and expenditure on tertiary education is often regressive. For the most part, the limited evidence shows some improvement in the progressivity of the distribution of public expenditure over time.

Taking the evidence on tax and government expenditure incidence together, since taxation is normally either progressive or neutral and expenditure is normally progressive, we can conclude that higher taxation and expenditure can generally be expected to improve the distribution of welfare. This is an important conclusion and counters the widespread image that elites monopolize government expenditures, and that, therefore, less government taxation and expenditure is more progressive than more. It follows that downward pressure on government taxation and expenditure, associated with globalization and the liberalizing agenda, is likely to worsen post-tax, post-benefit income distribution.[11]

The Distribution of Non-monetary Indicators of Well-being

Although there has been considerable progress in widening the definition and measure of progress beyond monetary income at a national level, notably with the UNDP Human Development Index, much less attention has been paid to the *distribution* of non-monetary aspects of well-being. Piecemeal evidence shows considerable inequalities in health and education. For example, it has been shown that the poorest electoral wards in northern England had death rates four times as high as the richest ones, while a study of civil servants in the United Kingdom found that death rates were three times as high among the lowest grades compared with the highest grades (Wilkinson, 1996). In the United States, age-adjusted mortality rates were found to be over 80 per 10 000 in the bottom decile of the white male population, compared with under 40 in the top decile (Davey *et al.*, 1996). In Brazil, infant mortality rates range from 90 per

1000 to 12 per 1000 in different areas of the same city. Similar differences are found for schooling, with, for example, nearly 60 per cent of the bottom quintile never having attended school in Nepal, compared with 13 per cent of the top quintile. In Brazil, all the top 30 per cent of the income distribution have attended school, while a fifth of the bottom 10 per cent have never attended school. Although the extent of inequalities in non-monetary indicators tends to be smaller than monetary income dispersion, their importance for well-being, as well as a precondition of improving future incomes, is likely to be greater.

There is strong two-way causation between the distribution of monetary income and the distribution of human development achievements. Societies with more unequal income distribution have higher death rates than those with similar incomes and more equal distribution. Indeed, among developed countries it is the equality of income distribution, not income levels, which is associated with longevity (Wilkinson, 1996). A positive relationship between income equality and longevity has also been found in developing countries (Flegg, 1982). Indeed, some research shows that infant mortality rates increase with rising incomes if the level of income among the lowest fifth of the population is kept constant (Waldmann, 1992). *Inequality* as such worsens health. Conversely, more inequality in health and education is likely to lead to a more unequal income distribution in monetary incomes.

VII   HORIZONTAL INEQUALITY: THE NEGLECTED DIMENSION

So far we have considered only *vertical* inequality, that is, the inequality among individuals or households in a society. *Horizontal inequality,* or inequality among groups, is also of huge importance to societal well-being. Groups maybe defined culturally and/or geographically, for example, by ethnicity, race, religion or location. The extent of inequality among such groups is a key determinant of social cohesion. There are many relevant aspects of such inequality, including inequality in income, assets, employment, access to social income and resources.

Horizontal inequalities are a major factor contributing to social instability and ultimately civil war. A graphic example was the Rwanda situation, where the Belgian colonialists had divided Tutsi and Hutu and given them unequal access to most types of resources. Similar horizontal inequalities are to be found in many other conflict-prone places, such as between Protestants and Catholics in Northern Ireland, Tamils and Singhalese in Sri Lanka and Muslims and Christians in Serbia. Horizontal inequalities are more likely to lead to conflict where they occur systematically along a number of dimensions, and where they are growing (see Stewart, 2000). For economies vulnerable to conflict (which includes most low-income economies), monitoring and addressing horizontal inequalities is essential to prevent violent group conflict. Yet, in practice, horizontal inequality is rarely identified or measured systematically. It should be noted that there can be a high degree of vertical inequality without substantial horizontal inequality if within a group inequality is high; however, generally, if a society has high horizontal inequality, vertical inequality is likely to be substantial. Given the heavy human costs of conflict, as well as the economic costs, tackling horizontal inequalities maybe at least as important as reducing vertical inequality.

VIII   GLOBAL INCOME DISTRIBUTION

So far we have focused entirely on income distribution within countries, which is of interest to national policy makers, and which determines the cohesion of a particular society. Global income distribution is of relevance to international policymakers concerned with matters such as aid distribution, the terms of trade and debt relief. As other chapters in this volume focus on this area (for example, see the contributions of Maizels and Nayyar), here we review developments briefly for the sake of getting a more complete picture.

World income distribution is substantially more unequal than that of particular countries, since it encompasses the big differences in income between countries as well as within them. According to an UNCTAD estimate, the top 20 per cent of the world population received 83 per cent of world income in 1990, and the world Gini coefficient was 0.74 (UNCTAD, 1997). Trends in the distribution of world income depend on the evolution of both inter-country income differences (that is, between-country inequality) and the distribution of income within countries. Most analyses suggest that inter-country income differences are the main contributor to the inequality which exists among the people of the world (Berry *et al.*, 1991), while changes in world distribution are likely to be much more influenced by changes in inter-country income gaps than by changes in intra-country inequality, because the former are so large and because they appear to change more quickly than do the intra-country gaps.

Berry, Bourguignon and Morrisson concluded that there was little change in the standard indicators of income inequality over the period 1950–77. An important aspect of the evolution of world distribution over this period was the fast growth of the largest low-income country, China. Estimates of distribution of income within the non-socialist world showed increases in inequality, with the bottom deciles losing together with the middle ones. In the period since 1980, the evidence suggests worsening world inequality with inter-country differences increasing. According to UNDP (1999), while thirty-three countries had growth rates in GNP per capita of over 3 per cent per annum for 1980–97,

59 countries had negative growth. For the decade of the 1980s, UNCTAD estimates that the world Gini coefficient rose from 0.68 in 1980 to 0.74 in 1990. This in fact underestimates the level and change in inequality because it includes only changes in distribution between countries, and does not include estimates of the increasing within-country inequality, documented above. However, a study using household data for 91 countries, adjusting for purchasing power parity, found a worsening of distribution from a Gini of 0.63 to 0.66 in 1993, with most of the increase due to rising differentials between countries (Milanovic, 1999).

Thus the impact of globalization seems to have been unequalizing between nations as well as within them. To some extent other influences were also responsible, such as the increase in the technology intensity of production and the rise in the rate of return to capital. Other factors, such as worsening commodity terms of trade, were more relevant to explaining rising inter-country inequalities than intra-country inequalitites.

IX CONCLUSIONS

There is broad empirical and theoretical support for the view that greater equality of income distribution is good for economic growth, for social cohesion, for poverty elimination and for health; in other words, that *in general, more equality promotes development*. It seems, therefore, that greater equality of income distribution is to be recommended on all counts. Yet the current situation is one of rising inequality in the majority of countries, among both developed and developing countries, which is associated with liberalization and globalization.

The evidence also suggests that governments can influence income distribution by their policies towards asset distribution, by the growth strategy chosen and by tax and expenditure policies. In general, higher levels of taxation and expenditure improve the distribution compared with the pre-tax system, even where the tax system is not notably progressive. Well designed, tax, expenditure and transfer policies can greatly improve the distribution of welfare. Within limits, also, empirical evidence suggests that higher taxes do not impede economic growth. Yet globalization is restricting governments' ability to counter the rise in inequality of primary monetary incomes by redistributive taxation and expenditure because of the feared impact on competitiveness, trade and capital movements. There is a sad irony in the situation because the rise in inequality and downward pressure on government expenditure is likely to reduce political stability, and also diminish expenditures on social and economic infrastructure, which are essential for sustained growth and social stability. A major policy challenge for the twenty-first century will be to tackle this dilemma.

One general conclusion from this is that coordinated regional, or better international, action would help promote equality without weakening the ability to compete. For example, regional coordination of domestic tax and benefit strategies would permit improved distribution without undermining competitiveness, as would regional coordination of minimum wages at an appropriate level. At an international level, coordinated taxation of international capital flows (including taxation of short-term capital and of multinational companies) and support for universal human rights to minimal standards of living would also contribute to improving income distribution, and to countering the immiserizing impact which globalization can have. A global economic environment requires a global social response. In general, the liberalizing and globalizing era of the late twentieth century has tilted the balance of power and benefits towards those with capital (physical, human and financial) against those without. This needs to be corrected.

However, while a regional and global response is needed, much can be done at the national level. Countries which have put human development and improved income distribution high on the agenda have not lost out in the global economy because the build up of human resources enhances their productivity. The types of policies likely to improve income distribution were identified above. They include agrarian-focused and employment-intensive growth strategies; high and widely spread expenditure on education; redistribution of assets; a structured market to direct education, training and asset accumulation towards deprived groups; and strong policies towards social protection and social income. Gender balance in each aspect is necessary to improve intra-household income distribution. It is essential to consider not just vertical income distribution but intra-household and horizontal inequalities as well.

Nonetheless, although it is fairly easy to identify the appropriate set of policies which would increase equality and improve social cohesion and economic growth, the prevalence of powerful global forces responsible for the general rise in inequality makes it difficult to be optimistic about the possibilities of countries switching to a more egalitarian pattern of development.

NOTES

1. This chapter has benefited greatly from the research assistance of Emma Samman.
2. The evidence is surveyed in Wilkinson (1996).
3. There is, of course, a lot of overlap among these alternatives.
4. Kaldor (1955–6) suggested that in a full-employment economy, higher investment would lead to a higher profit share, so that growth and inequality would be likely to be associated, although the causation in this model ran from investment to profits/savings, not the other way round.
5. Including Alesina and Rodrik (1994), Birdsall *et al*. (1995), Bourguignon (1995), Deininger and Squire (1996), Sarel (1997), Larraín and Vergara (1997).

6. Deininger and Squire (1996) produced a 'cleaned' data set, excluding 1200 out of 2000 observations. But the cleaning process inevitably introduces its own biases; for example, more equal countries are likely to produce more reliable data on income distribution as particular groups have less reason to conceal their incomes.
7. Data from Khan and Muqtada (1997).
8. This is also supported by a careful marshalling of evidence by Morley, one of the authors of the World Bank (1993) report, whose conclusion is slightly stronger than that of the World Bank: 'real minimum wages appear to have an equalising effect on the distribution' (Morley, 1995, p. 162).
9. A preliminary evaluation by the Confederation of British Industry, the main employers' organization, reports that the minimum wage introduced into Britain in April 1999 had not had adverse effects on employment in the first five months, or increased average earnings; it had had some effect in reducing wage differentials, and had led to modernization of work practices (upgrading skills) in some companies (*Financial Times*, 1/11/99).
10. However, government expenditure is often not 'well-targeted', when this is defined as occurring where the poor receive a higher proportion of benefits than their share of population (Chu *et al.*, 1999).
11. Grunberg (1998) explores the forces that reduce revenue as a result of globalization, including the reduction in trade taxes; financial liberalization, the globalization of income; tax competition, leading to a general fall in tax rates on individuals and companies; and the growth of the (untaxed) informal economy. Her aggregate evidence for the 1980s shows a small fall in the proportion of national income going to government in developing countries, but a quite significant rise in developed countries.

REFERENCES

Abowd, J., F. Kramarz and D. Margolis (1999), 'Minimum wages and employment in France and the United States', NBER Working Paper 6996, National Bureau of Economic Research, Cambridge, MA.

Adelman, I. and C.T. Morris (1973), *Economic growth and social equity in developing countries*, Stanford: Stanford University Press.

Ahluwalia, M. (1976), 'Inequality, poverty and development', *Journal of Development Economics*, 6: 307–42.

Ahmed, R. and F. Goletti (1998), 'Food policy and market reform in Vietnam and Bangladesh', *International Food Policy Research Institute (IFPRI) Annual Report*, Washington, DC: IFPRI.

Alesina, A. and R. Perotti (1994a), 'The political economy of growth: A critical survey of the recent literature', *The World Bank Economic Review*, 8.

Alesina, A. and R. Perotti (1994b), 'Income Distribution, Political Instability and Investment', National Bureau of Economic Research (NBER), Working Paper 4486, Cambridge, MA.

Alesina, A and D. Rodrik (1994), 'Distributive politics and economic growth', *Quarterly Journal of Economics* 109(2): 465–90.

Ali, Ali Abdel Gadir (1998), 'Dealing with poverty and income distribution issues in developing countries: Cross-regional experiences', *Journal of African Economies*, 7:2 (AERC Supplement): 77–115.

Anand, S. and S.M.R. Kanbur (1993a), 'Inequality and Development: A Critique', *Journal of Development Economic,s* 41(1): 19–43, June.

Anand, S. and S.M.R. Kanbur (1993b), 'The Kuznets process and the inequality–development relationship', *Journal of Development Economics*, 40(1): 25–52, February.

Anderson, D. (1982), 'Small industry in developing countries: A discussion of issues', *World Development*, 10(11): 913–48.

Atkinson, T. (1999), 'Increased income inequality and the redistributive impact of the government budget', paper prepared for WIDER project meeting on 'Rising Income Inequality and Poverty Reduction: Are they compatible?', WIDER, Helsinki, 16–18 July.

Behrman, J. (1993), 'Investing in human resources', in Inter-American Development Bank (ed.), *Economic and Social Progress in Latin America*, Washington, DC: Inter-American Development Bank.

Benabou, R. (1996), 'Inequality and growth', in B.S. Bernanke and J. Rotemberg (eds), *MacroEconomics Annual*, 11, Cambridge: MIT Press.

Berman, E., J. Bound and S. Machin (1997), 'Implications of skill-biased technological change: International evidence', IED Discussion Paper Series 78, IED, Boston University.

Berry, A. (1997), 'The income distribution threat in Latin America', *Latin American Research Review*, 32(2): 3–40.

Berry, A., F. Bourguignon and C. Morrisson (1991), 'Global economic inequality and its trends since 1950', in L. Osberg (ed.), *Economic Inequality and Poverty: International Perspectives*, New York: Sharpe.

Bertola, G. (1993), 'Factor shares and savings in endogenous growth', National Bureau of Economic Research Working Papers 3851, NBER, Cambridge, MA.

Besley, T. and R. Burgess (1998), 'Land reform, poverty reduction and growth: Evidence from India', The Development Economics Discussion Paper Series, 13, London School of Economics, STICERD.

Beyer, H., P. Rojas and R. Vergara (1999), 'Trade liberalization and wage inequality', *Journal of Development Economics*, 59: 103–123.

Birdsall, N. and R. Sabot (1994), 'Inequality as a constraint on growth in Latin America' (mimeo), Inter-American Development Bank, Washington, DC.

Birdsall, N., D. Ross and R. Sabot (1995), 'Inequality and growth reconsidered: Lessons from East Asia', *World Bank Economic Review*, 9.

Bloom, D.E., D. Canning and P. Malaney (1998), 'Population Dynamics and Economic Growth', HIID, Cambridge, MA.

Bourguignon, F. (1995), 'Comment on "Inequality, Poverty and Growth: Where do We Stand?"', Annual World Bank Conference on Development Economics, World Bank, Washington, DC.

Bourguignon, F. and C. Morrisson (1990), 'Income distribution, development and foreign trade: A cross-sectional analysis', *European Economic Review*, 34: 1113–32.

Bruno, M., M. Ravallion and L. Squire (1995), 'Equity and Growth in Developing Countries: Old and New Perspectives on the Policy Issues', paper prepared for the IMF Conference on Income Distribution and Sustainable Growth, World Bank, Washington DC, 1–2 June.

Burmeister, L., G. Ranis and M. Wang (1999), 'Group behaviour and development: A comparison of farmers associations in South Korea and Taiwan', paper prepared for WIDER Project Meeting on Group Behaviour and Development, WIDER, Helsinki, 10–11 September.

Card, D. and A.B. Krueger (1994), 'Minimum wages and employment: A case study of the fast food industry in New Jersey and Pennsylvania', *American Economic Review*, 84(4): 772–93.

Card, D., L. Katz and A.B. Krueger (1994), 'An evaluation of recent evidence on the employment effects of minimum and subminimum wages', *Industrial and Labor Relations Review*, 47(3): 487–96.

Chou, E. and L. Lau (1987), 'Farmer ability and farm productivity: A study of farm households in the Changmai Valley, Thailand, 1972–8', working paper, Washington, DC, World Bank.

Chu, K., H. Davoodi and S. Gupta (1999), 'Income distribution and tax and government spending policies in developing countries', paper prepared for WIDER project meeting on 'Rising Income Inequality and Poverty Reduction: Are they Compatible?', WIDER, Helsinki, 16–18 July.

Cornia, G.A. (1996), 'Transition and income distribution: Theory, evidence and initial interpretation', Research in Progress 1, WIDER, Helsinki.

Davey, S.G., J. Neaton and J. Stamler (1996), 'Socioeconomic differentials in mortality risk among men screened for the multiple risk factor intervention trial. White men', *American Journal of Public Health*, 86: 486–96.

Davis, D.–R. (1996), *Trade Liberalization and Income Distribution*, Cambridge, MA: Harvard Institute of Economic Research.

Deininger, K. and L. Squire (1996), 'A new data set measuring income inequality', *World Bank Economic Review*, 10(3): 565–91.

Deininger, K. and L. Squire (1997), 'Economic growth and income inequality: Re-examining the links', *Finance and Development*, 34(1): 38–41, March.

Deininger, K. and L. Squire (1998), 'New ways of looking at old issues: Inequality and growth', *Journal of Development Economics*, 57(2): 259–87.

Demery, L., B. Sen and T. Vishwanath (1995), 'Poverty, inequality and growth', ESP Discussion Paper Series 70, World Bank, Washington DC.

Dickens, R., S. Machin *et al.* (1994), 'The effect of minimum wages on UK agriculture', Discussion Paper 204, Centre for Economic Performance, London.

DiNardo, J., N. Fortin and T. Lemieux (1996), 'Labor market institutions and the distribution of wages, 1973–1992: A semiparametric approach', *Econometrica*, 64(5): 1001–44.

Dobb, M. (1956–7), 'Second thoughts on capital intensity of investment', *Review of Economic Studies*, XXIV.

Dorosh, P. and A. Valdes (1990), 'Effects of exchange rate and trade policies in agriculture in Pakistan', IFPRI Research Report 82, Washington, DC.

Drèze J. and M. Chen (1995), 'Widows and wellbeing in rural north India', in M. Das Gupta, T.N. Krishnan and L. Chen (eds), *Women and Health in India*, Oxford: Oxford University Press.

Drèze, J. and A.K. Sen (1991), 'Public action for social security: Foundations and strategy', in E. Ahmad, J. Drèze and A.K. Sen (eds), *Social Security in Developing Countries*, Oxford: Oxford University Press.

ECLAC (1992), *Social Equity and Changing Production Patterns: An Integrated Approach*, Santiago: ECLAC.

El-Ghonemy, R. (1990), *The Political Economy of Rural Poverty*, London: Routledge.

Fei, J., G. Ranis and S. Kuo (1979), *Growth with Equity: The Taiwan Case*, Oxford: Oxford University Press.

Fishlow, A. (1995), 'Inequality, poverty and growth: Where do we stand?', Annual World Bank Conference on Development Economics, World Bank, Washington, DC.

Flegg, A. (1982), 'Inequality of income, illiteracy, and medical care as determinants of infant mortality in developing countries', *Population Studies*, 36: 441–58.

Forbes, K. (2000), 'A reassessment of the relationship between inequality and growth', *American Economic Review*.

Freeman, R.B. and L.F. Katz (eds), (1995). *Differences and Changes in Wage Structure*, Chicago: University of Chicago Press.

Galenson W. and H. Leibenstein (1955), 'Investment criteria, productivity and economic development', *Quarterly Journal of Economics*, 69: 343–70.

Galor, O. and J. Zeria (1993), 'Income distribution and macroeconomics', *Review of Economic Studies*, 60: 35–52.

Ghiara, R. (1999), 'Impact of trade liberalization on female wages in Mexico: An econometric analysis', *Development Policy Review*, 17: 171–90.

Glyn, A. (1992), 'Stability, inegalitarianism and stagnation: An overview of the advanced capitalist countries in the 1980s', working paper, WIDER, Helsinki.

Gottschalk, P. and T.M. Smeeding (1997), 'Cross-national comparisons of earnings and income inequality', *Journal of Economic Literature*, 35: 633–87.

Grunberg, I. (1998), 'Perspectives on international financial liberalisation', Discussion Paper Series 15, United Nations, UNDP, Office of Development Studies, New York.

Guhan, S. (1992), 'Social Security for the unorganised poor: A feasible blueprint for India', Discussion Paper, UNDP and Indira Gandhi Institute of Development Research, Bombay.

Haddad, L. and R. Kanbur (1990), 'How serious is the neglect of intra-household inequality', *Economic Journal*, 100: 866–81.

Inter-American Development Bank (1999), *Facing up to Inequality in Latin America. Economic and Social Progress in Latin America, 1998–99 Report*, Washington, DC: Inter-American Development Bank.

Jones, O. (1998), 'The impact of minimum wage legislation in developing countries where coverage is incomplete', Working Paper 2, Centre for the Study of African Economies, Oxford.

Kaldor, N. (1955–6), 'Alternative theories of distribution', *Review of Economic Studies*, XXIII: 2.

Kanbur, R. (1998), 'Income distribution and development', World Bank Working Paper 98–13, and in A.B. Atkinson and F. Bourguignon (eds) (2000), *Handbook of Income Distribution*, Amsterdam: Elsevier.

Kanbur, R. and N. Lustig (1999), 'Why is inequality back on the agenda', paper prepared for the Annual World Bank Conference on Development Economics, World Bank, Washington, DC, 28–30 April.

Khan, A. and M. Muqtada (eds) (1997), *Employment Expansion and Macroeconomic Stability Under Increasing Globalisation*, London: Macmillan.

Khoo, L. and B. Dennis (1999), 'Inequality, fertility choice, and economic growth: Theory and evidence', Development Discussion Paper 687, Harvard Institute for International Development, Cambridge, MA.

Kuznets, S. (1955), 'Economic growth and income inequality', *American Economic Review*, XLV: 1–28.

Láchler, U. (1997), 'Education and earnings inequality in Mexico', World Bank working paper, World Bank, Mexico Country Dept, Washington DC.

Larraín, F.B. and M.R. Vergara (1997), 'Income distribution, investment and growth', Development Discussion Paper 596, Harvard Institute for International Development, Cambridge MA.

Learner, E.E. (1995), 'A trade economist's view of US wages and "globalization"', in S. Collins (ed.) *Imports, Exports and the American Worker*, Washington, DC: Brookings Institution.

Lewis, W.A. (1954), 'Economic development with unlimited supplies of labour', *Manchester School of Economic and Social Studies*, 22: 139–81.

Lipton, M. (1977), *Why Poor People Stay Poor*, London: Croom Helm.

Lipton, M. (1993), 'Land reform as commenced business: The evidence against stopping', *World Development*, 21(4): 641–57.

Lustig, N. and D. McCleod (1996), 'Minimum wages and poverty in developing countries: some empirical evidence', Brookings Institution Working Paper 125, Washington, DC.

Mehrotra, S., J. Vandemoortele and E. Delamonica (1999), 'Public Spending on Basic Social Services', manuscript prepared for UNICEF, New York.

Mesa-Largo, C. (1983), 'Social security and extreme poverty in Latin America', *Journal of Development Economics*, 28: 138–50.

Milanovic, B. (1994), 'Determinants of cross-country income inequality: An "augmented" Kuznets hypothesis', Policy Research Working Paper 1246, World Bank, Washington, DC.

Milanovic, B. (1998), 'Explaining the increase in inequality during the transition', World Bank Working Paper 1935, World Bank, Washington, DC.

Milanovic, B. (1999), 'True world income distribution 1988 and 1993: first calculations based on household surveys alone', World Bank Working Paper 2244, World Bank, Washington, DC.

Morley, S. (1995), *Poverty and Inequality in Latin America: The Impact of Adjustment and Recovery in the 1980s*, Baltimore: Johns Hopkins University Press.

Murphy, D., A. Shleifer and R.W. Vishny (1989), 'Income distribution, market size and industrialization', *Quarterly Journal of Economics*, 104(3): 537–64.

Neumark, D. and W. Wascher (1991), 'Evidence on employment effects of minimum wages and subminimum wage provisions for panel data on state minimum wage laws', *Industrial and Labor Relations Review*, 44: 55–81.

Oswang, T. (1994), 'Economic development and income inequality: A nonparametric investigation of Kuznets's U-curve Hypothesis', *Journal of Quantitative Economics*, 10: 139–53.

Panizza, U. (1999), 'Income inequality and economic growth: Evidence from American data', IADB working paper, Inter-American Development Bank, Washington, DC.

Paukert, F. (1973), 'Income distribution at different levels of development: A survey of the evidence', *International Labour Review*, 108: 97–125.

Perotti, R. (1993), 'Political equilibrium, income distribution, and growth', *Review of Economic Studies*, 60.

Persson, T. and G. Tabellini (1994), 'Is inequality harmful for growth?', *American Economic Review*, 84: 600–21.

Powelson, J.P. (1984), 'International public and private agencies', in J.D. Montgomery (ed.), *International Dimensions of Land Reform*, Boulder: Westview.

Psacharopoulos, G. *et al.* (1996), 'Poverty and income distribution in Latin America: The story of the 1980s', Latin America and the Caribbean Technical Department. Regional Studies Programme Report no. 27, World Bank, Washington, DC.

Rahman, S. (1999), 'Impact of technological change on income distribution and poverty in Bangladesh: an empirical analysis', *Journal of International Development*, 11 (7): 935–56.

Rama, M. (1996), 'The consequences of doubling the minimum wage: the case of Indonesia', World Bank Working Paper 1643, World Bank, Washington, DC.

Ranis, G. and F. Stewart (1987), 'Rural linkages in the Philippines and Taiwan', in F. Stewart (ed.), *Macro-Policies for Appropriate Technology*, Boulder: Westview.

Ranis, G. and F. Stewart (1993), 'Rural non-agricultural activities in development: Theory and application', *Journal of Development Economics*, 40(1): 75–102.

Ranis, G. and F. Stewart (1999), 'V-goods and the role of the urban informal sector in development', *Economic Development and Cultural Change*, 47(2): 259–88.

Ranis, G. and F. Stewart and A. Ramirez (2000), 'Economic growth and human development', *World Development*, 28(2): 197–219.

Robbins, D. (1995), 'Earnings dispersion in Chile after trade liberalization', Harvard University, Cambridge, MA.

Robbins, D. (1996), 'HOS hits hard facts: Evidence on trade and wage in the developing world', Harvard University, Cambridge, MA.

Roemer, M. and M.K. Guherty (1997), 'Does economic growth reduce poverty?', technical paper, Harvard Institute for International Development, Cambridge, MA.

Sarel, M. (1997), 'How macroeconomic factors affect income distribution: The cross-country evidence', IMF Working Paper, 97/152, International Monetary Fund, Washington, DC.

Schiff, M. and A. Valdes (1992), *The Political Economy of Agricultural Pricing Policy Volume Four. A Synthesis of the Economics in Developing Countries*, Washington, DC: World Bank.

Sen, A.K. (1968), *Choice of Techniques*, Oxford: Blackwell.

Sen, B. (1995), 'Growth and poverty reduction: macroeconomic experience', in World Bank (eds), *Social Impact of Adjustment Operation*, Washington, DC: World Bank, Operations and Evaluation Department.

Shah, A. and J. Whalley (1990), 'Tax incidence analysis of developing countries: An alternative view', *World Bank Economic Review*, 5(3): 535–52.

Shah, A. and J. Whalley (1991), 'The redistributive impact of taxation in developing countries', in J. Khalilzadeh and A. Shah (eds), *Tax Policy in Developing Countries: A World Bank Symposium*, Washington, DC: World Bank.

Spilimbergo, A., J.L. Londono and M. Székely (1999), 'Income distribution, factor endowments, and trade openness', *Journal of Development Economics*, 59: 77–101.

Stewart, F. (ed.) (1987), *Macro-Policies for Appropriate Technology*, Boulder, CO: Westview.

Stewart, F. and A. Berry (1999), 'Globalization, liberalization and inequality: expectations and experience', in A. Hurrell and N. Woods (eds), *Inequality, Globalization and World Politics*, Oxford: Oxford University Press.

Stewart, F. (2000), 'The root causes of conflict: some conclusions', in E.W. Nafziger, F. Stewart and R. Vayryenen (eds), *War and displacement: The Origins of Humanitarian Emergencies*, Oxford: Oxford University Press.

Stewart, F., H. Thomas and T. de Wilde (1990), *The Other Policy: The Influence of Policies on Technology Choice and Small Enterprise Development*, London: Intermediate Technology Publications.

Stolper, W. and P. Samuelson (1941), 'Protection and real wages', *Review of Economic Studies*.

Taylor, L. and P. Krugman (1978), 'Contractionary effects of devaluation', *Journal of International Economics*, 8: 445–56.

Teulings, C.N. (1998), 'The contribution of minimum wages to increasing wage inequality', working paper, Tinbergen Institute, Rotterdam.

Thompson, Robert L. (1998), 'Public policy for sustainable agriculture and rural equity', *Food Policy*, 23(1): 1–7.

UNCTAD (1997), *Trade and Development Report 1997*, sales no. E.97.II.D.8, New York and Geneva: United Nations.

UNDP (1999), *Human Development Report*, New York: United Nations.

Van der Hoeven, R. (1999), 'Economic reform under the Washington Consensus: Income inequality and labour market institutions', paper prepared for WIDER project meeting on 'Rising Income Inequality and Poverty Reduction: Are they Compatible?', WIDER, Helsinki, 16–18 July.

Waldmann, R.J. (1992), 'Income distribution and infant mortality', *Quarterly Journal of Economics*, 107:1283–1302.

Wilkinson, R. (1996), *Unhealthy Societies: The Afflictions of Inequality*, London: Routledge.

Wood, A. (1994), *North–South Trade, Employment and Inequality*, Oxford: Clarendon Press.

Wood, A. (1995), 'Does trade reduce wage inequality in developing countries?', (mimeo), Institute of Development Studies, Brighton, UK.

World Bank (1990), *World Development Report: Poverty*, Washington, DC: World Bank.

World Bank (1993), *Poverty and income distribution in Latin America: The story of the 1980s Report*, Washington, DC: World Bank, Technical Department, Latin America and the Caribbean.

World Bank (1995), 'Distribution and growth: complements, not compromises', *World Bank Policy Bulletin*, 6(3).

אין אוס
כלו בנן

11. Order, the rule of law and moral norms

Jean-Philippe Platteau

INTRODUCTION

As we have learned from evolutionary game theory, anonymous pairwise interactions among agents are generally not conducive to the sustained presence of
'nice traits' in the population. Biased pairing of individuals following some
cultural or geographical segmentation could, of course, solve the problem by
internalizing part of the externality associated with nice behaviour, yet at the
price of giving up the kind of conceptual framework that most closely resembles
market conditions. Retaining anonymity but at the same time assuming that the
probability is higher of meeting someone with whom one had a nice encounter
in the past leads to the conclusion that honest behaviour can be established, but
that this is far from a certain result. The problem with this rather strange combination of assumptions, however, is that it is not easy to substantiate
empirically: usually, we return to nice people because, in some way or other,
we can recognize them, or be informed about them, which amounts to saying
that a reputation effect is at work.

Now, regarding enforcement mechanisms based on reputation effects, there
exist a wide variety of situations in which such mechanisms can prove useful
to discourage cheating and thereby make market exchanges possible at
reasonable transaction cost. For example, Chinese businessmen residing in
Southeast Asian towns tend to exchange among themselves credit information
about indigenous customers, thereby reducing the frequency of their bad debts
(Szanton, 1998, p. 256; see also Hayami and Kawagoe, 1993; Hayami, 1998).
In the more complex situations in which the domain of exchange is so wide,
agents are so mobile, or economic transactions are so discontinuous that information cannot easily flow among potential traders, private third-party
mechanisms are needed to supplement communication networks. Yet, as has
been shown by Milgrom *et al.* (1990) in the specific case of a private judge
system known as the Law Merchant system (observed in the Champagne fairs),
there can be a number of rather stringent conditions to be fulfilled for a decentralized mechanism of information pooling to be workable. In particular, if the
benefits of honest behaviour are small compared with the one-time gain from
cheating, or if would-be opportunists heavily discount future incomes, the
decentralized punishment mechanism allowed by information pooling may not

be enough to discourage them from cheating. Moreover, agents' mistakes are susceptible to jeopardizing the kind of self-enforcing equilibria that may be produced in repeated games.

More importantly, nothing ensures that the right market governance institutions will be established. In point of fact, repeated game theory only shows that, in various situations, outcomes corresponding to these institutions are a possible equilibrium: it does not say that they will necessarily materialize. Evidently, if distrust is pervasive, nasty strategies (and these include cautious strategies that prescribe non-cooperation in the initial stages of the game) are likely to be followed by a significant number of agents, with the consequence that honesty-enforcing mechanisms are precluded (Gambetta, 1988, pp. 227–8; see also Binmore, 1992, p. 434).

There is undoubtedly a trust problem in the sense that a basic predisposition to trust must be present and be perceived for a cooperative equilibrium to prevail.[1] It is revealing that in Ghana, contrary to what was observed above in the case of Chinese businessmen, 'there seems to be no mechanism whereby information about clients' trustworthiness is shared among firms other than direct recommendation by common acquaintances'. Apparently, firms relish 'the idea that their competitors have to deal with the same deadbeats by whom they had been burnt' (Fafchamps, 1996, p. 441).

Unfortunately, the trust problem is especially difficult to solve in modern economies because market-like situations involving competition among many anonymous buyers and sellers (and complete contracts) tend to induce self-regarding behaviour while more personalized exchange settings tend to yield choices consistent with other-regarding or relational preferences (Lane, 1991; Schotter *et al.*, 1996; Bowles, 1998a, pp. 87–90; 1998b; Ledeneva, 1998, pp. 194–200). The evidence pointing to this tendency, whether from historical materials or from experimental psychology (see below), should not be construed as meaning that the market makes people intrinsically selfish, but rather that it evokes the self-regarding behaviours in their preference repertoires: individuals tend to behave selfishly in the market, altruistically in the family, and reciprocally in the workplace (Bowles, 1998b, p. 89). We shall soon return to this important point.

THE RULE OF LAW AS A NECESSARY COMPLEMENT TO SPONTANEOUS ORDER

The Need for Formal Law and State Enforcement

The most obvious way to get out of the above problem is through the emergence of the third party enforcement of legal provisions by the modern, centralized nation-state. Although recognizing that 'quite complex exchange can be realized by creating third-party enforcement via voluntary institutions that lower information costs about the other party', North has thus laid considerable stress on the fact that 'historically the growth of economies has occurred within the institutional framework of well-developed coercive polities'; the state was thus 'a major player' or a 'crucial actor in the process of economic specialization' that took place in Europe during modern times (North, 1990, p. 14; 1991, p. 107). Ultimately, indeed, institutions that can enforce agreements by the threat of coercion are required to sustain complex exchange because the transaction costs of a purely voluntary system of third-party enforcement would be prohibitive (North, 1990, p. 58; see also, pp. 35, 47, 59, 109).[2]

The development of the rule of law is unmistakably a central characteristic of the modern growth process of all the pioneer countries, as attested by the rising importance of laws for contract enforcement and respect of property rights, notaries for the recording of agreements, state courts for the resolution of disputes, and so on. In the Italian city-states, it was as early as the twelfth to thirteenth centuries that covenants and contracts became central to all aspects of life, 'and the ranks of notaries, lawyers, and judges burgeoned to record, interpret, and enforce these agreements'. In Bologna, for example, a town of roughly 50 000 inhabitants, as many as 2000 professional notaries were estimated to operate. Furthermore, an itinerant, professionally trained jurist–administrator elected for a limited term (known as the *podestà*), came to play a key role in communal affairs (Putnam, 1993, p. 126; Greif, 2002, ch. 5).

It bears emphasis that for North as for Friedrich Hayek (1993), effective law-enforcing agencies cannot be created by *fiat* but rather tend to arise from prolonged experiences with informal decentralized mechanisms invented by the civil society. It is the gradual and unusually successful blending of the voluntarist structure of contract enforcement via merchant organizations with enforcement by the state, and the progressive encoding into formal laws of behavioural patterns determined by private order institutions (including village-level regulations recorded in England's costumals or France's coutumiers), that constituted the main factor behind the rise into prominence of the Western world during the last few centuries (North, 1990, p. 41, 43; 1991, p. 107; Kriegel, 1995, pp. 72–8; Landes, 1998, p. 44).

Recent experience with Russia amply testifies that legal provisions and state enforcement mechanisms that are not built upon locally evolved mores and practices, but have been abruptly transplanted from the West, have few chances to take root. Reflecting upon the experience of transition economies over the last few decades, Katharina Pistor reached the following conclusion:

> It is now becoming apparent that the transplantation of formal law does not necessarily alter behaviour ... Where formal and informal institutions evolve over time,

they tend to complement each other. In the context of a political or economic regime change, however, new formal and preexisting informal institutions compete. Formal law may be rejected, or ignored and substituted with [sic] informal institutions that operate independently of and frequently in contradiction to the formal legal system. For formal law to be accepted and to affect behaviour, a constituency is needed, whose formation and strength in turn depend on consistent policy signals and effective mechanisms for the enforcement of new formal institutions. (Pistor, 1999, p. 2)

As the last sentence suggests, rejection of the new formal law may arise not only from its incompatibility with existing norms and practices but also from determined opposition by powerful groups whose interests would be hurt by the changes it is intended to bring about. For formal law does not always evolve in response to social demand but may be, and often is, designed to alter social behaviour or to reallocate political and economic rights (ibid. p. 3). In the latter instance, one must expect affected groups to challenge the new measures by using existing informal network relations to negotiate exemptions or simply ignore the law and hold on to existing control rights backed by informal institutions (ibid., p. 8).

In a recent paper, Berkowitz *et al.* (1999) have shown, on the basis of an econometric study using data from 49 countries, that the way in which the modern formal legal order that evolved in some Western countries was transplanted into other countries is a much more important determinant of legality and economic development today than the supply of a particular legal code. Legality is measured along the five following dimensions: the effectiveness of the judiciary, rule of law, the absence of corruption, low risk of contract repudiation and low risk of government expropriation observed during 1980–95. The precise conclusion reached by the authors is that, other things being equal, legality is better established in countries that have developed a legal order internally or in those that have familiarity with the country or countries from which they have taken the legal order, or again in those that have transplanted the external formal legal order with significant adaptation so as to make it appropriate to prevailing conditions. Conversely, countries that have transplanted an external formal legal order in a rather passive manner do not have good legal performances and their economic development is thereby adversely affected.

Legal Systems and Business Networks

It has been recently argued that the commercial legal system that is found in advanced market economies may be considered as a substitute to business networks. When the former develops, possibly out of informal contract enforcement mechanisms as suggested above, the latter become less necessary. Kali (1998) has thus shown that business networks, understood as groups of people trading with each other and obeying the norm of expelling anyone of them who has cheated once, are endogenous to the reliability of the legal system. If this reliability is high, the anonymous market is likely to set itself at a low-dishonesty equilibrium because opportunists choose to behave honestly. In these conditions, a business network which functions as a self-selection device for individuals of different types[3] is unenforceable. If, on the other hand, the legal system is largely unreliable, the opportunists behave dishonestly and a high-dishonesty regime comes to prevail. A business network becomes enforceable,[4] yet, in accordance with what has been said above about the existence of multiple equilibria, nothing guarantees that individuals will actually succeed in organizing themselves into such a personalized network. Thus, if communities do not exist or are too big or too heterogeneous, informal community-based trust mechanisms may be unenforceable and, consequently, there may be no other way to the market order than a system of individual legal responsibility backed by the state.

It is precisely at this point that the possibility must be considered that the relationship brought to light by Kali actually works in the other way around: thus, if we follow Greif's analysis, we would expect legal codes to evolve more quickly in 'individualistic' than in 'collectivist' cultures because cultures based on 'individualistic' beliefs cannot rely on effective multilateral reputation mechanisms and business networks. In other words, 'collectivist' societies are more effective than 'individualistic' societies when division of labour and trade opportunities are relatively limited. Yet, when division of labour becomes more developed and exchange more complex, 'collectivist' beliefs become an obstacle to further development, while 'individualistic' beliefs can then lead to an 'integrated' society in which inter-economy agency relations are established. This is apparently because the need for legal and political enforcement organizations, without which such relations cannot be sustained at reasonable costs, is more clearly felt and acted upon in 'individualistic' societies (Greif, 1994).

Taiwan Province of China provides a good contemporary example of a developing country where the existence of pervasive business networks (known as *guanxi*), rooted in a deep tradition of personalized relations and reciprocal commitments, has given rise to a dense web of extremely dynamic small- and medium-scale enterprises that do not need to rely on formal legal contracts such as are used in most advanced Western countries. In the words of Kao, 'In order to obtain trust, persons have to demonstrate certain qualities according to inter-subjective rules. These rules are not objectified, but are usually well recognized by the people involved. Because such informal, rather than formal, rules are used predominantly to regulate business activities, Western contractual relationships do not prevail' (Kao, 1991, p. 269). Interestingly, *guanxi* relationships, which are not confined to the family circle, are built up through gift exchanges typical of traditional village societies. Thus, when a person meets a potential partner with whom he has the right 'feeling', he does not use a contract to seal the deal; rather, he and his business partner reach an understanding that is sealed by reciprocating small gifts, drinks and banquets (Hamilton, 1998, p. 66).

In the aforementioned work of Kali, the implications of business networks for economic efficiency have been explored by comparing social welfare in two situations: when the anonymous market is the only exchange institution in the economy, and when business networks coexist with the anonymous market. He then demonstrates that the existence of a business network may produce a negative externality on the functioning of the anonymous market. This is because it absorbs honest agents, thereby increasing the density of dishonest individuals involved in anonymous market exchange. It is only when a business group is relatively large that economic efficiency is achieved.[5] The lesson is that informal contract enforcement institutions may be inefficient in general equilibrium even though they enhance efficiency in partial equilibrium.[6] Moreover, as the behaviour of many mafias attests, personalized networks, once formed, may have a vested interest in preventing any improvement of the legal system of codes and courts, thereby precluding the achievement of efficiency gains in the economy. In other words, they may be dynamically inefficient.

We have started from the point that informal governance systems may be problematic because they succeed only very imperfectly in discouraging cheating, or because even when they have that potential ability the suitable self-enforcing mechanism may fail to be established. It must now be added that the partial equilibrium result that informal contract enforcement institutions enhance economic efficiency is not robust to a general equilibrium extension. In particular, the existence of personalized business networks (see, for example, Woolsey-Biggart and Hamilton, 1992; Hayami and Kawagoe, 1993; Fukuyama, 1995; Hodder, 1996; Hefner, 1998; Hayami, 1998) does not constitute *prima facie* evidence that the market economy functions efficiently either in a static or in a dynamic sense. Hence the above-stressed need for the development of the rule of law.

That informal norms or mechanisms can play the role of substitutes for formal laws and institutions, and vice versa, is only one possibility that ought not to be overplayed. In many situations, indeed, it is more likely that social norms and laws are mutually supporting (Axelrod, 1986, p. 61), thereby vindicating the coexistence of the market, the state and the community. There are actually two sets of reasons why the fundamental problem of the market order cannot be solved satisfactorily by creating highly evolved political and juridical institutions (Elster, 1989a, p. 276). First, for small transactions, legal costs are typically too high to justify having recourse to legal procedures and court action (Fafchamps, 1996, p. 428). While laws often function best to prevent rare but large defections because substantial resources are available for enforcement (and while legal codification is often useful to clarify rights and obligations as well as to avoid mistakes), social norms are usually best at preventing numerous small defections where the cost of enforcement is low (Axelrod, 1986, p. 61). Second, two incentive problems tend to plague legal institutions. For one thing, as underlined by Arrow: 'It is not adequate to argue that there are enforcement mechanisms, such as police and the courts; these are themselves services bought and sold, and it has to be asked why they will in fact do what they have contracted to do' (Arrow, 1973, p. 24, cited by Williamson, 1985, p. 405; see also Arrow, 1971, p. 22; Phelps, 1975). For another thing, it is not because the law exists, even at the request of the people themselves, that it will be abided by them. The fact of the matter is that they have an incentive unilaterally to violate rules which they otherwise support.

In situations where fraud and deceit are widespread, people may be led to demand strong sanction systems so as to prevent rule-breaking and thereby reassure everybody that the rules are followed by others. Under their active or passive support, an authoritarian state bent on establishing or restoring 'law and order' may thus be called into being. As pointed out by Banfield (1958), it is in societies pervaded by distrust and 'amoral familism' (such as those of southern Italy) that people believe most in the need for a strong state to control their untrustworthy fellow citizens (see also Putnam, 1993, p. 112; Fukuyama, 1995, p. 99). The obvious difficulty with this solution is that it involves high administrative costs, creates a repressive climate around economic dealings, and risks entailing a generalized loss of freedom that people may later regret.

True, in order to economize on the costs of policing 'good behaviour', the state can decide to shift part of these costs to the citizens themselves. The easiest way to do this is through denunciation of deviant behaviour by the people themselves (possibly against some attractive rewards, material or symbolic) when the authorities define what is deviant behaviour. Insofar as not joining in this form of punishment is itself taken as an act of rebellion against the author-ities, a metanorm (Axelrod) is involved. Such a metanorm, however, appears to be especially perverse, not least because the vesting of prosecutorial powers in the public tends to be self-defeating. As a matter of fact, it ultimately creates distrust rather than trust and is bound to unleash witch-hunts by playing upon the worst human proclivities, those born of envious feelings, jealousy and pro-fessional rivalry. In the end, one does not know whether accusations of speculative behaviour, high treason or sabotage are not just fabricated pretexts to get rid of a personal enemy or contender, who cannot be won over through a fair contest, be it in the private or the public arenas of life.

Moreover, as attested by the experience of Stalinist USSR or of the Cultural Revolution in China, distrust tends not to be confined to economic dealings but to spill over into all spheres of human interaction. As a result, fear and suspicion infiltrate the whole society and individuals tend to withdraw from as much social intercourse as possible, to shun all risky ventures and to take refuge in private life (MacDonald, 1991, p. 123; see also Lane, 1991, p. 217).

Clearly, the 'Russian way' does not constitute an attractive solution to the trust problem. It is actually the product of a long history of strong central rule and state patrimonialism to which we shall soon return (see, for example, Anderson, 1974, ch. 6; Raeff, 1984; Platonov, 1985; Riasanovsky, 1993; Pipes, 1995, 1999; Hosking, 1997).

Good and Bad States: Some Lessons from European History

Before assessing the role of norms in the maintenance of the market order, it is useful to derive from the above discussion a number of important implications regarding the desired nature of the state in the perspective of a market-based development.

Insofar as state enforcement and legal provisions cannot be effectively imposed from above, and insofar as large chunks of everyday life must be governed by informal norms and practices (for example, private dispute settlement mechanisms), it is essential that central political power does not assume extreme forms of authoritarianism. This implies that it does not attempt to regulate all aspects of people's lives, that it relies on representative institutions through which the main interest groups of the country can make their voice heard, and that it promulgates laws that can be interpreted and implemented in an impartial and predictable manner. As the experience of Western Europe shows, representative institutions such as parliaments and courts develop gradually in the course of a protracted struggle through which the most influential sections of the society assert themselves by confronting a strong state power naturally bent on further entrenching its supreme position. More precisely, as a growing number of historians recognize today, 'the power to approve or reject grants of money for the support of the monarchy undoubtedly made some countries' representative institutions more powerful than others' (Bonney, 1991, p. 323). In other words, accountable government originated in political struggles between rulers and citizens about the linkage to be established between taxation and representation (Bates and Lien, 1985).

Just consider the case of England, as told by Douglass North and Barry Weingast (1989) or Charles Tilly (1992, pp. 153–9). Here, during the critical period of the seventeenth century, a major institutional evolution occurred that was to create tremendous opportunities for economic growth during the subsequent centuries. As a matter of fact, following the Glorious Revolution of 1688, a series of constitutional changes transformed the political regime from a system where the Crown had considerable leeway for imposing arbitrary measures on its subjects whenever it deemed fit, to a system where checks and balances were introduced to contain royal prerogatives, increase the powers of the parliament, establish the pre-eminence of the common law, and better ensure the independence of the judiciary. In short, the Revolution initiated the era of parliamentary supremacy, implying that the Crown could no longer claim to be above the law.

This supremacy thus 'established a permanent role for Parliament in the on-going management of the government', as a result of which the Crown could no longer call or disband the parliament at its discretion alone. More particularly, the parliament gained a central role in financial matters that was no longer to be constantly called into question by the Crown for reasons of expediency and opportunism. Since the exclusive authority of the parliament to raise new taxes was 'firmly re-established' and since at the same time the Crown's independent sources of revenue were also limited, the latter had to maintain successful relations with the parliament to achieve its own goals (such as the launching of wars). Its margin of manoeuvre therefore became severely constrained, all the more so because the parliamentary veto over royal expenditures was combined with the right to monitor how the funds they had voted were spent (North and Weingast, 1989, p. 816; McNally, 1988, pp. 8–11).

If the above transformation of the English constitutional system was to prove so critical for long-run economic growth prospects, it is because 'political rights were seen as a key element of protection against arbitrary violations of economic rights' (North and Weingast, 1989, p. 816). As stressed tirelessly by classical economists, most notably Adam Smith and John Stuart Mill, political rights are an inescapable way to secure property rights, protection of private wealth and elimination of confiscatory government. Interestingly, access to these protections were bought at a price, namely that of providing the government with sufficient tax revenue. Historically, Tilly argues, the need for reasonably strong and stable governments to solve a fiscal crisis, usually in situations dominated by armed conflicts with neighbouring countries, has been highly conducive to the adoption of representative institutions (Tilly, 1985,1992; see also Bates and Lien, 1985). On the other hand, it is not only the abuses of the Crown but also those of the parliament that were guarded against. Most notably, the political independence of the courts limited the possibilities for the parliament to introduce measures to regulate markets along the line of Colbert in France, since these would have clashed with the common law courts which predominate over economic affairs (North and Weingast, 1989, pp. 819, 829).

It is interesting to note that the above institutional transformations could easily have been missed. Indeed, the Crown nearly won the struggle against the parliament and, had a standing army existed in England, it would have been used by the Crown to suppress the opposition with the result that England would have probably followed the same fate as France and Spain. Yet this did not happen and, while in 1690 France was the major European power, in 1765 it was 'on the verge of bankruptcy while England was on the verge of the Industrial Revolution' (North and Weingast, 1989, pp. 830–31; McNally, 1988).[7] In France, the Estates General, a national representative assembly composed of clergy, nobility and a third estate of (primarily) townsmen, was doomed by the nobility's hopeless division over the spread of the Reformation, and the Estates' consequent inability to prevent civil war in the sixteenth and seventeenth centuries. Revealingly, Henri IV won the war with the support of a rival (but non-representative) institution, the *Parlement* of Paris (Bonney, 1991, pp. 322–3). As for Spain, its institutional evolution was deeply influenced by the centralized monarchy and bureaucracy prevailing in Castile where the role of the representative assembly (the Castilian *Cortes)* was minimized because, ultimately, it proved unable to force the Crown to summon it (North, 1990, pp. 113–14; Bonney, 1991, pp. 323–6).

Closest to England's experience was probably that of Sweden which possessed 'one of the most powerful and enduring representative institutions of Europe', the *riksdag*, which was composed not only of nobles, clergymen and townsmen but also, unusually for European assemblies, of peasants (Bonney, 1991, p. 326). The Swedish Crown eventually recognized that the *riksdag*'s explicit consent to new taxes and to conscription was needed and the latter assembly insisted that financial grants were made only for strictly limited periods so as to force the Crown to summon it regularly. During the constitutional crisis of 1650, the *riksdag* made it clear that its grievances would have to be met before it would grant new taxes. A generation later, the other three estates succeeded in undermining noble privileges exercised through the aristocrat-dominated council known as the *riksrad* (ibid., pp. 326–7).

Russia offers the opposite picture of a country where authoritarianism has always reigned supreme, with the dominant social classes strictly subordinated to central power. Control of populations highly dispersed over vast spaces lying under the constant threat of invasions by nomadic tribes may have determined this situation of extreme concentration of political power. In the terminology of Tilly, Russia was a 'coercion-intensive' state that relied heavily on sheer physical coercion to obtain the resources it needed from its subjects and to ensure compliance. Revealingly, in the aftermath of the conquest of Novgorod by Moscow's grand prince in the second half of the fifteenth century, the monarchy succeeded in eliminating allodial property on a large scale, replacing it with tenure conditional on service to the tsar (Martin, 1995, pp. 271–3). As a result of this suppression of private property rights in land, the Russian equivalent of the nobility (truly speaking, a service class) held both its land and its control over the serfs on royal sufferance. This was a fundamental factor in the country's historic evolution, since it meant that 'the Russian state grew and took shape without having to contend with entrenched landed interests' (Pipes, 1995, p. 172).[8] Marc Raeff goes as far as saying that 'the subjection of Russian society by the tsarist government started at the top', with 'nobles' being 'transformed into nothing less than the serfs or servants of the sovereign' (Raeff, 1984, p. 10). In the same vein, Pipes writes that, in some genuine sense, 'all

Russians lived in a servile condition'. Peasant serfdom in Russia 'was not an exceptional condition, but an integral aspect of an all-embracing system binding the entire population to the state ... [it] was only the most widespread and most visible form of bondage which pervaded every layer of Muscovite society creating an interlocking system without room for personal freedom' (Pipes, 1995, p. 105, 1999, ch. 4; see also Blum, 1961, ch. 9; Worobec, 1995, p. 29; Riasanovsky, 1993, pp. 183–95).

Especially noteworthy is the fact that, in order to get a complete grip on the localities, the rulers of Moscow prohibited their provincial administrators from holding office in any area where they had estates and rotated them at annual or biannual intervals. In this way, they prevented the establishment of any link between land property and administrative/political functions. Of course, hereditary office holding was totally unknown and the stern rule of temporary assignment of offices was applied to the highest levels of the service class, particularly the *voevody* (principal provincial officers combining administrative, military, fiscal and judiciary functions) (Pipes, 1995, pp. 96, 173). In such circumstances, not only peasants and merchants, but also service nobles, could never know for certain in advance what obligations they would have to discharge from one year to the next (Hosking, 1997, p. 57), a predicament that left them at the complete mercy of the central rulers.[9] In the words of Richard Pipes:

> Western royalty, too, would have preferred its nobility not to become entrenched in the provinces, but in most countries it was unable to prevent this from happening and so it concentrated on weakening the nobility's political influence at the centre and replacing it gradually with a bureaucracy. In Russia ... a dvorianstvo enjoying local roots would have challenged the very principle of monocracy, a basic ingredient of tsarist authority as historically evolved, and as such could never have been tolerated. (Pipes, 1995, p. 173)

Given their long experience of vulnerability and subservience to the imperial power, it is perhaps not surprising that, when the tsar's grip over them was somewhat relaxed –as happened under Peter III and Catherine II – the Russian nobles chose to solidify their economic and social privileges instead of attempting to acquire political rights and increase their contribution to the country's political life. In a striking contrast to their Western European counterparts, they thus continued to form a politically impotent class, unable to withstand the autocratic rule. Whereas, in Western Europe in general and in England in particular, the aristocrats dominated the countryside in the double capacity of administrators and proprietors, the Russian *dvorianstvo* 'enjoyed too little of either power to be able to stand up to the monarchy'. In other words, what Russia lacked was the meshing of landed wealth with administrative functions in the hands of a concentrated hereditary rural elite that enabled the latter, wherever it existed, to resist royal absolutism in its most extreme forms (Pipes, 1995, pp. 172, 177; Anderson, 1974, p. 338; Dixon, 1999, pp. 93–6).

According to the above account, Russia's failure to develop institutions of representative government can be traced back to a deep-rooted tradition of state patrimonialism that prevented the rise of any form (including feudalistic) of private property rights. As a consequence, no really independent class could form with which the state would have to learn to bargain for taxes. In a more recent book, Pipes summarizes his main argument as follows:

> the critical factor in the failure of Russia to develop rights and liberties was the liquidation of landed property in the Grand Duchy of Moscow, the principality which in time conquered all Russia and imposed on her a regime under which the monarch not only ruled the realm and its inhabitants but literally owned them. The fusion of sovereignty and ownership, a type of government known as 'patrimonial', vested all titles to the land in the hands of the monarch and allowed him to claim unlimited services from his subjects, noble and commoner alike. In marked contrast to the rest of Western Europe, where the authority of kings stopped at the boundary of private property, in Russia (until the end of the eighteenth century, at any rate) such constraint on royal power was unknown and, indeed, unthinkable. And when, toward the close of the eighteenth century, tsarism belatedly acknowledged private property in land, it encountered ... a great deal of hostility from both the educated elite and the mass of peasantry. The absence of property in land deprived Russians of all those levers by means of which the English succeeded in limiting the power of their kings. Since they required no taxes because all the land paid them rents and rendered them services, the tsars had no need to convene parliaments. Legal institutions which everywhere accompany property were rudimentary and served mainly as instruments of administration. The notion of individual rights was totally submerged by the notion of duties to the monarch. (Pipes, 1999, p. 160)

The luck of England was not only that, rather early, a parliament could fulfil a critical role in the country's political life, but also that the interest groups represented in it were not limited to big landlords. In addition to powerful nobles, the English Parliament did indeed comprise representatives of a commercially minded gentry (whom kings tried, over many centuries, to favour and promote opportunistically as a bulwark against the power of these nobles) and, increasingly from the eighteenth century, representatives of merchants mainly based in London (Tilly, 1992; McNally, 1988). In countries where conservative landlord interests collude with a strong central power, a rigid regime is established which stifles independent private initiatives on the levels of investment, risk taking, and technical, organizational and institutional innovations. The experience of Sicily, which curiously parallels that of Eastern Europe (see Brenner, 1985), springs to mind as an illustration of the above possibility. As a matter of fact, the conquest of Sicily by Arab and Norman invaders brought to an end a long period of economic prosperity which made this country a rich source of grain supply for all the Mediterranean. The problem came because the new rulers 'clamped on the island a system of alliance with militarily-active landlords that left little scope for cities and capitalists' (Tilly, 1992, p. 142). King Frederick II, who acceded to power in 1208, succeeded in subjecting cities and, according to Dennis Mack Smith, this policy helped to ensure that there was never any class of merchants or civic officials independent and vigorous enough to offset the landowning aristocracy; and this lack of challenge to the aristocracy was to be a fundamental factor in the political, cultural and economic decline of Sicily. 'Whenever strong government failed, it was the nobles and not the local cities which filled the vacuum of power. It was therefore foreign towns – Pisa, Genoa, Venice, Amalfi, Lucca – which dominated Sicilian commerce' (Mack Smith, 1968, p. 56 – cited by Tilly, 1992, p. 142).

The thriving cities of Northern Italy had a more lucky fate since Friedrich I known as 'Red Beard', lost his wars to bring them under his control, as a result of which these city-states remained independent. The consequences for Italy were dramatic. Indeed, while in the year 1000 southern Italy outstripped Northern Italy in agricultural productivity, population and urbanization, by 1500, after five centuries of absolutist rule in the south, southern Italy had just become 'a backwater next to the productive and urban north' (Bradford Delong, 1995, p. 10).

To take another striking example, the decision of Spanish Habsburg King Felipe II, called 'the Prudent', to send his lieutenant the Duke of Alva to impose royal power on, and suppress heresy, in the Low Countries proved to be a turning point in the differentiated evolution of this region. While Alva's government, the ill-famed 'Council of Blood', eventually crushed the widescale revolts it triggered in the southern half of the Low Countries, its efforts were foiled in the northern half where it was confronted by extensive water barriers and the navy of the embryonic Republic of the Netherlands led by Willem I Nassau ('William the Silent'). As a consequence, the northern provinces that were to become the modern-day Netherlands prospered while the southern provinces that were to become modern-day Belgium stagnated for centuries in spite of impressive past economic performances of cities such as Ghent, Bruges, and Antwerp (ibid.).

Another scenario arises when, instead of colluding with (proto-) central power, powerful nobles enter into conflict with it. When no decisive outcome is achieved, a lot of uncertainty is created which contributes to fragmented polities and law orders with predictably disastrous effects on economic growth. This happened typically in Poland and Hungary, where 'warrior nobles retained great power, including the ability to install and depose kings' (Tilly, 1992, p. 143). In Hungary, the towns remained strictly subordinate to their noble lords until, during the later fifteenth century, the Crown eventually succeeded in building a relatively centralized and effective war machine (ibid. p. 144). Yet, as cities were sparse and international trade played a minor role, there was no effective opposition of local merchants or capitalists to state power. Coercion prevailed, as in neighbouring Poland where outside of Gdansk, which prospered with the expansion of the Baltic trade, merchants 'were unable to break the grip of great landlords' (ibid. pp. 130, 132; see also Blockmans, 1994, p. 240–41). In the sixteenth century, the magnates' domination was so overwhelming that they were able to impose a refeudalization of the society without having to contend or bargain with state structures (Wyrobisz, 1994).

Contrast this situation with the position of merchants of Amsterdam, Dubrovnik, Venice, and Genoa, 'who could dictate the terms on which any state would operate in their territories' (Tilly, 1992, p. 130). As a matter of fact, 'until the sheer scale of war with nationally recruited armies and navies overwhelmed their efficient but compact military power, capital-intensive states prospered in a warlike world'. Whether city-states, city-empires (like Venice), or urban federations, they all created effective state structures and, without resorting to large bureaucracies, they built institutions representing their commercial oligarchies into the very organization of their states (ibid. pp. 150–51). Even though they were later (in the sixteenth and seventeenth centuries) to be absorbed into growing national sovereignties and their administrative, judicial and economic powers were thereby severely curtailed, these city-states could never be handled carelessly by the ruling dynasties (such as the Burgundy and the Habsburg) or princes (Blockmans, 1994, pp. 239–40). As pointed out by Wim Blockmans: 'even though areas with high urban potential were subjugated by monarchical states via conquest, internal war, or heritage, they did not become dependent towns like those in central Europe after 1450. Accumulated capital, existing social and political structures, and the increase in urban activity could not be annihilated by physical violence alone' (ibid. p. 244).

According to one influential account (Bates and Lien, 1985; Tilly, 1992; Moore, 1998,1999), it is because the landlords' power was based on landed property which is a fixed asset that this class had an adverse impact on the development of representative government. Contrariwise, merchants held mobile capital in the form of financial and trading assets. The precise argument is that there was particularly wide scope for shared gains from cooperation between rulers and owners of mobile assets. The latter had a direct interest in being protected against arbitrary and exploitative taxation to which they were especially vulnerable since their wealth was easy to confiscate. As for the former, if they were enlightened, they tried their best to retain within their jurisdiction existing capital owners and their business as well as to attract new capital owners from other political jurisdictions. Such inter-state competition, so the story goes, did not operate in the case of owners of real estate. In poor agriculture-based economies where there was little mobile capital and little prospect of attracting any, "rulers" objectives were more likely to be achieved through coercive taxation (and appropriation) and an (often unstable) alliance with landowners who were permitted wide discretionary power over the populations under their control' (Moore, 1999, p. 184).

The Growth-impeding Logic of the African State

State formation processes in developing countries are significantly different from what they were in Western Europe, where a Darwinian process of inter-state military competition coupled with an intra-state process of resource mobilization for war-making purposes led to a 'civilianization of government and domestic politics' (Tilly, 1992, p. 206). As aptly remarked by Tilly, many developing countries 'have acquired their military organization from outside, without the same internal forging of mutual constraints between rulers and ruled'. As a result,

> the new states harbour powerful, unconstrained organizations that easily overshadow all other organizations within their territories ... the advantages of military power become enormous, the incentives to seize power over the state as a whole by means of that advantage very strong. Despite the great place that war making occupied in the making of European states, the old national states of Europe almost never experienced the great disproportion between military organization and all other forms of organization that seems the fate of client states throughout the contemporary world ... In our own time, the analogy between war making and state making, on the one hand, and organized crime, on the other, is becoming tragically apt. (Tilly, 1985, p. 186)

Exploitation of great power rivalries during the Cold War period thus enabled many non-representative governments to obtain valuable support from abroad, including substantial aid flows that have had the effect of reducing the need to bargain with domestic groups for revenue and to mobilize their cooperation for the purposes of internal stability and effective rule (Luckham, 1996; Moore, 1998).[10] Thanks to their ability to thus bypass bargaining with their subject populations, 'large state edifices have grown up in the absence of significant consent or support from citizens'. And precisely because of a lack of strong ties between particular state institutions and major social classes within the population, new states have become 'more vulnerable to forcible seizures of power and abrupt changes in the form of government' (Tilly, 1992, pp. 207–8).

In many countries of sub-Saharan Africa, the problem is compounded by several interdependent factors that are worth delving into here. To begin with, many African economies have an essentially agrarian base which implies that taxes are harder to collect, especially where population density is low and the population remains subsistence-oriented. Revenue collection in these economies has therefore often relied on coercion, or has concentrated on export commodities where trade flows rather than scattered production activities could be taxed (Mokoli and Binswanger, 1999).

In addition, a significant number of countries in Africa possess considerable mineral resources that provide an alternative tax base to capitalistic production or mercantile wealth and should allow them to avoid coercive taxation of peasants and taxation of agricultural exports. Unfortunately, however, the presence of rich mineral sites is likely to induce private interests or groups to challenge the state's monopoly of coercive means with a view to arrogating to themselves the power to tax mineral wealth or to license the rights to exploit it (Moore, 1999, p. 186; Mokoli and Binswanger, 1999). That a natural resource advantage may easily turn against a country by causing chaos is tragically illustrated by the protracted state of civil war in Sierra Leone where, thanks to their control of rich diamond deposits, the rebels led by Foday Sankoh could obtain sufficient weaponry to extend their brutal rule over the major portion of the national territory. It is revealing that many of Africa's conflicts (in countries like Angola, the Democratic Republic of the Congo, Liberia, Mozambique, Nigeria and Sierra Leone) can be linked directly to contests for the control of natural resources such as diamonds, copper and oil, the extraction of which can continue even when it is subject to severe predation and the economic environment is disrupted (Binswanger and Collier, 1999).

Now, if the state can manage to appropriate a significant proportion of the resource rent, a predatory and authoritarian political regime can come into being simply because, as in the aforementioned case of international aid transfers, access to such ample revenues enables the political authority to dispense with the need to bargain with the population for tax proceeds, and thus enables it to resist popular demands for representative institutions and political accountability. Ample availability of natural resources and the resulting possibility of substantial 'rentier incomes' thus seems to provide a significant categorical divide among African states, between the mineral-based states where patrimonial, personal rule flourishes and other states where political authority is less authoritarian and less arbitrary (Moore, 1999, p. 181).

There are still other important reasons that explain why African countries have not been able to produce a growth-inducing political regime. To understand them, it is useful to take a retrospective look at their colonial and pre-colonial legacies. Two points are worth emphasizing here. First, African kingdoms ruled over some parts of sub-Saharan Africa during pre-colonial times. One can thus think of the forest kingdoms of West Africa (including the Ashanti and Abomey kingdoms in present-day Ghana and Benin, respectively), the Fulani emirates of (what was to become) Northern Nigeria or Northern Cameroon, the Tutsi kingdom of Rwanda-Urundi, the Sokoto Caliphate in Sudan, or the highly centralized kingdoms of Buganda (in what is now Southern Uganda) and Barotseland (in present-day Zambia). They were often grounded in a sharp division between chiefly strata (of which there could be several layers super-imposed on each other, as in the Ashanti kingdom in what is now a part of Ghana) and popular strata comprising farmers, artisans and traders.[11] Yet, with the notable exception of Ethiopia, their form of administration was essentially patrimonial, implying that there was no genuine professional bureaucracy. This is not surprising since illiteracy prevented the use of written codes and regulations. In addition, some of these states exercised only a loose control over distant provinces or turned out to be rather short-lived structures: thus, in East and West Africa, slave raiding gave rise to a number of temporary, small-scale, centralized polities which later collapsed (Goody, 1988, pp. 19–20; see also Coquery-Vidrovitch, 1985, pp. 98–100; Austen, 1987).

Whatever the level of political development achieved by these ancient African kingdoms, the fact remains that their boundaries were not coterminous with those of the independent states that Africans inherited at the end of the colonial period. This lack of correspondence not only prevented the consolidation of these ancient structures into modern states, but also gave rise to severe political and social conflicts at the time of independence. In the Gold Coast (Ghana), for example, a strong Ashanti subnationalism clashed with Gold Coast nationalism, as represented by the CPP led by Nkrumah. A rival party (the NLM) was founded with the backing of the great majority of Ashanti chiefs and the Asantehene to defend the interest of the Ashantis. Though it failed to gain power in the 1956 elections and to have its demand for a federation accepted, it left behind a legacy of bitterness, and probably inclined Nkrumah to adopt after independence emergency measures of an authoritarian kind, and to largely exclude the Akan ethnic group from the ruling circles (Chazan, 1988; Frimpong-Ansah, 1991, pp. 98–9; Tordoff, 1997, p. 86). The traditional kingdom of Buganda posed an even more serious threat to the integrity of Uganda. The problem was eventually solved in 1966 when the Kabaka, the traditional ruler of Buganda, was forcibly removed and his kingdom was dismembered as a unit of government. In Zambia, the government used 'a mixture of persuasion, threats and legal enactment to bring to an end the privileged position accorded to Barotseland under the agreement reached at independence in 1964' (ibid.).

Returning to the case of the Gold Coast, it is important to add that 'British administrators contradicted and undermined their own efforts to bolster the traditional rulers' authority' (Firmin-Sellers, 1996, p. 29). The intent of the colonial officials was to build upon the institutions of the erstwhile Akan state by delegating authority to traditional rulers and, in this way, to promote stability and minimize the costs of governing. Yet, at the same time, the British stripped the chiefs of any independent coercive authority (for example by allowing a chief's subjects to appeal decisions made in the chief's tribunal to a British court, thus effectively turning the British courts 'into a crucial legitimating force for the chief's decisions' – ibid.). Moreover, the British administrators refused to give the chiefs any direct influence over policy making (ibid. pp. 30–31).

Note that these centrifugal tendencies were an inescapable legacy to the new independent states since, after 1945 in particular, effective control of territory and populations ceased to be the the de facto condition for recognition by other states. In the words of Mick Moore,

> To be the legitimate successor of colonial rule was itself adequate to guarantee the recognition and the more substantial material resources, including international aid, that accrue to those holding governmental power. And in most of the ex-colonial world, but most strikingly in sub-Saharan Africa, Darwinian processes of inter-state competition were not only discouraged, but positively ruled out by the new international and regional systems. Governments that lost effective control of the populations and territories over which they nominally ruled did not as a matter of course fear wholesale predation on the part of their neighbours. There was conflict aplenty, but almost all internal (Moore, 1999, p. 178; see also Tilly, 1992, ch. 7).

Centrifugal tendencies were all the more important as the efforts of colonial rulers were generally aimed at increasing the power of local-level authorities over communities at the expense of pre-existing centralized political institutions such as kingship. This is illustrated, for example, by the deliberate attempts of the French colonial state to sap the authority of the Mogho Naba in Upper Volta (today's Burkina Faso) in order to foster division among lower-level authorities (the princes) within the ancient Mossi kingdom; or by its successful move to break up old political units in the highly centralized political system of Guinea's Fouta Djalon (Boone, 1994, p. 114; Tordoff, 1997, p. 32). Reinforcement of the power of local authorities was problematic not only because they were charged with maintaining law and order (including the power to fine, conscript, imprison and banish) by the colonial state to which they became directly accountable, but also because they were expected to advance the colonial economic agenda. The latter mission indeed implied that local chiefs, 'strongmen', or so-called 'warrant chiefs' (who were sometimes 'straw chiefs' directly appointed by colonial authorities when indigenous chiefs did not exist or when they were not deemed to be compliant enough) were vested with discretionary powers in allocating resources distributed by the colonial state (for example through agricultural cooperatives or mutual aid societies created at the behest of the colonial administration) as well as in mobilizing labour resources and collecting taxes on its behalf (Coquery-Vidrovitch, 1985, pp. 115–27; 1999, pp. 171–2; Bayart, 1989, pp. 99–101; Boone, 1994, pp. 115–19; see also Bates, 1976; Jackson and Rosberg, 1982; Berman, 1984; Skinner, 1989).

The pervasive role of localized and personalized modes of political control is a critical feature of colonial policy that was to have a profound and long-lasting impact on the social and political system of independent African states.

Through marketing boards and other forms of state trading monopolies that took over positions held by European merchant houses in the colonial period, but also through agricultural cooperatives and a host of rural development projects including settlement schemes, post-colonial states pursued the earlier policy aimed at concentrating control of rural surpluses in the hands of bureaucrats, politicians and other influential persons linked to new regimes (Boone, 1994, pp. 122–3; Bates, 1981; Bayart, 1989). Thus, for example, rural cooperatives distributing cheap credit and subsidized inputs are typically formed by local units of the governing party so that access to such advantages is contingent upon political loyalty. And where the institution of chieftaincy was abolished in response to popular discontent, the rural strongmen of the colonial period were replaced by rural administrators, party men and local notables or merchants tightly linked to the new state apparatus. Of course, the ability of local strongmen, whether urban or local, to secure access to state resources is a direct function of their ability to mobilize constituencies, followers and communities (Boone, 1994, pp. 123–4, 128).

When governments pre-empt important channels of potentially lucrative activities in the economy (for example, export crop purchasing, transport, real estate, mineral extraction), and when dynamic individuals eager to enrich themselves or to exercise their entrepreneurial talents are absorbed into the regime's rent-generating and collecting patronage networks, what obtains is a logic of 'politicized accumulation' that is narrowly linked to the inclusionary and cooptive strategies of regime consolidation described by Jean-François Bayart (1989) and Catherine Boone (1992), among others. Successful people are political rather than economic entrepreneurs (Janos, 1982) and such diversion of their creative energies into the political sphere obviously carries a high social cost. This is so not only because rent-seeking activities and monopolistic behaviour entail considerable efficiency losses, but also because the gradual emergence of an independent African bourgeoisie is thereby retarded and discouraged. As our analysis of the European experience has shown, by stifling the development of a genuine social class that will in due time have accumulated enough autonomous economic leverage to erect limits to state power, politicized accumulation actually prevents the long-term constitution of a growth-promoting state.

There is another disastrous long-term consequence of the above system in which accumulation of wealth is largely conditioned upon access to political power,[12] namely the political instability that is thereby generated. Unlike what obtained during the colonial era when supreme power stood indisputably in the hands of a single agent, the colonial state, power in post-independence Africa has been continuously contested because 'decolonization opened new struggles between and within loosely integrated, heterogeneous and often multiple coalitions for control over the state apparatus itself' (Boone, 1994, p. 121).

Contest takes place at the upper echelons of the hierarchical networks of patronage ties through which state resources continuously flow. It is true that African elites which succeeded in capturing power have tried their best to revamp and extend the system of parochial political control that had worked to fragment and isolate social forces during colonial times. Yet the very nature of the emerging state was bound to cause fierce struggles over the spoils of power that would increase rather than mitigate antagonisms between the disparate groups contained within post-colonial regimes (Sklar, 1979; Hyden, 1983; Young, 1986; Joseph, 1988; Staniland, 1986; Ravenhill, 1986; Bienen, 1987; Boone, 1994, pp. 126–7; Bayart, 1986, 1989; Kennedy, 1988; Herbst, 1990).

In particular, people compete for a share of the spoils by enlisting in factions defined with reference to their region of origin. Leaders of such factions conceived as 'a technique of elite competition' can thus invoke traditional sentiments to reinforce their appeal and win solid popular backing. Note that they are not necessarily coterminous with ethnics: patron–client networks may well cut across ethnic identities or comprise groups of people among whom ethnic and/or religious ties are not particularly salient. Also worth emphasizing is that, contrary to a common representation, 'ethnic groups are heterogeneous units and the individuals who belong to them have more than one cultural identity; which has relevance depends on the situational context' (Tordoff, 1997, pp. 92, 95, 106, 111).

The African political scene is thus the stage of cut-throat competition between rival networks of patronage articulated around regional factions, cliques or religious, ethnic, linguistic and economic groups. The merciless struggles for access to power and the wealth it secures to the winners make for weak states, despite appearances to the contrary created by the authoritarian modes of conduct followed by many African rulers, and by the concentration of coercive means in their hands. The problem comes from the fact that there is no well-established institutionalized mechanism for acceding to, and maintaining oneself in, power. All tricks are permitted so that democratic procedures, when they formally exist, are just debased versions of the models imported from the West. As a consequence, political regimes are chronically unstable even when there is no change of leader, and the rulers' time horizon is very short. In the desperate hope of clinging to power as long as possible, rulers spend most of their resources and energy in bribing their opponents into their personal clique and, if they fail, they do not hesitate to have recourse to graduated forms of intimidation that ultimately carry the threat of sheer physical elimination (Bayart, 1989).

Weakness of African rulers does not stem only from this climate of constant fear of being removed from power by rival factions, but also from their vulnerability towards their own supporters who need to be continuously rewarded to remain loyal (Booth, 1987).[13] In this fluid political set-up dominated by unregulated factional competition as well as by the instability of ruling coalitions composed of disparate elements recruited through coopting and cajoling, it is not surprising that many countries of sub-Saharan Africa appear as deeply fragmented polities. To say that in these polities local magnates hold fragmented sovereignty in their hands does not necessarily point to civil war situations such as those found in Somalia, Sierra Leone or the Congo. As attested by the leverage of the *marabouts* in Senegal, even in formally democratic and pacified countries, political fragmentation may run deep into the political fabric.

It is actually difficult to think of a political environment more uncongenial to long-term economic growth and development. At the bottom of the problem lies the explicit link between political power and wealth as well as the zero-sum game concept implicit in African politics: every group striving for power views other contending groups just as rival claimants in a purely distributive struggle, so that no arrangement or compromise with them is deemed desirable or possible. Since there are no perceived complementarities between the contending political factions, the situation is that of a zero-sum game akin to a state of political war.

The Relationship between Formal Law and Moral Norms

Thanks to their having been placed on a virtuous institutional trajectory, Western European countries were able to evolve cost-effective solutions to allow for the expansion of trade relationships and the rise of economic specialization. Two characteristics of these countries' experience deserve attention. First, the domain of public power is restricted, implying that many aspects of social intercourse which create opportunities for conflict could be organized by the individuals themselves, according to certain informal standards or fundamental rules for mutual tolerance. This is an essential feature because 'life in society, as we know it, would probably be intolerable if formal rules should be required for each and every area where interpersonal conflict might arise' (Buchanan, 1975, pp. 118–19). And, second, to the extent that formal rules are needed to resolve conflicts, the costs of operating law-enforcing agencies is not too high (ibid.; see also Shott, 1979, p. 1329).

These two achievements – the thriving of civil society and dynamic associative movements, on the one hand, and a good measure of law abidingness, on the other hand – would not have been possible without the continuous operation of moral norms conducive to the building up of trust. In fact, moral norms act as a substitute for, or a reinforcement of, state-engineered rules or control mechanisms, with the result that enforcement and punishment institutions become of secondary importance. The first effect (substitution) derives from the fact that individuals internalize public good considerations while the second one (reinforcement) arises from their conviction that the law represents the public good. In this perspective, civic consciousness appears as this attitude of respect for the law which tends to prevail among citizens who have such a conviction. When individuals thus place a high value on obedience to law, the announcement and enactment of the rules that constrain behaviour suffice to cause compliance. As we are reminded by Hausman and McPherson (1996, p. 57), Adam Smith did not fail to see that no legal system 'could rely purely on criminal sanctions for its enforcement. A widespread conviction that people ought to obey the law is essential to the maintenance of social order'.

From recent empirical studies conducted mainly in the United States, there is evidence that normative concerns, rather than purely instrumental considerations based on cost–benefit calculus, are an important determinant of law-abiding behaviour. In fact, voluntary compliance with the law depends on the extent to which people assess its legitimacy, and assessment of the law's legitimacy is strongly influenced by their assessment of the fairness of procedures used by the police and the courts. Procedural fairness, rather than distributive fairness (fairness of the outcomes themselves) or other aspects of procedures unrelated to fairness, such as expediency and predictability, seems to be the key to personal judgments of legitimacy understood as the perceived right of public authority to dictate people's behaviour (Tyler, 1990, chs 5–6).

Clearly, the fact that laws provide external validation of underlying social norms appears to be an important factor of effective implementation of the former. It also testifies that, in most situations, the law can only work as a supplement (and not a replacement) for informal enforcement of norms (Axelrod, 1986, p. 61).

THE ROLE OF MORAL NORMS

The Function of Moral Norms and the Motivations of Norm Following

Recently, a group of economic theorists interested in this topic have shown a predilection for viewing social norms as behavioural patterns which agents want to follow, given their expectations regarding others' behaviours, including the punishments meted out to players guilty of non-cooperative moves. Such an approach enables them to treat social norms as equilibrium outcomes of strategic interactions among actors rather than as social givens that are left unexplained. In more technical terms, norms are interpreted as Nash equilibria of particular games, defined as situations where agents' preferences or payoffs as well as the information structure of their interactions have been specified. In short, a social norm corresponds to a certain profile of strategies that are self-enforceable and sustainable once established (Kandori, 1992; Aoki, 2001, ch. 1; Greif, 2002).

Moral norms as they are understood in the remainder of this chapter are a different concept. They are not endogenous outcomes of interactions among individuals acting strategically within a given framework. After all, the behaviour of most people who refrain from driving away, without paying their bill, from a petrol station or a restaurant which they do not expect to visit again, or from taking free taxi rides, can obviously not be conceptualized as a game equilibrium. Neither does such a type of conceptualization square with the results from designed experiments that show relatively high rates of cooperation in PD-structured (prisoner's dilemma) games that are played only once or where defection cannot be detected, or that show significant levels of generosity even towards strangers.[14]

Rather than self-enforcing equilibria on which people coordinate, moral norms are viewed here as cultural beliefs that have the effect of truncating the players' strategy space or of modifying their preferences or payoffs. Let us first consider the truncating function of norms. What is meant here is that by ruling out some strategies because there are things that 'are not done', norms favour the selection of the cooperation equilibrium. Moral norms then provide the kind of 'friction' required to make the 'good' equilibrium more likely (Dasgupta, 1988, pp. 70–71). For example, in the initial stages of a repeated game, it is not considered ethical to cheat partners who belong to one's community because trust ought to be tried when one deals with people sharing common identity feelings. Subsequently, if partners have behaved honestly in the initial rounds, honest behaviour should be pursued. In other words, the tit-for-tat strategy is a sort of focal strategy suggested by the moral code inherent in community ties and, as we know, if everyone adheres to this strategy, the honesty equilibrium will be established.

On the other hand, a change of payoffs induced by the inculcation of moral norms makes the honesty equilibrium more likely. Here, one can think of the transformation of a prisoner's dilemma into an assurance game that may occur if such norms penalize any behaviour that exploits the benevolence or goodwill of a partner. A moral norm therefore appears as a social norm that forces or leads people to take others' interests into account.[15]

What is it that motivates people to follow a moral norm? One possibility is that 'people's desire to act on principles that no rational agent could reasonably reject, or their desire not to free-ride, but to do their part in practices of which they approve, can motivate them to follow norms, even when doing so will not benefit them materially' (Hausman and McPherson, 1996, p. 58). Thus the Kantian generalization principle, according to which an action is morally possible only if it can be universalized without self-contradiction, provides a good ground for moral behaviour: 'one ought to abstain from any action that would threaten to disrupt social order were everybody to undertake it or that one would not be prepared to see everyone else adopt'. The idea is therefore that the good consequences of a moral norm can motivate people to abide by it. Yet such an explanation suffers from the functionalist bias and remains incomplete as long as a proper account is not offered of the mechanisms by which the favourable consequences help produce or sustain the moral practice (Elster, 1989a, 1989b).

Because people are always somehow sensitive to the costs of honesty, morality does not usually mean unconditional commitment: 'each individual behaves the way he would wish others to behave, regardless of which way they actually behave'. This ethical principle indeed appears as too strong a tenet to form the basis of practical morality: honesty is too costly when people who behave honestly are constantly cheated. A more realistic code of moral behaviour is the principle of reciprocity or 'reciprocal fairness': according to this code, 'you behave the way which you would like the others to behave, but only if they actually meet this expectation' (Sugden, 1984, pp. 774–5; Elster, 1989a, p. 214). In other words, people want to be kind to those who have been kind to them (the positive reciprocity aspect) and to hurt those who hurt them (the negative reciprocity aspect) (Fehr and Tyran, 1996, p. 134; see also Rabin, 1993).[16] If we believe in experimental evidence, reciprocity appears as an empirically important motivational drive (see, for example, Eiser, 1978; Roth, 1988, 1995; Roth *et al.*, 1991; Dawes and Thaler, 1988; Frank, 1988, pp. 213–16; Camerer and Thaler, 1995; Fehr and Tyran, 1996; Fehr *et al.*, 1997, 1998a, 1998b; Rabin, 1998, pp. 21–4), a finding confirmed by questionnaire studies (see, for example, Kahnemann *et al.*, 1986; Agell and Lundberg, 1995) and by some anthropological works as well (for example, Bromley and Chapagain, 1984; Bagchia, 1992; Boehm, 1993).

Reciprocity is more likely in long-term relationships, not a surprising result since there are more opportunities for reciprocation of both the positive and negative kinds when parties interact longer. In addition, people seem to 'determine their dispositions towards others according to motives attributed to these others, not solely according to actions taken'. In particular, volition is central to the propensity to retaliate against negative actions (Rabin, 1998, pp. 22–3).

Another crucial finding is that, as already pointed out earlier in this chapter, the institutional context seems to affect human behaviour. Thus the impact of reciprocity is negligible if contracts are completely specified. In other words, competitive markets with completely specified contracts quickly converge to the competitive equilibrium, even if the resulting allocation is unfair by almost any conceivable definition of fairness (except, of course, the notion of fairness based on market clearing as a means to prevent waste). By contrast, reciprocity plays an important role when contracts are incompletely specified, even in the cases where incomplete contract situations are embedded in a competitive market. In other words, 'the existence of opportunities for reciprocation may significantly alter market outcomes' (Fehr *et al.*, 1998a, p. 19). For example, wages offered by firms in conditions of a large excess supply of workers never come close to the market clearing level when firms do not know the effort they would get from the workers who accept their contract. Again, this is because firms try to induce workers' positive reciprocity.[17]

The Role of Emotions

When transactions are one-shot deals that take place between strangers, the principle of reciprocal fairness can be taken to mean that the utility from abiding by a norm, or the disutility from violating it, rises with the level of adherence in the general population (Lindbeck *et al.*, 1996). Or, in the former kind of situations more specifically, someone who benefited from a favour becomes the others' benefactor, whereas a harmed person becomes non-cooperative (Fehr and Tyran, 1996, p. 134). However, as soon as we posit the presence of a certain proportion of inveterate opportunists in the population, it is only under special conditions that honest behaviour may be expected to become established and survive under the influence of reciprocal fairness motivations (without being able to eliminate fraudulent behaviour altogether). The sustainability of honesty becomes a more realistic prospect if, instead of simply following the principle of negative reciprocity which implies the giving up of honest behaviour as a result of bad experiences, agents are prone to punish dishonest people in a more straightforward manner; that is, if they adopt what Trivers (1971) has called 'moralistic reciprocity'.

The second-order public good problem of the nature of the incentives to punish non-cooperators then immediately arises. As a matter of fact, if punishment is costly while the benefits of honesty accrue to the population as a whole, why should selfish individuals choose to punish? This problem may be solved if a metanorm suggests the treatment of non-punishment as if it were another form of defection (Axelrod, 1986); that is, if moralistic reciprocators punish not only people who behave dishonestly but also those who fail to punish dishonest agents or who fail to punish non-punishers. When such strategies are common, it can pay to punish, even though the resulting spreading of honesty is not sufficient to compensate some individual punishers for the cost of punishing. If moralistic reciprocators are sufficiently numerous, the cost of punishing dishonest behaviour may be small, and the cost of being punished large (Fehr and Tyran, 1996, pp. 142–3).

Another possibility exists that has not escaped the attention of Axelrod (1986, pp. 57–8): a cooperation norm can be promoted and sustained if, instead of incurring a cost for the punishment of defectors, agents are rewarded for such an act, implying that they feel some sort of a gain from punishing (what he calls the 'internalization' mechanism). Honest people can thus be motivated to sanction fraudulent practices because they feel morally shocked or outraged by the behaviour of transactors who cynically exploit the benevolence of other honest agents. To relieve their feelings of indignation and anger (or what Axelrod calls their vengefulness), they are then apparently willing to incur personal costs: emotions drive these moral or self-righteous individuals to behave 'irrationally' (that is, in a reciprocally fair manner), but in a way that is ultimately beneficial to society. Or, to put it in another way, when a person is motivated by indignation, his act of punishment (such as his rejection of a bad offer in an ultimatum game) will give him the 'pleasure of revenge' (Elster, 1998, p. 69), so that the cost of punishment is only apparent or is compensated for by a pleasurable emotion. Moralistic reciprocity here appears as a propensity to behave honestly with other people sharing the same disposition, and a willingness to punish those who violate the ethical code of honesty, even at a personal cost.

The fact of the matter is that internal rewards and sanctions are often operating in individuals which are manifested in the form of self-satisfaction feelings aroused by abidance by the honesty code[18] and in the form of guilt feelings aroused by violation of this code. The other side of the guilt-feeling process is precisely the aforementioned reaction of indignation and moral outrage sparked by observations of cheating on the part of other individuals. Internal rewards and sanctions are generated by moral norms which have been internalized by the individuals (in Freudian terms, they form their superego), and provide society with a self-policing mechanism that exempts its members (or the state authorities) from the need to resort to external monitoring and punishment devices.

Internalization of standards may be said to arise when an individual actually conforms because of a personal attitude about the act itself, that is, when conformity becomes a motive of its own because it is intrinsically rewarding or because deviation is intrinsically costly (Weber, 1971, pp. 22–3; Opp, 1979, pp. 777, 792; 1982, p. 146; Jones, 1984, p. 89; Taylor, 1987, p. 13). Hence 'internalization refers to the aspect of the process of socialization through which attitudes, values, and behaviour patterns come to be maintained even in the absence of external rewards or punishments' (Jones, 1984, pp. 89–90; see also Aronfreed, 1968, 1969, 1970, p. 104; Bergsten, 1985, p. 115; Coleman, 1990, pp. 245, 293). As a result, moral norms are followed even when violation would be undetected, and therefore unsanctioned, because the moral act, which appears to be in conflict with the immediate or direct interests of the actor himself, is valued for its own sake (Griffith and Goldfarb, 1991; Elster, 1989a, p. 131, 1989b, p. 104).

To sum up, the effect of moral upbringing is (i) to inculcate in people preferences of the reciprocity type by leading them to adopt the others' viewpoint in situations where their own acts are susceptible to causing harm to others; (ii) to instil an optimistic rather than a cynical perception of other individuals, thereby contributing to establishing trust in the others' predisposition to abide by the same ethical code; (iii) to make external monitoring and punishment of dishonest behaviour less necessary owing to the desire to avoid guilt feelings and enjoy the pleasure of self-satisfaction; (iv) to drive people to resist the temptation to give in too easily to dishonest behaviour after they have had unpleasant experiences in which they were the victims of fraud and malpractices; and (v) to arouse feelings of moral outrage so that they are willing to detect and punish dishonest behaviour, even at a personal cost, and when they have not themselves been harmed by this behaviour.

Through these five effects, the inculcation of moral norms helps to establish an equilibrium dominated by honest behaviour. The first effect modifies individual preferences in such a way that the prisoner's dilemma game, where universal cheating is the only (Nash) equilibrium, becomes transformed into an assurance game, where honesty becomes a possible equilibrium outcome. By establishing trust, the second effect increases the likelihood that honest behaviour will be actually chosen by individuals with a reciprocity-type payoff structure. As for the last three effects, they help to establish the dynamic sustainability of the honesty equilibrium (for more details, see Platteau, 2000, chs 6–7).

Finally, it should be emphasized that market economies cannot function effectively if property rights (whether private or public) are not respected by a considerable majority of citizens. A situation in which individuals have the possibility to steal goods or assets belonging to other agents (or to the state), without incurring too high a risk of being detected, is not akin to a game (there is no strategic interaction) but to a single-person choice problem. It is straightforward that in such situations inculcation of moral norms helps prevent thefts. Yet, since moral beings are reciprocators, they are not ready to refrain endlessly from stealing if they somehow come to learn that many other individuals violate property rights. In other words, a game-like situation is created by the fact that individuals are sensitive to the way other people behave, and the game actually resembles the one used to study anonymous exchange between strategic transactors. Through the five above effects, moral norms thus increase the chances that an equilibrium comes into being where respect of property rights is pervasive.

Generalized Morality and the Market Order

From the above discussion, it is evident that inculcation of moral norms involves much more than purely cognitive learning. This is particularly true of primary socialization which an individual undergoes in childhood, since it takes place under circumstances that are highly charged emotionally (Berger and Luckmann, 1967, pp. 149–57). What needs to be emphasized now is that primary socialization creates in the child's consciousness a progressive abstraction from the roles and attitudes of concrete significant others (usually the parents) to roles and attitudes in general, implying that the child becomes able to identify 'with a generality of others, that is, with a society' (ibid. pp. 152–3; Lane, 1991, p. 82). This is an important aspect, since any moral rule includes an element of conceptual generality that involves the capacity to recognize the claims of others, and to impose such rules both on oneself and on others similarly situated (Griffith and Goldfarb, 1991).

If generalized morality is to be capable of sustaining order in a wide market domain, it is essential that concern for others or ability to see things from another's viewpoint be based on identity or loyalty feelings towards a large reference group. This is precisely the condition which Mark Granovetter finds problematic. He contends that norms of limited-group rather than generalized morality can tame fraud and deceit: in his own words, networks of relations, rather than institutional arrangements or generalized morality, 'are the structure that fulfils the function of sustaining order' (Granovetter, 1985, p. 491). Nonetheless, the ability to recognize the claim of a large generality of others is clearly present in the Christian ethical principle, according to which we ought not to do to other people what we would not like them to do to us. And Max Weber, as is well-known, has contrasted the achievement of generalized morality (what he called 'universally binding morality') in Western Europe in modern times with the limited domain of trust in traditional societies.

Weber's point is that the universal diffusion of unscrupulousness in the pursuit of self-interest was far more common in pre-capitalist societies than in their more competitive capitalist counterparts (Weber, 1970, quoted in Gambetta, 1988, pp. 215–16). While normative behaviour based on the principle of reciprocity ('I cannot expect others to deal honestly with me unless I am honest with them') was restricted to real kith and kin in the former societies, security of expectation or assurance has been provided by the pervasive influence of a code of generalized morality in the latter. Such a code can be considered as 'the great achievement of the ethical religions' which succeeded in destroying 'the fetters of the kin', an outcome which could not materialize in China where 'the fetters of the kinship group were never shattered' owing to the absence of a similar ideology (Weber, 1951, p. 237 – quoted in Pagden, 1988, p. 139). Note that reference to the case of China is probably unfortunate since, if this country had no established faith (it was indeed characterized by an extraordinary religious tolerance), it could rely on an effective lay morality (Confucianism) which the mandarinate and imperial court helped maintain and enforce over the centuries (Landes, 1998, p. 38).

In a similar line to that of Weber, Adam Seligman has recently emphasized the crucial role of Protestantism in 'privatizing morality'; that is, in placing an ever-increasing stress 'on the individual, the individual conscience, and the realm of the private as the arena of religious activity'. This revolution implied the rejection of the authority of ecclesiastical institutions and the grounding of religious life in the individual believer's inner ability to know religious truth. Most relevant to the present discussion, it led to the construction of new social identities stretching beyond the confines of traditional ties of the neighbourhood, the village or the parish (Seligman, 1997, pp. 138–41). Seligman thus points to a decisive shift from limited to generalized morality, when he speaks about the recasting of the bonds of 'community' as a shared tradition into new bonds of 'communality': 'Integrating all communal members in one collective definition, the boundaries between insider and outsider no longer ran through the community, but rather through each individual member', as a result of which 'the crossing of a boundary in the move from profane to sacred and from outsider to insider ... became less a public ceremony and more a private rite' (ibid., pp. 136, 141).

The historian Lawrence Stone similarly argues that in the period from 1560 to 1640, English society underwent 'a fundamental shift in human values and in the social arrangements that went with them'. This shift can be described as a change from a 'lineage society', characterized by bounded horizons and particularized modes of thought, to the more universalistic standard of values of a 'civil society'. The causes of this fundamental change are interdependent: 'the Reformation with its powerful drive for the Christianisation of society and its claim to overriding moral allegiance through the preaching of the Word; grammar school and university education in the rhetoric of Humanism with its stress on loyalty to the prince; Inns of Court education in respect for an abstraction, the common law, as superior to any private or local loyalties to individuals'(Stone, 1990, p. 100). In the context of the rise of the powers and claims of the state, encouraged by the Protestant Reformers, kin and client loyalties were thus increasingly subordinated to the higher obligations of patriotism and obedience to the sovereign (ibid., p. 93).

Other authors have highlighted the role of political doctrines in the diffusion of generalized morality. The ability to put others on a similar footing with oneself would thus lie at the heart of classical republicanism, a political doctrine (initially formulated by Nicolo Machiavelli and several of his contemporaries and later taken over by Alexis de Tocqueville) centred upon the notions of a well-ordered republic and public-spirited commitment to the common good. The emphasis on virtues of civic humanism or consciousness, and on the need to withstand the dictates of private interest whenever they undermine the public good, was expected to enable men from different kin groups to trust each other, thus making possible the operation of a 'commercial society' (Pagden, 1988, p. 139; McNally, 1988, pp. 40–43). The communal republics of Northern Italy during late medieval times served as a reference case for many founders of this political doctrine: thanks to a first and fervent allegiance to their own city-state, members of these mini-republics are supposed to have shown an unparalleled degree of civic engagement, as a result of which trust could be extended beyond the limits of kinship further than anywhere else in Europe in this era (Putnam, 1993, pp. 127–31; Fukuyama, 1995, p. 108). According to Skinner, the social ethos of Calvinism can actually be seen to constitute a special case of classical republicanism (Skinner, 1974). In other words, 'it was not a specifically Calvinist or Puritan work ethic which encouraged economic take-off in the Protestant cities of the seventeenth century, or Christianity itself in the medieval cities of north and central Italy, but the secular ethic of classical republicanism' (Pagden, 1988, p. 139).

A major lesson to draw from the above discussion is that it is inappropriate to account for 'the rise of the Western world' in modern times only in terms of a powerful 'cult of individuality'. Equally important is the fact that in Western Europe since the Middle Ages the emancipation of the individual (within the framework of national spaces) from feudal interference and from erstwhile networks of social and political allegiance went hand in hand with the development of generalized morality, in which abstract principles or rules of conduct are considered equally applicable to a vast range of social relations beyond the narrow circle of personal acquaintances. Thus, if attention is turned to the Protestant Reformation, it is essential to enlarge the conventional wisdom according to which it gave a big boost to personal autonomy, education, scientific inquiry, entrepreneurship and the thrifty use of money and time – all of which values foster capital accumulation and growth (see, for example, Landes, 1998, pp. 175–81) – to underline the transformation of social bonds that went with it, in particular, the 'privatization' of religion, and a moral allegiance that goes beyond the confines of kith and kin.

Countries that have a generalized morality but where individual emancipation is held under severe control by the custodians of the ruling doctrine, whether religious (as in Islamic countries where holy men govern society and religion reigns supreme) or lay (as in Ancient China where the mandarinate and imperial court, in their capacity to define the official doctrine, could judge individual thought and behaviour), are not in ideal conditions to develop: private initiative, innovation and dissent are strongly repressed as the whim takes the ruler.[19] The 'political secularization of faith', as Kriegel has called it, is also the trap that, unlike its Western counterpart, nineteenth-century Eastern Europe was not able to escape. The same pitfall drove into prolonged economic decadence inquisitorial Spain and the regions which were unfortunate enough to fall under its rule. This applies not only to the southern part of the Low Countries (see above), but also to neighbouring Portugal, where a period of remarkable advance in sciences and techniques was brought to a close when pressure from the Roman Church and Spain led the Portuguese crown to abandon its policy of religious tolerance at the turn of the sixteenth century, soon to fall under more direct Spanish influence.[20]

On the other hand, countries whose citizens have a large margin of freedom but where no public morality exists to place restraint on the harm which individuals can inflict upon each other – in particular, where there is no ethics preaching the respect of private property rights – are not in a good position to seize growth opportunities, as the example of present-day Russia or countries of the Caucasus attests.

A final word of caution: it must be reckoned that the borderline between limited-group and generalized morality is somewhat blurred because morality is rarely applied indiscriminately to all human beings. It is thus obvious that Western societies have typically ceased to apply their moral–ethical principles once they came into contact with non-European peoples on the periphery of 'their' world. The history of slavery and of colonial exploitation is there to remind us of this basic fact: for example, it was considered morally legitimate by Europeans to cheat American Indians on the grounds that they were lazy, irrational and unwilling to repay their debts (Ortiz, 1967, p. 203). This being said, if limited-group morality is understood as morality restricted to concrete people with whom one shares common identity feelings, while generalized morality is morals applicable to abstract people (to whom one is not necessarily tied through personal, family or ethnic links), one is on better grounds to argue that the Western world has a very particular history rooted in a culture of individualism pervaded by norms of generalized morality.

Reinforcement Processes

The Church (both Catholic and Protestant) obviously played a central role in the process of moral norm generation and maintenance throughout modern Western history. Its impact was all the more significant as (i) it promised a considerable reward (an eternal life of absolute happiness) for all those who were ready to incur personal sacrifices by behaving in other-regarding ways; and (ii) monitoring costs could be brought to a minimum insofar as God was thought to act as an impartial and free monitoring agent. Regarding the first aspect, the following must be noted: unpleasant experiences of dishonest dealings do not easily discourage believers if they are persuaded that, by continuing to behave morally, they will deserve special attention from God. There is an obvious analogy between this argument and the point made by Kant that ingratitude can stimulate giving, because the benefactor 'may well be convinced that the very disdain of any such reward as gratitude only adds to the moral worth of his benefaction' (Schoeck, 1987, p. 204, quoted in Elster, 1989a, p. 259). As far as the second aspect is concerned, the main effect is that the availability of a free monitoring device allows honesty to be sustained even in the presence of high costs of fraud detection. In the words of Frank:

> Teaching moral values was once the nearly exclusive province of organized religion. The church was uniquely well equipped to perform this task because it had a ready answer to the question, 'Why shouldn't I cheat when no one is looking?' Indeed, for the religious person, this question does not even arise, for God is *always* looking. (Frank, 1988, p. 250)

Two remarks are in order. First, all (external) manifestations of religiosity and clericalism are not necessarily correlated with cooperative (honest) behaviour or civicness. In certain historical or social settings, engagement in catholic groups and adherence to catholic rituals, for example, has been purely formal and even hypocritical, with the result that no genuine commitment towards taking the others' viewpoint into account was implied. Robert Putnam has thus recently argued that in Italy, at least, 'the most devout church-goers are the least civic-minded' (Putnam, 1993, pp. 175–6; see also pp. 107, 130). In fact, such hypocrisy has sometimes sparked off reactions by non-clerical movements which acted as more genuine defenders of moral tenets. Second, as has already been illustrated above, norms of generalized morality are not the exclusive province of organized religions. They have also been produced by non-clerical organizations, such as freemasonry. In addition, moral norm reinforcement may come from state agents or political leaders acting as norm reactivators.

LIMITED MORALITY AT WORK

Limited Morality and the Private Sector

Rural communities in areas with a long tradition of low population densities have a considerable ability to regulate many aspects of social and economic life, including all matters relating to land access. This remains true even when pressure on land resources increases. Unfortunately, there is a counterpart to this ability of rural communities to address successfully governance problems not easily amenable to market or state solution, namely their parochial character (see, for example, Bowles and Gintis, 1998, p. 23). This parochial character may lead them to adopt protective attitudes, and even to give in to chauvinistic tendencies if they feel too much threatened by outsiders or outside forces. Such attitudes and tendencies may take on the form of sheer malpractices and deceit – for example, double deals directed against strangers, sales of land parcels without informing the (stranger) buyer of the charges weighing on them (mortgage, in particular) and so on. In other words, traditional values according to which rural lands ought to remain in the hands of the 'sons of the village', since they are ancestral property, give rise to double standards reflected in norms of limited morality. And such norms are the cause of pervasive ineffi- ciencies that result from transaction costs and serious imperfections in land markets but also in other rural factor markets (see Platteau, 2000, ch. 4).

In tribal societies, morals typically differ according to whether one deals with kinsmen or with strangers. This double standard in ethical codes of behaviour is vividly manifested in the following concomitant facts: on the one hand, bargaining or haggling is considered to be aimed at exploiting and cheating the partners and, on the other hand, sheer commercial practices are permitted only with strangers. A merchant always steals, as has been noted with respect to Kapauka Papuans of New Guinea, and that is why trade inside one's tribe is badly looked at while trade conducted with non-kin brings social prestige as well as profit to the successful merchant (Pospisil, 1958, p. 127). The fact of the matter is that, in tribal ideology, to cheat one's clan is equivalent to cheating oneself, whereas cheating outsiders gives strength to the cheater's clan and weakens the clan of the cheated partner (Massoz, 1982, pp. 87–8). On the basis of his field observations in Kabylia province, Algeria, Pierre Bourdieu wrote in the same vein:

> Amicable transactions between relatives and allied people contrast with market trans-
> actions ... and 'the foodstuff or cattle of the fellah' are traditionally opposed to 'the
> foodstuff or the cattle of the market'; old informants can talk for ever about the guile
> and deceit commonly observed on the 'big markets', that is, in dealings with strangers.
> These are stories about mules that run away as soon as they have reached the new
> purchaser's destination; about oxen that are rubbed with a special plant so as to make
> them swell up and thereby appear fatter than they actually are; about related purchasers
> who collude to propose very low prices. (Bourdieu, 1980, p. 196 [my translation];
> see also Evans-Pritchard, 1940; Sahlins, 1963,1968; Polanyi, 1977, p. 59)

Limited morality is bound to affect the business sector by segmenting the domain of relationships within which business is viable. In the case of sub- Saharan Africa (SSA), Kennedy has thus observed that there exists 'a marked reluctance' to establish capital-pooling arrangements or business partnerships among non-kinsmen. This reluctance is to be mainly ascribed to 'the widespread fear that partners will cheat in some way or fail to pull their weight', which contributes to create an 'atmosphere of suspicion and pessimism concerning the motivations of others' (Kennedy, 1988, p. 166). Such a climate of distrust is highly detrimental to African capitalism insofar as, by preventing the estab- lishment of genuinely corporate forms of business associations, 'it closes one of the most important potential avenues to firm expansion and reduces the likelihood that indigenous companies can become sufficiently competitive to mount an effective challenge to foreign companies' (ibid.).

The latter argument, however, is not entirely convincing. As a matter of fact, intense familism combined with distrust of non-kin in traditional China anticipated the business culture of present-day Taiwan Province of China and Hong Kong (China) (Fukuyama, 1995, p. 89). Nonetheless, the fact that many Taiwanese firms are small- and medium-sized – largely as a result of their being based on family ties – did not prevent them from providing a major impetus to national economic growth, particularly in the export manufacturing sector (Hamilton, 1998). Something more subtle than sheer size probably accounts for the poor organizational performance of many African firms. Contrary to Chinese enterprises which are controlled by a restricted number of close relatives or members of the lineage, African businesses are generally opened to a large number of kin belonging to the extended family and the tribe of the owner(s). Problems arise because relations with kin entail multiple social obligations that may easily cause the ruin of such businesses. Indeed, if tribal ideology, through diffusion of values of limited morality, tends to make kinspeople more trustworthy than strangers, it also tends to discourage accumulation efforts through diffusion of strongly egalitarian social norms (Platteau, 2000, ch. 5). Close monitoring of the successful efforts of a kinsman gives rise to continuous harassment and to serious strains and tensions if the latter is not considered to be generous and fair enough with his subordinates.

Another crucial difference between SSA and Taiwan Province of China lies in the fact that, unlike the former region, the latter benefits from a host of institutions and informal mechanisms (such as the pervasive business networks mentioned earlier) that have enabled it to establish trust between separate economic entities, for example between small-scale family businesses or between them and large-scale upstream or subcontracting firms (Hamilton *et al.*, 1990; Hayami and Kawagoe, 1993; Hayami, 1998; Hamilton, 1998). The unwillingness to share information with other enterprises and the absence of multilateral punishment mechanisms to discourage cheaters, which Marcel Fafchamps (1996) and Abigaïl Barr (1999) noted for Ghanaian firms, are perhaps indicative of the lack of trust and cooperativeness beyond circles of acquaintances in sub-Saharan Africa. The only exception, notes Fafchamps in a revealing manner, concerns Accra's women fishmongers, whose situation is somewhat peculiar: 'they all belong to a closely knit neighbourhood, they share the same ethnic background, their husbands go to sea together, and they all sell in the same market' (Fafchamps, 1996, p. 441).

A more general lesson from the same study is that the lack of contractual discipline in Ghana is real and is reflected, *ex post*, in numerous delivery and payment delays. *Ex ante*, it is evident from the fact that firms often resort to unwieldy manners of doing business because they do not want to take the chance of a problem arising. Typically, they fall back on a 'flea market' mode of transacting: 'inspect the good on the spot, pay cash and walk away with it'. In other words, they avoid all transactions that involve delayed obligations that make breach of contract possible (ibid., pp. 441–4). A still more recent study using a larger set of survey data collected in several African countries (Burundi, Cameroon, Ghana, Ivory Coast, Kenya, Zambia and Zimbabwe) has as one of its conclusions that African managed firms face more problems with individuals than other firms, in particular firms run by Asian entrepreneurs, such as Indians in Kenya (Bigsten *et al.*, 1998). Moreover, firms that buy from family and friends encounter more late delivery problems, suggesting that relations based on family, friendship or ethnicity/kinship tend to raise the incidence of contract non-performance. At the same time, however, such relations make it easier for firms to solve disputes (through informal channels).

Limited Morality and the Public Sphere

Norms of limited morality are bound to affect not only the private but also the public sector. Nepotism and favouritism are often found to be major obstacles on the way to effective functioning of the bureaucracy and public enterprises. Codes of conduct emphasize the strength of ties to close social relations; procedural norms, when they exist, are particularistic; professional standards are low; reward and sanction mechanisms (including litigation) as well as taxation and subsidies are meted out in a specific way so as to make patronage effective instead of promoting economic efficiency and shared growth.

It is revealing that an important consequence of the declining role of kinship that was observed in England during the sixteenth and seventeenth centuries was the beginning of a gradual erosion of the moral legitimacy accorded to nepotism as a factor in recruitment to state and private offices. According to Lawrence Stone, it became increasingly difficult for younger and illegitimate sons of the landed society to find 'comfortable berths in the public service, either at home or in the colonies'. Each time 'there had to be a struggle, and each time there was competition to the ties of blood or marriage from the alternative principles of money and merit'. Moreover, 'the influence was primarily exercised by fathers for sons, or sometimes uncles for nephews, and only rarely for more distant members of the kin. It was thus a product of the bonding of the nuclear family rather than of the lineage' (1990, p. 97).

Large parts of the world have not yet completed the long evolution that causes a fundamental shift from particularistic to universalistic standards of values. Sub-Saharan Africa is a region well-known for the widespread prevalence of nepotistic practices. This is a logical outcome in a system dominated by patronage politics. Once established in key positions of the political power structure (at the level of the presidency, the politico-military hierarchy, the top civil servants, the ruling party officials and so on), it is the duty of the dominant faction, group or clique to remunerate a vast array of supporters, including the 'small men' who draw their livelihood from participating at the lowest level of this structure (Bayart, 1989, pp. 291–3). The methods used involve clear favouritism in the distribution of public jobs and subsidies (Bates, 1981, 1983; Teranishi, 1997) or a free run for fraudulent acquisition of riches through trafficking, racketeering, plundering and looting (Bayart, 1989).

The problem of favouritism is far from being the monopoly of sub-Saharan Africa. Many Asian countries, especially in South Asia, are fraught with this problem. Even though they have inherited the norms of the Western legal tradition due to more or less prolonged existence of a colonial state,[21] South Asian societies still remain under the strong influence of traditional patterns of social relations, in particular the principle of the primacy of family and caste relationships. Under these circumstances, it is not surprising that rights and obligations associated with these patterns still tend to predominate over the rules and norms rooted in the abstract individual (as opposed to the concrete person) which are the typical products of Western history. In one of his books, the Indian psychoanalyst Kakar has aptly described the essential nature of social relations in modern India. In particular, he has emphasized the persisting lack of a common code of generalized morality in Indian society. I cannot resist the temptation to quote him at some length given the great pertinence of his analysis in the context of this chapter:

> Among those Indians closely identified with the process of modernization, the well-educated urban elite who hold positions of power in modern institutions, the psycho-historical fact of the primacy of relationships, of family loyalties, of *jati* connections, is often a source of considerable emotional stress. For although intellectually the Indian professional or bureaucrat may agree with his Western counterpart that, for example, the criterion for appointment or promotion to a particular job must be objective, decisions based solely on the demands of the task and 'merits of the case', he cannot root out the cultural conviction that his relationship to the individual under consideration is the single most important factor in his decision. This conflict between the rational criteria of specific tasks and institutional goals rooted in Western societal values, and his own deeply held belief (however ambivalent) in the importance of honouring family and *jati* bonds is typical among highly educated and prominently employed Indians. And among the vast majority of tradition-minded countrymen – whether it be a *bania* bending the law to facilitate the business transaction of a fellow *jati* member, or a *marwari* industrialist employing an insufficiently qualified but distantly related job applicant as a manager, or the clerk accepting bribes in order to put an orphaned niece through school – dishonesty, nepotism and corruption as they are understood in the West are merely abstract concepts. These negative constructions are irrelevant to Indian psycho-social experience, which, from childhood on, nurtures one standard of responsible adult action, and one only, namely, an individual's lifelong obligation to his kith and kin. Allegiance to impersonal institutions and abstract moral concepts is without precedent in individual developmental experience, an adventitious growth in the Indian inner world. Guilt and its attendant inner anxiety are aroused only when individual actions go against the principle of the primacy of relationships,

not when foreign ethical standards of justice and efficiency are breached. (Kakar, 1978, pp. 125–6, added emphasis).

In Pakistan, reciprocal favours and limited morality are an essential ingredient of bureaucratic practice and they are formalized enough to have a name: *vartan bhanji*. In Baluchistan and the North-West Frontier Province, the two most tribal areas of the country, webs of traditional relationships are still pervasive and run through regional official agencies and municipalities. Thus, in a town like Peshawar, Pathan bureaucrats run their offices like the tribal *jirgas* they have been brought up with (Duncan, 1989, pp. 242–4).

The main contrast here is with East Asia, and Northeast Asia in particular, where the bureaucracy appears remarkably autonomous. There, bureaucrats 'were able to treat the government of their country as if it were the management of a household'. In the Republic of Korea and Taiwan Province of China, for example, political leaders, who ascended from a military background, regarded the building up of their country's industrial power 'as the first order of business', in a context dominated by geopolitical considerations – the strong determination to repossess mainland China, for Taiwan Province of China, and the need to defend itself in the context of the Cold War for the Republic of Korea (Aoki *et al.*, 1997, p. 26; see also Luedde-Neurath, 1988; White and Wade, 1988; Wade, 1990) – and influenced by a tradition of centralized governance (Hayami, 1997, p. 281). Recent research reveals that the absence of a politically powerful, dominant economic class was an important historical condition that favoured the emergence of effective and dedicated administrations in this part of the world (Woo-Cumings, 1997). They have been effective in the sense of being relatively little prone to rent-seeking behaviour, and they have been dedicated in the sense of having legitimized their control 'by the equal payment of growth dividends to all economic classes'. Interestingly, this model of 'shared growth' in Northeast Asia 'seems to be a profoundly path-dependent phenomenon that evolved from the unique historical conditions prevailing immediately after the Pacific War' (Aoki *et al.*, 1997, pp. 26–7; Aoki, 1997).

CONCLUSION

What the above analysis shows is that there is definitely nothing automatic about the rise of the market order. Such order rests on delicate conditions that are not easily forthcoming. The crux of the matter is that it needs to be embedded in a suitable sociopolitical fabric. The fabric required is certainly not unique and there are several configurations that are no doubt suitable for the purpose of sustaining a market order, as witnessed by the noticeable differences between East Asian, North American and Western European capitalist systems, for example. The fact remains, however, that the market can be perverted and deeply distorted if tried in a hostile environment, as evidenced most dramatically by the present-day experiences of ex-socialist countries lying to the east of Poland and Hungary, countries from sub-Saharan Africa, and some countries in Asia and Latin America.

No market order can function satisfactorily – that is, at reasonably low transaction costs – if there is not a right combination of rule of law and norms of generalized morality. The former requirement implies that a viable state structure is established that is able to enforce in an impartial manner rules and laws regarding respect of property, contract fulfilment, bank regulation, bankruptcies, control of abusive exercise of market power, and so on. This presupposes that the ruling elite, whether it has been democratically elected or not, has come to understand that its long-term interest depends on its being able to enlist the cooperation of dominated groups or classes on terms acceptable to them. If that objective is missed, the whole sociopolitical fabric will be threatened with the risk of political turmoil and popular uprisings, which is liable to lead to continuous changes of regime (think of the disturbed history of Chile) or, worse, to civil war ending in chaos, or in takeovers by extremist groupings acting in the name of the exploited masses. The last possibility is especially worrying in countries where the border between morality of laws and morality of faith remains tenuous. In such countries, indeed, as the recent experiences of Iran and Afghanistan testify, clerics may rise to power, driven by radical anti-market ideologies predicated on the need to protect the poor against corrupted feudalist–capitalist elites. Whichever the political trajectory that eventually obtains, the result is always chronic instability and an environment deeply adverse to investment and growth.

As for the second requirement, it means that exchanges can take place on a large enough scale only if people have come to adopt an attitude of moralistic reciprocity based on initial trust. This is because mechanisms of multilateral reputation, although extremely useful, cannot be expected to solve the trust problem in all circumstances. To admit that moral norms have a role to play in economic development is an embarrassing statement because nobody really knows how to make the right kind of norms emerge. Also it is important to stress again that there is no unique trajectory in this regard: for example, it would be absurd to contend that Africa needs to evolve the same norms as Western Europe or Asia. The crucial lesson from the European experience is that, in some way or other, societies that want to develop market-based specialization of economic activities require a shift from limited to generalized morality or, in Weberian language, from *Gemeinschaft* to *Gesellschaft*.

If we adhere to an evolutionary view of the Hayekian kind, one can make the point that norms of the required sort will eventually emerge in societies where the state is intent on long-term development. After all, the argument made in this chapter does not say that growth is arrested, but only slowed down in the absence of norms of generalized reciprocity. It could therefore be contended that, whatever the initial market imperfections resulting from uncontrolled opportunistic tendencies, the important fact is that markets somehow develop since they are bound to generate social norms that will have the effect of eventually mitigating incentive problems. True, such norms are likely to differ among societies and determine in them different growth trajectories, some more satisfactory than others, yet the crucial point is that growth occurs and is sustainable.

Unfortunately, even assuming that they are effectively at work, evolutionary processes may prove too slow to meet the challenges now confronting laggard countries. This is because the pressure of an external threat under the form of globalization creates a need to develop more quickly than can be achieved through an endogenous evolution of moral norms. History has nevertheless taught us that strong states relying on nationalistic ideologies can substitute for missing norms of fair behaviour. In fact, such norms might develop as a result of nationalistic fervour. For many countries of sub-Saharan Africa, however, this is not an easy path to tread. They are young nations that gather varied groups of population that are not used to living under the same rule. Political evolutions during both the colonial and post-colonial periods have generally failed to consolidate them as one would have wished.

The question therefore remains as to what support could be given to these young and fragile nations fraught with fragmented loyalties to help them to establish the right kinds of norms and political institutions. In particular, are present decentralization and liberalization efforts promoted by official and private donor agencies a step in the right direction? To the extent that they encourage the emergence of a sizable middle class with a growing measure of autonomy, they may be expected to lead to a situation where the state will be forced to adopt policies more congenial to long-term economic development. They could help to create also generalized trust by building up local entities that it is hoped, cut across kinship and ethnic boundaries. Whether these expectations are warranted and a genuine civil society can arise from institutional decentralization remains an open question. The answer will probably depend on the robustness of existing patronage networks, and the factional segmentation of the African polity in the face of such decentralization efforts.

NOTES

1. Adam Seligman defines trust as 'some sort of belief in the goodwill of the other, given the opaqueness of other's intentions and calculations' (Seligman, 1997, p. 43).
2. For instance, the way the (merchant) law provided protection of the *bona fide* purchaser (against the claims of the original owner of stolen or lost goods) from the beginning of the seventeenth century in England solved an important problem which confronted merchants

and hindered trade for many centuries in Europe (North, 1990, pp. 128–9; see also Rosenberg and Birdzell (1986, ch. 2).

3. There are three types of agents in Kali's model: two types behave mechanistically with regard to cheating, either honestly or dishonestly, while the third type, the opportunists, behave strategically on the basis of cost–benefit considerations.

4. 'Business in present conditions is so complicated and corrupt that reliability and really good contacts are highly valued,' said the president of a tourist company from Novosibirsk, the Russian Federation (Ledeneva, 1998, p. 157).

5. As a matter of fact, an increase in network size has two different welfare effects depending on the sphere of the economy. When the network creams off 'good' types (the honest agents and the opportunists who choose to behave honestly) and therefore worsens the pool of agents remaining in the anonymous market, the welfare of people involved in market exchange falls and honesty becomes easier to enforce within the network. The lump-sum entrance fee falls and, as a result, the welfare of the members of the business group is raised. Thus, as the size of the network increases, the welfare of its members rises at the expense of the people operating in the anonymous market. If the network is so large that the fraction of the population remaining in anonymous market exchange is small, it becomes an economically efficient institution. Otherwise, it is inefficient.

6. Another illustration of this possibility is provided by Kranton (1996) who makes the point that personalized exchange can persist even when it is inefficient for the economy. Note that her model is based on the assumption that in reciprocal exchange agents can only obtain the commodity produced by their trading partner.

7. France suffered a humiliating defeat at the end of the Seven Years War since it lost its New World colonies to England where the Crown, thanks to the stabilization of its relations with the parliament, was in a much better position to obtain funds without jeopardizing the economy.

8. The pedigreed families and clans (usually known as *boyars*) which originally owned *votchiny* (a *votchina* is a land estate which was the legal property of the *boyar*) were gradually uprooted, especially under Ivan IV, implying that their estates were transformed into so-called *pomest'e* lands which they and their descendants could retain only for as long as they continued to render satisfactory service to the tsar. Their status thus began to resemble that of the more humble *dvoriane*, who were initially employed as domestic servitors of the appanage princes (and most of whom were actually slaves) to be later transformed into nobles by the tsar to counterbalance the pedigreed families and clans (Pipes, 1995, ch. 4).

9. According to Pipes again, the imposition of service obligations on all holders of land (and owners of serfs) had profound implications for the future course of Russian history since it meant nothing less than the elimination of private property in land. 'This occurred at the very time when Western Europe was moving in the opposite direction. With the decline of vassalage after 1300, Western fiefs passed into outright ownership, while the development of trade and manufacture produced an additional source of wealth in the form of capital. In the early modern west, the bulk of the wealth gradually accumulated in the hands of society, giving it powerful leverage against the crown; in Russia, it is the crown that, as it were, expropriated society. It was the combination of absolute political power with nearly complete control of the country's productive resources that made the Muscovite monarchy so formidable an institution' (Pipes, 1995, pp. 93–4; see also Pipes, 1999, ch. 4).

10. It is estimated that, during the early 1990s, aid accounted for almost half the income of the typical government of those (mainly African) countries that the World Bank classifies as least developed (Moore, 1998).

11. For example, the medieval kingdoms of the Niger bend, such as the kingdom of Abomey, were built on the trade of salt, cloth and beads which were brought south from the Sahara across to West Africa, on the one hand, and gold, ivory and slaves which were taken back to the Barbary coast and from there into medieval Europe, on the other hand (Goody, 1988, p. 23; see also Coquery-Vidrovitch, 1985, p. 99).

12. Revealingly, the 1976 Nigerian constitutional draft held that politics opened up the possibility of 'acquiring wealth and prestige, of being in a position to distribute jobs, contracts, grants or gifts to one's kin and political allies' (Bayart, 1986, p. 123).

13. Hence the observation that, if African governments are primarily concerned with maintenance of political power and distribution of wealth to themselves and their supporters, 'the reason lies not in their special greed or malevolence but rather in the fact that rulers of new states cannot afford the luxury of disinterested public service because their position as rulers is fundamentally unstable' (Fieldhouse, 1986, p. 94).

14. Just to give one striking example, in their field experiments in New York city (during the spring of 1968), Hornstein and his colleagues found that, in what is typically a one-shot game, an astonishingly high 45 per cent of 'lost' wallets were returned completely intact to their owner by passers-by who came across them (cited by Frank, 1988, p. 216; for a more recent survey, see Ledyard, 1995).

15. In other words, moral norms differ from social norms (for example, a norm of etiquette) in the sense that they constrain the full-blown pursuit of self-interest in PD-structured situations.

16. Note that reciprocal fairness is neither purely egoistic behaviour (since reciprocators incur some personal cost in responding to other people's actions) nor purely altruistic behaviour (since 'gifts are exclusively presented to people who gave something before, or are supposed to give something back later') (Fehr and Tyran, 1996, p. 134).

17. Contract choices can obviously be affected by reciprocal behaviour. Firms may thus favour simple, non-incentive-compatible labour contracts that induce workers to provide effort beyond the level that is enforceable by incentive compatible devices (Fehr *et al.*, 1997; 1998b).

18. Thus the dean of a Faculty at the university of Akademgorodok (Russia) expressed his motivation to help by saying that 'If I am asked, I drop everything and help the other person, because I can imagine myself in his place. Indifference or refusal is a psychological trauma' (Ledeneva, 1998, p. 163).

19. The interruption of Islamic and Chinese intellectual and technological advance at critical times in their history (for example, the abandonment of the programme of great voyages in China during the early sixteenth century, or the fact that the Confucian doctrine supported and diffused by Chinese rulers abhorred mercantilistic practices) was decided at the highest level in an abrupt and irrevocable fashion and institutionalized in the minutest details (Landes, 1998, pp. 52–5, 96–7, 200; Jones, 1981, pp. 168–9).

20. *Stricto sensu*, the Inquisition was installed in Portugal only in the 1540s and it did not become 'grimly unrelenting' until the 1580s, after the union of the Portuguese and Spanish crowns in the person of Philip II (Landes, 1998, p. 133).

21. One may thus think of British India in which the Indian Civil Service and Western education have been solidly implanted by the colonial power, a significant event given the profound imprint that these two institutions have left on the elites of the post-colonial societies born of the old British Empire.

BIBLIOGRAPHY

Agell, J. and P. Lundberg (1995), 'Theories of pay and unemployment: Survey evidence from Swedish manufacturing firms', *Scandinavian Journal of Economics*, 97(1): 295–308.

Anderson, P. (1974), *Lineages of the Absolutist State*, London and New York: Verso.

Aoki, M. (1997), 'Unintended fit: Organizational evolution and government design of institutions in Japan', in M. Aoki, H.K. Kim and M. Okuno-Fujiwara (eds), *The Role of Government in East Asian Development – Comparative Institutional Analysis*, Oxford: Clarendon Press, pp. 233–53.

Aoki, M. (2001), *Towards a Comparative Institutional Analysis*, Cambridge MA: MIT Press.

Aoki, M., K. Murdock and M. Okuno-Fujiwara (1997), 'Beyond the East Asian miracle: Introducing the market-enhancing view', in M. Aoki, H.K. Kim and M. Okuno-

Fujiwara (eds), *The Role of Government in East Asian Development – Comparative Institutional Analysis*, Oxford: Clarendon Press, pp. 1–37.

Aronfreed, J. (1968), *Conduct and Conscience: The Socialization of Internalized Control Over Behavior*, New York: Academic Press.

Aronfreed, J. (1969), 'The concept of internalization', in D.A. Goslin (ed.), *Handbook of Socialization – Theory and Research*, Chicago: Rand-McNally.

Aronfreed, J. (1970), 'The socialization of altruistic and sympathetic behavior: Some theoretical and experimental analyses', in J. Macaulay and L. Berkowitz (eds), *Altruism and Helping Behavior*, New York, San Francisco and London: Academic Press, pp. 103–26.

Arrow, K. (1971), 'Political and economic evaluation of social effects and externalities', in M. Intriligator (ed.), *Frontiers of Quantitative Economics*, Amsterdam: North-Holland, pp. 3–25.

Arrow, K. (1973), *Information and Economic Behavior*, Stockholm: Federation of Swedish Industries.

Austen, R. (1987), *African Economic History – Internal Development and External Dependency*, London: James Currey, and Portsmouth: Heinemann.

Axelrod, R. (1986), 'An evolutionary approach to norms', *American Political Science Review*, 80(4): 1095–1111; reprinted in R. Axelrod (ed.) (1997), *The Complexity of Cooperation – Agent-Based Models of Competition and Collaboration*, Princeton, NJ: Princeton University Press, pp. 44–68.

Bagchia, A. (1992), 'Riding the free rider – A lesson from Barrackpore', *Economic and Political Weekly*, 27(34): 1778–80.

Banfield, E.C. (1958), *The Moral Basis of a Backward Society*, Chicago: The Free Press.

Bardhan, P.K. (1993), 'Symposium on democracy and development', *Journal of Economic Perspectives*, 7(3): 45–9.

Barr, A. (1999), 'Entrepreneurial networks in the Ghanaian manufacturing sector', paper presented at the Workshop on Group Behaviour and Development, World Institute for Development Economics Research (WIDER), Helsinki, 10–11 September.

Bates, R.H. (1976), *Rural Responses to Industrialization: A Study of Village Zambia*, New Haven: Yale University Press.

Bates, R.H. (1981), *Markets and States in Tropical Africa: The Political Basis of Agricultural Policies*, Berkeley, CA: University of California Press.

Bates, R.H. (1983), *Essays on the Political Economy of Rural Africa*, Cambridge: Cambridge University Press.

Bates, R.H. and D.-H.D. Lien (1985), 'A note on taxation, development and representative government', *Politics and Society*, 14(1): 53–70.

Bayart, J.F. (1986), 'Civil society in Africa', in P. Chabal (ed.) *Political Domination in Africa – Reflections on the Limits of Power*, Cambridge: Cambridge University Press, pp. 109–25.

Bayart, J.F. (1989), *L 'Etat en Afrique*, Paris: Fayard.

Berger, P. and T. Luckmann (1967), *The Social Construction of Reality*, Harmondsworth, UK: Penguin Books.

Bergsten, G.S. (1985), 'On the role of social norms in a market economy', *Public Choice*, 45(1): 113–37.

Berkowitz, D., K. Pistor and J.F. Richard (1999), 'Economic development, legality and the transplant effect' (mimeo), University of Pittsburgh, Department of Economics, Pittsburgh.

Berman, B. (1984), 'Structure and process in the bureaucratic states of colonial Africa', *Development and Change*, 15(2): 161–202.

Bienen, H. (1987), 'Domestic political considerations for food policy', in J. Mellor, C. Delgado and M. Blackie (eds) *Accelerating Food Production in Sub-Saharan Africa*, London and Baltimore: Johns Hopkins University Press, pp. 296–308.

Bigsten, A., P. Collier, S. Dercon, M. Fafchamps, B. Gauthier, J.W. Gunning, A. Oduro, R. Oostendorp, C. Patillo, M. Soderbom, F. Teal and A. Zeufack (1998), 'Contract flexibility and conflict resolution: Evidence from African manufacturing' (mimeo), World Bank, Washington, DC.

Binmore, K. (1992), *Fun and Games: A Text on Game Theory*, Cambridge, MA: D.C. Heath and Co.

Binswanger, H.P. and P. Collier (1999), 'Ethnic loyalties, state formation and conflict' (mimeo), World Bank, Washington, DC.

Blockmans, W.P. (1994), 'Voracious states and obstructing cities: An aspect of state formation in pre-industrial Europe', in C. Tilly and W.P. Blockmans (eds) *Cities and the Rise of States in Europe, A.D. 1000 to 1800*, Boulder, CO: Westview Press, pp. 218–50.

Blount, S. (1995), 'When social outcomes aren't fair: The effect of causal attributions on preferences', *Organizational Behavior and Human Decision Processes*, 63(2): 131–44.

Blum, J. (1961), *Lord and Peasant in Russia – From the Ninth to the Nineteenth Century*, Princeton, NJ: Princeton University Press.

Boehm, C. (1993), 'Egalitarian behavior and reverse dominance hierarchy', *Current Anthropology*, 34(3): 227–54.

Bonney, R. (1991), *The European Dynastic States 1494–1660*, Oxford: Oxford University Press.

Boone, C. (1992), *Merchant Capital and the Roots of State Power in Senegal 1930–1985*, Cambridge: Cambridge University Press.

Boone, C. (1994), 'States and ruling classes in post-colonial Africa: The enduring contradictions of power', in J.S. Migdal, A. Kohli and V. Shue (eds), *State Power and Social Forces – Domination and Transformation in the Third World*, Cambridge: Cambridge University Press, pp. 108–40.

Booth, D. (1987), 'Alternatives in the restructuring of state–society relations: Research issues for tropical Africa', *IDS Bulletin*, 18(4): 23–30.

Bourdieu, P. (1980). *Le sens pratique*, Paris: Les editions de minuit.

Bowles, S. (1998a), 'Endogenous preferences: The cultural consequences of markets and other economic institutions', *Journal of Economic Literature*, 36(1): 75–111.

Bowles, S. (1998b), 'Mandeville's mistake: The evolution of norms in market environments' (mimeo), University of Massachusetts, Department of Economics, Lowell, MA.

Bowles, S. and H. Gintis (1998), 'The moral economy of communities: Structured populations and the evolution of pro-social norms', *Evolution and Human Behavior*, 19(1): 3–25.

Bradford Delong, J. (1995), 'Overstrong Against Thyself: War, the State and Growth in Europe on the eve of the Industrial Revolution', University of California, Berkeley, mimeo.

Brenner, R. (1985), 'Agrarian class structure and economic development in pre-industrial Europe', in T.H. Aston and C.H.E. Philpin (eds), *The Brenner Debate*, Cambridge: Cambridge University Press, pp. 10–63.

Bromley, D. and D. Chapagain (1984), 'The village against the centre: Resource depletion in South Asia', *American Journal of Agricultural Economics*, 66(5): 868–73.

Buchanan, J.M. (1975), *The Limits of Liberty – Between Anarchy and Leviathan*, Chicago and London: University of Chicago Press.

Camerer, C. and R. Thaler (1995), 'Ultimatums, dictators and manners', *Journal of Economic Perspectives*, 9: 209–19.

Chazan, N. (1988), 'Ghana: Problems of governance and the emergence of civil society', in L. Diamond, L.J. Linz and S.M. Lipset (eds), *Democracy in Developing Countries*, Vol. 2. Boulder, CO: Lynne Rienner Publishers.

Coleman, J.S. (1987), 'Norms as a social capital', in G. Radnitzky and P. Bernholz (eds), *Economic Imperialism. The Economic Method Applied Outside the Field of Economics*, New York: Paragon House Publishers, pp. 133–53.

Coleman, J.S. (1990), *Foundations of Social Theory*, Cambridge, MA and London: The Belknap Press of Harvard University Press.

Coquery-Vidrovitch, C. (1985), *Afrique noire – Permanences et ruptures*, Paris: Fayot.

Coquery-Vidrovitch, C. (1999), *L'Afrique et les Africains au XIXème siècle*, Paris: Armand Colin.

Darley, J.M. and B. Latane (1970), 'Norms and normative behaviour: Field studies of social interdependence', in J. Macaulay and L. Berkowitz (eds), *Altruism and Helping Behaviour – Social Psychological Studies of Some Antecedents and Consequences*, New York, San Francisco and London: Academic Press, pp. 83–101.

Dasgupta, P. (1988), 'Trust as a commodity', in D. Gambetta (ed.), *Trust-Making and Breaking Cooperative Relations*, Oxford: Basil Blackwell, pp. 49–72.

Dawes, R.M. and R.H. Thaler (1988), 'Anomalies: Cooperation', *Journal of Economic Perspectives*, 2(3): 187–97.

Dixon, S. (1999), *The Modernisation of Russia 1676–1825*, Cambridge: Cambridge University Press.

Duncan, E. (1989), *Breaking the Curfew – A Political Journey Through Pakistan*, London: Michael Joseph.

Eiser, J.R. (1978), 'Cooperation and conflict between individuals', in H. Tajfel and C. Fraser (eds), *Introducing Social Psychology*, Harmondsworth: Penguin Books.

Elster, J. (1989a), *The Cement of Society. A Study of Social Order*, Cambridge: Cambridge University Press.

Elster, J. (1989b), 'Social norms and economic theory', *Journal of Economic Perspectives*, 3(1): 99–117.

Elster, J. (1998), 'Emotions and economic theory', *Journal of Economic Literature*, 36(1): 47–74.

Evans-Pritchard, E.E. (1940), *The Nuer: A Description of the Modes of Livelihood and Political Institutions of a Nilotic People*, Oxford: Clarendon Press.

Fafchamps, M. (1996), 'The enforcement of commercial contracts in Ghana', *World Development*, 24(3): 427–48.

Fafchamps, M. and B. Minten (1998), Returns to Social Capital among Traders (mimeo), Stanford University, Department of Economics, Berkeley, CA.

Fehr, E. and J.R. Tyran (1996), 'Institutions and reciprocal fairness', *Nordic Journal of Political Economy*, 23(2): 133–44.

Fehr, E., S. Gaechter and G. Kirchsteiger (1997), 'Reciprocity as a contract enforcement device: Experimental evidence', *Econometrica*, 65(4): 833–60.

Fehr, E., G. Kirchsteiger and A. Riedl (1998a), 'Gift exchange and reciprocity in competitive experimental markets', *European Economic Review*, 42(1): 1–34.

Fehr, E. *et al.* (1998b), 'When social norms overpower competition – Social exchange in experimental labor markets', *Journal of Labor Economics*, 16(2): 324–51.

Fieldhouse, D.K. (1986), *Black Africa 1945–1980 – Economic Decolonization and Arrested Development*, London: Unwin Hyman.

Firmin-Sellers, K. (1996), *The Transformation of Property Rights in the Gold Coast – An Empirical Analysis Applying Rational Choice Theory*, Cambridge: Cambridge University Press.

Frank, R. (1988), *Passions Within Reason: The Strategic Role of Emotions*, New York: Norton.

Frimpong-Ansah, J.H. (1991), *The Vampire State in Africa – The Political Economy of Decline in Ghana*, London: James Currey; Trenton: Africa World Press.

Fukuyama, F. (1995), *Trust – The Social Virtues and the Creation of Prosperity*, London: Hamish Hamilton.

Gambetta, D. (1988), 'Can we trust trust?', in D. Gambetta (ed.), *Trust-Making and Breaking Cooperative Relations*, Oxford: Basil Blackwell, pp. 213–37.

Goody, J. (1988), *Technology, Tradition, and the State in Africa*, Cambridge: Cambridge University Press.

Granovetter, M. (1985), 'Economic action and social structure: The problem of embeddedness', *American Journal of Sociology*, 91(3): 481–510.

Greif, A. (1994), 'Cultural beliefs and the organization of society: A historical and theoretical reflection on collectivist and individualist societies', *Journal of Political Economy*, 102(5): 912–50.

Greif, A. (2002), *Genoa and the Maghribi Traders – Historical and Comparative Institutional Analysis*, Cambridge: Cambridge University Press.

Griffith, W.B. and R.S. Goldfarb (1991), 'Amending the economist's rational egoist model to include moral values and norms', in K.J. Koford and J.B. Miller (eds), *Social Norms and Economic Institutions*, Ann Arbor: University of Michigan Press, pp. 39–84.

Hamilton, G.G. (1998), 'Culture and organization in Taiwan's market economy', in R.W. Hefner (ed.), *Market Cultures – Society and Morality in the New Asian Capitalisms*, Boulder, CO: Westview Press, pp. 41–77.

Hamilton, G.G., W. Zeile and W.J. Kim (1990), 'The network structure of East Asian economies', in S.R. Clegg and S.G. Redding (eds), *Capitalism in Contrasting Cultures*, Berlin: Walter de Gruyter, pp. 105–29.

Hausman, D.M. and M.S. McPherson (1996), *Economic Analysis and Moral Philosophy*, Cambridge: Cambridge University Press.

Hayami, Y. (1997), *Development Economics – From the Poverty to the Wealth of Nations*, Oxford: Clarendon Press.

Hayami, Y. (ed.), (1998). *Toward the Rural-Based Development of Commerce and Industry – Selected Experiences from East Asia*, EDI Learning Resources Series, Washington, DC: World Bank.

Hayami, Y. and T. Kawagoe (1993), *The Agrarian Origins of Commerce and Industry: A Study of Peasant Marketing in Indonesia*, London: Macmillan; New York: St Martin's Press.

Hayek, F. (1993), *Law, Legislation and Liberty*, London: Routledge.

Hefner, R.W., (ed.) (1998), *Market Cultures – Society and Morality in the New Asian Capitalisms*, Boulder, CO: Westview Press.

Herbst J. (1990), 'The structural adjustment of politics in Africa', *World Development*, 18(7): 949–58.

Hodder, R. (1996), *Merchant Princes of the East – Cultural Delusions, Economic Success and the Overseas Chinese in Southeast Asia*, New York: John Wiley and Sons.

Homans, G. (1950), *The Human Group*, New York: Harcourt Brace.

Homans, G. (1958), 'Social behavior as exchange', *American Journal of Sociology*, 65: 597–606.

Hosking, G. (1997), *Russia – People and Empire, 1552–1917*, London: Harper Collins Publishers.

Howe, A. (1984), *The Cotton Masters, 1830–1860*, Oxford: Clarendon Press.

Hume, D. (1740), *A Treatise of Human Nature*, (ed.) L.A. Selby-Bigge Oxford: Clarendon Press (1888).

Hyden, G. (1983), *No Shortcuts to Progress – African Development Management in Perspective*, Berkeley and Los Angeles: University of California Press.

Jackson, R.H. and C.G. Rosberg (1982), *Personal Rule in Black Africa*, Los Angeles: University of California Press.

Janos, A. (1982), *The Political Backwardness of Hungary, 1825–1945*, Princeton, NJ: Princeton University Press.

Jones, E.L. (1981), *The European Miracle: Environments, Economies and Geopolitics in the History of Europe and Asia*, Cambridge: Cambridge University Press.

Jones, S.R.G. (1984), *The Economics of Conformism*, Oxford: Basil Blackwell.

Joseph, R. (1988), *Democracy and Prebendal Democracy in Nigeria*, Cambridge: Cambridge University Press.

Kagan, J. (1984). *The Nature of the Child*, New York, Basic Books.

Kahnemann, D., J.L. Knetsch and R. Thaler (1986), 'Fairness as a constraint on profit seeking: Entitlements in the market', *American Economic Review*, 76(4): 728–41.

Kakar, S. (1978). *The Inner World*, Delhi: Oxford University Press.

Kali, R. (1998), 'Endogenous business networks' (mimeo), Institute Tecnologico Autonomo de Mexico, Department of Business Administration.

Kandori, M. (1992), 'Social norms and community enforcement', *Review of Economic Studies*, 59:63–80.

Kao, C. (1991), 'Personal trust in the large businesses in Taiwan: A traditional foundation for contemporary economic activities', in G. Hamilton (ed.), *Business Networks and Economic Development in East and Southeast Asia*, Hong Kong (China): University of Hong Kong, Centre of Asian Studies, pp. 234–73.

Kennedy, P. (1988), *African Capitalism – The Struggle for Ascendency*, Cambridge: Cambridge University Press.

Kranton, R. (1996), 'Reciprocal exchange: A self-sustaining system', *American Economic Review*, 86(4): 830–51.

Kriegel, B. (1995), *The State and the Rule of Law*, Princeton, NJ: Princeton University Press.

Landes, D. (1998), *The Wealth and Poverty of Nations – Why Some Are So Rich and Some So Poor*, London: Little, Brown and Co.

Lane, R.E. (1991), *The Market Experience*, Cambridge: Cambridge University Press.

Ledeneva, A.V. (1998), *Russia's Economy of Favours – Blat, Networking and Informal Exchange*, Cambridge: Cambridge University Press.

Ledyard, J.O. (1995), 'Public goods: A survey of experimental research', in J.H. Kagel and A.E. Roth (eds) *The Handbook of Experimental Economics*, Princeton, NJ: Princeton University Press, pp. 111–94.

Lindbeck, A., S. Nyberg and J.W. Weibull (1996), 'Social norms, the welfare state and voting', Institute for International Economic Studies, Seminar Paper, 608, Stockholm University.

Luckham, R. (1996), 'Democracy and the military: An epitaph for Frankenstein's monster?', *Democratization*, 3(2): 1–16.

Luedde-Neurath, R. (1988), 'State intervention and export-oriented development in South Korea', in G. White (ed.), *Developmental States in East Asia*, London: Macmillan, pp. 68–112.

MacDonald, I. (1991), *The New Shostakovich*, Oxford: Oxford University Press.

Mack Smith, D. (1968), *A History of Sicily. Medieval Sicily, 800–1713*, London: Chatto and Windus.

Martin, J. (1995), *Medieval Russia 980–1584*, Cambridge: Cambridge University Press.

Massoz, M. (1982), *Le Congo de Papa*, Liège: Editions Dricot.

Mathias, P. (1969), *The First Industrial Nation*, New York: Charles Scribner and Sons.

McNally, D. (1988), *Political Economy and the Rise of Capitalism – A Reinterpretation*, Berkeley, Los Angeles and London: University of California Press.

Milgrom, P., D. North and B. Weingast (1990), 'The role of institutions in the revival of trade: The law merchant, private judges, and the champagne fairs', *Economics and Politics*, 2: 1–23.

Mokoli, M. and H.P. Binswanger (1999), 'State Formation in the Democratic Republic of Congo' (mimeo), World Bank, Washington, D.C.

Moore, M. (1998), 'Death without taxes: Democracy, state capacity, and aid dependence in the fourth world', in M. Robinson and G. White (eds), *The Democratic Developmental State. Political and Institutional Design*, Oxford: Oxford University Press.

Moore, M. (1999), 'Taxation and economic development', in J. Degnbol-Martinussen (ed.), *External and Internal Constraints on Policy-Making: How Autonomous Are the States?*, Occasional Paper 20. Copenhagen: Roskilde University, International Development Studies, pp. 177–92.

North, D.C. (1990), *Institutions, Institutional Change and Economic Performance*, Cambridge: Cambridge University Press.

North, D.C. (1991), 'Institutions', *Journal of Economic Perspectives*, 5(1): 97–112.

North, D.C. and B.R. Weingast (1989), 'Constitutions and commitment: The evolution of institutions governing public choice in seventeenth-century England', *The Journal of Economic History*, XLIX(4): 803–32.

Opp, K.D. (1979), 'The emergence and effects of social norms. A confrontation of some hypotheses of sociology and economics', *Kyklos*, 32(4): 775–801.

Opp, K.D. (1982), 'The evolutionary emergence of norms', *British Journal of Social Psychology*, 21: 139–49.

Ortiz, S. (1967), 'The structure of decision-making among Indians of Columbia', in R. Firth (ed.), *Themes in Economic Anthropology*, London: Tavistock Publications, pp. 191–228.

Pagden, A. (1988), 'The destruction of trust and its economic consequences in the case of eighteenth-century Naples', in D. Gambetta (ed.), *Trust-Making and Breaking Cooperative Relations*, Oxford: Basil Blackwell, pp. 127–41.

Phelps, E. (1975), 'Introduction', in E. Phelps (ed.), *Altruism, Morality, and Economic Theory*, New York: Russell Sage Foundation, pp. 1–9.

Pipes, R. (1995), *Russia Under the Old Regime*, London: Penguin Books.

Pipes, R. (1999), *Property and Freedom*, New York: Alfred A. Knopf.

Pistor, K. (1999), 'The evolution of legal institutions and economic regime change', paper prepared for the Annual World Bank Conference on Development Economics in Europe on Governance, Equity and Global Markets, Paris, 21–3 June.

Platonov, S.F. (1985), *The Time of Troubles – A Historical Study of the Internal Crisis and Social Struggle in Sixteenth- and Seventeenth-Century Muscovy*, Lawrence: University Press of Kansas.

Platteau, J.P. (1994), 'Behind the market stage where real societies exist – Part I: The role of public and private order institutions', *Journal of Development Studies*, 30(3): 533–77.

Platteau, J.P. (2000), *Institutions, Social Norms and Economic Development*, Newark, NJ: Harwood Academic Publishers.

Polanyi, K. (1977), *The Livelihood of Man*, New York and London: Academic Press.

Pospisil, L. (1958), *Kapauka Papuans and their Law*, New Haven, CT: Yale University Press.

Putnam, R.D. (1993), *Making Democracy Work – Civic Traditions in Modern Italy*, Princeton, NJ: Princeton University Press.

Rabin, M. (1993), 'Incorporating fairness into game theory and economics', *American Economic Review*, 83(5): 1281–1302.

Rabin, M. (1998), 'Psychology and economics', *Journal of Economic Literature*, 36(1): 11–46.

Raeff, M. (1984), *Understanding Imperial Russia*, New York: Columbia University Press.

Ravenhill, J. (ed.) (1986), *Africa in Economic Crisis*, London: Macmillan.

Riasanovsky, N.V. (1993), *A History of Russia*, (5th edn), New York and Oxford: Oxford University Press.

Rosenberg, N. and L.E. Birdzell (1986), *How the West Grew Rich*, New York: Basic Books.

Roth, A.E. (1988), 'Laboratory experimentation in economics: A methodological overview', *Economic Journal*, 98(393): 974–1031.

Roth, A.E. (1995), 'Bargaining experiments', in A.E. Roth and J.H. Kagel (eds), *Handbook of Experimental Economics*, Princeton, NJ: Princeton University Press, pp. 253–348.

Roth, A.E., V. Prasndcar, M. Okuno-Fujiwara and S. Zamir (1991), 'Bargaining and market behavior in Jerusalem, Ljubljana, Pittsburgh and Tokyo: An experimental study', *American Economic Review*, 81: 1068–95.

Sahlins, M. (1963), 'On the sociology of primitive exchange', in M. Banton (ed.), *The Relevance of Models for Social Anthropology*, London: Tavistock Publications, pp. 139–227.

Sahlins, M. (1968), *Tribesmen*, Englewood Cliffs, NJ: Prentice-Hall.

Schoeck, H. (1987), *Envy*, Indianapolis, IN: Liberty Press.

Schotter, A., A. Weiss and I. Zapater (1996), 'Fairness and survival in ultimatum and dictatorship games', *Journal of Economic Behavior and Organization*, 31(1): 37–56.

Seligman, A.B. (1997), *The Problem of Trust*, Princeton, NJ: Princeton University Press.

Shott, S. (1979), 'Emotion and social life: A symbolic interactionist analysis', *American Journal of Sociology*, 84(6): 1335–60.

Singer, P. (1973), 'Altruism and commerce: A defence of Titmuss against Arrow', *Philosophy and Public Affairs*, 2: 312–20.

Skinner, E.P. (1989), *The Mossi of Burkina Faso: Chiefs, Politicians and Soldiers*, Prospect Heights, IL: Waveland Press.

Skinner, Q. (1974), 'Some problems in the analysis of political thought and action', *Political Theory*, 2(1): 277–303.

Sklar, R.L. (1979), 'The nature of class domination in Africa', *Journal of Modern African Studies*, 17(4): 531–52.

Smith, A. (1759), *The Theory of the Moral Sentiments*, (ed.), D.D. Raphael and A.L. Macfie Indianapolis: Liberty Classics (1982).

Staniland, M. (1986), 'Democracy and ethnocentrism', in P. Chabal (ed.), *Political Domination in Africa – Reflections on the Limits of Power*, Cambridge: Cambridge University Press, pp. 52–70.

Stone, L. (1990), *The Family, Sex and Marriage in England 1500–1800*, Harmondsworth: Penguin Books.

Sugden, R. (1984), 'Reciprocity: The supply of public goods through voluntary contributions', *Economic Journal*, 94: 772–87.

Szanton, D.L. (1998), 'Contingent moralities – Social and economic investment in a Philippine fishing town', in R.W. Hefner (ed.), *Market Cultures – Society and Morality in the New Asian Capitalisms*, Boulder, CO: Westview Press, pp. 251–67.

Taylor, M. (1987), *The Possibility of Cooperation*, Cambridge: Cambridge University Press.

Teranishi, J. (1997), 'Sectoral resource transfer, conflict, and macrostability in economic development: A comparative analysis', in M. Aoki, H.K. Kim and M. Okuno-Fujiwara (eds), *The Role of Government in East Asian Development – Comparative Institutional Analysis*, Oxford: Clarendon Press, pp. 279–322.

Tilly, C. (1985), 'War making and state making as organized crime', in P.B. Evans, D. Rueschemeyer and T. Skocpol (eds), *Bringing the State Back In*, Cambridge: Cambridge University Press, pp. 169–91.

Tilly, C. (1992), *Coercion, Capital, and European States -AD 990–1992*, Cambridge, MA and Oxford: Blackwell.

Tordoff, W. (1997), *Government and Politics in Africa*, London: Macmillan Press.

Trivers, R.L. (1971), 'The evolution of reciprocal altruism', *Quarterly Journal of Biology*, 46: 35–57.

Tyler, T.R. (1990), *Why People Obey the Law*, New Haven and London: Yale University Press.

Van Huyck, J.B., R.C. Battalio and R.O. Beil (1990), 'Tacit coordination games, strategic uncertainty and coordination failure', *American Economic Review*, 80(1): 234–48.

Wade, R. (1990), *Governing the Market*, Princeton, NJ: Princeton University Press.

Weber, M. (1951), *The Religion of China: Confucianism and Taoism*, Glencoe, IL: The Free Press.

Weber, M. (1970), *The Ethic*, London: George Allen and Unwin.

Weber, M. (1971), *Economie et société*, Paris: Plon (English version: *Economy and Society*, Berkeley: University of California Press, 1978).

White, G. and R. Wade (1988), 'Developmental states and markets in East Asia: An introduction', in G. White (ed.), *Developmental States in East Asia*, London: Macmillan, pp. 1–29.

Williamson, O.E. (1985), *The Economic Institutions of Capitalism*, New York: Free Press.

Woo-Cumings, M. (1997), 'The Political Economy of Growth in East Asia: A Perspective on the State, Market and Ideology', in M. Aoki, H.K. Kim and M. Okuno-Fujiwara (eds), *The Role of Government in East Asian Development – Comparative Institutional Analysis*, Oxford: Clarendon Press, pp. 323–41.

Woolsey-Biggart, N. and G. Hamilton (1992), 'On the limits of firm-based theory to explain business networks: The western bias of neo-classical economics', in N. Nitin and R.G. Eccles (eds), *Networks and Organizations*, Cambridge, MA: Harvard Business School Press.

Worobec, C.D. (1995), *Peasant Russia: Family and Community in the Post-Emancipation Period*, De Kalb, IL: Northern Illinois University Press.

Wyrobisz, A. (1994), 'Power and towns in the Polish gentry commonwealth: The Polish–Lithuanian state in the sixteenth and seventeenth centuries', in C. Tilly and W.P. Blockmans (eds), *Cities and the Rise of States in Europe, A.D. 1000 to 1800*, Boulder, CO: Westview Press, pp. 150–67.

Young, C. (1986), 'Africa's Colonial Legacy', in R.J. Berg and J.S. Whitaker (eds), *Strategies for African Development*, Berkeley, CA: University of California Press, pp. 25–51.

12. Regional cooperation in a changing global environment: success and failure of East Asia

Ippei Yamazawa

DEVELOPING ECONOMIES IN THE CONTEXT OF GLOBALIZATION

With major advances in information processing, telecommunications and transport in the second half of the twentieth century, firms have intensified their business activities across national borders and created production and distribution systems spanning the globe in a major shift to borderless manufacturing and marketing. A firm that is active only in its home market cannot possibly remain competitive, and this applies not only to the big firms but also to small- and medium-sized firms.

Developing economies have inevitably become involved in the process of corporate globalization today. Since economic development has been transmitted from advanced to developing economies through transfers of capital, technology and management know-how, globalization tends to accelerate this transmission and thus benefits developing economies. This is evidenced in the much higher growth rates and speed of catching up of some contemporary developing economies than those experienced by their predecessors before World War II.

However, not all developing economies have gained from globalization. Some have enjoyed rapid growth over decades, while others have remained underdeveloped for decades. Those economies that are not benefiting from globalization but, rather, suffering from its adverse effects usually have not yet developed the market mechanisms to gain fully from the opportunities it offers. Others suffer from frictions between global standards and local values in the process of exposing their economies and social systems to global competition. Furthermore, developing countries have become vulnerable to the global constraints and the amplified disturbances in factor supply movements that inevitably accompany globalization. However, the globalization trend is irreversible and developing economies can no longer develop behind protected walls. A balanced approach to globalization is needed for developing economies to take advantage of its benefits and avoid its evils.

The response of developing economies to globalization differs between regions, stages of development and resource endowments. Policy prescriptions are required through three levels: self-help at the national level; group efforts in regional integration or cooperation; and global support, such as that provided by UNCTAD and WTO, to cope with the global disturbances. It is important for economists not merely to discuss the theoretical responses needed but also to examine actual responses as witnessed in various parts of the world; to identify best practices in both taking advantage of globalization and avoiding its evils, and to prescribe effective means to respond to the challenges of globalization.

This chapter focuses on the second level, namely, the regional approach. Recent years have witnessed a proliferation of regional groupings in various parts of the world. In identifying the reasons for this increasing regionalism, the first thing to look at is corporate globalization and governments' responses to it. In responding to the corporate mobility mentioned above, governments are trying to sustain economic growth at home and to expand income and employment by seeking to attract both indigenous and foreign firms. They are having to dismantle impediments to trade and investment and standardize the regulations and practices that affect corporate activity, not only to attract foreign firms but also to keep their own indigenous firms from relocating to other countries where the business climate is better. Yet reaching global agreement on liberalization, deregulation and harmonization is a long and laborious process, and regionalism is seen as a practical short-cut to this end.

REGIONAL APPROACH: AN OVERVIEW

Open Economic Policies

The process of globalization had already started in the 1960s: a few East Asian economies, such as Hong Kong (China), Taiwan Province of China and the Republic of Korea, geared their development strategies towards outward-looking, export-oriented industrialization, and achieved high growth by the end of the decade. They were followed by several countries in Europe, Southeast Asia and Latin America in the 1970s, which, together with their East Asian predecessors, were designated as newly industrializing economies (NIEs) in an OECD report (OECD, 1979). Developed markets viewed their trade performance as an import threat, but in reality this performance responded to the outsourcing strategy of American and European multinational companies. The NIEs should thus be regarded as having pioneered the developing economies' response to globalization.

In the 1980s, the outward-looking strategy spread further, to socialist economies in Asia and Europe. Open economic policy became a new campaign for China in the 1980s, and other socialist economies followed suit, liberalizing their trade and inviting foreign investment to spur their economic growth. This policy spread further, to South Asia, the Middle East and Africa in the 1990s. East and Southeast Asian economies including China and Vietnam, continued to experience a 7–10 per cent annual GDP growth for a decade until 1997, and the World Bank (1993) hailed them as the 'East Asian Miracle'.

The Uruguay Round (UR) negotiations under GATT provided another spur to the developing economies' response to globalization. They were the first trade negotiations where major developing economies participated together with developed economies. Under GATT's Development Clause (Part IV), they were not obliged to commit themselves to substantial liberalization, but their East Asian members voluntarily implemented tariff reductions beyond their UR commitments in order to strengthen their response to globalization.

Spread of Regionalism

Regionalism has proliferated in the world since the mid-1980s. The European Union (EU) now has 15 members and has now undertaken the adoption of a single currency. The free trade agreement between the United States and Canada was renamed the North American Free Trade Agreement (NAFTA), and expanded to include Mexico in 1994, while Chile also expected to join before long. Inspired by these moves, the ASEAN countries have created the ASEAN Free Trade Agreement (AFTA), four Latin-American countries (Argentina, Brazil, Uruguay and Paraguay) have joined together to form 'Mercosur' (Common Market of the Southern Cone), and there are moves afoot for regional integration among the developing countries of the Middle East, Africa and South Asia. Indeed, UNCTAD (1995) listed twenty-two regional integration groups among the developing countries. Of course, some regions are more integrated than others, but most of these efforts for regional integration may be expected to lower or eliminate barriers to trade and investment to harmonize the member countries' domestic regulations, practices and procedures, and to seek a higher degree of policy coordination. These efforts aimed at promoting liberalization and facilitation among neighbours at the regional level.

At the same time, moves are also under way to promote liberalization and cooperation at the global level. However, these efforts are both slower and weaker than the push for regionalism. The UR negotiations, for example, were scheduled to take four years to complete but actually took seven years. Since then, GATT has evolved into the World Trade Organization (WTO), which now also covers services and intellectual property rights. The main accomplishment of the First WTO Ministerial Meeting in Singapore in December

1996 did not go beyond a reaffirmation of the participants' commitment to implement fully the UR Agreements. Meanwhile, as regionalism seems to be pushing ahead of globalism, some have expressed concern that this might not be in the long-term interests of the world economy, and that we should perhaps curtail regionalism and encourage globalism.

International economics textbooks typically describe regional integration as going through the five stages of a free trade area, customs union, common market, economic union and complete economic union. The regional groupings of NAFTA, AFTA and 'Mercosur' are all in the free trade area stage, with tariffs eliminated on trade within the region but all of the member countries maintaining their own tariffs on imports from outside. Since its founding in 1958, the Economic Commission (EC) has worked to eliminate intraregional tariffs and to set common tariffs for imports from outside the region. In 1992, the member countries signed the Maastricht Treaty, agreeing to eliminate over 280 physical, technical and fiscal barriers to the creation of a single market, and moved one step closer to the final stage of currency union.

New Pragmatic Approach

The forming of a free trade area typically has a trade-creation effect, as the elimination of tariffs stimulates trade within the region, as well as a trade-diversion effect, as it impedes trade with outside partners. Not surprisingly, non-members complain that the arrangement is discriminatory. Yet, in theory, it is fully possible for the trade-creation effect to invigorate the economies of the region, for example, by creating an increased demand for imports from outside the region; and there is no reason why the effect of such trade could not be to pull in more imports from outside partners than the trade diversion deters, in which case the free trade area would have a net trade-creation impact.

Empirical studies have shown that free trade areas do serve to enhance trade within the region, but there are no clear cases in which they have had a net trade-creation impact. Article 1 of GATT calls for most-favoured-nation treatment (MFN) for all trade partners, and Article 24 expresses the hope that regional liberalization will lead to global liberalization, allowing regional free trade agreements as exceptions to Article 1. However, this exception is conditional upon their covering substantially all of the trade in goods and services, on their setting a clear schedule for liberalization, and on their barriers to non-members being no higher or no more restrictive than before the free trade agreement's coming into force. This is very vague, and the EU, NAFTA and other free trade agreements are neither condoned nor condemned. Rather than trying to regulate free trade agreements through GATT and now WTO, it is both more realistic and more practical to monitor each agreement to ensure that it does not in fact lead to increased discrimination.

Of course, the advocates of regionalism argue that these agreements will expand intraregional trade, which will then lead to trade expansion worldwide. In fact, none of the free trade agreements or other regional groupings to date have suggested that they intend to stimulate intraregional activity by shutting out extraregional trade. Yet there have been a number of instances in which extraregional participants have been excluded from certain sectors (for example, as a result of NAFTA's very rigorous rules of origin regulations), and it is essential that such situations be monitored and publicized in order to reverse such protectionist trends.

To conclude this overview, the benefits of globalization are evident in the high growth performance of many developing economies, although its adverse impacts have not been monitored in empirical studies until recently. One of the few recent examples of the evils of globalization is the East Asian economic crisis, which brought to a halt the regions' decade-long miraculous growth. The following sections examine the beneficial and harmful effects of globalization on the growth performance of the East Asian economies over the past decade and offer prescriptions at three levels – national, regional and global – for tackling the challenges ahead based on these experiences.

THE EAST ASIAN 'MIRACLE': A SUCCESSFUL RESPONSE TO GLOBALIZATION

East Asian economies as a group, including China, experienced rapid GDP growth of 7–10 per cent per annum for a decade until 1997. It was preceded by the economic setback of the oil and primary products exporters in 1983–85 resulting from a global depression after the second oil shock in 1979/80. Many ASEAN members suffered from zero growth during this period and cautiously rescheduled their development plans to a lower rate of growth. But they quickly returned to high growth levels in 1987/8, partly helped by the rapid appreciation of the yen, and consequently by accelerated investment by Japanese firms in Southeast Asia. The World Bank (1993) praised their performance, calling it the East Asian 'miracle', and it was seen as an example of a successful response to globalization. The factors that contributed to this success are discussed below.

One was the good fundamentals these economies achieved for their continued development. Their savings ratios are as high as 32.7 per cent on average, compared with 26.1 per cent in other developing economies and 20.4 per cent in industrialized economies (IDE, 1999). And their investment ratios are even higher – 38.3 per cent on average – owing to their active entrepreneurship and to a sizable inflow of foreign capital. Their hard-working habits and traditional emphasis on higher education helped to enhance the level of qualified and skilled labour, and active entrepreneurship strengthened local responses to globalization. East Asian economies have been known for prudent management of their macroeconomic policies, and until recently this had kept their public debt and current account deficits at a minimum.

On the basis of these good fundamentals, East Asian economies implemented liberalization and deregulation policies. Tariffs and non-tariff measures restricting foreign access to their markets were removed unilaterally, and domestic regulations restricting foreign firms' activities at home were reduced or eased to attract foreign firms to operate within their borders. Nevertheless, they tended to retain governmental guidance and interventions in sectors of high growth potential. These remaining interventions conflicted with the free trade principle of GATT and the World Bank, but as they did not impede high growth in these economies, the World Bank (1993) accepted them as 'market-friendly' policies.

Paul Krugman (1994) contested the 'miracle' by pointing out that the high growth performance of East Asian economies was not accompanied by productivity growth but by an increase in factor inputs, and that, if the supply of labour and capital were to cease to increase, eventually East Asian growth would stop. His conclusion was based on an empirical study of low productivity growth of the manufacturing sector in Singapore and other ASEAN members states. However, he missed the point that, although the productivity of manufacturing had not grown remarkably, the sector still enjoyed a high productivity level, and that the productivity growth of an economy as a whole is sustained by an incessant flow of factors from low productivity sectors to high productivity sectors (EPA, 1998).

It is also important to note that, while almost all the East Asian developing economies achieved a 7–10 per cent annual growth of GDP, they did not grow independently. Rather, their growth was interrelated through steady expansion of trade and investment across borders. Their export and import trade source increased by 15–20 per cent annually, and the inflow of foreign direct investment (FBI) continued to grow by 18 per cent annually.

What was not highlighted in the argument for the East Asian 'miracle', but was crucial to its sustained miraculous growth for a decade, was the region's currency regime, which was de facto pegged to the US dollar. The stable currency value reduced uncertainty associated with foreign transactions, and assured foreign investors of the US dollar value of their invested assets in the region, thereby contributing to the steady expansion of trade and investment in the region.

THE EAST ASIAN ECONOMIC CRISIS: AN UNSUCCESSFUL RESPONSE

While the East Asian 'miracle' represents a successful response to globalization, the East Asian crisis of 1997 exemplified failure when the high growth of these economies was interrupted abruptly. Let us follow the changes in Asian exchange rates after July 1997 in Table 12.1. The run on the baht led the Thai government to abandon its peg with the US dollar and moved it to a floating rate on 2 July. As a result, the baht depreciated in the market by 14 per cent within a month and by a further 33 per cent by November that year. A similar run on the Indonesian rupiah, Philippine peso, Malaysian ringgit and Singapore dollar caused these currencies to depreciate by 27 per cent, 24 per cent, 26 per cent and 10 per cent, respectively, by November. The Taiwanese dollar and Korean won were also affected in October and November. In December 1997 and January 1998, another round of currency runs caused the rupiah to depreciate by 68 per cent, the baht by 56 per cent, the won by 42 per cent, the ringgit by 43 per cent and the peso by 36 per cent in seven months.

The market anticipated a devaluation of the Hong Kong dollar and China's yuan following the other Asian currency depreciations in October and November, but both economies resolutely kept their exchange rates unchanged. The yen depreciated by 29 per cent during the seven months to February 1998. This whole shift in currency rates reflected the strong position of the US economy and its dollar. The European currency (euro) also depreciated by 15 per cent, as did the German mark by 22 per cent during the same period.

Impacts on the Real Economy

The currency crisis disrupted the region's trade and investment and abruptly halted its economic growth. Thailand, Indonesia and the Republic of Korea, which sought rescue from the IMF, had to resort to severe contractionary policies and experienced slow growth. Other economies in the region responded to the currency crisis by raising interest rates, lightening their budgets and suspending development plans, along similar lines to the IMF's prescription. With their growth decelerating considerably, the East Asian 'miracle' disappeared. China and Hong Kong (China) maintained their exchange rates, but the currency crisis also had a severe impact on their real economies – so profound, in fact, that it was more appropriate to call it an economic crisis.

Big fluctuations in exchange rates have not left trade and investment in the region unaffected. In Thailand and the Republic of Korea, export prices declined abruptly and boosted manufactured exports. Exports of primary products increased in Malaysia and Indonesia, and overall exports increased in other Asian economies as well. To be sure, manufactured export prices did not decline

Table 12.1 Nominal exchange rates of Asian currencies against US dollar (January 1997 = 100, in US dollar per own currency)

		China	Hong Kong (China)	Indonesia	Japan	Malaysia	Philippines	Republic of Korea	Singapore	Taiwan Province of China	Thailand
1997	Jan.	100.00	100.00	100.00	100.00	100.00	100.00	100.00	100.00	100.00	100.00
	Feb.	100.03	99.90	99.58	95.95	100.20	99.91	98.04	99.08	99.67	99.15
	Mar.	100.00	99.91	99.13	96.24	100.61	99.95	94.83	97.91	99.70	99.07
	Apr.	100.00	99.89	98.60	94.04	99.72	99.82	95.11	97.57	99.42	98.68
	May	100.05	99.94	98.14	99.19	99.40	99.79	95.27	97.91	98.86	99.37
	Jun.	100.05	99.94	97.80	103.35	99.05	99.78	95.55	98.52	98.47	99.72
	Jul.	100.06	99.94	95.02	102.49	96.74	95.12	95.44	96.96	98.12	84.79
	Aug.	100.08	99.95	85.45	100.11	90.69	89.73	94.86	93.92	95.56	79.14
	Sep.	100.11	99.95	78.32	97.74	82.55	81.24	93.44	92.62	95.92	70.81
	Oct.	100.14	100.05	66.17	97.49	75.75	76.36	92.19	90.24	93.16	68.74
	Nov.	100.18	100.10	68.52	94.22	73.51	74.77	82.87	88.87	86.83	65.41
	Dec.	100.19	99.92	48.75	91.16	66.03	70.80	57.27	85.11	84.75	56.76
1998	Jan.	99.95	99.99	24.76	91.17	56.64	61.69	49.79	80.34	81.09	47.77
	Feb.	99.71	99.99	26.74	93.67	65.41	65.13	52.36	84.70	83.69	56.10
	Mar.	100.19	99.86	24.71	91.71	66.63	67.65	57.04	86.79	84.54	62.32
	Apr.	100.19	99.86	29.29	89.64	66.63	68.18	61.22	87.87	83.26	64.92
	May	100.19	99.86	23.62	87.43	65.41	67.03	61.06	85.73	82.16	65.80
	Jun.	100.19	99.95	17.68	83.96	62.30	65.15	60.91	82.82	85.75	60.68
	Jul.	100.19	99.96	17.14	83.86	59.91	62.99	65.69	82.08	85.96	62.41
	Aug.	100.19	99.95	20.02	81.59	59.34	61.15	64.77	80.06	85.12	61.83
	Sep.	100.28	99.95	22.31	87.69	65.55	60.96	61.92	81.33	85.47	64.07
	Oct.	100.19	99.95	28.87	97.30	65.56	61.36	63.60	87.64	83.12	67.40
	Nov.	100.19	99.95	31.13	97.88	65.56	65.89	65.87	87.64	84.40	70.50
	Dec.	100.19	99.95	30.86	100.34	65.56	65.84	70.15	87.11	85.00	70.91
1999	Jan.	100.19	99.95	27.46	104.28	65.56	69.18	72.39	85.56	85.11	70.20
	Feb.	100.19	99.95	27.42	101.17	65.56	67.86	71.47	84.55	84.30	69.36
	Mar.	100.19	99.95	26.92	98.53	65.56	67.64	69.16	83.08	85.48	68.53
	Apr.	100.19	99.95	27.99	98.52	65.56	68.82	70.48	84.06	83.45	68.37
	May	100.19	99.95	30.08	98.19	65.56	69.53	71.02	84.06	83.81	69.46
	Jun.	100.19	99.95	32.48	97.82	65.56	69.42	72.74	84.06	84.56	69.59
	Jul.	100.19	99.73	34.26	101.95	65.56	68.73	70.32	85.05	85.05	68.88

as much as their exchange rate depreciation. Production in manufactures in the Asian economies was highly dependent on imported parts and materials, the prices of which increased as a result of currency depreciation. This depreciation tended not only to raise the import prices of industrial materials (and foodstuffs in the case of Indonesia), but also to raise domestic prices and discourage exports. Furthermore, the depressed domestic economies dampened imports, as a result of which a trade deficit changed to a surplus in many economies. On the other hand, exports from China and Hong Kong (China) – which maintained exchange rates and export prices – were depressed, and exporters cried for help from the authorities. The impact of big depreciation had a strong 'beggar thy neighbour' element and inevitably tended to aggravate conflicts among Asian exporters.

In the first half of 1998, many East Asian economies fell into a trap, recording negative growth rates. During the preceding period of rapid growth they had benefited from a virtuous circle of exports and investment; exports led to growth, while the high prospect of growth encouraged investment in capacity expansion and improved competitiveness. This has now changed to a vicious circle of depressed exports which discouraged investment, and vice versa; the depression spread over the region and dampened exports which, together with low consumption (resulting from uncertain economic prospects), decreased aggregate demand and discouraged investment for the future. Individual economies have tried hard to get out of this trap, but it will take a strong stimulus of external demand, together with resumed currency stability and the recovery of a functioning financial system, for them to do so.

Often neglected by observers is the social impact of the crisis on poverty, education, health and nutrition, and social infrastructure. In these developing economies increased unemployment has resulted, not in the increased payment of insurance, but in households without any income, and increased poverty. It has tended to decrease the enrolment rate for elementary education. Household eating patterns have also been affected, and the malnutrition rate, especially among children, has increased. Public expenditure for these purposes has also been squeezed. The need to build a social safety net has often been stressed, but it is yet to be implemented. Owing to these adverse social effects, it will take the East Asian developing economies a longer time to return to their former growth paths (Alburo, 1999).

What caused the currency and economic crisis in East Asia? Many analyses have been done, which are summarized below. The causes of the crisis show defects in the East Asian economies' response to globalization.

Rapid Outflow of Foreign Capital

The currency crisis was, for the most part, triggered by a liquidity crisis which resulted from a large and rapid outflow of foreign short-term capital. Large amounts of short-term capital flowed into Asian emerging markets in the 1990s. This inflow was attracted by the promise of high returns, liberalized markets and the apparently stable values of the host currencies that were pegged to the dollar. However, as signals increased of weakened financial systems, accumulated external debts and possible defaults, foreign capital rapidly fled through the liberalized market channels.

The host governments tried to stop this outflow by selling US dollars to maintain their exchange rates. This quickly drained their dollar reserves, giving them no choice but to quit the dollar peg and let their currencies depreciate. However, as local currencies depreciated, external debt payments which fell due became an incessantly growing burden, thereby pushing banks and firms into genuine default. Three governments sought relief from the IMF to ease their liquidity crisis. The IMF, however, was originally designed to help finance current account deficits and was not prepared for disruptive capital outflows. The IMF rescue package came too late to prevent defaults and was conditional on severe reforms aimed at restoring their current account balances.

Excessive Inflow of Short-term Capital

In the 1990s, there emerged a huge loanable fund in industrialized economies ready for profitable investment abroad. At the same time, developing economies needed foreign funds for further development – to fill the domestic investment savings gap, and to finance deficits in the current accounts which had emerged over the preceding few years. Meanwhile, some East Asian economies had hastily liberalized their capital markets in order to attract portfolio investment, while their FDI was not completely liberalized, especially with regard to the right of establishment and other aspects of national treatment (Yamazawa, 1998a, 1998b). The rapid inflow of short-term capital caused excess liquidity in host markets, which could not be absorbed into long-term and productive investment projects. Instead, it flowed into risky investment in real estate and other non-competitive businesses, which resulted in local banks having a high volume of non-performing loans, aggravating financial weakness in the host economy.

This was an unlucky mismatch between demand and supply. Few foreign investors, except shrewd professional speculators, gained from the hasty inflow and outflow of funds during the currency crisis. If foreign funds had been invested in an orderly manner, they would have contributed to efficient industrialization of the host economies and brought investors high and stable returns. No developing economies are perfect in their economic systems and conduct. However, if foreign investors had been provided with sufficient information about host economies and conducted their investments with appropriate caution, excessive inflow and abrupt outflow could have been averted, thus avoiding the Asian economic crisis. There is no way to stop market forces, but are investor country governments not partly responsible for guiding their private investors with information about the developing economies in which they invest?

Deficiencies in the Economic Structure

East Asian economies still maintain the economic fundamentals, such as high saving ratios, hard working habits and active entrepreneurship, which supported rapid growth. However, a few major deficiencies in their economic structures and operation prevented sustained growth. Their financial system has developed non-competitively under governmental protection, and unsound government–business relationships have sometimes been aggravated by paternalistic industrial policies. These structural deficiencies were concealed during rapid growth but were revealed immediately after the crisis struck. They afflicted the arteries of economic growth and quickly brought it to a halt. These structural deficiencies should be corrected in order to prevent a recurrence of the crisis.

East Asian economies have been implementing a variety of structural reforms. Almost all of them have been strengthening their domestic financial system, encouraging the disposal of non-performing loans, even through providing public money and allowing non-bank financial corporations to go bankrupt. The governments of Malaysia and the Republic of Korea are pushing hard for the merger of smaller banks into a few competitive groups. The government of the Republic of Korea has gone further in streamlining the corporate governance of its business groups, the *chaebols*. Various institutional reforms are being attempted to improve their competitiveness. China has tackled the rationalization of its ineffective state-owned firms.

Problems with their industrial structure also need to be addressed. Many developing economies in East Asia successfully expanded their production and export of labour-intensive products in a relatively short period. However, their production has relied heavily on imported parts and materials, which in turn made these economies vulnerable to currency instability and frequent current account deficits. They have made significant progress in upgrading their industrialization in order to substitute for these imports. This has been necessary not owing to a lack of funds, but to the lack of capacity for absorbing technology and to the lack of skilled personnel. This structural deficiency would have stopped the East Asian 'miracle' sooner or later, even in the absence of the currency crisis.

Signs of the recovery of the real economy were witnessed across East Asia in May and June of 1999. Many economies, notably the Philippines, the Republic of Korea and Thailand, improved their growth rates, from negative growth in 1998 to positive growth. Industrial production has resumed once more and imports of industrial materials have been increasing. Foreign investments, both direct and portfolio, are rapidly returning to the region. The recovery has been more evident in the second quarter of 1999, even in Indonesia, where no effective reform measures have been implemented because of continued political disorder.

As regards the East Asian currencies, their exchange rates have become stable since September 1998. The competitive devaluation of ASEAN currencies and the Korean won against the US dollar has ceased, and these currencies have rebounded since their trough in January 1998. Political disturbances in Indonesia from March to May and rapid depreciation of the yen in June and July tended to delay the region's recovery, but since September 1998 we have witnessed the convergence of Asian currencies: exchange rates of the baht, ringgit, won and peso have been converging to a 30–35 per cent depreciation from the pre-crisis level, and the Taiwan and Singapore dollars have been converging to a 10–15 per cent depreciation (see Figure 12.1). Except for a speculated devaluation of the Chinese yuan, we may have got over the currency crisis in Asia.

Will these economies really be able to resume their pre-crisis growth path? In order to answer this question, we need to examine whether the causes of the crisis have really been tackled so as to prevent its recurrence.

REGIONAL COOPERATION: PAST, PRESENT AND FUTURE

So far, we have examined both the success and failure resulting from the East Asian response to globalization. We have mainly monitored individual efforts and found that regional cooperation was not the direct cause of either of them. Their success was achieved by the development efforts of individual economies: good fundamentals, open economic policy and cautious macroeconomics management. Their failure resulted from hasty liberalization by individual economies and their structural deficiencies. Nevertheless, their regional cooperation proceeded in parallel, indirectly affecting their response and helping their success. However, it did not prevent their failure. We now examine what role regional cooperation played throughout their miraculous growth and through the recent crisis.

High Growth as an Engine of Regional Cooperation

It is important to understand the unique characteristics of regional integration in East Asia. Regional cooperation groups involving developing economies in East Asia are the Association of South-East Asia Nations (ASEAN), formed in 1967, and Asia Pacific Economic Community (APEC), formed in 1989. Initially, ASEAN – comprising Indonesia, Malaysia, the Philippines, Singapore and Thailand – remained preoccupied with joint diplomacy and negotiation

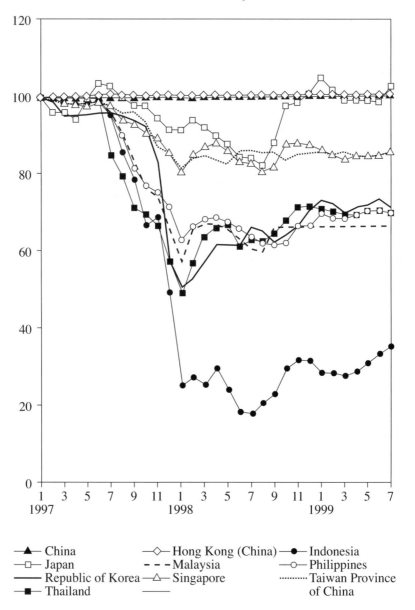

Source: EPA (1998).

*Figure 12.1   Nominal exchange rates of Asian currencies against US dollar
(January 1997 = 100, in US dollar per own currency)*

outside the region, and only since its twentieth anniversary in 1987 has the expanded grouping (now comprising ten member countries with the addition of Brunei Darussalam, Cambodia, Lao People's Democratic Republic, Myanmar and Vietnam) started to promote economic cooperation among its members. Its preferential trade arrangement (ASEAN PTA) has been strengthened, and various programmes for industrial cooperation, such as AIP (ASEAN Industrial Project), AICP (ASEAN Industrial Complementation Project) and AICO (ASEAN Industrial Cooperation), have been implemented.

On the other hand, APEC was launched in 1989 for economic cooperation. It was sparked by Europe's drive for economic union and consisted of twelve members: five advanced economies (Australia, Canada, Japan, New Zealand and the United States), six ASEAN members (its five original members plus Brunei Darussalam) and the Republic of Korea. In 1992, they were joined by China, Hong Kong (China) and Taiwan Province of China. APEC developed from an Australian proposal, and ASEAN members were initially hesitant to join because they were afraid that their own regional group would be overshadowed by this larger group. However, they have since adopted the APEC cause as their own and upgraded their ASEAN PTA to ASEAN Free Trade Arrangement (AFTA). AFTA aimed to reduce many tariffs to 0–5 per cent by 2008, and the goal for reduction was later accelerated to be completed by 2003.

In the last several years, APEC has made major progress in liberalization and facilitation. In 1993, the United States hosted the first Economic Leaders' Meeting in Seattle and proposed that work be started on the creation of an Asia Pacific economic community. The following year, the APEC meetings in Indonesia resulted in the adoption of the ambitious Bogor Declaration, which specified targets for liberalization within the region: by 2010 for the industrial countries, and by 2020 for the other members. The guidelines for implementing this were embodied in the Osaka Action Agenda adopted in 1995 at Japan's urging, and were further specified in the APEC Manila Action Plans in 1996. This voluntary liberalization is without precedent or parallel. Its comprehensive coverage requires not only the reduction of tariff and non-tariff barriers and elimination of regulations on services and investment, but also the harmonization of rules and standards and other facilitation measures. All eighteen members announced their individual action plans (IAPs) at the APEC meeting in Manila in 1996 and started to implement them in January 1997 (Yamazawa, 1998b). Unlike the EU and NAFTA, APEC does not have a treaty to back it up or a blueprint to guide it. Rather, it is gradually organizing and getting structured, starting with the areas that all of the members can agree upon, which means that it is still largely undefined.

AFTA and APEC have provided a favourable environment for individual member economies to pursue an open economic policy and they have supported the steady expansion of trade and investment in the region contributing to the

East Asian 'miracle'. At the same time, looking at it another way, the miraculous growth of the region's economies underlay the speedy formation of AFTA and APEC and provided a strong basis for their successful development.

Weak Financial Cooperation in the Region

For the last decade the East Asian economies have been watching over the financial aspects of rapid growth, mainly through their individual efforts at maintaining the dollar peg and through their prudent management of macroeconomic policies, but all of them were caught by the current crisis. As regards ASEAN, financial cooperation was totally lacking from its agenda, and ASEAN finance ministers met for the first time in 1998. As all its major members were caught by the currency crisis, they were not capable of helping each other.

Both ASEAN and APEC were totally unprepared for the Asian currency crisis. Increased interdependence between East Asian economies through steady expansion of trade and investment had been accompanied by rapid financial integration in terms of increased flow of foreign capital across money and capital markets in the region. The de facto dollar peg and capital account liberalization supported this integration process. Financial cooperation facilitated this integration but did not work in time to prevent the crisis.

Major efforts towards financial cooperation in the Asia Pacific region have been made through the Executives' Meeting of East Asia and Pacific Central Banks (EMEAP), the APEC Finance Ministers' Meetings (FMM), and the Pacific Economic Cooperation Council (PECC) Financial Market Development (FMD) Taskforce. The EMEAP started in the 1980s and conducted frequent exchanges of information. It also aimed at building a network of repurchase arrangements in order to cope with any possible currency and financial crisis. The APEC/FMM started in 1994 and has had regular exchanges of information and policy forums regarding financial development in the region (APEC, 1995). The PECC/FMD organized an expert group on developing financial markets and has promoted personnel training; its analyses and recommendations provided an input into the APEC/FMM (PECC, 1997).

It was from these dialogues that the proposal for an Asian Monetary Fund was developed, which called for Asian APEC members to establish a common fund in order to prepare better for a liquidity crisis in the region. But it failed to materialize because of the strong objections of some non-Asian members who did not want to see an increase in fund-pooling outside the IMF.

It was only in November 1997 that the APEC leaders suggested, in their Vancouver Declaration (APEC, 1997), that cooperation in both financial and real sector cooperation should be promoted in parallel and incorporated into the full APEC process. Deputies to finance ministers and central bank governors of fourteen APEC members met a week before the APEC summit and set a Manila framework for cooperation in finance and macroeconomic policies to be endorsed by the heads of states (MAFCBD, 1997). A second meeting was held in late August 1999 to further develop this aspect of cooperation. But APEC began to help East Asia to return to high growth only in the later phase of the crisis.

The Need for Closer Financial Cooperation

It is difficult for individual developing economies to get integrated success-fully into the world of globalized financial market and huge capital flows. Even after recovery from the present hardship, East Asian economies may be caught again by a currency crisis in the absence of effective financial cooperation. They require a closer regional cooperation framework than that provided by their earlier currency regime. Two years after the crisis, there are rumours of a possible devaluation of the Chinese yuan. The yuan is overvalued in comparison with other East Asian currencies and, in spite of repeated denials by the Chinese government, it may be devalued. If this were to happen (which could be at any time), it could trigger competitive devaluation of other East Asian currencies.

East Asian governments should jointly undertake a realignment of their exchange rates along the line of the Plaza or Smithsonian Agreements. In addition, it is preferable for the current US dollar exchange rate for the yuan to remain unchanged while other Asian currencies are revalued, so as to correct the current undervaluation of their real exchange rates. This will correct the current overvaluation of the yuan and allay concerns about its possible devaluation.

This region-wide arrangement would result in a stable set of cross exchange rates between East Asian currencies. Individual currencies would be pegged jointly with a currency basket that includes the US dollar, the yen and the ECU, with their composition reflecting their weights in trade and investment in the region. A common wide band of 5–10 per cent should be allowed for individual currencies in order to enable them to adjust in response to changes in the market.

In addition, East Asian economies should introduce a minimum coordina-tion of macroeconomic policies among themselves. This means that they need to set targets for their inflation rate and to introduce a set of maximum ratios for their government debts, balance-of-payment deficits and external debt to GDP. These target ratios need to be sustained through mutual surveillance and early warning in order to avoid the recurrence of large macroeconomic distur-bances. It is important to make the market believe in the sustainability of the stable currency regimes in East Asia for some length of time.

Regional Facilitation, and Economic and Technical Cooperation

The currency crisis was a stumbling block for the East Asian developing economies in their efforts to meet the challenge of globalization. Neither

ASEAN nor APEC could help them to avoid it in time, but both are now emerging to help them to get back on the growth path. Closer regional cooperation will enable these economies to respond more effectively to globalization and to gain more from its benefits while minimizing its harmful effects.

As regards liberalization and deregulation, neither ASEAN nor APEC have changed direction in spite of the crisis. The ASEAN Summit in Hanoi in December 1998 confirmed the commitment to pursuing liberalization through AFTA. While a few economies were reported to have reversed their liberalization of a few sensitive sectors, many APEC members have kept their commitments to the UR agreements and have continued to pursue their unilateral liberalization as expressed in their individual action plans. While the resistance by vested interest groups to reforms increased and protectionism gained momentum in the crisis-hit economies, this joint commitment has helped individual members to stick to their liberalization plans.

The advantage of APEC is its aim to implement facilitation and economic and technical cooperation (Ecotech) together with liberalization, as stipulated in the Osaka Action Agenda (APEC, 1995). The facilitation includes rationalization of customs procedure, harmonization of rules and standards, streamlining visa procedures, and so on. Ecotech is concerned with mainly technical cooperation in human resource development, trade and investment promotion, and environmental protection. These cooperative activities need to be implemented in parallel with liberalization measures. Unlike liberalization, they do not meet strong resistance from vested interest groups at home. In cases where developing economies are not capable of implementing them effectively owing to a lack of human resources and technological know-how, APEC has provided an effective framework for assistance. Furthermore, since facilitation measures need to be implemented jointly in a concerted manner, APEC has been promoting them in Collective Action Plans, making it more likely that the facilitation measures will progress steadily towards achieving the Bogor targets noted above (Yamazawa, 1998b).

Facilitation and Ecotech constitute a 'plus element' over WTO and ordinary free trade agreements (FTAs). Since its inception, APEC has been oriented towards facilitation and Ecotech because it contains many developing economies. The essential elements of Ecotech are stated as follows: 'APEC economies will pursue economic and technical cooperation in order to attain sustainable growth and equitable development in the Asia Pacific region, while reducing economic disparities among APEC economies and improving the economic and social well-being of all our people' (APEC, 1995).

On the other hand, other regional cooperation groups which consist of only developing economies are not capable of extending such help to other members. ASEAN could not provide such assistance within the group and only gave new members longer periods to complete committed tariff reductions. Even NAFTA, which is composed of both advanced and developing countries, lacks such assistance from the advanced to the developing members. East Asian developing economies should thus take the best advantage of what regional cooperation offers through APEC.

A THREE-TIER PRESCRIPTION FOR THE GLOBALIZATION CHALLENGE

East Asian developing economies have been a pioneer group in responding successfully to globalization, benefiting from its opportunities and minimizing its harmful effects. Other developing economies will follow suit in their wish to achieve economic development. Thus prescriptions for East Asian economies will be relevant to other developing economies as well.

It is important to note that the mere resumption of production, employment and growth rates is not sufficient for recovery in the East Asian developing economies. In order to prevent a recurrence of the currency crisis and get back along a path of steady growth which they began in early 1999, they need to eliminate the factors that caused the current crisis. The following is a summary of prescriptions for achieving this at three levels: the national, regional and global levels.

At the national level, their economic fundamentals still remain valid and will support the revitalization of their economies. However, their structural deficiencies need to be corrected in the process of recovery. Their financial systems need to be strengthened so as to endure occasional disturbances in the market. The governance of their business firms needs to be improved in order to make them more competitive *vis-à-vis* multinational firms without governmental assistance. In addition, a temporary freeze on the convertibility of capital accounts may be needed to combat any serious speculative attack.

At the regional level, developing economies, by definition, are not fully capable of making all these efforts on their own. They need assistance in various forms: technical assistance for liberalization and facilitation, strengthening individual financial systems, and moral support or joint commitment for pursuing structural reform. These cooperation measures are already being implemented through APEC. The APEC Leaders' Declaration in Auckland in 1999 endorsed their commitment to utilizing the grouping to its full extent in this direction. The APEC leaders emphasized the 'competition principles' in nurturing better and efficient markets – both domestic and international – and made commitments to provide assistance for 'capacity building' by the developing members (APEC, 1999; PAFTAD, 1999). APEC finance ministers must strengthen their cooperation in order to avoid recurrence of the currency crisis in the region by stabilizing exchange rates, quickly providing rescue funds in the case of liquidity crises, and establishing a network for macroeconomic policy cooperation. Multiple alignment of exchange rates between regional currencies and jointly pegging their currencies to a currency basket, as mentioned earlier, should also be pursued in the context of regional cooperation.

At the global level, several tasks still remain to be undertaken in order to combat the currency and economic crisis. A stable regional currency regime relies critically on deliberate control of volatile capital movements, which is beyond the capability of regional cooperation. A routine procedure should be introduced to prevent disruptive capital movements from engendering a liquidity crisis in a member economy. There is a need to introduce appropriate regulatory measures against disruptive capital flows.

The IMF should be strengthened so that it can provide a quick rescue fund for a member economy trapped in a liquidity crisis. Some form of regional arrangement for borrowing and repurchase should be worked out in the region to supplement the IMF. It is also indispensable to maintain stable exchange rates among major currencies: the US dollar, the euro and the yen. The Group of Seven meetings of finance ministers and central bank governors and the IMF all have roles to play in this area, including a minimum coordination of macroeconomic policies among major players.

Cooperation at the *global* level is also needed to deal with other issues which developing economies in various regions have in common. International organizations, such as UNCTAD, WTO and the World Bank, as well as regional development banks, have to promote liberalization and facilitation for economic development, while providing needed technical assistance for all developing economies. Such assistance is provided by APEC for its developing members, but it should also be provided for all developing economies which do not have easy access. These organizations should also work for other types of global issues, such as the effects of greenhouse gases, the population explosion and possible food shortages. A task force of APEC (the Food, Economic Development, Energy, Environment and Population Group) is already addressing these global issues, and its efforts should be globalized to deal with them effectively.

Self-help is indispensable for developing economies to respond effectively to the challenges of globalization. At the same time, regional cooperation can help them in these efforts, and a global regime must be strengthened to enable them to benefit from globalization. The recent experience of East Asian economies is an example of how this can be made possible.

REFERENCES

Alburo, F.A. (1999), 'The Asian Financial Crisis and Philippine Responses: Long-run Consideration', *The Developing Economies*, 37(4), December.

APEC (1995), 'Joint Ministerial Statement of the Second APEC Finance Ministers' Meeting', Asian Development Bank Institute meeting, Bali, Indonesia, 15–16 April.

APEC (1997), 'APEC Economic Leaders Declaration: Connecting the APEC Community', Asian Development Bank Institute meeting, Vancouver, Canada, 25 November.

APEC (1999), 'Auckland Challenge: APEC Leaders' Declaration', Auckland, New Zealand, September.

EPA (1998), *Kaigai Keizai Deta* (Overseas Economic Data), June, Tokyo: Economic Planning Agency, Government of Japan.

IDE (1999), *Strengthening Cooperation among Asian Economies in Crisis*, March, Tokyo: Institute of Developing Economies/JETRO.

Krugman, P. (1994), 'The myth of Asian economic miracle', *Foreign Affairs*, 73(6): 62–78, November–December.

MAFCBD (1997), 'A New Framework/or Enhanced Asian Regional Cooperation to Promote Financial Stability – Agreed Summary of Discussions', Meeting of Asian Finance and Central Bank Deputies, Manila, November.

OECD (1979), *The Impact of Newly Industrializing Countries on Production and Manufactures. Report of the Secretary-General*, Paris: Organization for Economic Cooperation and Development.

PAFTAD (1999), *APEC: The Challenges and Tasks for the Twenty First Century, Summary and Recommendations*, July, Osaka: Kansai Economic Research Center.

PECC (1997), *Financial Market Development: A Road to Pacific Economic Growth*, Singapore: Pacific Economic Cooperation Council.

UNCTAD (1995), *State of South–South Cooperation: Statistical Pocket Book and Index of Cooperation Organizations*, Geneva: United Nations Conference on Trade and Development.

World Bank (1993), *The East Asian Miracle: Economic Growth and Public Policy, (A World Bank Policy Research Report)*, New York: Oxford University Press for the World Bank.

Yamazawa, I. (1998a), 'Economic integration in the Asia Pacific region', in G. Thompson (ed.), *Economic Dynamism in the Asia-Pacific: The Growth of Integration and Competitiveness*, The Open University's textbook series, London: Routledge.

Yamazawa, I. (1998b), *APEC's Progress toward the Bogor Target: A Quantitative Assessment of 1997. IAP/CAP*, Tokyo: PECC Japan Committee.

13. Economic governance institutions in a global political economy: implications for developing countries

Peter Evans

INTRODUCTION[1]

Increased openness to trade and financial flows has spread around the world over the course of the past few decades, working together with accelerating technological change to create new worldwide economic dynamism in a variety of sectors. Openness has had positive political as well as economic consequences. Backward-looking elites find it harder to use local political machines to shield their assets from more forward-looking competitors. Opaque, arbitrary and capricious governments pay a higher economic price than they did fifty years ago. Nonetheless, the new globalized political economy still leaves much to be desired (see Nayyar, in the present volume).

Some of the failings of this new economy are exactly what one would expect from a market which starts from a foundation of vastly unequal endowments and then allows capital and goods to move freely while keeping workers largely trapped inside national boundaries. Growing inequality both within and between nations is not surprising, but it is still disturbing.[2] Another cause for concern is the volatility of the new global financial markets, whose devastating impact on developing economies has been demonstrated most dramatically in the 1997–8 Asian financial crisis. Perhaps most puzzling is the failure of the globalized economy to match the record of growth produced by the less open world economy of the post-World War II 'Golden Age' of capitalism (roughly during the period 1945–73).

Clearly, openness alone is not enough. For market-based production and exchange to deliver more widespread increases in well-being, something more complicated than simply making national borders more economically permeable is required (Rodrik, 1997). The global political economy is built on information flows and market exchanges, but it is also built on an intricate set of rules whose maintenance and enforcement require concrete organizations, both at the global and the national level. The governance institutions that formulate and enforce national and global rules are as important as the rules themselves. Unless rules are coupled with robust organizations, market actors cannot depend on predictable enforcement. Unless problems of inequity and volatility are addressed in institutional terms, they will grow worse. The time to start thinking about these global performance problems in institutional terms is long overdue.[3]

Institutional questions are particularly important today because the world is in the midst of a general process of institution building at the global level. The global governance institutions currently under construction may well eventually come to play a role at the global level analogous to the role that nation-states gradually acquired within their national territories over the course of the last 400 years. It would be foolish, indeed irresponsible, not to take advantage of this moment of opportunity to give the most thorough consideration to the way global governance institutions might best be structured.

Reviewing the full range of evidence and arguments on global governance institutions would be a massive undertaking. This chapter has more modest goals. It uses a single organization – the WTO – as a prism for examining a very limited set of questions about institution building in the current global political economy. I will not try to assess the degree to which the rules and dispute settlement mechanisms associated with the WTO have contributed to increased openness or whether they have reduced or inadvertently contributed to biases in the law and practice of international trade. Instead, I will look at the political tensions surrounding the actual and potential institutional role of the WTO. I will consider first the WTO's relationship with prior modes of economic governance (that is, the nation-state) and then the politics surrounding the possible expansion of the WTO's governance role in the future in a way that would address inequality as well as openness. Three questions will serve as guideposts along the way:

1. Does the emergence of the WTO as a governance institution undermine the traditional governance role of nation-states?
2. Could the WTO become a forum for addressing developing country concerns with growing first world/third world disparities?
3. Could the WTO become a vehicle for attacking growing global inequality through the mechanism of 'core labour standards'?

All three questions are political and organizational. All three discussions, but particularly the latter two, are designed to provoke debate and expand the current range of discussions regarding the future of the WTO as an organization. Before turning to these questions, however, a brief general consideration of the WTO as an organization is in order.

THE WTO AS AN ORGANIZATION AND POLITICAL ENTITY

Four features of the WTO as an organization need to be underlined. First, and most obvious, is its centrality to global economic governance; second is the surprisingly democratic character of its formal decision-making procedures; third are the tensions and contradictions between formal and informal realities, both in terms of its governance role and in terms of its decision-making procedures; finally, and perhaps most important, is its political vulnerability, as is the case with global governance institutions in general.

The formally democratic character of the WTO (in contrast to the IMF, for example) is, at first, surprising. Formally, each of the WTO's 135 member states has an equal vote. Since there is no equivalent to the Security Council, this makes the WTO in theory even more democratic (in the Westphalian sense) than the United Nations. Its governing 'General Council' allows representatives of all major countries (with the notable exception of China and Russia) to participate in relative equality (at least formally) and the WTO ministerial conferences have been accompanied by extensive public debate.

If we turn from theory to practice, oligarchy comes closer than democracy to describing decision making at the WTO. The precedent established in GATT that all decisions are made by consensus allows the United States and other major nations to set the agenda. Nonetheless, informal oligarchy remains in tension with formal democracy, and this tension creates some interesting potential for change.

The contrast between formal and informal realities also applies to the WTO's power and centrality to the global trading system, but in a different way. As the organizational embodiment of GATT, the WTO is the central forum for regulating international trade (see Krueger, 1998). As Ruggie (1994) has nicely underlined, regulating international trade has come to include passing judgment on 'trade-related' domestic policies, which can mean anything from environmental regulations to tax laws. This creates the impression that the power of the WTO might even extend inside domestic boundaries. Furthermore, unlike organizations such as the International Labour Organization (ILO), the WTO has the ability to legitimize sanctions if its rulings are not followed. It is, therefore, a legitimate reflection of the general perception of the importance of WTO when a former member of the WTO secretariat (Blackhurst, 1997, p. 533) writes of its 'emerging role as the pre-eminent international economic organization'.

What is surprising is that, if we look at the WTO in *formal* terms, it does not appear to be a very powerful organization: its legal power is strictly limited and its founders were very careful to avoid threats to sovereignty. The WTO was given no formal power to dictate national trade policies or even punish (directly) countries that refuse to abide by the obligations for openness that they have legally agreed to follow. Its only formal power is to legitimize the right of countries to engage in bilateral trade sanctions when their interests have been damaged by trade restrictions that violate the WTO agreements.

If the WTO is seen as powerful, it is because it is viewed as the embodiment of the interests of the world's major economic powers. The WTO exists because powerful national players wanted to focus the politics of international trade disputes on an international organization whose decisions are likely to be considered legitimate, precisely because it is formally democratic, and because its decision makers are bureaucrats not beholden to any particular country. The WTO's *informal power* then lies in the fact that it is the concrete representation of the informal consensus and solidarity that makes the international trading system work.

Being viewed as the 'agent' of powerful international interests is an enviable position in many respects. At the same time, however, the fact that the WTO is the most prominent formal reflection of an informal consensus makes it an obvious target for any nation or group that disagrees with the informal consensus. Those aggrieved by the effects of international trade have no other place to go to at the global level. Being the most obvious concrete public organization to hold accountable for the consequences of the otherwise acephalous international trading system creates an obvious potential for political discomfort. Such discomfort is further increased by the ambivalence with which global governance institutions are viewed by national political leaders.

In the current political climate, the idea of 'free markets' is without doubt ideologically hegemonic, but infringements on sovereignty remain politically problematic. Consequently, organizations that must provide the institutional underpinnings for 'free markets' benefit only partially from the ideological hegemony of free markets. As Steven Weber (1999) has pointed out, these organizations, as organizations, attract little political loyalty. The supposedly anachronistic institution of the nation-state looks charismatic when compared to the average global governance institution. If global governance organizations are to fulfil their missions, they must somehow counterbalance their own political vulnerability.

The WTO (like other global governance institutions) exists because the more sophisticated, internationalist currents in the leadership (including both politicians and corporate managers) of the United States and other developed countries realized that a global market requires a complex set of institutional underpinnings. As the 'realist' theory of international relations (Waltz, 1979) correctly underlined, aWestphalian world has strong elements of anarchy at the global level. Anarchy does not lend itself to stable market relationships, let alone to long-term investments. Reducing the level of anarchy in order to get the stability and predictability necessary for a global economy to operate is the whole point of global governance institutions. Stability and predictability require that the strong as well as the weak accept some level of constraint. Institution-alization is a trade-off whereby the strong accept constraint in order to get reliable consent from weaker players (as well as from each other).

Such sophisticated internationalism is, however, far from universal among key political elites. One of the central reasons for the political vulnerability of global governance institutions is the peculiar ideological character of the nation that is the hegemonic economic, political and military power of this 'new world order' – the United States (Evans, 1997). There is a powerful current of elite ideology within the United States that is both profoundly distrustful of any kind of public governance institutions and deeply apprehensive of anything that might reduce the absolute sovereignty of the United States itself. This segment of the conservative political elite is completely supportive of free markets, but has little appreciation of the institutional infrastructure necessary to make such markets work, particularly at the global level. Distrust of government in any form, combined with deep-seated xenophobia, turns any institution of global governance into the enemy.

Hostility from traditional conservatives (principally in the United States) who will be hypersensitive to any WTO actions considered to infringe on US sovereignty is almost inevitable. At the same time, an increasingly active civil society has begun to take a serious and vociferous interest in the politics of globalization. If passivity and defence of the status quo are the WTO's only response, frustrated civic groups have every reason to try to get their national governments to withdraw support from the organization. A progressive–conservative alliance of political groups, whose only point of agreement is that the WTO should be dismantled, is far from fanciful, especially in the United States.

This political fragility is a cause for concern, but also an impetus to organizational innovation. The quest for organizational survival should stimulate bolder and more creative thinking on the part of the WTO and its supporters about how its role might evolve in a way that would generate a broader base of political support. Thinking about relations with member states must come first, of course. Unfortunately for the WTO, the current politics often disregards the WTO's formal inability to threaten sovereignty and starts from the assumption of a zero-sum relationship between national power and global governance. Questioning the existence of such a zero-sum relationship is a good starting point in any re-examination of the WTO's role.

GLOBAL AND NATIONAL ECONOMIC GOVERNANCE: IS IT A ZERO-SUM RELATIONSHIP?

Despite the careful framing of its charter to make it clear that the WTO could not impinge on the sovereignty of member states, a firm belief has spread that in the 'post-WTO world' developing countries can no longer embark on ambitious, independent development strategies that run counter to openness. In some quarters, this belief is coupled with relief based on the expectation that the era of the interventionist 'developmental state' is over, and that developing countries will now return to the traditional wisdom of the Anglo-Saxon model of the 'nightwatchman state'. In other quarters, there is despair, based on the belief that third world States can no long attempt aggressive national strategies aimed at counter-balancing the natural tendencies of global markets to exacerbate existing disparities between first and third worlds. Both reactions are almost certainly wrong.

The willingness of national political elites to attempt aggressive strategies aimed at fostering local capital accumulation may well have declined over the course of the last twenty years. There is unquestionably more fear of enacting policies that might elicit a negative reaction from 'the markets'. Be that as it may, it is a dangerous mistake to extrapolate from these trends and conclude that the capacity for national economic governance has become irrelevant. While the nation-state's role in economic governance is changing (World Bank, 1997), reports of the demise of the nation-state are, without doubt, premature. Despite evidence that the nation-state's pre-eminent power and authority have been eroded in important ways (for example, Cable, 1995; Strange, 1995), arguments for the persistent importance of the nation-state (for example, Evans, 1997; Fligstein, 1996; Wade, 1996a) are equally cogent.

The additional extrapolation that the erosion of the economic power of the nation-state can be attributed to the growth of the power of global governance institutions like the WTO is even harder to defend. Such extrapolation ignores the content of WTO rules, misses the difference between globalization and global governance, and misreads the history of economically effective third world states. As Amsden points out in the present volume, a close reading of the WTO rules shows that very few of the strategies utilized by 'developmental states' in the 1970s and 1980s are disallowed. In the case of very poor countries, the latitude available for policies designed to promote local economic transformation is almost unlimited. To the extent that globalization has produced more timid economic policies, the shift is not due to the effects of the WTO as an institution.

A variety of influences are reshaping the nation-state's role. Most of them are only tangentially related to the WTO. Most obviously, shrinking roles reflect a salutary recognition that states will be better off if they bring what they try to do in line with what they are capable of doing. For states whose past performance has demonstrated governance capacity – primarily the so-called 'developmental states' of East Asia[4] – more complicated political and ideological dynamics are at work, but again they are largely independent of the institutional role of the WTO.

Globalization (as distinct from global governance institutions) has undoubtably put pressure on states to bring their economic policies into closer conformity with Anglo-Saxon orthodoxy. Liberalization of capital markets, and an explosive increase in the volume of international financial transactions, have turned the wisdom of 'the markets' into a self-fulfilling prophecy. If policies are considered too heterodox, they are likely to have deleterious effects simply because market opinion will be reflected in adverse capital flows and the disruption that they imply. Only the small minority of states that have maintained a modicum of control over their capital markets (for example, China, Malaysia and Vietnam) have leeway in the face of the self-fulfilling prophecy.[5]

Closely related to the problem of the self-fulfilling prophecy are the limitations imposed by the increasing hegemony of Anglo-Saxon models of state behaviour among the domestic economic elites of developing countries (including state bureaucrats).[6] Especially following the 1997–8 'gestalt shift', in which East Asian developmental states were redefined in the public mind as homes of ineffectual 'crony capitalism' (see Wade, 1998), belief in the efficacy of state economic action has been strongly undermined. The vulnerability of developmental states, as demonstrated in the 1997–8 crisis, opened political space for a new generation of United States trained economists to bring traditional Anglo-Saxon views of the state's role to the fore. Policy makers in other developing countries were encouraged by the international media to read the lesson of the Asian crisis, not as a cautionary tale about the dangers of opening capital markets without first developing the appropriate regulatory apparatus, but rather as evidence that state involvement in economic governance should be reduced.

This response is misguided. It encourages policy makers to forget about the governance assets accumulated over the years of institution building that went into the construction of the modern nation-state when thinking about problems of global governance. The value of capable state apparatuses built around meritocratic recruitment, long-term career rewards and government–business relations, which combine scepticism with communication, and support with discipline, is validated both by the long-term accomplishments of the East Asian developmental State (Amsden, 1989; Wade, 1990; Akyüz, 1999) and by systematic comparative examination of the covariation between bureaucratic performance and economic performance in a larger set of nations (see World Bank, 1997; Evans and Rauch, 1999; Rauch and Evans, 2000).

Acknowledgment of this basic lesson focuses attention on the central importance of capacity building at the national level. For developmental states, recuperating the prior capacity of the state apparatus becomes the problem, not figuring out ways of diminishing it. For less fortunate states, the problem remains how to put into practice the obvious lesson that reliable governance capacity at the national level is the keystone for effective markets and economic growth.

A capacity-building approach focuses attention on the importance of reconciling the tasks of institution building at the national level and the challenge of constructing governance institutions at the global level, in a manner that will produce a positive-sum relation rather than a zero-sum relation. This approach is also consistent with the more sober and reflective arguments that have been made by analysts at the global level with regard to the requirements of an effective 'new financial architecture'. For example, Eichengreen (1998, p. 8) argues that 'increasing regulators' capacity [at the national level] to supervise the financial sector' is one of the preconditions for the benefits of open capital markets to outweigh the risks, as far as developing countries are concerned.

The conclusion is straightforward. It is a mistake to view the relationship between national and global governance institutions as a zero-sum struggle to divide some fixed amount of control. It makes more sense to look closely at complementarities. Unless capable institutional foundations can be built (or sustained) at the national level, the kind of international regime that is currently under construction may well be unviable. This straightforward conclusion leads, in turn, to the more difficult question of complementarity in the other direction. If governance capacity at the national level is essential in order for the WTO to achieve its goals, is it also possible that enhancing the capacity of the WTO might facilitate the ability of developing countries to achieve their perennial goal of trying to reduce the gap that separates them from advanced industrial countries?

COULD THE WTO SERVE AS A FORUM FOR DEVELOPING COUNTRIES TO ADDRESS GROWING FIRST WORLD/THIRD WORLD DISPARITIES?

Some view the WTO as the instrument through which the advanced industrial countries in general, and the United States in particular, impose the interests of their business elites on the rest of the world. Others consider it to be the neutral provider of collective rules and norms which benefit all trading nations. While the two views seem diametrically opposed, they are not.

All trading nations have an interest in the existence of some set of transparent rules which are considered legitimate by their trading partners. To this extent the WTO is a collective good. At the same time, no set of rules is neutral. Any actual set of rules represents a selection from the theoretical universe of possible rules, and the selection process will benefit some countries (and groups within nations) more than others. Since the economic power of the United States and the advanced industrial countries cannot help but be reflected in the process of negotiating the rules, it would be odd if the resulting set of rules did not differentially reflect the interests of these nations. The fact that the initial rule-making priorities of the WTO regime focused on intellectual property rights and trade in services – both issues which are primarily of interest to the United States and other advanced industrial countries – is consistent with this premise.

Accepting the fact that international trade rules cannot help but reflect particular interests raises two connected questions. The first question is whether the less powerful are worse off with an institutional form of global governance like the WTO than they would be without it. Some nongovernmental organizations, such as Public Citizen, argue that they are worse off (see Wallach and Sforza, 1999), but they are probably wrong.

The 'WTO regime' (in the specific sense of a trade regime formulated and implemented under the organizational auspices of the WTO) must be compared not to some idealized global economic democracy but to the most likely alternative – a globalized economy shaped primarily by the bilateral efforts of the United States and other advanced industrial countries. When the contrast is put in these terms, it is reasonable to argue that implementation via an organization like the WTO creates more opportunity for third world states to continue to pursue distinctive economic policies. It is even more plausible to argue that having a body like the WTO as an institutional filter increases the ability of third world states to defend themselves against arbitrary actions that conflate 'free trade' and the self-interest of US firms to the disadvantage of poorer countries. From the point of view of the third world (including would-be developmental states), the kind of institutionalization embodied in the WTO is almost certainly preferable to a regime regulated primarily by the unmediated power of the hegemon on the basis of 'realpolitik'.

In a purely 'realpolitik' world, where powerful countries simply bullied the weak into signing whatever agreements the strong considered to be in their interests, there would be no need for a WTO. The WTO may sometimes reinforce bilateral bullying, but it also constrains bullying. In the end, it is more about establishing norms and building consensus than it is about the raw exercise of power. In any given bilateral dispute, the WTO makes it more cumbersome rather than easier for the United States to realize its preferences with regard to the global trade regime.

The second, and more interesting, question is whether institutionalization may create new, unintended opportunities for weaker players to modify the rules to better reflect their interests. In other words, could the WTO serve as a forum in which developing countries could push for rules that would better address growing first world/third world disparities? To answer this question we must return to the tension between formal democracy and informal oligarchy that characterizes the WTO as an organization. Obviously, it would put the United States and the advanced industrial countries in a difficult political position if a large block of developing countries were to push for an issue to be put to the vote on grounds that it was not possible to achieve a consensus. In short, the formal rules provide a basis for political threat.

Is it unthinkable that such a threat would prove effective in practice? The recent experience of trying to select a director-general for the WTO would suggest not. A series of straw votes made it clear that the candidate favoured by the developing countries had enough votes so that – even if the votes would never be officially counted – the developing countries had no reason to back down. The result was an embarrassing stand-off necessitating the appointment of an interim director-general. In the end, a compromise was reached.[7] The fight made it clear that if developing countries were to decide collectively to push for something it would not be easy for the United States and the European Union (EU) simply to ignore their position.

Is it likely that developing countries would succeed in extracting an equivalent compromise on a substantive issue, such as reducing EU agriculture subsidies? Probably not, but the barriers to success have less to do with the WTO than they do with general obstacles to concerted developing country political action. First, as Amsden argues in the present volume, the tendency of developing country political leadership is towards overconformity with global rules rather than towards challenging them. Second, any movement to challenge would have to transcend the serious collective action problems generated by the diversity of concrete interests, which are subsumed under the general rubric of 'developing countries'.

What is important to underline here is that the primary obstacles to effective political action on the part of the developing countries would exist whether or not there was a WTO. The effect of the WTO as an institution may well be positive. It is a forum in which collective action is possible in principle. Indeed, the formally democratic structure of the WTO should be an incentive for developing countries to work towards identifying shared interests and overcoming the myriad obstacles to collective action. The more countries rely in practice on the WTO to resolve trade disputes, and the more thoroughly institutionalized it becomes, the greater the incentive to try to utilize it as a mechanism for collective redress.

One might, of course, argue that, if the developing countries ever actually succeeded in using the WTO to pursue collective interests, the more advanced countries would simply withdraw from the organization. This, however, seems unlikely, as abandoning the WTO would be a major shock to investor confidence in the predictability of global political economy – something the advanced industrial countries would certainly avoid at all costs. Once again, it would be a trade-off between the benefits of institutionalization and the costs of constraint.

The conclusion is ambiguous. The WTO provides a potentially quite useful forum in which developing countries might explore ways of reshaping the rules aimed at reducing first world/third world disparities, but it is doubtful whether developing countries will ever take advantage of this potential. It may well be that 'civil society' will be more aggressive in testing the political potential of the WTO, despite the fact that it is nation-states which are enfranchised by the WTO charter.

COULD THE WTO BECOME A FORUM FOR ADVANCING 'CORE LABOUR STANDARDS'?

The idea that the political leaders of developing countries might be able to make use of the WTO to advance shared interests is radical, but the idea that 'civil society' might find in the WTO a vehicle for pursuing interests, which are defined socially rather than nationally, is even more so. As it stands, environmental groups are vehement in defining the WTO simply as 'the enemy', to be exposed and destroyed, if possible. For other groups in civil society, the WTO has only recently appeared on the political radar screen. Nevertheless, the possibility of expanding the WTO's conception of what constitutes a legitimate 'free market' beyond a narrow definition of property rights is likely to become part of future debates on this organization's role.

The idea that certain basic human rights transcend sovereignty and must be addressed at a global level is increasingly accepted. The possibility that core labour standards could also become part of the minimal set of global norms that cannot be abrogated by nation-states (sovereignty notwithstanding) cannot be dismissed. As soon as the possibility of enforcing core labour standards is debated, attention cannot help but turn to the WTO.

The argument is simple. The global definition of 'free markets' already includes a broad range of restrictions (for example, buying and selling parts of the human body, cocaine, or even the labour power of non-citizens, are all highly restricted.) There is no logical reason why the absence of 'core labour standards' – most crucially the right to organize – should not be considered a trade-related aspect of unfair competition in the same way that the absence of intellectual property rights is considered to be a trade-related violation of the rules of fair competition. Preventing workers from organizing reduces producers' costs, just as not requiring producers to pay royalties reduces their costs. Both can be considered subsidies (Wachtel, 1998). So far, the WTO has, of course, been careful to avoid acknowledging the logical possibility of becoming involved in broader definitions of legitimate competition in global markets, but the possibility continues to lurk in the background.

At the WTO's first Ministerial Conference in Singapore in 1996, the Scandinavian countries were, predictably, in favour of including core labour standards in the WTO's mandate. More surprisingly, the United States tried (unsuccessfully) to include references to a commitment to 'core labour standards' in the WTO's mandate. The response was the epitome of cautious avoidance. The Conference came out with a declaration stating: 'We renew our commitment to the observance of internationally recognized core labour standards'. Of course, the Ministerial Statement was careful to keep the commitment rhetorical, insisting that labour standards were 'not their department' but that of the ILO. Still, the issue is not likely to go away. President Clinton pushed for WTO participation in protecting basic labour standards once again at the 1998 WTO Ministerial Conference in Geneva.

The politics surrounding the question of core labour standards and the WTO are intricate, but the basic pro and con positions are relatively simple. Those who are satisfied with their global economic performance under existing rules are steadfastly opposed, because they do not want to do anything that would jeopardize what they see as the crucial, and already difficult, basic mission of increasing trade openness. In this view, burdening the WTO with any additional task could sink the basic mission. Even the Agreement on Trade-related Aspects of Intellectual Property Rights (TRIPS) is sometimes seen as a mistake. A mission as contentious as core labour standards would definitely be too risky from this point of view.

For those who are disturbed by undeniable increases in global inequality, the idea that global governance should not be risked is not compelling. In this view, the mission to be accomplished is to increase global equity and well-being – a mission not being accomplished by existing governance. Global governance must, therefore, be extended in a direction that produces better results for equity and well-being. Core labour standards are the most obvious possibility for extension.

For developed country labour movements, which have seen their bargaining power eroded by globalization, using global governance institutions as a way of seeking redress makes good sense. The WTO is an obvious target for such an effort. Wachtel (1998) argues that 'the WTO could become a critical venue for advancing workers rights worldwide', and that, therefore, 'Organized labor and its friends would do well to make the WTO a priority issue.' Richard Freeman (1999), while sceptical of the likelihood of global labour standards being enforced to a degree that would result in widespread material benefits to third world workers, still agrees with Wachtel that labour should push organizations, such as the WTO, to put standards on their agenda. In Freeman's (1999, p. 31) view, 'campaigns for labour standards just might be the wedge for bringing workers' concerns directly into discussions of how we run global trade and finance, and that could make a big difference'.

Whether labour has a chance of succeeding depends on how these debates filter through national politics, particularly the national politics of the United

States. The 'reformist' stance of the United States on core labour standards in the 1996 and 1998 Ministerial Conferences makes political sense (especially for a Democratic administration). From the point of view of the US labour movement, which is a central constituency for the Democratic Party, institutionalizing core labour standards is a bedrock issue. For the corporate constituency, whose interests the administration must balance against those of labour, the issue is much less salient. While US transnational corporations (TNCs) are beneficiaries of the inability of labour in developing countries to organize effectively, the more sophisticated US TNCs are aware that labour costs are a sufficiently small fraction of total costs, so that the diffusion of 'core labour standards' would be, at most, a minor detriment to their global profit rates. From the point of view of the US administration, then, supporting core labour standards is a political winner. The same logic applies to the political leadership of the EU.

For developing country political elites, the calculus is, of course, quite different. Given the economic logic of globalization, anything that might threaten access to developed country markets is terrifying. Standards in any area (whether health and safety, environment or labour) are viewed primarily in terms of this threat. At the same time, enhancing the power of local labour would threaten the political and economic privileges of the established elite in most developing countries. Since core labour standards are really about protecting the right to organize, and even minor and sporadic international pressure on behalf of this right would be a boon to third world labour movements, established political elites are likely to see 'core labour standards' as a threat to both their local power and the economic strategies that they have adopted in response to globalization.

Developed country labour does not have a chance to win at the global level on core labour standards unless it can build effective alliances with developing country labour movements around the issue. A serious effort in this direction should find a receptive audience in developing countries. Third world workers would certainly value the opportunity to make their own choices as to whether they want to participate in a 'race to the bottom' on wages, with the aim of maintaining export market shares, or whether they would prefer to try to stimulate local investments in increased productivity by pushing local wages higher. A better protected right to organize, through international legitimation of core standards, would increase their ability to make such a choice. Following this logic, third world labour has a clear interest in allying itself with developed country labour and opposing the position of their own national elites.

None of this suggests a high probability of getting 'core labour standards' onto the WTO agenda. Even with substantial support from developed country labour movements, it is hard to imagine third world labour movements gaining sufficient political clout to change the position of their governments in international forums. Nonetheless, the value of the battle may be independent of the probability of success in getting new global rules in place.

Insofar as a political battle over core labour standards is one that gives developed country labour new incentives to build alliances with their counterparts in developing countries, it is a fight that might be considered to have value independently of the outcome. Just as Richard Freeman (1999) sees the value of a fight over core labour standards in terms of getting labour a place at the bargaining tables where global governance is shaped, those who lament the lack of first world/third world labour solidarity might see the primary value of a core labour standards campaign as a way to stimulate an increase in alliances across the first world/third world divide. In this vision, the WTO plays a useful role by providing an institutional target, regardless of whether or not it ends up trying to enforce labour standards.[8]

Developed country labour has obvious incentives to engage in a fight to get core labour standards onto the global governance agenda, by pressuring developed country governments and by building alliances with third world labour movements. There are good reasons to argue that the positive side-effects of the strategy would make it worthwhile, even if it did not succeed. The arguments in favour of such a strategy do nothing, of course, to address fears of defenders of the current set of global rules who believe that, were the fight ever won, the resulting political burden would bring down the fragile structure of the WTO. Once again we are brought back to the dangers and opportunities inherent in the current period of institution building at the global level.

OPPORTUNITIES AND DANGERS OF EXPANDING GLOBAL GOVERNANCE

Three premises provided the starting point for this discussion. First, we are in a period of institution building at the global level that constitutes a unique opportunity for exploring new solutions to global problems. Second, the biggest challenge facing global governance institutions is to find ways to reverse the trend towards growing inequality (within and between countries) that has characterized the current process of globalization. The simple pursuit of openness now seems very unlikely to meet this challenge; innovative ways of thinking about how to structure global markets are, therefore, essential. Third, because global governance institutions are 'under construction' politically as well as organizationally, they are vulnerable, and the danger of their being undercut by opposition from a variety of different positions must be taken seriously. Building political alliances with a broader range of nation-states, as well as groups representing civil society, is probably essential to ensuring the survival of governance organizations, but alliance building involves risks as well as opportunities.

Three questions provided the vehicle for exploring the implications of these premises with respect to the WTO. They were designed to provoke debate about the relationship of the WTO with nation-states and with civil society, particularly the labour movement, which, despite the emergence of myriad new groups and agendas, remains the single largest organized group in civil society. In both cases, opportunities for building new relationships that might help expand and strengthen governance in a way that would respond to the inequality problem are clear. In both cases, it is clear that extraordinary political will and skill would be required to take advantage of these opportunities.

The first question was the easiest to answer because it involved looking at the relationship of new global institutions with existing national governance institutions. The question was whether the growing role of global institutions should be seen as threatening the traditional role of national institutions, or whether a synergistic positive-sum view of the relationship is possible. My conclusion was that it is a mistake to view the WTO regime as having a zero-sum relationship with the strength of governance institutions at the national level. Effective operation of the WTO regime depends on encouraging and strengthening the growth of organizational capacity at the national level. Otherwise global markets will lack the fundamental layer of local regulatory capacity that provides the essential first line of protection against unacceptable volatility. Global governance institutions will be undercutting their own institutional infrastructure unless they work to strengthen national institutions, particularly in developing countries.

The second question asked whether developing countries might be able to use the WTO as an instrument for expanding global governance in a direction that would speak more directly to questions of inter-country inequality and 'catching up'. The answer was that neither the formal structure nor the informal international politics of the WTO exclude this possibility. Were the developing countries to transcend their internal divisions, construct a common agenda and pursue it with real political determination, the formally democratic structure of the WTO would make it difficult to exclude their agenda. At the same time, the centrality of the WTO to the economic agenda of the developed countries would make it very costly for the developed countries to abandon the WTO altogether. Nonetheless, it is hard to imagine the crystallization of the political will and skill required to expand global governance in a direction that would specifically benefit the developing countries.

The third question – whether the WTO might become a forum for designing more broad-based definitions of what constitutes a legitimate market that would include 'core labour standards' – is even harder to answer. The formal structure of decision making within the WTO offers little leverage, but the fact that such expansion is favoured by key political constituencies (that is, the labour movement) within the advanced industrial countries increases the likelihood of the issue working its way into the informal agenda-setting process.

Answers to the third question depend on assessments of vulnerability. Expanding conceptions of global governance is one way of expanding the base of political allies. Convergence between the interests of global governance institutions and those of labour or other groups is less implausible than it might seem at present. In the end, institutions like the WTO are in the business of regulation. Labour has a clear interest in stronger global regulation, providing, of course, that labour rights are included, along with property rights, as part of the regulatory regime.

A global compromise, in which a broad alliance in support of global governance institutions would be created by combining the protection of labour rights with support for property rights, cannot be considered an outlandish possibility. Such a compromise would be quite 'rational' from the point of view of the transnationally oriented elites, which form the core political constituency for global governance. It would, after all, amount to the re-creation, on an expanded scale, of the 'embedded liberalism' (Ruggie, 1982) that underlay the post-World War II 'Golden Age' of capitalism.

All of this leads us to three possible future scenarios. The first, and always most likely, is a continuation of the status quo: global governance would remain focused as it is; worsening distribution and failure to extend improvements in well-being to a wider share of the world's population would also continue as it is; and so would political vulnerability. A second, more pessimistic, scenario cannot be excluded. Political vulnerability could lead to the creation of a coalition of conservatives defending sovereignty and progressives infuriated by failure to deal with questions of equity. The current project of global institution building could collapse (just as national institution-building projects have collapsed in certain territories). Deterioration of global governance institutions would make it more difficult to build institutional capacity at the national level. The results, in terms of global growth and overall welfare, would be worse than the current status quo. The third, more optimistic, scenario is, not surprisingly, the least likely. New political alliances would allow global governance institutions to address a broader range of issues, facilitating improved distributional performance both within nations and between them.

Trying to formulate concrete strategies for avoiding the pessimistic scenario and making the optimistic scenario more feasible would go far beyond the mandate of this chapter. The purpose here has been only to suggest that global governance institutions like the WTO are 'works in progress', whose future evolution will depend on the combined political imagination and ingenuity of all those who are stakeholders in the global political economy. Expanding global governance in a way that might address the current failings of globalization is a political and institutional challenge. Thinking about the existing array of global organizations as sites of political opportunity, rather than simply new sources of constraint, is a way to begin addressing the challenge.

NOTES

1. I would like to thank the other participants in the UNCTAD X High-level Round Table for their cogent criticisms of an earlier version of this chapter. I would also like to thank Malcolm Fairbrother for his invaluable help on the research for the chapter.
2. For data and discussion of rising levels of global inequality, see Stewart, this volume, UNCTAD (1997), Korzeniewicz and Moran (1997).
3. A number of forms of 'institutional analysis' have been developing in parallel for some time. The 'new institutional economics' of Douglass North (1990) and Oliver Williamson (1985) has tried to counteract the institutional tone deafness of Walrasian economics. Economic sociology (for example, Block, 1990,1996; Fligstein, 1996; Granovetter, 1985; White, 1981) provides a different approach. The tradition of comparative historical analysis in sociology, economics and political science also provides a rich source of institutional insights (Evans, 1995; Evans *et al.*, 1995). The 'neoliberal institutional' (for example, Keohane, 1984) and 'social constructivist' (for example, Ruggie, 1998) traditions in political science have tried to bring institutionalist perspectives to bear on international organizations. Despite this panoply of potential intellectual assets, analysis of contemporary global economic governance institutions is only just beginning to develop. (See Finnemore, 1996, or Barnett and Finnemore, 1999, for some promising examples.)
4. There is, of course, a vast body of literature on these states, which will not be reviewed here. See, for example, Akyüz (1999), Amsden (1989), Chang (1994), Evans (1995), Kim (1987), Koh (1995), Quah (1982, 1984, 1993), Wade (1990), World Bank (1993).
5. It is interesting to note that these countries have also enjoyed exceptionally good records of economic development relative to other developing countries.
6. On the Republic of Korea, for example, see Amsden (1994) or Chang (1998).
7. Instead of one candidate serving a four-year term, two candidates will serve three-year terms successively (Mike Moore served from 1999 to 2000 and Dr Supachai will serve from 2002 to 2005).
8. The 'labour side agreements' in the North American Free Trade Agreement (NAFTA) offer an interesting precedent here. Despite being extremely weak, they have still had the effect of helping to stimulate cross-border solidarity between the US and Mexican labour movements (Kay, 1999a, 1999b).

BIBLIOGRAPHY

Akyiiz, Y. (ed.) (1999), *East Asian Development: New Perspectives*, London: Frank Cass.

Amsden, A. (1989), *Asia's Next Giant: South Korea and Late Industrialization*, New York: Oxford University Press.

Amsden, A. (1994), 'The spectre of Anglo-Saxonization is haunting South Korea', in L.-J. Cho and Y.H. Kim (eds), *Korea Political Economy: An Institutional Perspective*, Boulder, CO: Westview Press, pp. 87–125.

Barnett, M. and M. Finnemore (1999), 'The politics, power and pathologies of international organizations' (unpublished).

Blackhurst, R. (1997), 'The WTO and the global economy', *World Economy*, 20: 527–44.

Block, F. (1990), *Postindustrial Possibilities: A Critique of Economic Discourse*, Berkeley: University of California Press.

Block, F. (1996), *The Vampire State and Other Stories*, New York: The New Press.

Boli, J. and G.M. Thomas (1999), *Constructing World Culture: International Nongovernmental Organizations Since 1875*, Stanford: Stanford University Press.

Cable, V. (1995), 'The diminished nation state: A study in the loss of economic power', *Daedalus*, 24(2): 23–54.

Castells, M. (1997), *The Information Age*, 3 vols, Oxford: Blackwell.

Chang, H.-J. (1993), 'The political economy of industrial policy in Korea', *Cambridge Journal of Economics*, 17(2).

Chang, H.-J. (1994), *The Political Economy of Industrial Policy*, London and Basingstoke: Macmillan.

Chang, H.-J. (1998), 'Korea: The misunderstood crisis', *World Development*, 26(8).

Chang, H.-J., H.-J. Park and C.G. Yoo (1998), 'Interpreting the Korean crisis: Financial liberalisation, industrial policy and corporate governance', *Cambridge Journal of Economics*, 22(6).

Eichengreen, B. (1995), *Globalizing Capital: A History of the International Monetary System*, Princeton, NJ: Princeton University Press.

Eichengreen, B. (1998), 'Capital controls: Capital idea or capital folly' (unpublished).

Eichengreen, B. (1999a), *Toward A New International Financial Architecture: A Practical Post-Asia Agenda*, Washington, DC: IIE Press.

Eichengreen, B. (1999b), *An Independent and Accountable IMF*, London: CEPR Press.

Evans, P. (1995), *Embedded Autonomy: States and Industrial Transformation*, Princeton, NJ: Princeton University Press.

Evans, P. (1997), 'The eclipse of the state? Reflections on stateness in an era of globalization', *World Politics*, 50(1): 62–87.

Evans, P. (2000), 'Counter-hegemonic globalization: Transnational networks as political tools for fighting marginalization', *Contemporary Sociology*, 29(1).

Evans, P. and J. Rauch (1999), 'Bureaucracy and growth: a cross-national analysis of the effects of "Weberian" state structures on economic growth', *American Sociological Review*, 64(5): 748–65.

Evans, P. (1995), with Atul Kohli, Peter Katzenstein, Adam Przeworski, Susanne Rudolph, James Scott and Theda Skocpol, 'The role of theory in comparative politics: A symposium', *World Politics* 48(1): 1–49.

Finnemore, M. (1996), 'Norms, culture, and world politics: Insights from sociology's institutionalism', *International Organization*, 50(2): 325–47.

Fligstein, N. (1996), 'Markets as politics: A political–cultural approach to market institutions', *American Sociological Review*, 61: 656–73.

Freeman, R. (1999), 'What role for labor standards in the global economy?', unpublished draft discussion paper, NBER, Cambridge, MA.

Granovetter, M. (1985), 'Economic action and social structure: The problem of embeddedness', *American Journal of Sociology*, 91(3): 481–510.

Haworth, N. and S. Hughes (1997), 'Trade and international labor standards: Issues and debates over social clause', *The Journal of Industrial Relations*, 39(2): 179–95.

Kay, T. (1999a), 'Labor relations in a post-NAFTA Era', unpublished, Berkeley, CA.

Kay, T. (1999b), 'Overview of NAO submissions', unpublished, Berkeley, CA.

Keck, M. and K. Sikkink (1998), *Activists Beyond Borders: Advocacy Networks in International Politics*, Ithaca, NY: Cornell University Press.

Keohane, R. (1984), *After Hegemony*, Princeton, NJ: Princeton University Press.

Kim, B.K. (1987), 'Bringing and Managing Socioeconomic Change: The State in Korea and Mexico', PhD dissertation, Department of Political Science, Harvard University, Cambridge, MA.

Koh, G. (1995), 'A sociological analysis of the Singapore administrative elite: The bureaucracy in an evolving developmentalist State', PhD dissertation, University of Sheffield, UK.

Korzeniewicz, R.P. and T.P. Moran (1997), 'World-economic trends in the distribution of income, 1965–1992', *American Journal of Sociology*, 102(4): 1000–1039.

Krueger, A. (1998), *The WTO as an International Organization*, Chicago: University of Chicago Press.

North, D. (1990), *Institutions, Institutional Change and Economic Performance*, New York: Cambridge University Press.

Quah, J. (1982), 'The public bureaucracy and national development in Singapore', in K.K. Tummala (ed.), *Administrative Systems Abroad*, Washington, DC: University Press of America.

Quah, J. (1984), 'The public policy making process in Singapore', *Asian Journal of Public Administration*, 6: 108–26, December.

Quah, J. (1993), 'The rediscovery of the market and public administration: Some lessons from the Singapore Experience', *Australian Journal of Public Administration*, 52(3): 320–28.

Rauch, J. and P. Evans (2000), 'Bureaucratic Structures and Bureaucratic Performance in Less Developed Countries', *Journal of Public Economics*, 75: 49–71.

Rodríguez, F. and D. Rodrik (1999), 'Trade policy and economic growth: a sceptic's guide to the cross-national evidence', NBER Paper 7081, National Bureau of Economic Research, Washington, DC.

Rodrik, D. (1997), *Has Globalization Gone Too Far?*, Washington, D.C.: Institute for International Economics.

Ruggie, J. (1982), 'International regimes, transactions and change: Embedded liberalism in the postwar economic order', *International Organization*, 36(2): 195–231.

Ruggie, J. (1994), 'At home abroad, abroad at home: International stability and domestic stability in the new world economy', *Millenium: Journal of International Studies*, 24(3): 507–26.

Ruggie, J. (1998). *Constructing the World Polity: Essays on International Institutionalization*, New York: Routledge.

Steinberg, R. (1995), 'Consensus decision-making at the GATT and WTO: Linkage and law in a neorealist model of institutions', BRIE Working Paper 72, University of California, Berkeley Roundtable on International Economy, Berkeley, CA.

Strange, S. (1995), 'The defective State', *Daedalus*, 24(2): 55–74.

UNCTAD (1997), 'Income inequality and development', *Trade and Development Report, 1997*, pp. 103–50; United Nations publication sales no. E.97.II.D.8, New York and Geneva.

Wachtel, H (1998), 'Labor's stake in the WTO', *The American Prospect*, 37: 34–8, March–April.

Wade, R. (1990), *Governing the Market: Economic Theory and the Role of Government in Taiwan's Industrialization*, Princeton, NJ: Princeton University Press.

Wade, R. (1996a), 'Globalization and its limits: Reports of the death of the national economy are greatly exaggerated', in S. Berger and R. Dore (eds), *National Diversity and Global Capitalism*, Ithaca, NY: Cornell University Press, pp. 60–88.

Wade, R. (1996b), 'Japan, the World Bank and the art of paradigm maintenance', *New Left Review*, 217, May/June.

Wade, R. (1998), 'The Asian debt and development crisis of 1997: Causes and consequences', *World Development*, 26(8): 1535–53.

Wallach, L. and M. Sforza (1999), *Whose Trade Organization? Corporate Globalization and the Erosion of Democracy*, Washington, DC: Public Citizen.

Waltz, K. (1979), *Theory of International Politics*, Reading, MA: Addison-Wesley.

Weber, S. (1999), 'Ethics, actors, and global economic architecture: What is the role of international organizations?', discussion paper for Carnegie Council Workshop, June.

White, H. (1981), 'Where do markets come from?', *American Journal of Sociology*, 87: 517–47, November.

Williamson, O. (1985), *The Economic Institutions of Capitalism*, New York: The Free Press.

Wolfe, R. (1999), 'The World Trade Organization', *Trade Politics: Environments, Issues, Actors and Processes*, New York: Routledge.

World Bank (IBRD) (1993), *The East Asian Miracle: Economic Growth and Public Policy (A World Bank Policy Research Report)*, New York: Oxford University Press for the World Bank.

World Bank (IBRD) (1997), *World Development Report: The State in a Changing World*, New York: Oxford University Press.

Index